Seventies Rock

Freddie Mercury's dynamic vocals demanded a vast soundscape in support, but Queen guitarist Brian May was up to the challenge. Though Queen was justifiably recognized for their studio craft, May's ability to recreate on stage the towering guitar sound that characterized Queen albums was a remarkable feat.

Seventies Rock

The Decade of Creative Chaos

Frank Moriarty
Foreword by Brian May

TAYLOR TRADE PUBLISHING
Lanham • New York • Oxford

First Taylor Trade Publishing edition 2003

This Taylor Trade Publishing paperback edition of Seventies Rock is an original publication. It is published by arrangement with the author.

Published by Taylor Trade Publishing
A Member of the Rowman & Littlefield Publishing Group
4501 Forbes Boulevard, Suite 200
Lanham, Maryland 20706

Distributed by National Book Network

Library of Congress Cataloging-in-Publication Data

Moriarty, Frank.
    Seventies rock : the decade of crative chaos / Frank Moriarty; forward by Brian May.—1st Taylor Trade Pub. ed.
        p. cm.
Includes discography (p.) and index.
    ISBN 1-58979-024-3 (pbk. : alk. paper)
    1. Rock music—1961–1970—History and criticism. 2. Rock music—1971–1980—History and criticism. I. Title: 70s rock. II. Title.

    ML3534.M68 2003
    781.66'09—dc21

                                    2003007365

Printed in the United States of America

∞ ™ The paper used in this publication meets the minimum requirements of American National Standard for Information Sciences—Permanence of Paper for Printed Library Materials, ANSI/NISO Z39.48-1992.
Manufactured in the United States of America.

This book is dedicated with love to my wife, Leigh Anne, who was born too late and had to settle for me instead of Cream drummer Ginger Baker. As a result, she's heard far more talk of Atomic Rooster and Jo Jo Gunne than most people ever will, and even survived a close encounter with Slayer in the pit at Ozzfest. Her patience and understanding are appreciated immeasurably.

Contents

Acknowledgments

As is the case with any large book, this one was made possible through the contributions of many people.

Obviously, there would be no book without a publisher, so thanks are due first and foremost to Michael Dorr at Taylor Trade Publishing for his interest in the project from the very beginning, and to Ross Plotkin for his efforts during and after its creation. Stephen Driver ensured this book had a smooth production path, while Hector DeJean laid the groundwork for its reception into the marketplace. Raven Moore Amerman's careful and insightful editing was an invaluable contribution.

Without the kind attentions of Sara Bricusse and Sally Frost, this book would not have benefited from the thoughts of Brian May. And thanks naturally go to Brian himself, for his love of rock and willingness to participate in a project outside the recording realm.

Robert Matheu of *Creem* magazine was also most helpful. As a *Creem* photographer he shot many images that visually defined rock music. In fact, the work of all the writers and photographers who contributed to that groundbreaking magazine is an important legacy. *Creem* magazine truly was rock in the 1970s. Recently, Robert has reactivated *Creem* (www.creemmedia.com) at a time in rock history when it's needed most.

Larry Crane's fascinating recording magazine *Tape Op* (www.tapeop.com) regularly provides insight into the works of many of rock's greatest producers and engineers, revealing that there is far more to great albums than the brilliance of the musicians alone.

Dan and John Taylor were tireless proofreaders, catching mistakes, offering thoughtful suggestions, and generally biting their tongues when they came across something they disagreed with—and as the topic is rock music, that must have happened fairly often! My wife, Leigh Anne, also did her share of reading, and she had the dubious pleasure of hearing all about every trial and tribulation I faced while writing this book.

Any quotes that are not attributed directly in the text came from one of two fascinating compilations of rock star quotations. *Small Talk, Big Names: 40 Years of Rock Quotes* by Myles Palmer (Mainstream Publishing, 1993, www.mainstreampublishing. com) captures rock stars talking about themselves, from the early days of Elvis through the beginning of the 1990s. *Mouthing Off: A Book of Rock & Roll Quotes* by John D. Luerssen (The Telegraph Company, 2002, www.thetelegraphcompany.com) brings the conversations into the new millennium. Both books are captivating and fun to read, for we all know rock stars are liable to say anything. My thanks to the publishers of both books.

Finally, a big "thank you" to my brother Gordon for his ongoing free advice, and to my parents, Ralph and Joyce, who ensured that their son had a good education, which he promptly applied to mentally cataloging the countless developments of rock music in the 1970s.

Well, somebody had to do it . . .

Foreword

I have a lot in common with Frank Moriarty. We have many of the same heroes and share the same enduring love of the first waves of musical wonder that swept over us when we were kids. Frank went on to be primarily a journalist, and I went on to be primarily a musician. But he likes to play, and as anyone who has visited my website knows, I like to write! My relationship with rock journalists (in fact, most journalists!) has normally been cool to say the least. But there are some guys who continue to write out of a true passion for real rock music, and Frank Moriarty is one of this select bunch. He managed *not* to become too cool to get excited!

Those of us fortunate enough to have lived through the extraordinary explosion of the New Art of Rock during the past fifty years all have our own viewpoints—none of us truly experienced *all* of it; that would have been impossible. But each of us has our own album of precious mental scraps, images, feelings tied forever to moments in time and place, always ready to be triggered off when we hear an echo from the past—a fragment, a spluttering guitar riff, an inspired vocal line—and we are back there, feeling that for a second eternity is revealed to us! (Ahem, as Frank would say . . .)

Frank has had his own wonderfully colorful journey through all this madness, and he has put this scrapbook together with honesty and undiluted passion—need I say more?

Dip in and enjoy!

BRIAN MAY
London, England
January 2003

Introduction

I got Experienced at the age of thirteen.

On April 12, 1969, to be precise. For reasons entirely unclear to me when looking back all these years later, my parents' church decided to take a busload of teenagers to see The Jimi Hendrix Experience at Philadelphia's Spectrum Arena. Was it because the tour was christened "Electric Church?" Was it an attempt to show that the church could be hip? I'll probably never know why they did it, but God, if you had anything to do with it, thanks!

On that night, I found a new religion in the waves of sound that Jimi launched from his guitar. I had abandoned my assigned seat in the next-to-last row of the next-to-the-roof balcony and had wormed my way onto the floor before The Experience's arrival on stage. A pretty, blond hippie girl let me share standing room on her sixth-row seat, and thus was I baptized into the heavenly realm of rock and roll.

Oh, I was indoctrinated in a major way. It was painfully obvious from one look at my high school yearbook several years later. There's my photo, one of me sitting on a frozen waterfall, wearing a Jo Jo Gunne T-shirt that I made myself with the help of a stencil and a permanent black marker (remember, these were the days before rock wear could be picked up in any shopping mall). Beneath the photo appears a convoluted lyrical excerpt from a Procol Harum album, telling a story about the Dalai Lama and the meaning of life. Ahem . . .

But as the years went on, my love of rock never faded. In fact, my musical tastes haven't changed so much as they've expanded. In one memorable week in 2001, I saw concerts by Eric Clapton, The Lincoln Center Jazz Orchestra, The Allman Brothers Band, Slayer, Pantera, and John Hammond. That was a good week!

As a teenager in the 1970s, though, I began to seek ways to get closer to the musicians who made these incredible sounds. Writing for various now-long-defunct newspapers and magazines, and doing photography as well (that included smuggling my disassembled Minolta in my socks and underwear to shoot at no-cameras-allowed concerts by David Bowie and The Spiders from Mars), I began to experience close encounters with rock's high and mighty.

Among the cherished memories: An evening at Hurrah's in New York with said Mr. Bowie. Getting punched by Robin Trower's brother in the Spectrum's photo pit. Posing for snapshots with Grace Slick. Getting the cold shoulder from Mountain's Leslie West, one of my favorite guitarists, when I tried to tell him how much I dug Mountain. Sneaking in the loading dock door of Philadelphia's Civic Center following a Leon Russell concert and getting to meet one of rock's all-time unsung heroes, bassist Carl Radle, who was shyly embarrassed that some kid was a big fan of his playing. Sitting at the feet of the members of Return to Forever in Pennsylvania's famed Main Point Club night after night as Chick Corea's band pushed fusion in new directions. Attempting to teach Yes' Rick Wakeman how to mimic a David Bowie pose that involved framing one's eyes with one's fingers. Enjoying breakfast in a tiny diner surrounded by Bruce Springsteen and the E Street Band. Having John McLaughlin approach for a chat immediately after a Mahavishnu Orchestra show, only to have a massive and very angry security guard literally pick me up and throw me over two rows of seats. I guess he'd had enough jazz-rock fusion for one night.

One memory, though, is especially clear. I was interviewing Irish musician Rory Gallagher, one of the greatest blues-rock guitarists ever. As we talked, Rory sat playing his Fender Stratocaster, a guitar that was truly a battered road warrior of an instrument but one that spoke volumes at the behest of Gallagher's fingers. Not knowing much about guitar technique at that time, I asked Rory about one move he frequently made. Gallagher's response was to hand me his guitar, saying, "Here—I'll show you!"

I'll never forget the feel of that guitar in my uneducated hands—the scratches on its surface, the warmth of the wood. I wanted to play so badly, but by then, years of watching guitarists at the virtuoso level of Hendrix, McLaughlin, and Gallagher made it seem like an insurmountable task.

Then came punk rock.

When The Clash embarked on their first American tour, some friends and I were determined to meet them, and we did so simply by walking in the door of their hotel where we encountered the entire band lounging in the lobby. They were in no hurry at all and seemed to be enjoying the conversation. I happened to mention to their guitarist, Mick Jones, that I had always wanted to play guitar. His reply set off the light bulb above my head: "Why don't you, then? I'm no better than you are." There I had it: The punk attitude summed up in one exchange.

Taking Jones' advice, I bought a black Fender Telecaster just like the one The Clash's Joe Strummer played, and I set about learning with single-minded determination how to play it.

In the years that followed, I was fortunate to play with some fairly well known bands in Philadelphia. There was Informed Sources, a band in the first wave of hardcore U.S. punk, and then the adventurous three-guitar explorations of Bunnydrums.

I point this out in the context of this book in the hopes of invalidating that old insult about rock critics being know-it-all music fans who take up that vocation because they can't play music themselves. You've probably seen it along these lines: "Those that can, play. Those that can't, write." Well, I can, but I see no reason not to play *and* write.

The influences of the 1970s rock world are to me fundamental. In fact, when my metal band Third Stone Invasion had the opportunity to record our CD after signing with J-Bird Records in 1999, I thought it would be the ideal time to make a concept album, one thematically and sonically unified into a single, evolving suite of songs. And so I got a good firsthand lesson at just how hard it is to make an album like that, even with modern studio technology and digital computer-based recording

applications. The challenges Pete Townshend must have overcome to record *Quadrophenia* and connect all the disparate parts
into a seamless whole on tape in 1973 are mind-boggling.

But *Quadrophenia* is just one selection from a dizzying array
of music in that groundbreaking decade.

It was a decade that began with the greatest musicians in
rock and roll striving to reach ever greater levels of creativity. It
ended with many of those artists dead and buried, and rock
and roll itself staggering in the wake of fundamental musical
upheavals that seemed to travel at the very speed of sound.

My goal with this book is to try to bring some perspective to
a time that played out like chaos unleashed. And although it
did seem like unstructured invention, look closely and you can
see that a subtle and intricate cause-and-effect process led to
the highs and lows of one of the most creative ten-year periods
in music history.

Was there one constant that characterized rock and roll
throughout the 1970s? Yes—it was constant upheaval. Evolution
occurred at an astonishing pace. Jazz, classical, soul, country—
rock's stylistic thirst in the 1970s was unquenchable. Its artists
were like mad scientists, eager to combine disparate elements in
unpredictable experiments, constantly seeking to discover
sounds that had never been heard before, consumed by the
sheer joy of wanting to see what would happen. Sometimes the
experiments yielded works of staggering genius; others were
failures of titanic proportions.

This book is not a history of everything that happened, of
every note played by every artist. But it does aim to enlighten
and expose some of the most significant or underappreciated
bands, artists, and events. Of course, like all such projects, the
standard warning applies: this book is a work of opinion—
namely, mine.

To all the bands and musicians mentioned in this book—even
the ones I didn't care for—thanks for existing in that decade of
rock. Without all of you, the music world of the 1970s might
have sunk into that most dangerous of musical climates—one
of boredom.

Thirty years after seeing Jimi Hendrix, in my musical mind
I'm still that kid sitting on a frozen waterfall in a homemade Jo
Jo Gunne T-shirt. My hope is that in these pages you'll find mu-

sic so exciting you'll be inspired to break out your permanent markers to make your own rock T-shirts. Yeah, I know you don't need to make them when you can order any band's shirt on the Internet, but it shows you really, really care.

I haven't read much Leo Tolstoy, but I've got a good quote from him to wrap things up. I have to admit I didn't find it in a book. Instead, I came across it in the liner notes of an album by former Genesis guitarist Steve Hackett (*Watcher of the Skies*, Guardian Records). If you substitute the word "art" with the word "rock," it does a pretty good job of explaining what this book is all about.

"The purpose of art is to demonstrate that which in argument would appear incomprehensible."

Rock on!

1970
1
Passing the Torch

The note hangs in the thick air, a banshee shriek emanating from some unimaginable electronic creature. It soars and twists, morphs and pulses. Given birth through a spontaneous union of feedback and signal processors, the resulting cacophony erupts into being through hundreds of watts of Marshall amplification.

The stunned audience inside New York City's Fillmore East stares at the source of this nearly unbearable note, one note that seems to viscerally communicate all of the emotions of war: terror, anger, shame, danger, chaos.

Almost impossibly, its origin is a slight African American man standing to the left of the theater's stage, cradling a Fender Stratocaster guitar. His eyes are closed in concentration, a slight grimace clouding his features. One hand rests in delicate repose on the guitar's pitch-changing tremolo bar. The other is wrapped high around the guitar's neck, remarkably long, calloused fingers pressing a single thin guitar string against the instrument's fret board. That physical action is communicated, passed on as the guitar's pickups sense the string's vibration. The electronic pulse flashes through the guitar's cable, streaks into a series of interconnected boxes of circuitry, then is launched into the guitar's amplifiers before racing on to the speakers, which instantly convert the impulse into a nearly tangible sound that explodes like fireworks over the heads of the audience.

The man with the guitar seems nearly frozen from the effort of generating this incredible sound, but suddenly he sways, the exertion signaling the launch of a second consecutive howling volley of sound. And then, for the next three and a half minutes, Jimi Hendrix uses his new song "Machine Gun" as the soundscape for one of the greatest and most intense electric guitar solos ever captured on tape.

It happened on January 1, 1970. Hendrix was seeing 1969 out and ringing the new decade in with a series of four shows at the Fillmore East theater on New Year's Eve and New Year's Day.

As the new decade began, the rock world was on the brink, about to tumble into ten long years of furious invention and reinvention. The inception of this new era of chaotic sonic turmoil was brilliantly reflected in the emerging music of Jimi Hendrix. What the Fillmore audience heard that night—and what a wider audience was exposed to when the *Band of Gypsys* album was released in April for the United States and in June for Europe—was a radical new manifestation of Jimi's music.

Jimi Hendrix began his ascent to rock stardom only after years of paying dues. His will to creatively express himself through his instrument was suppressed by the basic need to survive. By late 1966, Hendrix had backed up artists ranging from Ike and Tina Turner to Little Richard to The Isley Brothers. He'd grown tired of the long bus tours and the lack of respect for his own music. His exploratory talents had only appeared in drips and drabs, leaking out from the rigid musical arrangements mandated by his host of short-term employers. And though he'd been in the studio for a few brief sessions—first with saxophonist Lonnie Youngblood in 1964, then on various other dates, including one forgettable session with Hollywood starlet Jayne Mansfield—he had never had the opportunity to craft the sounds he heard in his head. So he took refuge in New York's Greenwich Village.

It was there, playing a small club called Café Wha? with blues guitarist John Hammond, that Hendrix was spotted by a member of the established British rock hierarchy. Bassist Chas Chandler of Eric Burdon and The Animals could hardly believe what he heard when he walked into the dim club.

Though The Animals were unarguably stars, Chandler, like Hendrix, was disillusioned with his current musical situation.

Chas had pondered giving up the stage and the screams of the fans, trading them in for artist management. The question was, whom to manage? But when Linda Keith, a friend of ruling rock aristocrats The Rolling Stones, insisted Chas come see an unknown guitarist in the Village, he instantly was struck in his heart by Hendrix's talent.

From that moment, things happened quickly. An enthused Chandler arranged for Jimi to come to England, where the two men set about the creation of a new band designed to showcase the music Hendrix had longed to create.

Guitarist Noel Redding was counted in on the condition that he make the transition from six strings to four as a bass guitarist. The drummer's throne came down to two choices: Aynsley Dunbar, who had played with highly respected British blues artist John Mayall, or Mitch Mitchell, a former child actor who had drummed with Georgie Fame and the Blue Flames until the band's demise. Impressed by both drummers, Hendrix and Chandler literally tossed a coin. Mitchell was in. Chandler devised the unique spelling of Hendrix's first name and, christening the band "The Jimi Hendrix Experience," he put the final piece in place.

Over the next three years, the life of Jimi Hendrix sped by at a dizzying pace. He became the most famous rock star in the world as his albums *Are You Experienced*, *Axis: Bold as Love*, and the monumental double album *Electric Ladyland* established him as the leading voice of creativity in popular music. But there were problems.

The touring pace of The Experience was exhausting, particularly in the United States, where gig-to-gig transport was accomplished the old fashioned way—logging thousands of miles by automobile. Unlike today's rock tours, carefully laid out like military campaigns, The Experience criss-crossed the United States in haphazard fashion. The band sometimes wondered if their management office was booking the tours using the map-as-dartboard method. They were forced disciples of a five-step program: drive in, unload the gear, play the gig, load up, drive on.

Each night, audiences would call out for Hendrix to burn his guitar, as he had famously done at 1967's seminal Monterey Pop Festival. The act—"I'm going to sacrifice something I love," Jimi had said—had been documented in the accompanying film of the festival. It took little time before the image of Jimi Hendrix, poised over his shrieking guitar, urging the flames higher, had become one of the defining images of rock and roll. But Hendrix was a musician maturing at an intense speed, and he had grown beyond the need to perform pyrotechnic stunts on demand.

Finally, after a particularly grueling stretch of touring in the first half of 1969, The Experience ground to an ultimate, debilitating halt. The band's final performance, on June 29, took place at Mile High Stadium in Denver, Colorado, with police and the audience battling under roiling clouds of tear gas. As conditions worsened and the situation threatened to erupt into a full-scale riot, The Jimi Hendrix Experience were loaded into the back of a rented truck just like the equipment they so often moved. They were nearly crushed as the crowd surged against the escaping vehicle. The next day, bassist Noel Redding returned to England.

Drummer Mitchell dug playing with Hendrix enough to stick around to see what would happen next, and he was back behind the kit when Jimi next surfaced in the public eye at New York's massive Woodstock festival in August. Jimi's spontaneously christened Gypsy Sun and Rainbows band included two old buddies from Hendrix's stint in the army, bassist Billy Cox and guitarist Larry Lee. Further augmented by percussionists Juma Sultan and Jerry Velez, Hendrix and company took the stage at eight in the morning on August 18 as the festival wound to a soggy and exhausted close in the light of the morning. And though he did touch on some of his earlier hits like "Purple Haze" and "Fire," the Jimi Hendrix that performed at Woodstock was clearly moving into uncharted rock waters. The proof came in moments like the beautiful octave chordal structures, influenced by jazz guitarist Wes Montgomery, that framed the haunting new ballad "Villanova Junction." And then there was the aggressive 6/4 rhythm of "Jam Back at the House." It had a beat, but—unlike most rock songs of the period—people were highly unlikely to find a way to dance to it.

Jimi and Mitch reasoned that, as they were no longer The Jimi Hendrix Experience, many of the expectations associated with that name should no longer apply. Though The Experience had often stretched out instrumentally in concert on songs like "Red House" and "I Don't Live Today," there now was a clean slate. The influence jazz drummers such as Elvin Jones and Philly Joe Jones had on Mitch Mitchell's playing had been obvious from The Experience's earliest recordings, but now Mitchell had artistic freedom to push his drumming on free-time explorations right alongside the guitar.

Jimi's ears were always wide open to new sounds and approaches, and he had incessantly jammed over the past three years with hundreds of musicians, ranging from Miles Davis sideman John McLaughlin to Rahsaan Roland Kirk. As a youth, Kirk had dreamed of playing three wind instruments at once, and he set about making the dreamed skill a reality. Kirk's ability to create three-part harmonies while using circular breathing to endlessly sustain notes paralleled Jimi's use of drone notes to counter melodies, just one of several revolutionary techniques in Hendrix's exponentially growing aural arsenal.

The Woodstock performance was crowned by Jimi's interpretation of the traditional "Star-Spangled Banner," in which he made use of the entire palette of textures and tones available for his experimentation. It was stunning on several levels, ranging from Hendrix's mastery of the less-than-dependable guitar technology of the era to his translating the song's traditional lyrical images into pure sound. When Jimi played the notes of "the rockets' red glare, the bombs bursting in air," he used sound to create those very images. It was sonic visualization— and it was creative expression being articulated in a manner unlike that of any of Jimi's rock contemporaries.

Several weeks after Woodstock, on September 9, Hendrix was a guest on ABC television's late night *Dick Cavett Show*. Cavett was quick to bring up the "Star-Spangled Banner" performance, one that was already being considered controversial in that time of polarization between generations.

"All I did was play it," Hendrix said, practically rolling his eyes when asked about the topic. "I'm an American, so I played it. I used to have to sing it in school—they made me sing it in school, so it was a flashback."

When Cavett pressed, explaining to Hendrix that people didn't like unorthodox renditions of the national anthem, Hendrix broke in. "No, it's not unorthodox," he insisted.

"It's not unorthodox. I thought it was beautiful—but there you go . . ."

Mitch Mitchell returned to England shortly after the Woodstock festival, understandably having had his fill for one year of playing extremely amplified rock music in arenas, stadiums, and rock festival settings. Mitchell promised to return in 1970, but for immediate playing Hendrix needed someone he could count on. Jimi had frequently jammed and recorded with drummer Buddy Miles, so, with four New Year's dates booked and Mitchell unavailable, it made sense for Hendrix to ask Buddy to join Cox as a new rhythm section. Thus was born Band of Gypsys.

Freed from the constraints of The Experience and at least slightly encouraged by his Woodstock performance, Hendrix originally planned to recruit members for a new band that he envisioned as a loosely affiliated group of musicians. The identity of the players would change as they came and went over time, but the ever-evolving project would survive no matter the lineup.

"The fact of calling it Gypsys means it could even expand on personnel," Jimi said. "I might not even be there all the time. Buddy might not even be there all the time, but the core, the whole, the child will be there."

Future plans aside, the Band of Gypsys that set foot on stage at the Fillmore on New Year's Eve was the traditional bass-drums-guitar rock power trio. But the sounds they made were anything but conventional.

Over the four shows, Hendrix's playing was at its most exploratory and powerful. Comparing the content of the songs that were repeated among the four concerts reveals radical revisions of the material from show to show.

The fact that the stage was set for such creation was partially due to the ambience of the Fillmore and the fact that the band had the opportunity to settle in for the shows, fine tuning their sound at their own pace. That was a luxury that The Experience, chasing gig after gig, never had. For once Hendrix wasn't forced to show up, rush through a sound check, and hit the stage in a tight time frame. But also key was the interplay between Cox and Miles, a sultry rhythm section that was rooted in deep funk. The stylistic change in drumming was fundamental, as Buddy Miles sank deep into the groove, playing in the pocket, all about the beat in a technique that was diametrically opposed to Mitch Mitchell's free flights of jazz fancy.

Fully half of the Band of Gypsys album was culled from the third Fillmore show, and that performance—and perhaps Jimi's career—reached its artistic peak with "Machine Gun."

Jimi had performed "Machine Gun" twice the previous night, once in each of that evening's shows. Though many elements were present in those versions—and would be in a fourth take at the second show this New Year's Day—everything coalesced in this third performance of the song, the Band of Gypsys sounding like a group that had spent years rather than mere days honing themselves into a brutally potent force.

The societal events that led up to this milestone of Jimi's creativity had been boiling for years. Change and uncertainty abounded in the United States, a nation being torn apart by drastic cultural shifts and political dissention. The country had been enmeshed in the maddening conflict in Vietnam, and for the first time the public saw imagery of war each night on the dinner-hour television news. This was not rah-rah footage accompanied by the stirring martial music of Second World War newsreels; this was footage of scared young men wading through swamps and jungles, of atrocities committed on innocent victims, of napalm consuming acres of lush forests in roaring flames and thick black smoke. The times were charged, and Jimi used "Machine Gun" to focus the darkness of the United States at the dawn of 1970 into an electrifying, hypnotic vision of power, terror, and defiance.

Literally hundreds of thousands of words have been used by scores of writers trying to sum up what Jimi conjured in this one song on this one night. But perhaps the essence of the song—its most visceral power—came in that series of howling notes Jimi unleashes roughly three and a half minutes into the song. The lyrics leading up to this moment had told of families being killed, bullets ripping through the air—but as he did so often in his career, Jimi turned to his instrument to paint a picture. With terrorizing, unending sustain, Jimi's Marshall amps summoned forth noise unlike any ever heard from a guitar, his new Uni-Vibe effect pulsing and pitching the sound with a disconcerting, unearthly quality. "You'll be going just the same," Jimi had sung seconds before, "three times the pain—and your own self to blame." This was the sound of that pain, that blame. The solo snakes away from this devastating introduction, climbing, diving suddenly, roaring back up and twisting in aural panic. And as he created this most moving of passages, Jimi stood almost completely still, pulling this interpretation from some rarefied source that most musicians only dream of finding.

By the time "Machine Gun" ended nine minutes later, on one last blast of carefully controlled feedback followed by a series of nearly gentle growls, the audience appeared to be in shock. For a few moments, they even forgot to applaud.

"It was like a movie about war without the visuals," guitarist Vernon Reid of the band Living Colour told *Jazz Times*. "It had everything—the lyrics, the humanism of it, the drama of it, the violence of it, the eeriness of it, the unpredictability of it. I can't imagine what it was like to have been in the Fillmore East and have that happen . . ."

But for all the promise of Band of Gypsys—and the brilliant creative achievements over those two evenings in New York—the band did not last out the month.

The fifth and final performance by Band of Gypsys came at Manhattan's Madison Square Garden on January 28. It was a peace movement benefit concert called the Winter Festival for Peace. As was typical of that era, the scheduling of the acts was muddled, and Band of Gypsys did not climb onto the Garden's stage until the early hours of the morning. By then, Jimi had become ill, allegedly from having his drink spiked with acid by a hanger-on during the long wait backstage. In a shambles, Band of Gypsys self-destructed on stage.

"That's what happens when Earth fucks with space," Jimi said before being led off the stage. "Never forget that, never forget that."

Although Jimi Hendrix's "Machine Gun" was one of the most visceral—if not overtly political—songs of a troubled era, other artists consciously steered clear of associating their works with any specific period of time or current event.

"My strength is not political writing," Paul Simon said in the liner notes of *Old Friends*, a career retrospective of his work with his vocalist partner Art Garfunkel. "Those songs were about the mood of the times, but they weren't political."

Two days before Hendrix's disastrous Winter Festival for Peace show, the sixth and final album by Simon and Garfunkel was released. The duo had taken a dramatically different path than many of their harder-rocking brethren. While other artists were striving for bigger and more complicated sounds, Simon and Garfunkel backed off on arrangement complexity and stripped their sound down to reveal their folk roots. They then framed the result in carefully devised studio productions that succeeded brilliantly, if subtly.

Paul Simon and Art Garfunkel had known each other since grade school, and immediately became friends and working partners. Recording as Tom and Jerry, they released their first single, "Hey, Schoolgirl," in 1957. And it was in that era that both young men became immersed in the factory-like hit-making scene that existed within New York's Brill Building, at 1619 Broadway in Manhattan.

By 1962 the Brill Building housed more than 150 music businesses and was the heart of American popular music. It was possible for a writer to come up with a song, sell the song to a publisher, find musicians and record a demo of the song, and arrange for a hot artist to record the song—all without ever leaving the building's confines. The hits that came out of this somewhat incestuous environment make up a cross-section of Top 40 chart toppers in the 1950s and 1960s, and the songwriters who penned these hits include legendary teams like Goffin and King, Leiber and Stoller, Pomus and Schuman, and Barry and Greenwich, working for groundbreaking producers including Phil Spector and publishers such as Don Kirshner.

Both Simon and Garfunkel were fascinated by what was happening in New York's Greenwich Village folk scene, and both men had traveled to England, where they worked with British folk legends like Martin Carthy, Bert Jansch, and Davey Graham. Yet there was no escaping the fact that the sensibilities of the Brill Building were fundamental to their approach.

Simon and Garfunkel began devising a meticulous recipe of ingredients. One part was folk music instrumentation, seasoned with the related lyrical influences of the Bob Dylan and Joan

Baez Greenwich Village scene. That was blended with the hallmarks of the Brill Building realm: a catchy vocal turn backed by a strong and memorable chorus, Brill songwriting prerequisites.

The concept paid off with tremendous success, beginning with "The Sound of Silence," which took the duo to number one on the charts in 1965. It was to be just the first of several ascents to the top of the charts.

But five years after that initial smash, and after almost twenty years of working together, relations between the two men were strained in 1970. Perhaps it was reflected in their material, through songs sung from the viewpoint of the coolly detached narrator. The messy emotions at the heart of certain songs appeared suppressed and internalized, hermetically sealed and then shoehorned neatly into tidy pop masterpieces. Though their fifth album, *Bookends*, had been released early in 1968, it took nearly two years to record and release their final album, *Bridge over Troubled Water*.

When the album came out, a certain cynicism and evidence of the tension that was splitting the duo apart colored some of the music. Indeed, "Keep the Customer Satisfied" came across as a thinly veiled litany of dissatisfaction about life on the road and the expectations of the duo's massive audience.

Despite the conflicts of personality, art, and commerce, two tracks on the new album stood out as crowning achievements in Simon and Garfunkel's body of work. The album's title track was a monument to thoughtful arrangement and the studio craft, meticulously constructed by the duo and their longtime studio collaborator Roy Halee. Its grand finale was held off until the last possible moment, maximizing the impact of the song's metamorphosis from stark piano ballad to string-driven crescendo, a sweeping climax that would have made Phil Spector proud.

"The Boxer" was more obviously a example of the characteristic Simon and Garfunkel style. The voices of the two men were recorded almost conversationally, overlaid together to create a single voicing hybrid that delivered Simon's narrative of independence and determination. A repeating phrase generated by strings, vocals, woodwinds, and percussion grew in force and urgency, building in the song's latter moments before abruptly falling away to reveal once again the gentle pattern of

Simon's acoustic guitar that had introduced the song almost five minutes earlier.

Simon's guitar presence was the foundation of Simon and Garfunkel's music, the pulsing heart of their masterful productions. Most casual rock fans would never look at him in the way they did Eric Clapton or Jimmy Page, because to discover the strength of his deceptively simple approach required careful and attentive listening.

"You can't underestimate the power of Paul's guitar playing, the way it developed at that time," Art Garfunkel said in *Old Friends*. "You could take so many things and put it to that guitar."

In 1970, you could walk up to any rock fan and get an immediate response to the words, "Deaf, dumb, and blind boy." The Who's 1969 smash album *Tommy* told the tale of just such a character, and the recording rivaled anything on offer from Simon and Garfunkel in the sophistication of both its performance and its recording arrangements. Pete Townshend, lead guitarist and creative visionary for the British band, found himself labeled a genius for creating the first "rock opera" through this unified suite of songs.

But as the old saying goes, "You can dress them up but you can't take them out."

On The Who's stage, sophistication didn't have a chance. Opera or not, violence ruled the roost.

"It's hard to appreciate just how dangerous The Who were in those days," Brian May of Queen recalled on his band's Internet site. "Frightening. The way a truly great rock band has to be.

"Townshend would be thrashing his instrument, crashing it into the floor, the mic stands, the amplifiers and himself. Keith Moon would be thrashing the kit, looking like a mad pixie suspended above his drums, which could at any moment be kicked across the stage. Broken sticks were flying everywhere."

Vocalist Roger Daltrey would hurl his microphone around in an ever-widening circle, whipping it like a high-speed scythe that threatened a devastating impact with any band mates or audience members unfortunate enough to enter into its arc. And through it all, black-clad bassist John Entwistle—known as The Ox—would stand to the side, nearly immobile, impassively watching the chaos unfold all around him.

The Who in full-throttle performance were like absolutely nothing else in rock music. And as 1970 began, they were poised to become the biggest rock band in the world. The Beatles had finally collapsed under the weight of superstardom and personality conflicts, although the official announcement would not come until later that year. The Rolling Stones, after the disastrous free Altamont festival in California in December 1969, had been perceived as either ignorant or totally incompetent, if not both. Blind Faith, the supergroup formed from the ashes of Cream and Traffic, had quickly imploded under a crush of audience expectations. The time was right for someone to step up, and with the recording of a live concert on February 14, 1970, The Who did just that.

Townshend had been eager to record the band live, and he proceeded to commit a number of American shows to tape in the course of The Who's 1969 tour. But faced with the ear-numbing task of auditioning countless hours of performances, Townshend instead decided to start from scratch. The game plan was simple: play two shows in England early in 1970, record both, and pick the best material. When it turned out that the tapes of the Hull City Hall show on February 15 were useless due to technical problems, the choice was made even simpler. It was the February 14 show at Leeds University or nothing.

But what a show it was.

Before a rowdy, shouting audience—likely receiving their first and perhaps only exposure to "opera"—The Who performed the entirety of Tommy's twenty songs, sandwiched in between thirteen other numbers. It was a two-hour performance, the recording of which documented a band at their most virile and exhilarating.

Unlike his blues-based contemporaries, Townshend relied more on chords and parts of chords in his solos, shying away from the fleet-fingered scale runs that characterized the work of guitarists like Eric Clapton and Jeff Beck. Instead of a single piercing note, Townshend's amps would blast out the sound of a raw gaggle of guitar strings, the clamor threatening to disintegrate into sheer noise. His brilliant rhythm playing drove the band, crossing over from staccato bursts to glorious open chords that rang out with rich harmonic breadth.

Entwistle's bass, loaded with his preferred Rotosound bass guitar strings, spoke with a voice unique in rock and roll. His sound boasted a complexity that has not been heard since, an unlikely jumble of brittle high end, clanging middle, and truly thunderous bottom.

With The Ox rooting the band, Keith Moon was unleashed. And that is the only way to portray his approach to drumming. Moon's job description did not include the words "time keeper"—his gig with The Who is best described as lead drummer. With eyes bugging out and sweat-drenched hair whipping back and forth, Moon attacked his drums with a physical ferocity. In any live song by The Who, Moon can be heard pulling off countless nearly impossible percussion rolls and flourishes. But listen to the same song on a different night, and a totally different array of highlights will go crashing past. As incapable of repeating himself as he was of playing "normal" drums, Moon carved a unique rock niche, one in which he remains the sole resident.

At the front of The Who's stage stood Daltrey, the voice of Townshend's visions. Other rock singers might dance about in fey sways to the beat; Daltrey staked his claim, feet planted firmly, belting out the lines with workmanlike confidence.

And on this February night, it was all captured on tape with stunning clarity. Though the album's material was heavily edited—to present the entire concert on vinyl would have required three LPs—*Live at Leeds* offered a revealing look at The Who's imposing onstage strengths.

When *Live at Leeds* hit the store racks in May 1970, the cover sleeve was thin buff-colored cardboard, rubber-stamped in the corner with the band's name and the album title—a parody of the bootleg albums of concerts and unreleased studio sessions that were beginning to be sold via the underground collector network. Inside the sleeve was an array of Who documentation, from bills for smoke generators to a copy of The Who's contract to perform at the Woodstock festival.

The package was fun to explore, but what really mattered was the music. With this documentation of their onstage supremacy, The Who had raised the bar for rock and roll. In the liner notes for the CD reissue of the album, Townshend aptly described *Live at Leeds* as "the sound of a tremendous machine working almost by itself."

The Who had an opportunity to climb to the top of the rock pile, and they made the most of it with *Live at Leeds*. Traffic, meanwhile, was just trying to get back on the road in 1970.

Though fairly successful, the band would likely never reach the level of adulation that greeted their countrymen. Yet Traffic's vocalist and keyboardist, Steve Winwood, was highly regarded in musical circles.

First emerging into prominence as the teenage whiz kid vocalist of the Spencer Davis Group, Winwood had an old man's voice in a young man's body. His soul-stirring vocals belied his age and made instant fans of rock aristocracy like Jimi Hendrix and Eric Clapton. And though Jimi did augment his Experience with Winwood's organ on the groundbreaking *Electric Ladyland* album in 1968, it was Clapton who had the opportunity to form a band with Winwood in 1969 after the demise of both musicians' primary bands, Cream and Traffic.

Blind Faith was the result, a band guilty of starting a rather dubious trend, that of the rock supergroup. Throughout the 1970s the pattern repeated itself: first take a few well-known members from shattered bands, then record an album that, based on the participants' pedigrees, should have been great, and finally, split up the supergroup based on the disappointing reaction to said lackluster album. Blind Faith were the pioneers of that formula, with Clapton and Winwood joined by Cream's mercurial drummer Ginger Baker and bassist Rick Grech from Family.

The band convened to record *Blind Faith* in 1969, an album highlighted by Winwood's emotional vocals on the urgent "Sea of Joy" and the melancholy acoustic ballad of doubt and loss, "Can't Find My Way Home." But the lack of an entire album's worth of first-rate material led to the plodding presence of jam-based filler. Expecting a monumental work of stirring genius, the public reacted with lukewarm enthusiasm.

Under the standard pressure from management and the record companies to promote the album in both Europe and the United States, Blind Faith—a band that had yet to take the time to gel—hit the road. It was a fatal move.

"When it came down to it, we failed because we couldn't resist requests for the hits," Winwood recalled. "Ginger did a drum solo and they thought it was Cream, so we chucked in an old Cream song, then I put in a Traffic song, and the identity of the band was killed stone dead."

Retreating from the Blind Faith experience, in 1970 Winwood returned to familiar waters. He reformed Traffic after playing again with fellow Traffic-mates Jim Capaldi and Chris Wood during a brief stint in Ginger Baker's own Blind Faith follow-up, Air Force.

For Winwood and company, there had been one positive result from Blind Faith's existence, and that was the tremendous exposure the rock media had given the names Steve Winwood and Traffic in the process of hyping Blind Faith. When the reformed Traffic—missing only guitarist Dave Mason from their original lineup—released *John Barleycorn Must Die* in 1970, there was a bigger market ready to spend money on Traffic product.

The album was an altogether more successful project than Blind Faith's effort. The familiarity among the musicians was obvious, but after spending creative time in the company of others, the group's inventiveness was spurred. The album covered a lot of musical ground, from the sly instrumental jazz of the opener, "Glad," to the driving "Freedom Rider." An interesting stylistic deviation was the album's title track, a moving traditional English folk song that was later found on albums by Martin Carthy and Steeleye Span.

Throughout the *Barleycorn* album, Winwood was in exceptional vocal form, and it was understandable why Hendrix and Clapton had both come knocking at his door in recent months. More crucial as far as the band's continued survival, the relaxed album established Traffic as a commercial entity in the United States. The big payoff came with the band's next recording, *The Low Spark of High Heeled Boys*, released in 1971 and featuring an expanded band lineup. Though that particular disc

barely dented the British charts, in reality England was a relatively small market. In the United States—the market that really mattered from a financial standpoint—*Low Spark* climbed
to number seven on the charts.

On April 30, 1970, a surprising escalation of the bloody Vietnam conflict took place when President Richard Nixon ordered
combat units into Cambodia.

"We take these actions," Nixon said in his address to the
American people, "not for the purpose of expanding the war
into Cambodia, but for the purpose of ending the war in Vietnam, and winning the just peace we all desire."

The move was met with shock by a large segment of the
American public, and peace demonstrations—already taking
place on campuses across the United States—intensified in reaction to Nixon's decree.

As the sun rose on May 4, Kent State University and the town
of Kent, Ohio, had been through three difficult days. There had
been riots in the town as peace protests turned violent, and the
ROTC building on campus was destroyed in an act of arson.
The campus was occupied by the Ohio National Guard, who
were charged with suppressing any violent actions.

Just before noon, more than 1,500 students had gathered on
the campus commons. The National Guard dispersed them toward a parking lot, then the troops appeared to be returning to
the commons. Suddenly, twenty-eight of the guardsmen
turned, opening fire on the students. When the thirteen seconds
of gunfire ended, four students were dead, one was paralyzed,
and eight others lay wounded. Some students who had merely
been walking to and from class, not even part of the demonstration, were hit by the rifle fire.

In a time when American troops were fighting a war that
seemingly could not be won, when students were being shot
down by guardsmen, the popular music of the day—light musical trifles by Tony Orlando and Dawn, The Partridge Family,
Anne Murray, and The Carpenters—suddenly sounded as

meaningless as it truly was. Listening to pop to escape was one thing, but if ever there was a time for music to reflect current events, this was such an occasion.

One of the first groups to respond to the bloodshed at Kent State was Crosby, Stills, Nash, and Young.

Soon after the inception of Crosby, Stills, and Nash—whose first tour included 1969's Woodstock Festival—Neil Young was recruited into the band, expanding the group and reuniting Stills with his former band mate from Buffalo Springfield. There was plenty of peace and love imagery on the first Crosby, Stills, Nash, and Young album, *Déjà Vu*, but the shocking violence at Kent State demanded an attitude that was the polar opposite of songs like "Our House" and "Teach Your Children." Young was up to the task, writing the grim, powerful song "Ohio" and arranging for the band to record it within weeks of the incident. Suddenly, the music of Crosby, Stills, Nash, and Young had a defiant backbone, wrapped in churning guitars and propelled by an urgent beat. By July, the somber vow of outrage began to climb the charts, with its repeated chorus, "Four dead in Ohio," acting as a memorial to those lost in the tragedy. It was also the initial indication that Young was well on his way to becoming the most significant voice of the group.

Even before students were being shot on campuses, there were rock artists who used their status as musicians to make political statements. Some of the statements came out of the times, as honest attempts at pointing out flaws and injustice. Others were plotted out as savvy career moves, attempts to connect with "the kids" and revitalize record sales. One of the strongest statements—and riskiest, considering the success the band had obtained in the pop charts—came from Steppenwolf.

Steppenwolf was led by legally blind German immigrant John Kay, who had grown up in Toronto and Buffalo before relocating to rock-and-roll-crazy Los Angeles. Once the band built up a head of steam in the viciously competitive Hollywood club scene, a record deal they signed with ABC/Dunhill led to the recording of two of the iconic singles of the 1960s. "Born to Be Wild" and "Magic Carpet Ride" were blaring blasts of rock and roll at its finest, songs that careened along on noisy, syncopated rhythm pulses. Psychedelic guitars ignited in solos, and Kay's gruff voice promised danger. It was dizzying stuff that sold in droves.

So when, in 1970, Kay and company elected to do an entire album of songs about the decline and potential fall of the United States, it certainly wasn't considered a canny career move. But Steppenwolf, never highly regarded as a something-important-to-say "album band," aimed to change that perception with *Monster*.

"Time was once again our enemy," Kay recalled on the band's Internet site of the rushed recording of *Monster*, "which made it necessary that we recorded this project in an unusual fashion. The guys came up with one track after another while I was trying to keep up with my vocal parts and lyrics. Since this was supposed to be a concept album, I had to write within certain guidelines so that the lyrics fit within the concept."

The album wasted no time blasting the state of political affairs in the United States, beginning with the highly charged three-movement suite of songs, "Monster/Suicide/America." Clocking in at ten minutes, the music ranged from delicate chordal arrangements to the grinding, heavy crunch of blues rock in "Suicide," ultimately resolving to the repeated question, "America, where are you now?" The question remained unanswered as "America" slowly faded out to silence.

To prove their political point, Steppenwolf released "Monster" as a single. Not surprisingly, most Americans found it nowhere near as catchy as "Born to Be Wild." Though the weighty piece stalled at number thirty-nine on the charts, Kay and company reaped personal and creative satisfaction from their work. A bold and dangerous move from a band that had it made, "Monster/Suicide/America" remains the highlight of *Monster*, Steppenwolf's fourth—and most creative—album.

Of course, even when demonstrations weren't leading to deaths on college campuses, everybody had their own opinion about the United States' actions in Vietnam and the rest of

Southeast Asia. The United States often seemed divided—sometimes straight down political lines, other times along generational boundaries. But there were other conflicts afoot in 1970. Among them was the always-thorny issue of race relations. The subject was particularly contentious given the riots of the late 1960s, and white Americans were nervous about a growing militancy among many urban blacks.

Although the great soul singer James Brown could not be described as militant, it was obvious that Brown had become aware of which way the wind was blowing. Brown's ample talents yielded the creation of colorful nicknames—Godfather of Soul and King of Soul—and a string of hits early in the 1960s with songs like "Papa's Got a Brand New Bag" and "Please Please Please." But by the end of the decade, James had found "soul power" and was recording "Say It Loud, I'm Black and I'm Proud" and "Soul Pride."

In 1970, though, there was significantly more than a mere topical shift to be heard in Brown's music.

James Brown found himself in a lurch in March. His solid ring of band members, an inner circle that had surrounded the Godfather with a funky good time for years, was suddenly shattered. Longtime sax player St. Clair Pinckney left after almost ten years with Brown, as did bassist "Sweet Charles" Sherrell. But the biggest blow came when longtime band leader Maceo Parker decided to get into his own groove, splitting with more of the castle guard to form the appropriately named Maceo and All the King's Men.

Default band leader and organist Bobby Byrd got the call to shore up the decimated Brown band. The much-needed musical reinforcements arrived in the somewhat dubious form of a Cincinnati-based band called The Pacemakers, previously known as The New Dapps and The Blackenizers. James Brown Productions often signed new talent, and this bar band was one such outfit under incubation. Ready or not, it was star time for The Pacemakers.

"Bobby Byrd called, 'Hey fellas, y'all ready to gig with James?'" bassist William "Bootsy" Collins recounted to Cliff White in the liner notes to Brown's *In the Jungle Groove* CD. "There I was on the phone, my mouth hung wide open. 'With James!?'"

One key aspect had characterized Brown's musicians since his earliest days in show business: professionalism. James expected nothing but the best—tight precision, a zero-tolerance policy on mistakes, and an impeccable image. Things were about to get interesting.

Bootsy and company—including Collins' guitarist brother "Catfish"—had to drive night and day direct from Ohio to reach their first gig in Georgia.

"When we got there we had to go straight on stage," Collins recalled. "We had on jeans and T-shirts, looking crazy . . . As soon as we got on stage and plugged in, James calls out, 'Cold Sweat, hit it!' and that was it. Suddenly we're James Brown's backing band. No rehearsals, nothing."

Funny thing was, the "crazy-looking" band instinctively knew how to get way, way down. The feel was different from James' old-school band, but these kids knew their way around a deep funk vamp, and their enthusiasm grew on the great soul man.

It became one of the most powerful phases of James Brown's career, with the master exhorting everybody to "Get Up, Get Into It, and Get Involved" or "Give It Up or Turn It Loose." Ringleader Byrd's hoarse shouts demanded that listeners pay close attention, all while a band whose members were known as Chicken, Hasaan, Catfish, Cheese, Jabo, and, of course, Bootsy, funked up the Godfather's classic material.

All too quickly, though, one of the greatest parties in funk history reached a hung over conclusion. Chief among the culprits was the youngsters' predilection for drug experimentation, principally with acid.

"One night with James I thought the neck of my bass guitar turned into a snake," says Bootsy. "I didn't want no part of it and went back to the dressing room in the middle of the show. That pretty much cooled my deal with the Godfather."

Still, Brown's willingness—by necessity, to be honest—to work with and teach the new generation of funksters laid important groundwork. Soon after his stint with James Brown, Bootsy would hook up with George Clinton for the landing of the Parliament/Funkadelic/P-Funk mother ship, a mind-boggling synthesis of the flamboyant genius of Jimi Hendrix and the deep funk of the Godfather of Soul.

The influence of James Brown was all-encompassing, spreading even to the critical ears of the legendary jazz trumpeter and band leader Miles Davis.

"I listen to James Brown," said Miles Davis in the liner notes to *The Columbia Years*. "They swing their asses off. No bullshit. All the white groups have a lot of hair and funny clothes—they got to have on that shit to get it across."

But despite his somewhat derogatory comments, the often-cantankerous Davis was listening closely to rock, taking in both the new musical influences and the technical means by which the sounds were created. In particular, Davis was listening to Jimi Hendrix.

"Jimi Hendrix can take two white guys and make them play their asses off," Davis noted. "You got to have a mixed group—one has one thing, and the other has another . . ."

In 1970, Miles Davis' new project was about to have a "mixed group" of unprecedented pedigree.

Davis had a big burden on his shoulders. His groundbreaking efforts with arranger Gil Evans on albums like *Birth of the Cool* and *Sketches of Spain* were justifiably considered milestone albums of jazz, as was his freer work with sax master John Coltrane. Many listeners considered him the captain of jazz, charting its course into the future. But jazz traditionalists must have questioned whether they were aboard the Titanic when they heard Davis' 1969 album *In a Silent Way*. And when *Bitches Brew* arrived in 1970, it seemed that Davis had deliberately plowed jazz into an iceberg floating in rock music's waters.

Silent Way had offered just two tracks over a core band relying to a great extent on the instrumentation of rock music. *Bitches Brew* took things considerably further, becoming a landmark album for both its content and its personnel.

Among the musicians Davis chose to steer jazz in an entirely new direction were keyboardists Chick Corea, Joe Zawinul, and Larry Young; bassists Dave Holland and Harvey Brooks; saxophonist Wayne Shorter; drummers Lenny White, Don Alias, and Jack DeJohnette; and British guitarist John McLaughlin.

The gulf between jazz and rock in England was much smaller than in the United States, and many of the big guns in British rock had served time in a number of jazz combos. Jack Bruce and Ginger Baker had, prior to forming Cream, been working with guitarist McLaughlin and later sax player Dick Heckstall-Smith in keyboardist Graham Bond's famed Graham Bond Organisation. Shortly after Cream's dissolution, Bruce again stretched out his jazz chops in 1969 while working with McLaughlin in master percussionist Tony Williams' band Lifetime. There's no doubt Bruce and McLaughlin were nudging each other into both jazz and rock directions while playing in the fiery Lifetime. And a sizeable piece of the complicated jazz-rock puzzle fell neatly into place through the presence of Larry Young as Lifetime's keyboardist. When Davis went shopping for his *Bitches Brew* crew, he found both Young and McLaughlin in one convenient location.

When the first of three days of *Bitches Brew* sessions commenced—on August 19, 1969, a mere twenty-four hours after Jimi Hendrix walked off the Woodstock stage—many of the musicians had either never worked with Davis or never worked with each other. It was an environment ripe for uncharted exploration, and the band quickly got to work discovering where they were going.

Davis had a unique methodology, preferring to record sections or segments, later determining if a given piece stood on its own or if it required partnering with other components. The twenty-minute opening track, "Pharaoh's Dance," was comprised of multiple cuts and loops—groundbreaking thinking at a time when maximizing the creative use of a studio was not necessarily standard jazz practice. The album's title track was recorded much the same way.

"He would have us play," Harvey Brooks remembered in the liner notes to the remastered *Bitches Brew*, "and we would finish a section and he would say, 'Go on! Go on!' and we would keep playing. Miles knew what he wanted to do—he had a plan before he went into the studio."

Upon release in 1970, *Bitches Brew* confounded many listeners. In fact, some jazz and rock listeners found rare common ground in their assessment that much of *Bitches Brew* was at the least meandering, if not totally meaningless. But the key was that no one had ever made an album like this—and the people who got it, really got it.

Complexity aside, anyone should be able to appreciate the more accessible sounds like "Spanish Key," with the sparring of McLaughlin's guitar, Shorter's airy saxophone, and Corea's roiling keyboards. It works in breathtaking fashion, with the three soloists making way for Miles' trumpet as it flies in above the fray, a clarion call heralding a fundamental shift in the music of both jazz and rock.

In those moments, Miles Davis was laying out the whole blueprint for jazz-rock fusion.

On June 7, the unimaginable happened. Onto the hallowed stage of the Metropolitan Opera House in New York strolled the four members of the fresh-from-Leeds The Who. With the invitation to play the venerable concert hall, their rock opera *Tommy* received the ultimate in validation. For the Met's high-toned surroundings to house rock and roll was dramatic evidence of how respect for the band had evolved. Human evolution, on the other hand, was obviously lagging far behind, as evidenced by the continuing existence of the rock festival.

Despite the rain-drenched muck of Woodstock and the terror and death of Altamont, where Hell's Angels had rampaged, plenty of promoters were ready and willing to dip their toes into the festival game. Curious, considering that, as the 1967 Summer of Love faded into a distant memory, things were getting ugly in the American subculture. Those who kept track of what the drugs of choice were pointed to a decided swing toward more rambunctious chemicals like speed and the dynamic duo of downers and booze. A significant number of the hippies who had been so peaceful in the summer of 1967 were getting kind of surly—and when they were taking a lot of speed, they were surly for days at a time.

At the Atlanta International Pop Festival in Byron, Georgia, the kids were really getting down. All the way to the ground, that is, as a good portion of the 300,000 in attendance suffered heat stroke when temperatures easily spiked past the hundred-degree mark. Instead of acid tabs, salt tablets were the pill of choice. The Fourth-of-July-weekend festival was then clobbered by rain, which generated mud, which guaranteed that the remainder of the weekend would be passed in a steamy sauna atmosphere.

By day two, Atlanta—like Woodstock—had been declared a free festival, leaving one to wonder how festival promoters ever envisioned making any money organizing these thankless events.

Among the artists who dared venture onto the sweltering stage were Woodstock veterans Jimi Hendrix and Ten Years After, along with home-state heroes the Allman Brothers Band. But it was a newer band that caused one of the biggest stirs of the superheated weekend, and that was Grand Funk Railroad—Grand Funk for short.

Grand Funk had been warmly received in Atlanta in 1969, and they hit the festival stage on July 5, 1970, as conquering heroes. Named after the Grand Trunk Western Railroad, Grand Funk hailed from Flint, Michigan, and played big, dumb, loud rock befitting the city's industrial working-class heritage. Like California's Blue Cheer in the late 1960s, Grand Funk was a people's band, practically guaranteed to get bad reviews from any rock critic. It didn't matter to the audience, though, and the band's fourth album, 1970's *Live Album*, captures every ponderous nuance of the Grand Funk experience.

Live Album is perhaps the best documentation of what a 1970 concert actually sounded like, with a low-fi P.A. system's volume cranked up to eleven and a howling audience at peak hysteria. In fact, the recording sounds as though the extent of Grand Funk's preparation to record their live album was to make sure the cassette recorder had fresh batteries. As such, it's a glorious artifact.

A power trio among power trios, bassist Mel Schacher, drummer Don Brewer, and guitarist Mark Farner went for the throat when they hit the stage. Farner played a custom-built guitar with Grand Funk, which isn't surprising given that no normal guitar could possibly generate the gnarly tones of *Live Album*. It's heard to best effect on the solos, passages that typically climax with a multinote chromatic ascension up the guitar neck, capped by Farner stabbing at his fuzz pedal. That action yields the crowning glory: a buzzy, feedbacking cacophony nearly drowned out by the audience's lusty approval.

Had the apes of Stanley Kubrick's *2001: A Space Odyssey* encountered *Live Album* and a cheap 1970 stereo in place of the monolith that so stirred them in the film, the result would have been much the same: furious bone tossing and frenzied snarling. Grand Funk appealed to the lowest common denominator, and they did so expertly with carefully crafted, hefty riffage on songs like "Paranoid" and "Inside Looking Out."

There were many rumors that *Live Album* documented Grand Funk's performance in the heat of the 1970 Atlanta festival, but the album's recorded announcements that "the fire marshall" wanted the aisles cleared pointed to the recording's true origins, from three Florida gigs in June. Any fire marshall would have immediately recognized the futility of aisles in Atlanta's crowd of 300,000.

Nevertheless, *Live Album* is one of the enduring recordings of the 1970s. It is a record that, regardless of actual playback volume, simply sounds loud.

Across the ocean in 1970, rock festival experimentation was underway as well, although with a unique "isle" motif. A "gathering of the tribes" drew 500,000 people to East Afton Farm on the Isle of Wight, off the southern coast of England, from August 26 to 30, 1970.

Among the artists who made the sojourn to the small island was singer-songwriter Joni Mitchell, who had a memorable and tearful meltdown on stage when the audience did not react to her songs with the sensitivity she apparently required. Fortunately, less emotional artists with thicker skins also performed. Miles Davis brought the core of his *Bitches Brew* crew to forcibly expose the captive audience to his new sounds. The Who performed *Tommy* yet again, and Jimi Hendrix also played, running the gamut from brilliant to dreadful as he battled equipment woes during a two-and-a-half-hour festival-headlining set.

And for those who couldn't make it to these intimate little concerts with a few hundred thousand close friends—or those who just had the common sense to stay home—films documenting both Woodstock and Altamont were projected on movie screens across the country in 1970. Woodstock set new standards in filmmaking, with brilliant use of split screen techniques. *Gimme Shelter* focused not only on The Rolling Stones' disastrous free festival, but also on the band's 1969 tour and the recording of a new album. Still, the most moving moments came when the members of The Rolling Stones were filmed watching the unedited footage of the violence that erupted around the stage as the Hell's Angels "security guards" clashed with the audience. Singer Mick Jagger spoke of being disturbed by the footage, but the sadness in the eyes of drummer Charlie Watts required no words.

On the evening of June 4, 1967, the audience in London's Saville Theatre was abuzz with excitement. The Jimi Hendrix Experience was about to begin their concert, and the hum of the warmed-up amplifiers could be heard behind the curtains. But the excitement over Hendrix's imminent arrival was ramped up an extra notch, for among the crowd sat none other than Paul McCartney. The hysteria of Beatlemania had matured a bit, but interest in the band was still intense—just three days earlier, The Beatles had released their highly anticipated new album, *Sgt. Pepper's Lonely Hearts Club Band.*

"The curtains flew back," McCartney later recalled, "and Jimi came walking forward playing 'Sgt. Pepper.' It had only been released on the Thursday, so that was the ultimate compliment. It's a shining memory because I liked him so much anyway, he was so accomplished. I put that down as one of the greatest honors of my career."

McCartney's comment, and his obvious respect, only begins to convey the importance of Jimi Hendrix to the rock world of 1970. Most significantly, this importance wasn't reflected solely in record sales and concert tour grosses—the influence of Hendrix's work on his fellow musicians was seismic. But that influence was about to be taken away.

Late on the morning of September 18, 1970, Chas Chandler, the man who had brought Hendrix to England and produced Jimi's first two albums, climbed aboard a train to Newcastle.

"When I arrived me father was waiting for me, which he never did," Chandler recounted in *Jimi Hendrix: Electric Gypsy* by Caesar Glebbeek and Harry Shapiro. "'I came to get you away from all the reporters.' 'Reporters?' 'Don't you know?' 'Know what?' 'Jimi's dead.'"

Under circumstances that, to this day, are surrounded by intrigue and confusion, the greatest electric guitarist in rock's history—and arguably rock's most important star in 1970—was dead from an overdose of sleeping pills.

Hendrix had gone to bed late, staying in a downstairs room in the tiny Samarkand Hotel in London, a room he was sharing with a young German named Monika Dannemann. Though questions about the events of the early morning hours on that September 18 may never be fully answered, there is no disputing that Hendrix accidentally took a fatal dose of Vesparax. The sleeping tablets belonged to Dannemann, and they were a German brand with which Hendrix was likely unfamiliar. The label on the pill bottle was printed in German, preventing Jimi from seeing that the pills were far more powerful than most such sleep aids—the normal dosage was one-half of a tablet. Jimi was unaware of the drug's strength, and it cost him his life.

"It's funny the way most people love the dead," he had told the British music newspaper *Melody Maker* eighteen months before. "Once you're dead, you're made for life. You have to die before they think you're worth anything . . ."

The musical loss was a staggering blow to rock music, but the death of Jimi Hendrix would prove to have equally tragic personal repercussions on the life of another of rock music's greatest instrumentalists.

On September 13, 1970—five days before Jimi Hendrix died—guitarist Paul Kossoff was celebrating his last night as a teenager. Standing on stage at England's Fairfield Hall in Croydon, Kossoff—or "Koss" to his band mates in Free—was continuing his ascension to the ranks of rock's elite guitarists. As with a gig in Sunderland earlier in 1970, the Croydon show was being recorded for an upcoming live album, and the band were also in the studio laboring away at the creation of their next album of new material.

Free had come together just more than two years before. Kossoff, the son of esteemed British actor David Kossoff, was playing with a band called Black Cat Bones when he met Simon Kirke. Kirke, a drummer, boldly informed the guitarist that it would be in the best interests of Black Cat Bones to fire their current drummer and place Kirke into the position. Kossoff took the advice. And when Koss later jammed with a band called Brown Sugar, he met singer Paul Rodgers. In April 1968, Koss, Rodgers, and Kirke played together and reached a decision—to form their own band. A bass player was recommended, and into the mix came sixteen-year-old Andy Fraser. Free was born.

In a time when hype was common, Free earned their popularity the old-fashioned way—they gigged until they were ready to drop. Though they were quickly signed to Chris Blackwell's Island Records and did manage to work their way onto the bill of some high-profile shows—including a support role at the 1969 edition of the Isle of Wight festival—Free spent most of their time driving endlessly up and down the United Kingdom, stuffed into a transport van. Their sleep was usually little more than catnaps taken while nestled amongst the amplifiers, guitar cases, drums, and other tools of their trade.

When *Fire and Water*, their third album, joined its predecessors in the record stores in June 1970, a foundation of fans was in place. But that foundation swelled exponentially due to the presence of one song, "All Right Now." A mindlessly simple boy-meets-girl tale—and therefore instantly attractive to fans of pop music—the song moved audiences from the first time Free played the song. It quickly sailed into rarified atmosphere in both the British and American charts, logging sales of more than a million copies in just four weeks.

But "All Right Now" was not the archetypal Free song. Their hit was light-hearted fluff, more obviously so when heard in light of earlier Free material like the weary, stark "Mourning Sad Morning" and the heavy blues "Worry," with its messages of death on the wind.

Indeed, the remainder of *Fire and Water* was more in line with Free's prior studio track record. From the first notes of "Fire and

Water," the album's lead-off title track, the loping sound of Free offers an obvious divergence from the work of other guitar-bass-drums lineups descended from the prototype of all power trios, Cream. Though Free did borrow one aspect of Cream's approach—the prominence of Fraser's bass in the overall sonic balance—where Cream would typically venture into realms of frantic instrumental combat, Free preferred to keep things open and austere. The wide-open spaces gave Koss room to weave his emotional, pained playing, the guitar notes laden with his uniquely quivering vibrato.

"The empathy he had!" recalled recording engineer Richard Digby-Smith in the liner notes to the reissue of Free's *Highway* album. "Amazing you could have a guitar that loud, that powerful, and play so delicately, so harmonically rich . . . Free were quite inspired. Quite chilling sometimes. The beauty of it could bring a grown man to tears."

That beauty was prominent on the darker moments of *Fire and Water*, as the band crafted a haunting, delicate atmosphere in "Oh I Wept" and in their masterpiece ballad, "Heavy Load." Rodgers' restrained vocal approach was devastatingly effective, able to transport listeners into a musical world of shadowy moods, and he avoided the over-the-top tendencies of his rock-front-man contemporaries in favor of this intimate communication.

Of course, Free had not built a fan base on ballads alone—the months spent on the road found the band playing more than their share of shows in front of rowdy audiences with little patience for songs of emotion, no matter how well crafted. "Fire and Water" and "Mr. Big," with an unusual lead bass solo urging the song towards its climax, characterized the aggressive side of the band. Driven by Kirke's deceptively simple drumming, Koss and Fraser brought new weight to heavy blues progressions, completing the package and making *Fire and Water* one of the most effective and artistically successful albums of the decade.

Despite the success the band had found, though, it was while Free was recording *Highway*, the follow-up to *Fire and Water*, that a single event would change the band forever.

Sharing the insecurities that plague most musicians, Paul Kossoff was uncertain where he stood when weighed against his fellow guitarists. Free's sudden success—with "All Right Now" selling so many copies that the band was immediately given a billing of prominence at the 1970 Isle of Wight festival—made for a heady time for the young player, but also a difficult one. Suddenly, Koss was seeing his name alongside those of guitarists like Eric Clapton, Jeff Beck, and Jimmy Page. Was he good enough to be mentioned in the same breath?

Despite those doubts, there was one thing Koss was certain of—his admiration and respect for Jimi Hendrix. To Koss, the music of Hendrix was everything. So when the terrible news of Jimi's death reached Koss' ears, he was far more than just saddened.

"He was pretty near to tears," Simon Kirke recalled in the Free history *Heavy Load* by David Clayton and Todd Smith. "I still believe that a lot of spirit went out of Koss then. I could see the change in him, the psychological thing, not the physiological, and the change was very apparent. They were very spiritually close, or to Koss it seemed that way . . . So it hit him very hard. He went almost on this death wish thing. He wouldn't eat and he got into a terrible state."

Kossoff was determined to fly to Seattle to attend Hendrix's funeral. The band pleaded with him to return to the studio instead—there was an album that had to be finished under deadline.

Koss eventually relented and returned to work. But his attitude was strikingly different, his mood solemn and grave. The aura of morose depths that sometimes permeated Free's music—depths that had shadowed the most heartrending moments of Kossoff's moving solos—began to consume him. The death of Jimi Hendrix, sadly, would become the catalyst of Paul Kossoff's own dark spiral.

Jim Morrison of The Doors, bare-chested and confident, coolly staring down the camera. Jimi Hendrix on stage at Woodstock, eyes squeezed shut in rapt concentration. Duane Allman playing his unplugged Les Paul in a moment of solitude stolen in a Holiday Inn bathroom. Pete Townshend on stage in San Francisco, arms outstretched in pure rock god posturing. Eric Clapton and Ginger Baker in deep discussion while recording *Disraeli Gears*.

This is rock and roll, communicated viscerally in the nonverbal, nonmusical language of shadow and light—photography. It was through photography that many rock star personalities came to be defined, and it happened only because photographers of the era had unrestricted access to the most private moments of rock stars. The greatest and most moving of the rock portraits depicted candid moments, unstaged and unblinking looks into the lives of the musicians. It was not always a pretty sight.

The cameras of San Francisco's Jim Marshall captured an astounding number of the images that represented rock music on the printed page. His greatest gift was in reminding the viewer that these musicians, for all the trappings of stardom, were still just people, whether in the throes of glorious creation or wretched excess. But of all the thousands of photographs Marshall has shot over the years, perhaps his most memorable picture evokes the pain that imbued so much of Janis Joplin's music.

In the image, Janis reclines on a ripped vinyl couch, backstage at San Francisco's Winterland in 1968. She's alone, holding a bottle of Southern Comfort, cast in the harsh glare of a string of bare light bulbs above her head.

"When I showed Janis the picture of her lying back with the bottle in her hand," Marshall recalled in his book *Not Fade Away*, "she said, 'Jim, this is how it is sometimes. Lousy.'"

Janis often alluded to the loneliness of stardom, a stardom with negative facets made all the more prickly by the fact that Janis was one woman working in a male-dominated business.

"On stage, I make love to 25,000 different people," she once said. "Then I go home alone."

In 1970, Joplin was attempting to reenergize her career. She had arrived in California from Texas in 1966, and almost immediately helped define the San Francisco Sound while gaining stardom in Big Brother and the Holding Company. But the merely competent capabilities of the Big Brother band sent Janis in search of musicians who could realize the soul-influenced music she wanted to make. Most of 1969 was spent working and touring with The Kozmic Blues Band, a grouping more or less assembled for her rather than by her. But the horn-driven aggregation was inconsistent, and their performances ran the gamut from ecstatic to erratic. As the new year dawned, Janis and manager Albert Grossman set out to assemble a real band.

Retaining two members of the Kozmic Blues Band and selecting three other musicians, Janis assembled The Full Tilt Boogie Band. The lineup differed from the norm, designed around a core of guitar-bass-drums but augmented by two keyboardists. As the band and Janis got to know each other on the road in the summer of 1970, The Full Tilt Boogie Band came together, integrating into a tight ensemble. They could rock with authority, but their foundation was in the rhythm and blues of great instrumental combos like Booker T and the MGs. The enthusiastic crowd reactions told Janis that she now had the one thing missing in her career to this point—a band capable of making a great album.

The final piece of the recording puzzle came into place just after the tour ended, when Paul Rothchild was signed as the producer of Joplin's next album. After producing groups like The Paul Butterfield Band early in his career, Rothchild boldly stepped into the industry spotlight through his innovative work as producer of The Doors. Rothchild had helped propel Morrison and company to superstardom; with the maturing talent of a star like Janis, combined with a band that was both excited and exciting, the potential to create a landmark album was obvious.

Throughout September, 1970, the recording sessions progressed at Sunset Sound Studios in Hollywood. At last, Janis had strong material—some written by Janis herself, other songs contributed by musicians like Nick Gravenites and Bobby Womack—and a band capable of working together, crafting the kind of arrangements needed to build a creative whole that worked on every level.

On October 4, though, Rothchild was worried. It was nearly six in the evening, and Janis was very late arriving at the studio. He finally asked Full Tilt's road manager, John Cooke, to go check on Janis and find out if she was in her room at a motel near Sunset Boulevard. When there was no answer to

Cooke's knocking, he summoned the motel's manager to gain entrance to the room. They found Janis Joplin lying wedged between the bed and the nightstand, dead of a heroin overdose at the age of twenty-seven.

In shock, but unable to forget how thrilled Janis had been in the last few weeks, the album participants made a difficult decision. Rothchild and the Full Tilt Boogie Band continued work on the album, which would be christened *Pearl* after Janis' nickname. Most of the production work had been done by the time of Joplin's death, as the album was nearing completion. In fact, there was just one song for which Janis had not recorded a vocal take, and that was Gravenites' "Buried Alive in the Blues." When *Pearl* was released and climbed to number one on the album charts, its song lineup contained "Buried Alive in the Blues," sadly now the instrumental it had never been intended to be.

Much like Janis, Jimi Hendrix had also been immersed in a period of intense work prior to his death three weeks before Joplin's. His dream studio—Electric Lady Studios, on Eighth Street near Greenwich Village in New York—had finally become operational after months of delays. It opened only weeks before Jimi left the United States on his final European tour.

As with Paul Rothchild and the Joplin project, Hendrix engineer Eddie Kramer and longtime drummer Mitch Mitchell found themselves with the melancholy task of bringing a deceased artist's music to fruition. Jimi's music would fill the rooms of Electric Lady as Mitchell fine-tuned his drum tracks, creating an eerie atmosphere where loss and creativity uneasily coexisted. When *The Cry of Love* was released months later, it pointed to some of the bold new directions in which Jimi had intended to guide his music.

Across the Atlantic, it seemed fitting that the album George Harrison was creating as his first release since the dissolution of The Beatles was to be titled *All Things Must Pass*. For indeed The Beatles had passed, as had Jimi and Janis—and much of rock's innocence.

When Harrison's album emerged in December, his opus was something of a monument to excess. *All Things Must Pass* sprawled across three albums, the collection packaged in a big black box. The impression was that every moment of studio time had been deemed worthy of inclusion—hence the presence of one LP subtitled *Apple Jam*, a documentation of various loose jam sessions. Many of rock's leading musicians had an opportunity to contribute to the recordings, and George worked with the legendarily eccentric producer Phil Spector to fabricate the fabled Spectorian "wall of sound" as the underpinning for songs like "My Sweet Lord," "Hear Me Lord," and the title track.

Despite a somewhat hefty price tag and the rather daunting prospect of sitting through six sides of anybody's music, *All Things Must Pass* had shoved its way straight to number one by the first week of 1971.

It may have seemed that the music world was harmoniously in tune with the former Beatle's search for his Lord. Not quite. Though Harrison had shown that he was seeking transcendence and transition through spirituality, there was a new band in England with eyes firmly fixed on the darkness of the human condition. They were called Black Sabbath, and the mere mention of their name would soon strike fear into the hearts of a generation of parents.

The sudden resonance is indescribably horrifying, its momentum unstoppable. A single dark, molten chord erupts, forged from a simple two-note formation yet bearing more weight than an orchestral crescendo. A rumbling bass lopes beneath the chord, morphing itself into a ghastly counterrhythm. The thunder of massive drums is locked in with the bass, fused in an unholy alliance of noise and lumbering energy. A pattern emerges, taking form as a relentless repetition, and, descending from high above the fray, a howling air raid siren grows in volume, forecasting disaster, hopelessness, and terror.

Welcome to the first minute of Black Sabbath's *Paranoid*. And all this came from humble origins in the unlikely form of a Birmingham, England, blues band called Earth.

Earth was formed only after an immediate dislike between vocalist John "Ozzy" Osbourne and guitarist Tony Iommi stretching back to school days was finally put to bed. The quarrelsome duo were joined by the rhythm section of Terrence Michael Butler, soon to be known as "Geezer," on bass, and Bill Ward on drums. The foursome set about playing blues clubs in the north of England and also engaged in a lengthy stint at Hamburg, Germany's Star Club, where The Beatles had cut their teeth more than a decade before.

After discovering that the name Earth was already in the possession of another outfit, the 1935 Boris Karloff film *Black Sabbath* provided a much more descriptive moniker. Signing with the Vertigo label in England, the newly rechristened Black Sabbath entered the studio to record their first album. To say the band was on a tight budget is an understatement—Sabbath had a whole three days to get the record done, spending the princely sum of roughly one thousand dollars in the process.

Much like Free, Black Sabbath was building a reputation based on the live gig circuit. The endless succession of shows in pubs and run-down halls seemed to add up to little more than a thankless task at times, but their debut, *Black Sabbath,* began to climb the charts during the first part of 1970.

The group was scheduled to return to the studio in July, presented with a lengthier opportunity to further define the Black Sabbath sound for posterity—though their first album had clearly revealed the band's British blues roots.

"To me, Sabbath was always just a really heavy blues band. That's all we were," bassist Geezer Butler told *Bass Dimensions.* "We just took those blues roots and made them heavier, because we were into Hendrix and Cream, who were like the heaviest bands around at that time. We just wanted to be heavier than everybody else!"

Black Sabbath began to achieve their goal through the use of volume and pacing. The volume part was easy—more amplification running on full power. The pacing took some thought. As the band developed the songs for their second album, they began to turn away from clichéd blues progressions. This was accomplished either by slowing the speed of the songs to a deadening crawl, thereby emphasizing carefully thought-out series of ominous notes, or by powering along with all three instrumentalists unified in the leaden throes of a heavy staccato pulse. Over it all, Ozzy's vocal cords emitted a tortured, harpy wail, tonal qualities perfectly suited to undertaking the conveyance of the dark truths of Butler's increasingly sinister lyrics.

When the band completed the recording of *Paranoid*, Sabbath saw the album quickly embraced by the public upon its September release. Though the group was marketed in such a way as to encourage the image of Black Sabbath as a Satan-worshipping gang of dangerous black massers, in truth the lyrics of *Paranoid* dwelt on more pedestrian rooted-in-reality topics, heavily focusing on drugs and war. Still, with song titles like "War Pigs," "Electric Funeral," and "Hand of Doom," it was clear that Black Sabbath was embarking on a career arc dramatically different from that of other bands.

The success of Black Sabbath offered proof of the turbulent waters that rock music found itself treading as 1970 came to a close. *Paranoid* had quickly risen to number one on the British album charts, and in the United States the album would soon ascend to number twelve. There were obviously listeners ready to embrace music crafted with a new aggression and attitude, but was Black Sabbath to be the band that would steer rock in a new direction?

In their brief life span of just more than two years in the late 1960s, England's Cream had left a legacy that influenced everyone from Jimi Hendrix to Black Sabbath while laying the groundwork for the ascension of hard rock throughout the 1970s. But the brilliant trail blazed by the trio had taken its toll on the personalities of Eric Clapton, Ginger Baker, and Jack Bruce.

"The group was dead by the time we did the *Goodbye* album," drummer Baker recalled of the group's acrimonious split in the liner notes to the career retrospective box set *Those Were the Days*. "When Cream died, it died. Short of murder, we couldn't solve a problem between us."

"After Cream it felt like a great weight had lifted off us," bassist and vocalist Bruce recalled in the book *Cream* by Chris Welch. "It had been such an intense period of activity. I suppose we should have split up for a while and then come back together again . . . But that didn't happen . . . We all became involved in our own things and grew apart."

Though Baker and Clapton were soon back out on the road in Blind Faith, Bruce was seeking some normalcy in his life, "as opposed to living out of a suitcase." But seeking domestic calm after surviving Cream's near-nonstop existence on the road didn't mean Bruce was forsaking his taste in adventurous music.

As he prepared to record his first solo album, Bruce moon-lighted in The Tony Williams Lifetime, playing jazz cross-pollinated with both rock instrumentation and—almost more importantly—amplification. Joining Bruce and master drum-mer Williams in the project were keyboardist Larry Young and guitarist John McLaughlin, key players in Miles Davis' groundbreaking electric bands. Although Bruce enjoyed the challenge of The Lifetime's high-wire antics, the Scottish bassist had something different in mind.

Though Cream was highly regarded for their breathtaking onstage instrumental jousting, in the studio the band was ca-pable of crafting concise, beautifully melodic songs like "We're Going Wrong" and "As You Said." That sense of harmonious composition was just as much a part of Bruce's overall vision of music as was his experimentation with jazz. So it should come as no surprise that on 1971's *Harmony Row,* Bruce saw fit to use elements of both musical spheres in his quest to realize a unique middle ground.

Just after his association with the Williams project, Bruce had begun his search for the right balance on 1969's *Songs for a Tai-lor*, a strong first post-Cream solo album that had featured a va-riety of players ranging from Cream producer Felix Pappalardi to sax player Dick Heckstall-Smith, who had played with Bruce and Ginger Baker in the old Graham Bond Organisation. For *Harmony Row*, though, Bruce chose to work exclusively with a core unit of two musicians who also had contributed to the first album, drummer John Marshall and guitarist Chris Spedding.

The result was a stimulating mix, showing off the lyrical strengths of Bruce and his songwriting partner Pete Brown while allowing the three musicians free reign to enter into dis-tinctive territory. Over Bruce's probing bass and Marshall's freely swinging drums, Spedding squarely contrasted his own style against the jazz leanings of the rhythm section. Spedding somehow fit perfectly, allowed by Bruce to give his playing un-conditional range, from beefy rock chops to fleet runs in the R&B and rockabilly styles of the great American guitarists Steve Cropper and James Burton. Though songs like "A Letter of Thanks" and "You Burned the Tables on Me" largely played to the ample jazz strengths of the participants, they stayed firmly anchored in strong songwriting rather than acting as skeletal frames for demonstrations of instrumental prowess. If one track summarizes the success of the overall experiment, it is "Morning Story," where the trio creates an urgency in the chord evolution while Bruce's vocals soar into the same rarified air they had ventured into so frequently with Cream.

On paper, it shouldn't have worked, considering the divergent pedigrees of the musicians. But it was the kind of adventurous pairing of contrasting styles that commonly led to fascinating work in the 1970s. Instead of creating tension, the disparate elements brought by Bruce and his accompanists combined into a tuneful and creative coexistence. That synchronization elevated *Harmony Row* to esteemed status while eclipsing the higher-profile albums released by Bruce's Cream cohorts.

Ironically, it was the American tour of Cream's Baker and Clapton in Blind Faith that would prove to have a major impact on rock in the early 1970s—although it wasn't for the brilliant performances of rock's first supergroup. Instead, it was due to the presence of one of the tour's opening acts, Delaney and Bonnie.

Eric Clapton had been struggling with the trappings of rock stardom long before the Blind Faith tour, and when he met Bonnie and Delaney—"down-home ordinary cats" as he referred to them—the duo and their band were like a fresh breath of country air. Delaney Bramlett hailed from Mississippi; Bonnie O'Farrell's Southern roots only stretched as far south as Illinois, but she was on the same musical page as her husband. Playing rootsy, soul-inspired rock, the duo's second album was produced by Booker T and the MGs' Duck Dunn and a studio musician acquaintance of Delaney's named Leon Russell.

The critical reaction to the album, *Accept No Substitute,* helped get the duo on the Blind Faith tour, where Clapton became enthralled with the band's laid-back style. In fact, he was so taken with Delaney and Bonnie that, after Blind Faith's collapse, he took on the role of side man for the duo's European tour. The relaxed touring pace and lack of pressure was so attractive that

Clapton's good pal George Harrison began coming along for the ride, one documented on *Delaney & Bonnie & Friends on Tour with Eric Clapton*. In turn, Harrison and Clapton both used the Delaney and Bonnie band as core musicians on their *All Things Must Pass* and *Eric Clapton* albums.

Paraphrasing Harrison, all things must indeed pass, and that included Delaney and Bonnie's prized band. With an upcoming tour already booked, blues shouter Joe Cocker found himself in need of a band. Cocker had gained acclaim from an inspired performance on Woodstock's stage, one that was glowingly featured in the accompanying film documentary. Leon Russell volunteered to help the singer—and did so by convincing the Bonnie and Delaney band to defect to the Cocker camp en masse.

When Cocker's album *Mad Dogs & Englishmen* was released, joined by a film that premiered on January 22, 1971, an important gathering of musical talent was documented. By the time Cocker's two-month tour was underway, the band numbered eleven, augmented by ten vocalists pressed into service as Cocker's "choir." In reality, the assemblage was a bit like The Church of Ray Charles, with its soul revue concept given a thoroughly modern aura of marijuana smoke and light shows. But the ensemble crackled with excitement, and the sheer power of the entire group at full flight was undeniable.

In the wake of the tour, solo stardom was assured for troupe keyboardist Russell and singer Rita Coolidge, and members of the band went on to play with artists ranging from The Rolling Stones to John Lennon.

Eric Clapton, of course, had kept his keen eyes on the proceedings. As soon as the Cocker tour reached a conclusion, he snatched up two of its key members, bassist Carl Radle and drummer Jim Gordon, for a new project with keyboard player Bobby Whitlock, himself recently of the decimated Delaney and Bonnie band.

The newly named Derek and the Dominos retired to Miami's Criteria Studio, where ace producer Tom Dowd was charged with documenting the proceedings. He had his hands full.

"Tom couldn't believe it, the way we had these big bags laying out everywhere," Whitlock said in the liner notes to *The*

Layla Sessions, recalling the band's copious drug consumption. "It was scary, what we were doing, but we were just young and dumb and didn't know. Cocaine and heroin, that's all—and Johnny Walker."

Fueling much of the debauchery was Clapton's dubious mental state. He had managed to fall fanatically in love with Patti Harrison, wife of his good friend George. It was a consuming obsession that was bound to come to no good end—but it was just the thing for torturing "Derek" into peaks of anguished creativity.

Where the Eric Clapton album had been as sittin'-on-the-porch laid back as any Delaney and Bonnie album, the album Clapton and his Dominos knocked out in Miami—*Layla and Other Assorted Love Songs*—seethed with a fire and passion that had been missing from Clapton's playing since the glory days of Cream. Songs like "Why Does Love Got to be So Sad" and "Keep on Growing" roiled and boiled instrumentally as Clapton and Whitlock hoarsely and fervently shouted the lyrical exchanges. And when the pace slowed, as on "Bell Bottom Blues" and "Have You Ever Loved a Woman," Clapton's expressive instrumental communication revealed a new understanding of the pain at the heart of real blues. The album was crowned by its title track, a song which has become one of the most enduring of the 1970s.

Like any band running flat-out on a highly combustible fuel of drugs and inflamed passions, the end was near, and it came sooner rather than later for Derek and the Dominos. After vainly attempting to record a second album in May of 1971 at Olympic Studios in London, the Dominos fell for the final time. One of Clapton's last memories of the aborted sessions is of Whitlock standing outside the guitarist's door, screaming for Clapton to emerge as he hid inside, too paranoid from drugs to answer the door.

In the end, though, Clapton did get the girl—he married his Layla, Patti, in August, 1978, after she left Harrison for Clapton.

One of the fieriest elements of the Derek and the Dominos' *Layla* album had been provided by a guest Domino, a bearded young guitarist born in Nashville named Duane Allman.

Duane had followed a long and twisting path before he wound up playing alongside Clapton, one of his guitar heroes. After several fitful attempts at getting musical momentum going with his brother Gregg—in bands like The Allman Joys and Hour Glass—Duane made his way to the improbable rural Alabama locale known as Muscle Shoals. There, under unlikely circumstances, a tiny recording studio had become a hit-making factory.

It began in 1966, when Percy Sledge cut "When a Man Loves a Woman" at the cinder-block Fame studio. The song became a hit for Atlantic Records, beginning an association between the label and the studio that saw artists like Wilson Pickett and Aretha Franklin dispatched to Alabama for recording purposes. The Muscle Shoals Rhythm Section became known as one of the premier studio backing bands, especially for rhythm and blues and soul music. But when Duane Allman got a call in November 1968 to track some Pickett sessions in Alabama, he brought a new dimension to the Muscle Shoals Sound.

Despite Duane's unorthodox persona—long hair and colorful clothes were still likely to ruffle feathers in the deep South, and Duane's manner had earned him the nickname Skydog— the other members of the Fame studio band knew Allman was something special. He was immediately invited to move to the area and join the studio's musical staff. Over the next few months Allman honed his chops, contributing brilliant lead and slide guitar to a wide range of albums by artists ranging from Boz Scaggs to King Curtis. But Duane's talent was too vast to be contained in the four walls of a little Alabama studio, no matter how great the end results.

Jerry Wexler of Atlantic Records and manager Phil Walden encouraged Duane to get his own band together, and after moving to Jacksonville, Florida, Allman began to solidify the lineup. Drummer Jaimoe—short for Jai Johanny Johanson— made the move with Duane to Florida, in pursuit of bassist Berry Oakley. Oakley didn't want to leave his band Second Coming because of his musical relationship with guitarist Dickey Betts, so Allman invited both Oakley and Betts to join his new project. With second drummer Butch Trucks also on board, in March 1969 Duane was finally able to convince his brother Gregg to leave California, where the younger Allman had remained since the dissolution of Hour Glass. The final piece was in place—they were now The Allman Brothers Band.

The band's first two albums revealed a growing competency, but like many of the bands that found success in England through constant touring, The Allman Brothers made their reputation through hard work on the road.

"In 1971 we did two-hundred-and-twenty-seven dates," Kim Payne, a key member of the band's road crew, recalled in Scott Freeman's band history *Midnight Riders*. "You'd get the equipment tore down and loaded up and then you'd get to the next gig just in time to set it all up again. I've slept soundly lying down behind a line of amplifiers, and them sumbitches would be booming."

With an instinctive communication between the band's players now having been honed by two years on the road, it just made sense to record the band on stage, freed from the constraints of a recording studio and in their natural environment where anything might happen.

On March 12 and 13, 1971, a truck full of equipment belonging to New York's Location Recorders was poised to capture The Allman Brothers Band performing at New York's Fillmore East. Promoter Bill Graham had been an early supporter of the band, so the choice of venue was copasetic. And producer Tom Dowd, who had helmed the band's second album, *Idlewild South*, was set to oversee the live recording.

Doing two shows each night, and not wrapping things up until the very early morning hours, The Allman Brothers Band lived up to their stellar live reputation.

"In my heart and in my mind I knew they had played wonderfully and that this would be an incredible album," Dowd recalled in the liner notes for the MFSL/Ultradisc reissue of *The Allman Brothers Band at Fillmore East*.

Indeed, *Fillmore East* became one of the most important live albums of the decade, although the record company dragged their heels at the prospect of a double live album—particularly one that the band's manager, Phil Walden, wanted to release at a cost just slightly higher than that of a single album. But

Walden won out, and any lingering doubts were quietly swept under the rug when the album immediately ascended to number thirteen in the *Billboard* charts. By the end of the summer, just weeks after its release, *The Allman Brothers Band at Fillmore East* had easily reached gold record status.

What the hundreds of thousands of fans who bought the record heard was a band at a stunning peak of improvisational creativity. When Duane or Dickey took a solo, the other instinctively fell into the rhythm role, carefully building chordal drama to emphasize the lead lines. And what leads they were. Both guitarists, armed with Gibson Les Pauls, had discovered an amazing tone that was almost keyboard-like in its sustain yet still retained a biting squawk that emphasized each note. Both Betts and Allman maintained a keen sense of a song's melodic structure when they took the lead, easily flowing from major scales to blues scales to relative scales. And no matter how feverish the pitch or what frenzied heights the peak of a solo reached, neither guitarist lost sight of the need to keep what they were playing rooted solidly in synergistic musical approaches.

Gregg Allman's dexterous work on his Hammond organ was equally crucial to the band's sound. The younger Allman brother avoided the tendency of many organists to overplay, subtly coloring the songs with partial chords and stabbing emphasis notes. But when it was his turn to step out, Gregg revealed a smoky, jazz-like influence in some solos; a commanding, raunchy, rhythm-and-blues earthiness in others. And there were no vocals earthier than Allman's, his hoarse voice bearing an old man's weariness and belying his true age.

Supporting the entire band with a constantly evolving foundation, the rhythm section of Jaimoe and Trucks created a rolling rhythm bed, one that surged and urged and persuaded the songs forward. Instead of devolving into a cacophonous percussive disaster, the two drummers complemented each other's styles, knowing by intuition when to press and when to lay back.

But the unsung hero of the Allman Brothers Band was bassist Berry Oakley. Throughout the live album, Oakley played in an incredibly melodic style that was most reminiscent of Motown Records' brilliant bassist James Jamerson. Oakley weaved his bass over, under, and deep within the chord changes, nailing target notes that urge whole sections of songs into new vistas and tempos. How important is a good bassist to the engine room of a great rock band? One listen to Oakley's performances on "Hot 'Lanta" or "In Memory of Elizabeth Reed" will provide an abundantly clear answer.

The sum of these strengths was a band that, at full flight, was fully unified and quite capable of reaching spectacular heights. Equally significant was the fact that The Allman Brothers Band, while playing songs that frequently exceeded the ten-minute mark, successfully found a mass audience. It was a reflection of a time when attention spans were long enough to welcome quests for improvisational excellence.

Sadly, Duane Allman was never given the chance to further develop his prodigious talents. Just seven months after his band recorded the *Fillmore East* concerts—and with his name now spoken in the same breath with names like Clapton, Page, and Beck—Skydog was killed in a motorcycle accident near his Georgia home. He was just twenty-four years old.

Though The Allman Brothers Band frequently navigated the blues sphere of influence—*Fillmore East* included takes on Blind Willie McTell's "Statesboro Blues" and T-Bone Walker's "Stormy Monday"—another American band had begun their career with respectful blues worship, if not outright imitation.

The J. Geils Band—named after founding guitarist Jerome Geils—hailed from Boston. Their lead singer was a rail-thin, compelling motor mouth who called himself Peter Wolf. Wolf had perfected his ability to unleash a torrent of hip jive talk while DJ-ing on local radio stations—but the rock and roll stage provided a sympathetic environment for Wolf to evolve his act to the next level. More importantly, though, Wolf and Geils brought to their musical house party an encyclopedic knowledge of the blues' founding fathers. With keyboardist Seth Justman, bassist Danny Klein, drummer Steven Bladd, and harmonica whiz Magic Dick, the vocalist and guitarist cut a debut album for Atlantic Records that stood tall as white blues evolution in its highest form.

Rather than rip off riffs and lyrics from the blues masters and then rename the thinly disguised proceedings in an attempt to avoid plagiarism charges—a charge most famously leveled at Led Zeppelin—The J. Geils Band was happy to cover the works that they considered holy ground while giving credit where credit was due. And the band looked the part of blues musicians; in an era of long hair and flamboyant clothes, The J. Geils Band favored a street-tough image of black clothing, leather jackets, and sunglasses.

On *The J. Geils Band*, the group mixed cover versions in with their original material, new songs that were highly influenced by their musical heroes. Produced by Atlantic Records staff producers Brad Shapiro and Dave Crawford, the album utilized a tried-and-true recording methodology: set up the microphones, stand back, and let the band rock.

"Like a lot of bands cutting their first albums, we were ready," Seth Justman said in the liner notes to *Anthology*. "A lot of the versions you hear on the record were first takes and the whole thing took just three days."

The immediacy of the sessions shines through. On the instrumental "Ice Breaker" the soloing and rhythm instruments exchange sonic locations within the mix, but that was as gimmicky as things got on a beautifully recorded album that works because of its simplicity. In a time when many bands restlessly experimented with studio technology, on this album there was nothing more complex than the rich reverb cloaking Geils' guitar in the album's spooky centerpiece, a menacing rendition of John Lee Hooker's "Serves You Right to Suffer."

The J. Geils Band followed up their 1970 debut with *The Morning After*, which found them easing into rock star territory. Their record company flew the group to Los Angeles to record, where they were teamed with producer Bill Szymczyk. Though the follow-up album did not have the shimmering clarity of sound and intimacy that characterized their debut, it did show off the band's rapidly maturing songwriting. Among the record's contents was a first for the group—a chart hit in "Looking for a Love," which just eked into the Top 40 pop charts.

Still, the greatest strength of The J. Geils Band—their onstage charisma—could never be captured in the studio. From the time they began playing in bars until they completed their matriculation to stadiums, the J. Geils Band was an outstanding live unit. In concert, Peter Wolf maniacally cut loose, a blur of motion inspiring general audience hysteria as his cohorts whipped the frenzy further with raw, hyper blues grooves.

Most bands waited until their careers were well established before releasing a live album, but the J. Geils Band quickly used just such a recording to cement their reputation. Within months of the release of *The Morning After*, in front of a crazed Detroit mob that was as revved up as the band itself, the J. Geils Band recorded *Full House*, documenting one of their hyperactive live blowouts to superb effect.

The live album set the stage for the band's success throughout the decade. Right through their career, though, the group never strayed far from their gritty R&B and blues roots.

While The J. Geils Band spread the gospel of the blues in the country where the style itself was conceived, in England the blues had arguably played an even more crucial role in the shaping of British rock and roll. The fact that the blues mattered at all in England was largely due to a single band leader, John Mayall. Mayall's band had served as a virtual incubator for future rock stars for more than a decade.

Mayall had moved in 1963 to London from Manchester on the advice of fellow British blues player Alexis Korner, following the dream of making a living playing the blues. Soon after his London arrival he recorded his debut single, but the first tremendously influential recording of Mayall's career came in 1966 when he partnered with Eric Clapton for the release of *Blues Breakers*.

Clapton, having fled the pop success of his stint with The Yardbirds, fancied himself a dourly serious blues musician. In Mayall, he found a kindred spirit. Aligning themselves in 1965, they recorded the *Blues Breakers* album. In its tracks, the young guitarist played with such fire and fury that many guitar fans still consider this to be the apex of Clapton's entire career.

Clapton soon moved on to other styles of music, although his work always remained rooted in blues. Mayall continued as a blues traditionalist. Though his band The Bluesbreakers often seemed to have a revolving door, through the portal came an astonishing array of Britain's most talented musicians. Members of bands like Fleetwood Mac, Free, Cream, and The Rolling Stones all played in the Mayall lineups of the 1960s. Like James Brown, Mayall had a reputation as a difficult band leader, but there was no arguing with his ability to realize his rootsy vision through a consistently elite array of talent.

In 1971, Mayall was most deservedly given his due with the release of *Back to the Roots*. In sessions recorded in both Los Angeles and London, many of the luminaries who had shared stages with Mayall—and used his band as a springboard to stardom—joined with him once again to create an all-star celebration of blues music. The lineup of guitarists alone—Clapton, Mick Taylor of The Rolling Stones, and Harvey Mandel of Canned Heat—was indicative of the esteem in which Mayall was held. The double album's eighteen songs ranged from piano boogie solo takes to fiery instrumental exchanges between the guitarists and a new Mayall discovery, blues violinist Sugarcane Harris.

Though many of The Bluesbreakers' alumni went on to use their education in the blues as a starting point for further musical journeys, John Mayall remained true to the blues in its most raw and pure form. It was that passion which enabled him to always discover something new in the infinite variations of a deceptively simple style of music.

From the very earliest days of rock and roll, it was obvious that the new musical form had been fathered by blues music. But in the 1970s, a new—and highly unlikely—form of music began to steer rock music in uncharted directions. In a search for respect and sophistication, a growing number of rock musicians were listening to—and borrowing from—classical music.

Chief among these proponents was a young keyboard player named Keith Emerson. Like most gigging musicians in England, Emerson had done his time in an assortment of rhythm and blues and pop bands. But when he formed The Nice, things began to get interesting.

From their inception in 1968, The Nice hinged on Emerson's leadership and flamboyant keyboard grandstanding. The band did have their fair share of cheap stunts in their stage repertoire, stunts that included the burning of an American flag, which found the group banned from London's historic Royal Albert Hall in a blizzard of free publicity. Still, serious attention was focused on The Nice's sober attempts at "real" music. Albums by The Nice featured "Rondo" with its revved-up Mozart, a spin through Sibelius' "Intermezzo," and a bludgeoning of Leonard Bernstein's "America." Although Bernstein was none too pleased with the attention rockers were giving his music, Jimi Hendrix was intrigued by The Nice, as were a growing number of rock fans drawn to the classical sphere.

Emerson split up the band in 1970, promptly forming a new powerhouse in the "serious rock" realm, Emerson, Lake, and Palmer, or ELP. The trio included vocalist and bassist Greg Lake, late of King Crimson, and Carl Palmer, who had drummed in The Crazy World of Arthur Brown—a crazy world indeed, due to Mr. Brown's tendency to enter the stage wearing a specially constructed flame crown that launched pyrotechnics high overhead. After that experience, even Emerson's inclination to stab his Hammond organs with daggers seemed relatively tame.

ELP made their debut at the 1970 Isle of Wight festival, performing a little ditty known as Mussorgsky's "Pictures at an Exhibition." They capped off their sojourn through one of classical music's most enduring symphonic works with a barrage of cannon fire. When the smoke cleared, the buzz around the band was so great that supposedly Jimi Hendrix, in the days just before his death, was investigating the possibility of Emerson, Hendrix, Lake, and Palmer.

After releasing a self-titled debut album—which debuted the new Moog synthesizer to most listeners' ears—and scoring a hit with the Lake ballad "Lucky Man," in 1971 ELP released their second album, *Tarkus*.

Aside from a bit of a Bach borrow here and there, on *Tarkus* ELP were now crafting their own themes. Yes, they were under the influence of classical music, but Emerson in particular was struggling to create something new. And the band's overall sound was evolving into a coherent whole. Palmer's drumming was athletic and powerful, a perfect foil for Emerson's growing arsenal of instrumentation. And where other keyboardists considered the role of the Moog to be that of showstopper solo instrument, by *Tarkus* Emerson was integrating the synthesizer, the organs, and his pianos into a wide-ranging palette of tones that he effectively balanced.

Vincent Crane was listening with interest. He had been organist in the psychodrama insanity of The Crazy World of Arthur Brown, where he had met drummer Palmer. Soon after Brown's smash hit "Fire," the two men had fled the troubled outfit to form the curiously named Atomic Rooster. Almost immediately, Palmer flew the Atomic Rooster coop to chase the greener pastures of ELP, but Crane brought in Paul Hammond as a replacement, a drummer he had spotted in a drum competition sponsored by influential British music newspaper *Melody Maker*. John Du Cann completed the picture on guitar and lead vocals.

Crane was doubtless encouraged by the success of ELP, but Atomic Rooster was its own band. For one thing, Crane was a bit of an instrumental traditionalist, eschewing the Moog technology in favor of basic organ and piano. And where Emerson had flipped for classical scores, Crane was still guided by the influence of British jazz combos like the famed Graham Bond Organisation, the seminal group in which Jack Bruce and Ginger Baker had backed Bond's sly organ work.

There was one other prime influence on Atomic Rooster, and that was the cheerful, optimistic attitude of Black Sabbath. So when the second Atomic Rooster album was released in 1971, it bore the heartening title *Death Walks behind You*. On the title track and elsewhere in the album's grooves, Crane and his cohorts engendered the sound of a keyboard-based power trio that packed a lumbering weight, contrasting starkly with Emerson and company's classical complexities. In the same way that Black Sabbath had been blues-influenced, Atomic Rooster was jazz-influenced. What both bands had in common, however, was a moody intangible factor that made them each darkly different from other bands on the scene.

Darkness, though, was a constant in the mind of John Entwistle, the bassist for The Who. When given a chance to place one of his own songs on an album by The Who, The Ox tended to channel directly from a fantasy world of spiders and hell. The problem was, with Pete Townshend churning out rock operas, Entwistle's recording opportunities were few and far between. The obvious solution: a solo album.

When you are the bassist in one of the world's premier bands, guitarists will knock down walls for the opportunity to link their name to your reputation. But for his album, Entwistle opted to keep things in the family. Dave "Cyrano" Langston had left his high-ranking post in Cyrano and the Bergeracs, a 1960s pop combo, to become The Who's first roadie. Entwistle decided to repay that loyalty by handing the guitar chores to Cyrano. Drummer Jerry Shirley, on loan from Humble Pie, completed the lineup.

When *Smash Your Head against the Wall* was released, it was met with a lukewarm reaction. The title track was the album's most blunt and powerful, riding a grinding riff straight from the Black Sabbath playbook. In typically charming Entwistle fashion—and hopefully with tongue planted firmly in cheek—the bassist outlined how he planned to deal with a troublesome female acquaintance. Familiar ground was covered with a rendition of "Heaven and Hell," a standard number from The Who's live gigs. This version was slowed down and drenched in echo, providing an alternate view of Entwistle's melancholy vision.

Though dark lyrics and heavy music seemed to be all the rage in the United Kingdom, there was a singer in the United States who was busily plotting out his own rock and roll strategy, one that would make the British rock morbidity look like tea time at Claridge's.

On February 4, 1948, in Detroit, Michigan, baby Vincent Furnier came into the world. To this day, that name means little to all but Vince's biggest fans—but soon enough Furnier would begin doing business under a new name that the entire world would come to recognize.

By Vince's teen years, the Furnier family had moved west to Phoenix, Arizona, where he ran track for the team at Cortez High School. But the young man was also under the influence of Beatlemania, and in a defining moment performed a Beatles parody at a talent show with some friends. The reaction from the crowd had a big impact, convincing Vince and his pals that perhaps they should take rock and roll a bit more seriously. And thus was born The Earwigs, who soon became known as The Spiders, and later were called The Nazz. What's in a name? Well, seeing as how Philadelphian Todd Rundgren had landed a record deal for his new band, also known as The Nazz, a potential lawsuit.

By this time singer Furnier, along with drummer Neal Smith, guitarists Michael Bruce and Glen Buxton, and drummer Dennis Dunaway, had been making a serious effort at establishing themselves in the rock world. They'd had a regional hit in Arizona as The Spiders, playing raw garage rock influenced by The Rolling Stones and The Yardbirds, then made a run at the vibrant Hollywood music scene around the Sunset Strip in their Nazz days. Success was hard to come by, and a lack of audience respect and hungry late nights were plentiful for the young band. Now they were facing yet another name change.

Many stories have arisen over the years concerning the origins of the band's new name, a name that came to identify both the group and Furnier, to the point that its true genesis may never be known. But regardless of how it was chosen, the name is one of the most instantly recognizable in rock music: Alice Cooper.

With the new name came a new plan—to embrace shocking behavior, and make this group unlike any other in rock and roll. For some reason, Alice Cooper seemed to be uniquely suited to make progress toward that goal, to the point where the band attracted the interest of Frank Zappa. Zappa himself had developed a reputation for outrageousness and pushing the limits, so much so that he and his band, The Mothers of Invention, joined The Nice on the list of acts banned from the Royal Albert Hall. How could a musician so enamored with pushing the limits not fall in love with the Alice Cooper concept, with a band of masculine men dressed as women playing shambling, noisy rock? Zappa signed Alice Cooper to his new Warner Brothers spin-off label, Straight Records.

"The very first time I called myself Alice Cooper, with the makeup smeared everywhere," recalled the man himself, "I was wearing a pink clown outfit with furry afro hair. I must've looked like the scariest thing on two legs."

Alice Cooper could clear a room in a big hurry—and that impressed Shep Gordon. Gordon was a novice manager who figured that any band capable of actually driving people out of a concert in a matter of minutes really had something. It simply needed to be perfected. Gordon and the band laid out their plot for best generating outrage and spectacle.

Two albums for Straight—*Pretties for You* and *Easy Action*— failed to go anywhere. Despite the efforts of Neil Young producer David Briggs on *Easy Action*, the band's sound seemed to be taking them nowhere fast in Hollywood. So Gordon and the band decided to relocate to Alice's birthplace, Detroit.

Detroit had already proved it was a city on a tougher rock page than the rest of the world. The violent revolutionary posturing of The MC5, the chaos of The Stooges, the mania of Ted Nugent's Amboy Dukes, the thunderous Grand Funk Railroad— all of these rough bands called Detroit home. It looked like safe haven for Alice Cooper.

Through a single incident, Alice quickly—if accidentally— earned a bad reputation, one that fit right in with Detroit's image as rock's dark alley in a bad neighborhood. At the 1969 Toronto Rock Revival, someone had the bright idea to throw a live chicken on stage in the midst of the Alice Cooper set. No farm boy, Alice mistakenly believed chickens could fly. He scooped up the bird, and helpfully cast it into a takeoff trajectory. Naturally, the bird made an uncontrolled descent into the audience, which rather brutally dispatched the fowl. The story began to mutate, taking on a rumor-laden life of its own. The media proclaimed: Alice Cooper, Chicken Murderer.

It was in this atmosphere that Shep Gordon was trying to land a producer for the band's next album. Not surprisingly, no one wanted to work with a band of cross-dressing chicken killers. One of Gordon's targets was Jack Richardson, at Toronto's Nimbus 9 Productions studio, where The Guess Who had recorded their hit records. Richardson resisted; Gordon persisted. Finally Richardson agreed to dispatch an assistant producer, nineteen-year-old Bob Ezrin, to witness the band.

Perhaps it was because of his youth that Ezrin came away from the show a convert to the Cooper cause. He volunteered to produce the band himself, and an intense period of wood-shedding ensued, followed by the recording. The result was the third Alice Cooper album, *Love It to Death.*

Ezrin and the band had partnered their way into a new sonic trademark for the Alice Cooper band. It was accessible but still retained the rough rock shading. On songs like "Caught in a Dream" and "Long Way to Go," Ezrin succeeded where others had failed by revealing the band as strong players and, even more importantly, as excellent songwriters. Those high standards were demonstrated in "I'm Eighteen," Alice's aggressive paean to adolescent chaos, which hovered in the upper reaches of the pop singles charts.

The band's stage show was also maturing, cast in a newly organized manner that relied more on theatrics than chaos. For the *Love It to Death* tour, Alice—who had evolved into an emotive rock vocalist—sang the album's climactic "Ballad of Dwight Fry" in a straightjacket as he portrayed a violent psychopath escaping from his bonds at song's end and murdering a nurse. Alice then, of course, paid for his onstage transgressions by being strapped into an electric chair and executed. The press and an entire generation of parents were horrified by this new presentation from The Band that Kills Chickens. The kids were enthralled.

"I've never been known to do anything straight," Alice informed *Creem* Magazine's Barbara Charone in 1977. "We're just advancing. We used to do it on a slighter level because we couldn't afford the props. I remember in the old Detroit days, we'd go out in the alley of Eastown Theatre and get stuff out of the garbage cans for props and build the stage around it."

Success having ended the band's forced reliance on castoffs for stage sets, Alice and company set about the task of preparing for their fourth album. With the band having laid the foundation for stardom with *Love It to Death*, everyone was well aware that this next album was crucial. With Bob Ezrin behind the board once again, Alice Cooper went to Chicago and got to work.

When *Killer* was released in 1971, it was obvious that a further refinement had taken place. Though each album side led off with scorching rockers—"Under My Wheels" and "You Drive Me Nervous"—the bulk of the album was more complex. The songs were designed to form integral parts of the new Cooper stage show, but material like "Halo of Flies" and the deliberately shocking "Dead Babies" also displayed a new sophistication in the band's music. There were interesting tempo changes, mood shifts, and a thoughtful implementation of dynamics. Regardless of Alice Cooper the show, Alice Cooper the band had become quite a creative and powerful rock group.

"I've been influenced by stage plays, musicals, TV themes and movie themes," Cooper said. "But basically, I'm a rock 'n' roller. I like the Yardbirds, old Them, The Who, and Chuck Berry. I've taken the basics and added some theatrics."

Regardless of Alice's logical explanation of what he did for a living, there was no way that a major rock group singing about dead babies was going to fly under the radar on tour, especially when the accompanying album featured a unique calendar poster of Alice being hanged. His stage makeup had evolved, from cartoonish stars emanating from his eyes to two evil black orbs, capped off with menacing grimace lines tracing down from the corners of his mouth. Modeling this new look, Alice hung from the noose, his eyes nearly shut, blood spilling from his mouth and pouring across his bare chest.

"Weekend Rocks to the Weird Limit" proclaimed the headline as the *Philadelphia Inquirer* sounded the alarm over the impending arrival of the *Killer* tour, coming "in a blaze of put-down and hostility and electrified shrieking and hostility." And, of course, chicken killing was prominently referenced.

Alice Cooper appealed to a newer, younger audience thirsting for aggression and spectacle in concert, but those spectacles were carefully coordinated and planned. As Alice himself had discovered, it was difficult to control chaos. But one rock singer had often tried—Jim Morrison of The Doors. And although there is no questioning the originality of Cooper's theatrics, on songs like "Killer" the musical influence of Morrison could be heard.

Though The Doors were still one of rock's elite bands in 1971, the group faced a decidedly uncertain future. In March 1969, The Doors had performed a typically riotous concert in Miami. The did-he-or-didn't-he question would linger for decades, but in the aftermath of the concert Morrison was charged with having exposed himself on stage. The charges for "lewd and lascivious behavior in public" were serious ones, including one felony charge. It appeared well within the realm of possibility that Morrison would log jail time. In the wake of the hoopla surrounding the charges, events like the "Rally for Decency"—a concert featuring such purified musicians as Anita Bryant and The Lettermen held at Miami's Orange Bowl stadium—reflected the growing animosity much of the world had for Morrison's increasingly erratic antics.

The charges crippled the band's ability to tour, and Morrison's well-known alcohol-consumption skills had the singer reaching new lows. The band retreated to the studio and recorded *Morrison Hotel*, their fifth studio album. Despite Morrison's condition, the album was a strong one, stripping down the large-scale horn and string arrangements that had choked parts of its predecessor, *The Soft Parade*. But the court charges from the Miami concert ominously hung over the singer, and it was difficult to plan anything until the legal events played out for better or worse.

On August 10, 1970, the court proceedings began at last, continuing for well over a month. During the lengthy process, The Doors did manage to play two concerts, one in California and the other at the Isle of Wight festival in England, where they were a star attraction. While on stage in front of the massive crowd, his band mates recall, Morrison simply went through the motions in an uninspired performance.

On September 20, the verdict came in—guilty on the misdemeanor charges of indecent exposure and public profanity.

Morrison's lawyers immediately appealed, concerned that the singer might actually be forced to serve the six-month prison sentence.

Late in the year, The Doors returned to the studio for what would prove to be a final studio album. There they faced the latest blow—longtime producer Paul Rothchild announced that he had decided to produce Janis Joplin's new album instead of The Doors' work. Rothchild did not hide the fact that he did not care for the band's new music.

In the wake of Rothchild's decision, it was up to the band and Bruce Botnick, who had engineered all of their albums, to produce the new album. The Doors had every reason to enter the studio in a bad frame of mind. Instead, ensconced in their own Doors Workshop in Los Angeles, the band felt an invigorating freedom, with no real producer to question their creative decisions. Morrison had told the *Los Angeles Free Press* that the band intended to record a blues album. "That's what we do best—just your basic blues."

When *L.A. Woman* emerged in stores in April 1971, there was ample evidence that The Doors had, as promised, taken a further step back to basics. Morrison, borrowing one of the oldest sentiments of the blues, sang that he'd "been down so long that it looks like up to me." If so, the despondency was being channeled into a vital, liberating new album.

L.A. Woman was recorded almost entirely live in the studio in a matter of weeks, as opposed to the months a Rothchild production typically demanded. The Doors sounded like a real live band, one faithfully captured at a creative peak. The Doors' core—keyboardist Ray Manzarek, drummer John Densmore, and guitarist Robbie Krieger—played with an audible ease and familiarity, augmented by bassist Jerry Scheff and rhythm guitarist Marc Benno. On songs like the title track and "Love Her Madly," Densmore kept the rhythm section swinging while Manzarek added atmosphere under Krieger's spiraling solos. Morrison sang the new songs with authoritative passion, rising from his alcoholic depths and transcending the reach of his inner demons.

L.A. Woman entered the *Billboard* album charts on May 8 and began a steady climb upward, eventually peaking at number nine. In light of the band's album sales, it seemed that the summer of 1971 would be an ideal time for the foursome to reestablish themselves as an essential creative force on the rock music scene. There was just one problem—Jim Morrison had more or less disappeared.

Aware that the life he was leading had ample potential to kill him, Morrison had fled to Paris, France, a month prior to *L.A. Woman's* release. He was seeking a respite from the Los Angeles life and his reputation as the self-destructive "Lizard King." Morrison and his longtime companion Pamela Courson arrived in Paris on March 11. Hoping to find some anonymity, Morrison shaved the beard that had masked his features in recent months, then existed quietly in Paris for several weeks.

On July 3, 1971, Pamela and Jim saw a movie, then returned to their apartment. Late in the evening, Pamela went to bed while Morrison stayed awake, nostalgically listening to albums by The Doors. When he came to bed he complained of not feeling well. After he became ill, at Jim's request Pamela drew the singer a bath. With Jim in the water, Pamela returned to bed. She later awoke, alarmed that Morrison was not beside her. She tried the bathroom door—it was locked. She was afraid of what she suspected was on the other side of the door—the lifeless body of Jim Morrison, dead at age twenty-seven.

The official cause of death was listed as heart problems. Alternate stories of Jim Morrison's last night have centered on a novice's misuse of heroin. The bottom line was still the same—after the deaths of Janis Joplin and Jimi Hendrix, the world of rock music had lost its third superstar in less than a year.

Word of Morrison's death began to circulate in fits and starts. Some reports had Morrison dead, others had him fine but hospitalized, and a third variation reported that the entire story was a hoax. Finally, on July 9, Bill Siddons, manager of The Doors, confirmed that he had just returned to Los Angeles from Paris and the funeral of Jim Morrison.

"In Paris he'd found some peace and happiness and worked L.A. out of his system," Siddons said in a statement. "It may be hard to understand, but it was hard to live here and live what everybody thought he was. There was no service, and that made it all the better. We just threw some flowers and dirt and said goodbye."

The mysterious circumstances and the rumors swirling around the story of Jim Morrison's death led to a cottage industry of Morrison sightings among those who claimed the singer had staged his own death. Dead or alive, Morrison would never be seen on stage again.

Mick Jagger, as lead vocalist of The Rolling Stones, was in the strange position of watching many of his rock and roll competitors die off. But increasingly vital signs of life were being shown by The Stones' two biggest challengers for the title "Greatest Rock Band in Existence," longtime rivals The Who and the newly-ascended-to-superstardom Led Zeppelin. All three bands released important albums in 1971.

"I always think of The Rolling Stones as a rock and roll band," Jagger has said, "and every time they say a ballad should be the single it worries me."

What, Jagger worried? Not from the looks of the liner photo gracing the interior of *Sticky Fingers*, a shot that captured Mick in the midst of an oh-so-bored yawn.

If ballads made him worried, though, Jagger had no reason for concern with the lead-off single from the Stones' new album, their first release on their own Rolling Stones Records. They simply chose to unleash the two most raw, dynamic songs from *Sticky Fingers*, "Brown Sugar" and "Bitch." The former swaggered; the latter drove hard, but both showcased The Stones with all of their strengths on full display.

"The best rock and roll music encapsulates a certain high energy—an angriness—whether on record or onstage," observed Jagger. "Rock and roll is only rock and roll if it's not safe."

This single sounded anything but safe. Keith Richards' brilliantly intuitive rhythm guitar skills propelled both tracks, riding on the infallible rhythm section of bassist Bill Wyman and reticent powerhouse drummer Charlie Watts. Over it all, Jagger the ringmaster hoarsely called out the typically risqué lyrics in his own inimitable phrasing.

The album's companion tracks covered a vast range of musical territory, including the country shuffle of "Dead Flowers,"

the stark horror of death and addiction infusing "Sister Mor-
phine," and the ambling drive of "Can't You Hear Me Knocking." But arguably the strongest track of a very potent album
was "Sway," a song that nearly staggers into existence before
blooming into a beautiful and moving extended fade out. In
"Sway," the Stones reaped the full benefits of new lead guitarist
Mick Taylor's tutelage under John Mayall, as Taylor cast a striking, melodically evolving solo over the swelling string arrangement scored by Paul Buckmaster.

In ordinary times, *Sticky Fingers* might easily have stood as
album of the year. But 1971 was not an ordinary time—the big
bands were all hard at work.

"We are intending to produce a fiction, or a play, or an opera
and create a completely different kind of performance in rock,"
The Who's Pete Townshend pronounced in a January 1971
press conference. An ambitious declaration, but after recording the first rock opera with *Tommy* and producing one of
rock's most aggressive live albums with *Live at Leeds*, what else
was left?

Townshend's "different kind of performance" was to be
called Lifehouse, a grand scheme involving a near-future story
line in which the youth joined together to discover the glory of
rock. The Lifehouse would be where the music would be
shared, audience and musician unified as they rose together
onto another spiritual plane buoyed by the Universal Chord. At
least, that was the plan.

Townshend envisioned Lifehouse happening as a living,
breathing event, part recording, part film, part personal experience. In the end, it was too great a vision—and perhaps too
vague—to be realized as a concrete entity. So the musical roots
of Lifehouse became *Who's Next*, released in August.

"It was a compromise album," Townshend told the British
music newspaper *Sounds* in 1972. "I felt it was making the best
of what we had at the time—the whole theatre project, the film
idea—all those new numbers were part of a bigger scheme."

The bigger scheme had shrunk even further when producer
Glyn Johns convinced Townshend to reduce a planned double
album into a single, pointing out that the leftover narrative
threads from Lifehouse were now so tenuous as to be nearly
unnoticeable to listeners.

What remained on *Who's Next*, though, was inarguably brilliant. If *Live at Leeds* had captured the band at their brutal and chaotic live peak, *Who's Next* was the manifestation of that force having been captured and focused into a luminous studio creation.

The album begins with a hypnotic, repeating synthesizer pattern. Known as a guitarist, Townshend may have seemed an unlikely candidate to carry the banner for synth use in rock and roll, but Pete's meticulous programming of the primitive (by today's standards) instruments colored much of *Who's Next*. And the emphasis was on programming—most of the synthesizer appearances in rock to date had been in solos intended to make a band sound modern; Townshend took on the laborious task of creating synth-based soundscapes to support entire songs. That Townshend could hear the potential of the instrument, and then took the untold hours necessary to bring his vision to fruition, speaks volumes about the intensity with which he approached projects by The Who.

Laid upon the groundbreaking synth foundations, the typically exceptional elements of The Who—Moon's volleys of percussive detonations, Entwistle's thunderous bass domination of the lower frequencies, the unique technique of Townshend's chordal guitar approach—were given authoritative voice by Roger Daltrey, who offered compelling evidence that he was quite likely the most commanding of rock's vocalists.

The songs of *Who's Next* became musical legends from this era of rock—songs like "Baba O'Riley," "Behind Blue Eyes," and the album's stunning and powerful finale, "Won't Get Fooled Again." They have attained this rarified status because they exist at a level of near-perfection in the realms of songwriting, recording, and performance.

In the bright light of that creativity, other bands may have been intimidated by the brilliance of *Who's Next*. But not Led Zeppelin, a band that had no doubts about their own place in the rock spectrum.

"At our very worst, we were better than most people," judged bassist and keyboardist John Paul Jones. "And at our very best, we could just wipe the floor with the lot of them."

Led Zeppelin was obviously not lacking in confidence. Then again, it's not bragging if it's a fact. To be honest, they did do some floor wiping with the release of the band's fourth album on November 8, 1971.

Formed by studio musician and Yardbirds guitarist Jimmy Page upon the dissolution of that band—in which he had inherited the lead guitar post once held by Eric Clapton and later Jeff Beck—Led Zeppelin brought Page together with goldilocked vocalist Robert Plant, then laboring in the psychedelic-tinged Band of Joy. Plant in turn brought along his band's beefy drummer, John Bonham. The fourth member of the new band was a soft-spoken multi-instrumentalist named John Paul Jones, a young man Page had known from various studio sessions. In the world of British studio musicians, Jones was highly regarded for both his playing and his arranging skills.

During a brief contractually obligated Scandinavian tour in 1968, the newly formed group was rather unimaginatively billed as The New Yardbirds. Soon thereafter, a more suitable name—Led Zeppelin—was adopted after a joke by The Who's Keith Moon, who stated that the band would "go down like a lead zeppelin."

Far from going down, Led Zeppelin took off. Two strong albums of high-energy blues-based rock established the band in 1969, the debut album being one of the most powerful first efforts in rock's history. *Led Zeppelin III* in 1970 then allowed an acoustic side of the band to reveal itself, emerging in the midst of the high-volume, amps-set-on-stun thunder.

Unlike The Rolling Stones, whose two-guitar lineup and heavy use of rock and roll piano and horns gave the band an ensemble attack, and The Who, now using dense layers of synthesizers to swell their sound, Led Zeppelin remained for the most part a stripped-down power trio with a vocalist. But there was an interesting visual tension when the band climbed on stage—Plant's airs of fantasy and fearless revelations of his feminine side diametrically opposed Roger Daltrey's image as a working-class bloke who just happened to sing for The Who.

The fourth Led Zeppelin album got down to business in typically high-octane fashion with "Black Dog." After a rhythmically complex Page riff establishes direction, the band begins cruising at a lumbering pace, driven hard by John Bonham's physically battering drumming. Robert Plant's sexually charged lyrics are telegraphed via a high, keening banshee shriek, and the rhythm repeatedly starts and stops. Page contributes one of his uniquely halting solos, and returns with more stylized blues runs as the track finally hulks off into the distance.

"Rock and Roll" follows, a second flat-out rocker. But then things begin to take an interesting turn. "The Battle of Evermore" pairs Plant with Fairport Convention vocalist Sandy Denny, whose range challenges Plant's upper register as Page and Jones provide a churning bed of mandolin and acoustic guitar.

The album's first side closes with "Stairway to Heaven," a song that has, sadly, become something of a cliché. Page's brilliant production, carefully layering instruments with each passing verse until he has crafted a vibrant, breathing aural structure, exemplifies one of the high points of his career. The guitar solo alone is exceptional and emotional, its phrasing and construction uniquely identifiable as Page, standing as one of the most beautifully constructed passages recorded in rock music. And beneath Page's layers of guitar, Jones plays inventive and exciting bass lines, working around the song's chords and sounding almost like the great Motown bassist James Jamerson had stepped into Led Zeppelin.

By the time the album's final track, the hypnotic and hallucinatory blues "When the Levee Breaks" was ushered in on Bonham's truly thunderous drums, it really didn't matter that Led Zeppelin had probably never seen a levee in their lives. What counted was that Led Zeppelin had made their own strong bid for rock immortality. The record streaked up the charts, settling comfortably at number one.

"No one ever compared us to Black Sabbath after this record," quipped Jones.

How much music industry power does a band capable of making number-one albums wield? Despite the marketing problems they knew would ensure, Led Zeppelin refused to supply a title for the album. It is still officially referred to as the "untitled fourth album."

In August, George Harrison staged one of the key musical events of 1971 with his concerts at New York's Madison Square Garden benefiting the impoverished country Bangladesh. Along with the by-now de rigueur ex-Bonnie and Delaney alumni, Harrison used the magnetic appeal of his status as a Beatle to lure the reclusive Bob Dylan back on stage. And joining in on guitar was Eric Clapton, who had remained virtually invisible since the demise of Derek and the Dominos three months earlier.

Clapton was riding a wave of substance abuse that would worsen before it got better, leading the guitarist into new depths both personally and professionally. Though the relationships among Clapton and his Cream-mates Ginger Baker and Jack Bruce had grown acrimonious in the band's final months, it could not have been worse than the condition Clapton now found himself in.

Felix Pappalardi had witnessed Cream's collapse firsthand. A protégé of Atlantic Records' famed producer Ahmet Eretgun, Pappalardi was asked to work with Cream when they arrived in New York to record their second album. Though Felix was unfamiliar with the band—then hardly a household name in the United States—he and the trio hit it off, wrapping up *Disraeli Gears*, one of rock's most influential albums, in just five days. From that point on, Pappalardi was nearly a fourth band member, producing and performing on *Wheels of Fire* and the farewell *Goodbye* album.

Pappalardi thought he knew what had destroyed rock's premier power trio. Felix felt it was essential for only one band member at a time to step out, while that player's band mates rallied behind him in a solid support role. In Cream, there were times when Clapton, Bruce, and Baker were essentially all soloing at once.

After producing a solo album by new talent Leslie West in the wake of Cream's downfall, Pappalardi flew to London to work on Jack Bruce's solo debut, *Songs for a Tailor*. That album complete, Felix returned to the United States and found Leslie West in hot pursuit. West, a guitarist heavy in both his style and his physical stature, persuaded the tall and thin Pappalardi to try a live band. Leslie invited his friend Corky Laing to join on drums, and Steve Knight was added on organ. Thus was born one of the premier bands of the decade, Mountain.

At first, audiences balanced the band against Cream, comparisons that were inevitable due to Felix's background. But Mountain had a distinctive sound that quickly began to emerge, and their 1970 album *Climbing* set the stage for the group's two 1971 albums, *Nantucket Sleighride* and *Flowers of Evil.*

Pappalardi was exceptionally bright, and had a strong knowledge of classical music theory. In the studio, as he produced his new band's albums, he concentrated on finding ways to make Mountain sound different. One approach used to great effect was to employ classically themed chord or note progressions as melodic devices. Once constructed, it was time to turn West loose to cut a typically blues-based solo. The result was a divergent contrast of moods that somehow worked.

The sound of Mountain so impressed Pete Townshend that he considered making *Who's Next* a collaboration with Pappalardi and West. Tapes of Felix's production of The Who, with Leslie playing lead guitar, reveal songs like "Won't Get Fooled Again" and "Love Ain't for Keeping" taking on a different but equally powerful aura.

Despite the brilliance of Pappalardi's production techniques and his songwriting partnerships with West, on stage was where Mountain's reputation was made. They were brutally loud, but where Cream concerts sometimes devolved into high-volume chaos, Mountain stood unified, with each member of the foursome buying into Felix's "support whoever is out front" mantra. Usually, it was West carrying the day—a musician who lacked Felix's music education, but made up for it with a fiery, intense style.

"To tell you the truth, man, I don't know the names of the chords I play," West admitted to *Guitar Player*'s Fred Stuckey in 1972. "I can't read music; I can't even look at a chord positioning in a book and play it."

But if anything, that provided freedom to Mountain.

"The thing I love is mistakes," Pappalardi said in 1970's *Superstars in Their Own Words,* "because we've come to a point in chromatic music where that's where the new things come from, from overt mistakes . . . That's what makes a great improviser, somebody who can get into a bind while improvising and know enough to work his way out of it. And that's what makes beautiful things, beautiful solos."

Mountain's expertise at improvisation was aptly—and powerfully—presented on the second side of *Flowers of Evil* in the twenty-five-minute "Dream Sequence." West and Pappalardi locked together as a single entity, using band material as jumping-off points, and plunged fearlessly into ground-shaking passages that virtually defined the phrase "heavy rock." Laing's syncopated drumming contributed a nimbleness to the rhythm, while Knight, rather than soloing on his keyboards, played his role with subtle colorings placed amidst the sonic gale of the band's leaders. And as proof that Pappalardi played improvisation like he talked it, tapes of "Dream Sequence" from shows of the same era reveal totally different approaches from concert to concert, as Mountain boldly pursued any musical path that their inspiration revealed.

While Mountain strove to reach new peaks of hard rock artistry, Ohio's James Gang were also emerging from the power trio mold cast by Cream.

The James Gang received an indoctrination to recording with their debut *Yer' Album*, then replaced bassist Tom Kriss with Dale Peters before revisiting the studio to record their second album, *Rides Again*. Returning as producer was Bill Szymczyk, whose reputation would grow with each passing year in the 1970s.

Szymczyk had become fascinated with sound as a sonar man in the Navy, and when he returned to civilian life he began engineering demos in the fast-paced world of New York's pop factory, the Brill Building. From there he had moved into rock production, scoring his first major success by casting bluesman B.B. King in a contemporary light on the hit "The Thrill Is Gone."

"*Rides Again* was a logical extension of *Yer' Album* in that the band was in a very creative phase and we had been introduced to the world of record production by Bill Szymczyk," guitarist Joe Walsh said in the liner notes of the CD remastering of the second album. "The spontaneous performance ability was still there, but we also were laying basic tracks, overdubbing, and editing stuff together to make 'pieces' of music like 'The Bomber.'"

"The Bomber" was a lengthy assemblage of parts, including an echo-drenched pass through Vince Guaraldi's "Cast Your Fate to the Wind" in midexploration. The rest of the album was more song-based, contrasting harder material like "Funk #49" against pensive, delicate tracks like "Ashes the Rain and I," which featured strings coordinated by highly regarded arranger Jack Nitzsche.

Though *Rides Again* displayed a growing sense of sophistication in the studio, *Live in Concert*, released late in 1971 in the wake of the uneven *Thirds*, proved that The James Gang followed the same party line as most power trio lineups: on stage, louder equals better.

Live in Concert was an accurate documentation of the noisy maelstrom that was The James Gang in person. When they wanted to, the band easily rivaled Mountain or Led Zeppelin on the heavy rock scale. The dark tones of Walsh's Gibson guitars were overdriven and amplified to titanic levels of volume, with Peter's bass matching Walsh decibel for decibel. Behind the two string men, drummer Jim Fox proved that he was The Gang's secret weapon. Fascinated by African and other exotic forms of percussion, band founder Fox displayed an unusual style that, while far from lacking in brute force, ventured off into unexpected directions. But Fox was clever, never using his superior drumming skills to distract audiences from the group effort—he simply and subtly provided his power trio new dimensions in their rhythms.

Through concerts like the one documented on *Live in Concert*, The James Gang began to garner rave reviews—one of which came from no less an authority than Pete Townshend. The Who's guitarist specifically requested that the band join his group on tour. Once in that enviable position, no doubt the James Gang saw all manner of conspicuous consumption of substances not necessarily legal. But though the 1970s rock world was rife with sordid tales of drug abuse, there were two major bands who preferred to visit their demons through an alcoholic haze—and both bands shared a common point of origin.

The Small Faces was a British band formed in 1965, which, despite finding little success in the United States, had struck it big in England. But by 1969, tensions had grown within the band to the point where singer and guitarist Steve Marriott simply walked off the stage in mid-song, never to return.

Freed from The Small Faces, Marriott called guitarist Peter Frampton, laboring away in his own band called The Herd, and suggested they form a new group. The result was one of the greatest of the British hard rock bands, Humble Pie.

Humble Pie's triple-threat song topics—girls, blues, and booze—was transmitted via a heavy guitar approach bottomed out by bassist Greg Ridley, who had defected from Spooky Tooth, and potent drummer Jerry Shirley. Though Frampton could rock hard, the young guitarist also had a taste for softer acoustic music. Fortunately, Marriott kept that tendency in check, steering the band on a path toward gritty and grimy rock, best heard on the raucous 1971 album that finally established Humble Pie in the United States, *Performance—Rockin' the Fillmore*. Fueled by Marriott's raspy vocals and a twin lead guitar attack, *Performance* set new standards in the glories of big, dumb rock.

But speaking of raspy singers and raucous rock, The Small Faces did not simply implode in the wake of Marriott's departure. Instead, they brought in two refugees from The Jeff Beck Group, guitarist Ron Wood and singer Rod Stewart.

After shortening the band's name to Faces, drummer Kenny Jones, keyboardist Ian McLagan, and bassist Ronnie Lane teamed up with Wood and Stewart in crafting a legacy of sloppy, low-down rock that existed in an atmosphere of drunken debauchery. Heard to best effect on 1971's *A Nod Is as Good as a Wink . . . To a Blind Horse*, Faces were characterized by McLagan's rollicking piano and Wood's admirably distorted guitar, which on this album had a rich, full, and filthy tone that remains unequalled. Above it all, Stewart exhorted his mates onward through wildly rude songs like "Stay with Me" and "Miss Judy's Farm."

So intensely decadent were the lifestyles of both Humble Pie and Faces that they were inevitably doomed to implosion.

Peter Frampton turned the Humble Pie lead guitar duties over to Colosseum's Clem Clempson soon after *Performance*, leaving to establish a solo career. Although Humble Pie went on to record the wonderfully raw *Smokin'* in 1972 with Clemson, it was all over for the great rockers within three years, as the fast living led to increasing strain on the band's interpersonal relationships.

Faces faced more than just substance abuse issues—Rod Stewart was cultivating an increasingly successful solo career. Albums like *Never a Dull Moment* and *Every Picture Tells a Story*—whose title song proved beyond a shadow of doubt that it was indeed possible to rock hard with acoustic instruments—were more consistent than Faces' studio output and were making Rod a superstar. That created a growing tension in the band, although, curiously, Rod's Faces mates often appeared on the solo albums. The once-great band could only soldier on for a final uneven studio album, 1973's *Ooh La La*, descending from the bawdy heights of *A Nod Is as Good as a Wink*. Lane quit in 1973, replaced by an associate of Free, Japanese bassist Tetsu Yamauchi, who played with the band for their final year.

Neil Young once sang of the benefits of burning out rather than fading away; Faces and Humble Pie were early rock and roll case studies of that very theory.

In the autumn of 1971, inflation in the United States had reached such rampant proportions that President Richard Nixon declared a ninety-day freeze on prices and wages.

Though many artists were understandably concerned about the effect of a harsh economic climate on record sales, two former chart toppers in particular found themselves on uncertain footing. Both The Beach Boys and Sly and the Family Stone found hard rock bands like Mountain and The Who on one side, with the soft fluff of The Osmonds, Olivia Newton-John, and John Denver on the other. The dilemma facing Beach Boys leader Brian Wilson and Sylvester "Sly Stone" Stewart was simple: how to stay relevant.

That had not been a problem for The Beach Boys in the 1960s, when even The Beatles looked toward new releases by that band to see how high the creative ladder had been raised. Wilson's symphonic rock compositions used complex melodic structures and were presented to spectacular effect through the group's luxuriant harmonies. But by 1971, The Beach Boys were seen as has-beens. They felt a desperate pressure to evolve, and the impact of that pressure was clearly seen between *Sunflower*, released on August 31, 1970, and *Surf's Up*, released 364 days later.

On *Sunflower*, The Beach Boys still seemed cheerfully untouched by a world of Altamonts and Black Sabbaths—after all, Ozzy Osbourne and company were unlikely to be found singing songs about a little bird who whistles outside someone's window.

The album did have its share of genuine highlights, among them "Slip on Through," with its propulsive, soul-like structure framed by the group's hallmark vocal harmonies; "This Whole World," which, despite its somewhat corny sentiments, boasts an entertaining chordal structure; and "Add Some Music to Your Day," about the preponderance—and importance—of music in human culture. The latter was perhaps closest in structure to previous Beach Boys hits like "Sloop John B," but beautiful in its restrained performance.

Some people may justifiably wonder why a band that was capable of creating the lush, near-ambient sound washes of the tonal experiment "Cool, Cool Water" would even care if they were relevant. But in the midst of the times, and witnessing the actions of their fellow artists, The Beach Boys felt desperate to connect with the underground culture.

"We got a little arty about it," Brian Wilson said in an interview with Richard Cromelin in the October 1976 issue of *Creem* magazine. Noting the band's conscious creative changes, Wilson conceded, "It got to the point where we were too selfishly artistic and we weren't thinking about the public enough. It got to that level. Partially because of drugs . . ."

Wilson was leading a hermit-like existence, yet in an attempt to maintain a connection with the band's sun-and-sand tradition, he had turned one room of his home into a makeshift beach.

"It's true that I did have a sandbox in my house," Wilson admitted. "It was the size of one room and we had a piano in the sand. The story about staying home and writing in the sandbox is all true . . ."

Wilson's fellow Beach Boys who weren't stuck in the sand saw the rampant cultural changes going on and thought it was high time they told it like it was. As a result, there was a deep split between Brian's songs and those penned by Beach Boys determined to reattain hip status.

Ironically, *Surf's Up* seemed to answer *Sunflower's* "Cool, Cool Water" via lead-off track "Don't Go Near the Water," a lament about water pollution—and a rather obvious attempt to identify with fashionably prominent environmental concerns. The relevance campaign continued with "Student Demonstration Time"—the Mike Love-penned endorsement of student disobedience set to the tune of "Riot in Cell Block #9" by Jerry Leiber and Mike Stoller—and with "Lookin' at Tomorrow (A Welfare Song)" by Al Jardine and Gary Winfrey.

In fact, it wasn't until the final three tracks of *Surf's Up* that Brian Wilson's own music emerged. The band's spiritual leader towed the prevailing party line in his own dire song about pollution, "A Day in the Life of a Tree." But then, rising above the contemporary morass, came "'Til I Die," a pensive, atmospheric questioning of universal issues of existence. Earlier in the record, Brian's brother, Carl, had contributed "Feel Flows," itself a trippy, oblique-but-engrossing ode to peace and well being.

Taken together, "'Til I Die" and "Feel Flows" were gorgeous songs pointing to new directions in sound that might have made The Beach Boys vital voices in music's future. Had they followed such a path, their songs would have been noteworthy not for topicality, but for the beauty of their craft, while still maintaining touch with the group's imposing heritage. Sadly, though, with the exception of a few brief moments of brilliance, for The Beach Boys the years ahead would be notable only for creative decline.

Drug use no doubt contributed to the eccentricities of Brian Wilson's homebound existence, and similar problems had led to a radical shift of direction in Sly and the Family Stone's music.

When *There's a Riot Goin' On* was released in 1971, gone were the exuberant, horn-driven blasts of soul that had powered hits like "Dance to the Music" and "I Want to Take You Higher." In the eighteen months since the release of the band's last smash album, *Stand!*, Sly Stone had moved to Los Angeles and rented a mansion with a recording studio in the attic.

"It was havoc," sax player Jerry Martini told Joel Selvin in *MOJO* magazine. "It was very gangsterish, dangerous. The vibes were very dark at that point. There was a cloud flying over that place. There was a cloud flying over Sly from the time he moved down to Los Angeles to this day . . ."

Though he faced new creative competition when Kenny Gamble and Leon Huff, with arranger Thom Bell, began to develop "the Philly Sound," Stone was chronically late for concerts. And if he showed up at all, he was often surrounded by armed, shady characters. Sly increasingly tried to dictate the lives of band members through a haze of drug-addled decisions. And in that atmosphere, *Riot* was recorded.

The supercharged R&B that had characterized Sly and the Family Stone was now replaced by sneakier funk, music creeping about on Sly's staccato clavinet keyboard and given voice through the hoarse falsettos of "Like a Baby." Even bassist Larry Graham—who, along with Bootsy Collins, was one of the most essential practitioners of an instrument so vital to this form of music—sounded well reigned in. Many of the album's vocals were garbled in stoned street talk, as on the bizarre "Spaced Cowboy," which featured Sly yodeling through the chorus when he wasn't croakily slurring the verses. Stone fronted an attitude which would prove influential in funk and soul music in years to come, but this album's release confused a good segment of the record's buyers, who expected more accessible material. Still, the initial rush of sales sent the album to number one on the charts. It was to be Sly's last breath taken in that rarified atmosphere.

For most rock fans, The Who's *Tommy* was about as big a work as could be easily digested—but for those with a hunger for more, there was always a stroll down the avant avenue of *Escalator Over the Hill*, a "chronotransduction" by jazz composer Carla Bley and writer Paul Haines.

Spread over three full albums, *Escalator* told the story of . . . Well, quite what it was all about was subject to interpretation. But there were similarities to Joe Cocker's *Mad Dogs & Englishmen* tour—the respected Bley was able to assemble a bohemian army of scores of musicians, playing in assemblages ranging from rock power trio ensembles to near-orchestral groupings. Among the bizarre array of participants was the raucous young Argentinean saxophonist Gato Barbieri, country-tinged vocalist Linda Ronstadt, Andy Warhol starlet Viva, bassist Jack Bruce, and guitarist John McLaughlin.

Though *Escalator* was intriguing, McLaughlin was a musician on the verge of participating in ventures that would have far greater impact than Bley's work.

Having played guitar since the age of eleven, McLaughlin passed through some of the same circles as the British rock royalty. This background included a stint with the groundbreaking Graham Bond Organisation, where he had first met Bruce and drummer Ginger Baker. But where others followed the call of rock stardom, McLaughlin remained focused on music alone. By the late 1960s, though he was laboring in virtual obscurity, McLaughlin's imposing talents were well known among British guitarists.

"I would say he was the best jazz guitarist in England then," Jimmy Page told *Guitar Player's* Steve Rosen in 1977. As a bastion of England's studio scene, Page had a professional interest in keeping a close eye on the competition. "He was easily the best guitarist in England—and he was working in a guitar shop."

By 1970, word of his talent was getting around, McLaughlin having recorded with Miles Davis, jammed with Jimi Hendrix, and performed with Bruce in the Tony Williams Lifetime. He'd played straight jazz, but had also been exposed to the world of electric and electronic instruments.

Significantly, McLaughlin was open-minded about the talents of rock musicians.

"A revolutionary force who single-handedly shifted the whole course of guitar playing," he noted of Jimi Hendrix.

Having already covered a lot of musical ground, and armed with an extensive catalog of both jazz and rock influences, McLaughlin felt there was an entirely new realm ripe for exploration—all he needed to do was assemble the expedition.

For the foundation of his new project, McLaughlin turned to muscular drummer Billy Cobham.

"Billy was the first man I talked to about coming into my new band," McLaughlin told *Downbeat*'s Burt Korall. "I had met him several times with Miles and on dates with other people. He impressed me so much. I was very happy when he said he would join me."

McLaughlin then sought a violinist, auditioning any rock or jazz album with a lineup that included such a player. When he heard The Flock's Jerry Goodman, another piece of the puzzle fell into place. Czech keyboardist Jan Hammer, then working with Sarah Vaughan, was next recommended to McLaughlin, and the final member, bassist Rick Laird—who had been house bassist at the vital London jazz club Ronnie Scott's—was an old acquaintance. The name of the new band came from McLaughlin's studies with guru Sri Chinmoy: The Mahavishnu Orchestra.

The band's first gigs were at the Gaslight club in New York's Greenwich Village. The reaction was immediate: The Mahavishnu Orchestra was held over for weeks while the band recorded their debut, *The Inner Mounting Flame*. Upon the album's release late in 1971, the rest of the world was exposed to the radical new sounds that had thrilled New York's music denizens.

The Mahavishnu Orchestra performed music that was cerebral and kinetic—one moment gliding through serenely beautiful melodies, the next careening through tricky, abrasive passages. McLaughlin and Goodman would typically play runs in harmony, issuing fiercely dynamic themes, accented by twinkling fills from Hammer's Fender Rhodes electric piano. Cobham played with an athlete's force, but his staggering power was harnessed under precise control and discipline. The result was a devastating combination. Bassist Laird somehow managed to keep his fellow musicians earthbound, an imposing task in a band in which the high-volume, white-hot intensity of the music made it seem as though ascension to the heavens was a very real possibility.

Though *The Inner Mounting Flame* sold slowly at first, its momentum was unstoppable. The arrival of The Mahavishnu Orchestra was like a comet smashing into the surface of an ocean. Soon, the consequences of McLaughlin's project would hit rock music like a tidal wave, altering forever the way many rock musicians viewed their creative craft.

1972

3

Electric Warriors

On December 7, 1971, a young man who would soon be eternally known in one song's lyrics as "some stupid with a flare gun" exercised very bad judgment during a Frank Zappa concert in Switzerland. And British band Deep Purple—guitarist Ritchie Blackmore, vocalist Ian Gillan, organist Jon Lord, bassist Roger Glover, drummer Ian Paice—were witnesses to the chain of events that followed.

This second career lineup of Deep Purple found themselves in Montreux, ready to track their third studio album. After first recording a rather bombastic live album with the Royal Philharmonic Orchestra, 1970's *Deep Purple in Rock* had established the group as leaders of the British hard rock movement, and the follow-up, *Fireball,* had done equally well. But there was a sense that, with the right album, superstardom awaited.

Much of the interest in Deep Purple was focused on Blackmore's bold guitar attack. And when Blackmore played, you had no choice but to hear him.

"My setup is pushing out about 500 watts—I guess that's maybe 1000 watts in American ratings, but it's all distortion," Blackmore boasted of his heavily modified Marshall amps to Martin Webb in *Guitar Player.* "The people at Marshall said it's the loudest amp they'd ever heard. . . . That's why every two weeks things just tend to disintegrate."

The band planned to use a large hall known as the Casino to try to capture their massive aural character, setting up their gear on the stage and recording to a mobile truck full of recording equipment rented from The Rolling Stones. Claude Nobs, involved in Montreux's music scene as a promoter of both the city's famed jazz festival and concerts at the Casino, was happy to welcome Deep Purple to the city. He stood by, ready to help them set up as soon as the Casino concert he'd booked with Frank Zappa was over. To pass the time, Nobs provided Deep Purple and their crew with tickets to the Zappa concert.

Safely ensconced in deluxe seats, the band members settled in to watch the afternoon show. Zappa's band included vocalists Mark Volman and Howard Kaylan, the core of the 1960s pop group The Turtles, along with drummer Aynsley Dunbar, who'd lost a slot in The Jimi Hendrix Experience on the results of a coin toss that favored Mitch Mitchell.

Amazingly, in the midst of Zappa's set, someone stood up and—for reasons unknown—fired off a flare gun. Several moments later, smoke was seen wafting from a false ceiling over the audience. The decision was made to evacuate the building, Zappa quipping that perhaps the culprit was Arthur Brown, the famed eccentric vocalist notorious for his flame-spewing pyrotechnic helmet.

At first the fire appeared small, but after everyone was safely outside the building, larger flames suddenly erupted. In a matter of moments, the Casino was gone, as was all of Zappa's gear and Deep Purple's intended recording site.

Between his duties in the wake of the fire, Claude Nobs vowed to help Deep Purple find a new place to cut their album. First he directed the group to an older theater known as the Pavilion. The band made it through a single night of high-volume recording amidst the ornate surroundings before general neighborhood outrage dictated another relocation.

At last the band found a home at the empty-for-the-winter Grand Hotel. With The Stones' recording truck parked outside, Deep Purple rigged up a makeshift studio in empty rooms and corridors.

"Cables running into all the rooms, the residents [of the neighborhood] couldn't believe it when they saw all the equipment," Blackmore recalled in the remastered release of the album the band recorded in Montreux, *Machine Head*. "During playbacks, I had to go through half a dozen doors, down a fire escape at the back of the hotel, across a courtyard where it was snowing at the time, and into the mobile."

Despite the primitive—and chilly—conditions, Deep Purple recorded a masterpiece hard rock album. On full display was Blackmore's fiery brilliance, breaking new ground through the incorporation of classical scales and aggressive, bottom-dropping-out tremolo bar attacks. Lord's organ blared its proudly raunchy voice, adding an edge of fury to classical-inspired touches. Gillan cemented his reputation as one of rock's leading vocalists, able to span the range from conversational blues to leather-lunged shrieking.

Equally as important as the band's front line, Deep Purple's rhythm section of Glover and Paice was a large part of what set the band apart from their contemporaries. Many hard rock bands could—and did—rely on thudding pacing from drummers and bassists who followed chord changes with monotonous, zombie-like plodding. But Paice and Glover were fleet and nimble—heavy in sound, yet able to play with a song rather than just play it.

And the instrumental track the band recorded on the night that led to their eviction from the Pavilion? With the addition of Gillan's man-on-the-scene lyrics, the song became "Smoke on the Water," an account of the fire at the Casino and the band's Swiss recording travails. Propelled by one of rock's greatest guitar riffs, the song stormed into the top five of the American charts by mid-year.

Before hitting on this most dynamic personnel lineup, Deep Purple was for a time fronted by singer Rod Evans, whose vocal style helped the band score a hit in the United States with "Hush" in 1968. Evans resurfaced in 1972, behind the microphone with the cerebral Los Angeles heavy rock band Captain Beyond.

Joined by Iron Butterfly members Larry "Rhino" Rheinhart on guitar and Lee Dorman on bass, and teamed with drummer Bobby Caldwell, Captain Beyond arguably commanded one of the first successful expeditions into the realm of "art rock" or "progressive rock"—"prog rock" for short—where musical complexity scores big points. And with song titles like "Thousand Days of Yesterdays (Intro)/Frozen Over/Thousand Days of Yesterdays (Time Since Come and Gone)" and "I Can't Feel

Nothin' (Part I)/As the Moon Speaks (To the Waves of the Sea)/Astral Lady/As the Moon Speaks (Return)/I Can't Feel Nothin' (Part II)," it was obvious there was complexity in abundance. Captain Beyond offered more than the standard rock riff-a-rama.

Unlike Deep Purple's music—with Blackmore and Lord blasting out unified, classically inspired melodic runs over the typically swinging Glover/Paice rhythm section—Captain Beyond got the entire band into the act. The scorching guitar solos were nestled amid an array of evolving time signatures, complex chord designs, and intricately planned out pieces of music. It was heavy, but it was also impressively difficult.

Cactus had also been cultivating their own heavy canon of rock, but it was far removed from Captain Beyond's approach and lacking any connotation with the word *cerebral*. Their 1972 album *'Ot 'n' Sweaty* would prove to be the band's last, a half-live half-studio album with a distinctly schizophrenic personality.

The 1970 brainchild of two founders of Vanilla Fudge—bassist Tim Bogert and drummer Carmine Appice—Cactus had released three hard-driving blues and boogie albums by the time they took the stage at Puerto Rico's Mar y Sol festival in 1972. But the band that appeared under tropical skies was radically different from the group's original lineup. Gone were vocalist Rusty Day and guitarist Jim McCarty, who had led the band through thunderous onslaughts like "Evil" and "Parchman Farm." In their place were singer Pete French, with Werner Fritzschings on guitar and Duane Hitchings on keyboards.

To an audience that had traveled so far to have a good time, it probably didn't matter. The new version of Cactus exploded on stage, blasting through every cliché at their disposal. French, who had joined and then split from Atomic Rooster just after *Death Walks behind You*, spent the majority of his time cheerleading the audience, while Fritzschings and Hitchings predictably played what was expected of them. It wasn't spontaneous, nor was it brilliant improvisation, yet it was effective and high-energy. The album's live side stands as an alluring artifact of state-of-the-art stage craft in 1972.

Sadly, the same can't be said for the five studio tracks. Equally cliché-ridden, but lacking any discernable pulse, the album's second side gave listeners no reason to flip over 'Ot 'n' *Sweaty* if it landed live side up on turntables. And virtually upon release of the album, Appice and Bogert split to form the latest rock supergroup, Beck, Bogert, Appice. Like most of Jeff Beck's projects, the trio was soon put to an end, fated to termination by the temperamental-but-brilliant guitarist's unpredictable whims. Hitchings carried on with the Cactus name briefly, resurfacing later in the decade with Rod Stewart as cowriter of the cloying smash hit "Do Ya Think I'm Sexy?"

While Cactus was in the throes of dissolution, Johnny Winter found himself without a band as well. The albino-like blues guitarist from Beaumont, Texas, had gained acclaim after an article about the unsigned musician in *Rolling Stone* led to a record contract with Columbia. Eventually Winter hooked up with members of The McCoys, a band that had a number-one pop hit in 1965 with "Hang on Sloopy." In the quite oddly named Johnny Winter And, though, the ex-McCoys were certainly not expected to be a pop band. Winter's revved-up blues were expressed in a hail of guitar notes that elevated him to superstar status, and the album *Live—Johnny Winter And* was a top seller in 1971. Shortly after the album's release, Johnny Winter And split up, with drummer Bobby Caldwell heading off to Captain Beyond.

It seemed like a good time for Johnny to check in with his younger brother Edgar, and that's just what he did on *Roadwork*. Edgar had parlayed his high-profile appearances on Johnny's early albums into his own record deal, and in 1972 had assembled a horn-driven R&B band called White Trash. *Roadwork* captured the band at several gigs, including one at Harlem's famed black showcase the Apollo Theater, in which the audience sounds quite amused to be viewing a band called White Trash. The material ranged from the gospel of "Save the Planet" to the greasy funk of "Cool Fool." If the vocal histrionics are occasionally over the top, at least the band was razor-sharp. And *Roadwork* was assured of a launch high into the charts thanks to Johnny's guest appearance, featured prominently on the album's cover despite his single-song participation on the grooves within.

Within a few months, Edgar would tire of the big White Trash sound and streamline his efforts into a tight hard rock outfit featuring Ronnie Montrose and Rick Derringer—formerly second guitarist with Johnny Winter And, and himself a guest on *Roadwork*. The Edgar Winter Group's *They Only Come out at Night* would yield a massive instrumental hit in "Frankenstein," powered by one of the primary riffs for the ages and appropriately gimmicked-up with an abundance of synthesizer stuntage.

To the west of the Winters' hometown, Houston's ZZ Top were building the foundation for a career that would see the band's original lineup last for decades. From the opening notes of ZZ Top's *First Album* in 1970, the trio sketched a course from which they would seldom stray. With the workmanlike bass of Dusty Hill providing the deep bottom, and Frank Beard's drumming contributing agile syncopation, guitarist Billy Gibbons took traditional blues runs and gave them a high-voltage reinvention. The band's travels ranged from Tex-Mex territory to harder rock terrain, but they seldom veered far from the heart of the blues.

In 1972, ZZ Top entered the studio to record their third album, *Tres Hombres*. Largely on the strength of the song "La Grange," a pumping, quasi-instrumental spiritually descended from John Lee Hooker's style of vamping blues, the "Li'l Ole Band from Texas" transferred their popularity in that state to the rest of the nation.

While prominent artists from the Lone Star State reveled in their roots, a host of new bands on both sides of the Atlantic sought to establish themselves as major hard rock forces. For the most part, they failed. Still, their efforts should not be forgotten; bands like Dust, Budgie, and Sir Lord Baltimore all recorded hard rock albums that helped sketch out the blueprint for heavy metal.

One of the last prime hard rock power trios had members from both the United States and the United Kingdom. Based on their pedigree, their 1972 debut *Why Dontcha?* should have been just the first listen to one of the greatest supergroups of all time, but it didn't work out that way.

West, Bruce & Laing—respectively, Leslie from Mountain, Jack from Cream, and Corky from Mountain—proved to be a highly erratic aggregation with a body of work that varied wildly from rousing to rubbish. Despite Jack Bruce's typically stirring vocals and incendiary bass, the songs not written by Bruce seemed to miss the compositional and arranging skills that Felix Pappalardi had brought to both Mountain and Cream. Not that Leslie wasn't fully capable of writing pounding riff-based rockers—he'd come up with many such anthems in Mountain's catalog. But there was something intangible missing in the project, and West, Bruce & Laing never came close to consistently matching the heights of Mountain in the studio or the excitement of Cream on stage.

Captain Beyond had tentatively dipped their toe in the uncharted American waters of prog rock, but in England, progression was the name of the game, with a host of bands elevating themselves—and rock music—above the riffs of the commoners.

The definition of prog rock was fluid. But where at one time most bands figured they had it made if their lineup included a jazz- or classically oriented keyboardist, the growing influences of musicians like Miles Davis and Mahavishnu Orchestra were stretching the boundaries of prog rock. A survey of those doing prog rock business in 1972 reveals a wide range of experimentation from the exotic to the avant-garde.

Ginger Baker, after surviving the disintegration of both Cream and Blind Faith, piloted his own Ginger Baker's Air Force through 1970. It was a free-form, jazz-inspired gathering of musicians that included Blind Faith bassist Rick Grech and influential band leader Graham Bond, and reunited Chris Wood and Steve Winwood, thus leading directly to the reformation of Traffic.

But Baker was a drummer with a taste for the exotic, and he proved this by dissolving Air Force and entering into a creative relationship with Fela Ransome Kuti. On 1972's *Stratavarious*, the unlikely alignment of a British drummer with a Nigerian jazz musician cum political revolutionary yielded an album with precious little rock, one that instead was a heady concoction of pure jazz with African elements.

So enamored was Baker with Mother Africa that he soon moved to the teeming city of Lagos, Nigeria, to study firsthand the music of Africa. And though the *Stratavarious* album was far from being a smash hit, Baker's fellow musicians were listening, hearing the sound of cultural barriers being smashed in what was a blueprint for the "world music" movement that arose twenty years later.

An alternate direction for jazz exploration in a rock context was provided by Good God, a Philadelphia band that recorded a single—yet essential—self-titled album for Atlantic Records. Along with four original numbers, the quintet covered Frank Zappa's "King Kong" and John McLaughlin's "Dragon Song." Since the release of Miles Davis' first electric works, it had become more common to find jazzers working in a rock context. By playing jazz without a strict jazz background, though, Good God took things in the opposite direction.

Ironically, the very next Atlantic Records catalog number after the one given to Good God was issued to the British band Yes, for their fifth album, *Close to the Edge*.

The band was formed in 1968, based on a proposed collaboration when singer Jon Anderson first met bassist Chris Squire in London's Marquee Club. The duo advertised for other musicians, recruiting drummer Bill Bruford via classified ad in the music newspaper *Melody Maker*. When keyboardist Tony Kaye and guitarist Peter Banks joined up, the first lineup of Yes was complete. They quickly established a high profile, one that brought them the prestigious opening slot at the farewell performance by Cream at the Royal Albert Hall late in 1968.

Critical encouragement greeted the band's first two albums, *Yes* and *Time and a Word*, released in 1968 and 1969 respectively. In an effort to better themselves, Yes made the first of myriad personnel changes when Banks was dismissed in favor of Steve Howe, a guitarist Anderson had spotted at another London club, the Speakeasy. Further progress was made with 1971's *The Yes Album*, a six-song album with tracks stretching out to nine-minute lengths.

Soon after, Yes had the opportunity to make a crucial personnel change. With Kaye leaving the band, Yes pursued renowned keyboardist Rick Wakeman, a classically trained pianist at the Royal Academy who had achieved critical notoriety as a member of The Strawbs, a band fronted by Dave Cousins. The Strawbs merged progressive elements and classical influences, but applied them to a traditional British folk framework. Cousins' voice was suitably ancient in tone, lending credence to songs with titles like "The Hangman and the Papist" and "The Shepherd's Song." The experimentation was unique and artistically successful, and The Strawbs prospered long after Wakeman's departure, particularly on their early-1970s albums *Grave New World*, *Bursting at the Seams*, and *Hero and Heroine*.

Armed with Wakeman's exciting contributions, Yes recorded its commercial breakthrough, *Fragile*. *Close to the Edge* came on its heels in 1972, an album that charted in the top ten in both the United States and England.

The Yes sound was characterized by an intricate interplay of lead and rhythm instrumentation. Where most bands relegated the bass guitar to the background, in Yes it was Squire's rumbly-yet-rattly bass sound that propelled the band forward. Howe's guitar approach differed from his contemporaries in that his solos took fleet leaps of the fingerboard that were more jazz-inspired than blues-based, while Wakeman used classical elements filtered through both traditional keyboards and the new wave of synthesizers that were de rigueur in prog rock. Above it all, Jon Anderson's high, longing voice placed a near-angelic lightness above the weight of the band's collective sound. The singer added visual contrast in concert by cloaking himself in gauzy white stage wear that further cemented a minstrel-like image.

"Twentieth century rock audiences are far more intelligent than half the audiences who go to classical concerts," Wakeman ventured to Jaan Uhelszki in *Creem* magazine in 1975. "Classical concerts are like churches; the only people who go to them are the converted. Rock and roll audiences will give anything a try—they want to see and hear something different, yet performed and presented properly."

Also gaining momentum in the same orbit traveled by Yes was a newer band called Genesis. Upon the release of the third Genesis album, *Nursery Chryme*, star keyboardist Keith Emerson directed a highly publicized compliment their way. The remark helped ensure that a growing audience was on hand for 1972's *Foxtrot*.

The music of Genesis at this stage was one part gothic, one part fairy tale, with the remainder consumed by complicated song construction, as in *Foxtrot's* twenty-minute climax "Supper's Ready." Vocalist Peter Gabriel—already gaining renown for his outlandish stage presentations—had a voice that sounded dusty and primordial, and it nestled in snugly among Tony Banks' stately keyboard washes. Steve Hackett's guitar provided an edge to the band, while bassist Michael Rutherford and drummer Phil Collins cooked up a billowing head of progressive steam.

Based on the strength of their recordings and the carefully designed theatrical aspects of their concerts—as the lofty final section of "Supper's Ready" neared its grand conclusion, a silver-clad Gabriel was lowered from the heavens amidst clouds of smoke—Genesis were clearly elevating prog rock performance standards.

Of course, the whole idea of prog rock came about through the infusion of classical elements in rock music, so it was logical—or inevitable—that orchestra players would somehow get involved. Deep Purple had watched as their *Concerto for Group and Orchestra* was met with unconvinced reviews; Procol Harum was next to try the full orchestra treatment via *Live with the Edmonton Symphony Orchestra*.

Procol Harum had rocketed into prominence on the strengths of the Bach-inspired single "A Whiter Shade of Pale." Driven by Gary Brooker's clearly potent vocals, the song climbed to number one in England and into the top five in the States. This established a career for the band as they ran the stylistic gamut from an early dependence on blues-based material to later classical experimentation.

On August 6, 1971, in Edmonton, Canada, Procol Harum's grandest experiment yet was realized—the recording of a live album with a full orchestra and choir. The centerpiece was the nearly twenty-minute "In Held 'Twas I," from the band's *Shine on Brightly* album. Rarely performed live, the massive work had more or less written itself in the studio.

"All the ideas were there, but it wasn't completely written before we started to record it," Brooker said of the piece to Richard Cromelin in *Creem* magazine in 1972. "I think we'd written about half of it before we started to record it and the other bits came as we went along. It's so long that we never knew what was going to happen until we finally finished it."

Though the live-with-orchestra version does have a certain bombastic appeal to it, the most successful track on the album is the title track from Procol Harum's third album, *A Salty Dog*.

Band lyricist Keith Reid recalled, "'A Salty Dog' was just an idea that came from . . . Cleveland; we were playing a place, and carved up on the wall it said, 'Great God, skipper, we done run aground.' So that stuck in my mind and it ended up turning into 'A Salty Dog.'"

The eerie tale of a sea voyage in the dangerous age of sailing ships, "A Salty Dog" found Brooker's expressive vocals wonderfully supported by the orchestra's breathtaking crescendos. The mood evolves from despair, as the crew passes the place "where ships come home to die," to a soaring resolution as Brooker dramatically conveys the relief and joy of returning to loved ones on dry land. One of the most beautiful songs of the rock era—or any era—"A Salty Dog" showed that the unlikely pairing of rock band and orchestra could work if the material was right.

Unlike the successful conclusion of the voyage recounted in "A Salty Dog," *Live with the Edmonton Symphony Orchestra* sank with all hands aboard when it was released in England in May 1972. The album logged just a single week in the British top fifty. Surprisingly, though, in the United States it became a top seller, claiming gold album status and residing in the top five of the album charts.

Though Procol Harum received support from a real orchestra in Edmonton, England's newly formed Electric Light Orchestra was not an orchestra at all. Jeff Lynne and Roy Wood, the two leaders of the quirky band The Move, decided that exploration of rock elements using classical instrumentation might prove interesting. They drafted Move drummer Bev Bevan, horn player Bill Hunt, and violinist Steve Woolam to create a new band.

The debut album from Electric Light Orchestra was released in 1972, self-titled throughout the world but known as *No Answer* in the United States. It seems that a secretary with the United States record label was asked to call someone with the British label to inquire what the band was calling their debut.

No one answered the telephone extension, and her handwritten notation of that fact was mistakenly recorded as the album's title.

Regardless of title, the album began with the paranoid, doomy "10538 Overture." With French horns resounding, Wood sawed away at layers of overdubbed cello, the tonal frequency of the instrument finding a clear home amidst the ranges of the guitars, bass, and drums. It was a lesson The Beatles had learned late in their career, and Electric Light Orchestra used that knowledge as a starting point.

Beyond that, the entire album sounded as though it was recorded in some kind of alternate universe, and even co-creator Lynne says of the album, "This was a pretty wacky album, so innocent yet so bold. It goes to some very strange places." With its mix of classical and folk instruments set to odd arrangements—like the truly mind-bending "Battle of Marston Moor (July 2nd 1644)"—*No Answer* is about as far removed from rock as rock records get.

England's Jethro Tull was much more identifiable as a rock band, though leader Ian Anderson had his problems with the band's back catalog.

"Some of the songs on *Benefit* I still really like, but it was a bit too much like what a rock group is supposed to be," Anderson said of the group's third album to Cameron Crowe in *Creem* magazine in January 1975. "By that time we were doing all right, we were playing to some sizable audiences and indulging the illusion that we were a name group. That's a very dangerous thing. We played it too safe with *Benefit*. It could have been a lot more adventurous.

"*Aqualung* was an attempt to move on," Anderson said of 1971's follow-up album. "It was a different kind of music than we played before. The playing wasn't so hot and the production was dismal, but the songs were good. I don't dislike it."

Though Anderson wasn't overly thrilled with the album, the public was; songs like the title track, with Martin Barre's beautifully lyrical guitar solo, and the near-metal crunch of "Locomotive Breath" helped establish the band as stars in the United States. As a result, many rock fans were looking forward to the next album of Jethro Tull songs. That presented a dilemma for the group, one that all bands face when an album is a hit.

"Not being a successful album for us personally, and yet being a very well received album kind of upset things," Barre noted of *Aqualung* at the time. "Do you follow the same formula and risk that unhappy feeling in the studio, or do you carry on as you had planned with something different?"

In the end, Jethro Tull went with something different: one single song consuming an entire album, *Thick as a Brick*.

"When we started recording *Thick as a Brick*, we didn't know the end result would be a concept album," Barre later recalled in an interview included with the anniversary CD release of the album. "It just started life as another Tull album, and we learnt the music in the way that we learnt music for *Aqualung*, *Benefit*, other albums. But it developed along the way, mainly because we were splicing all the bits of music together to make it continuous. I don't think we were ever aware of what direction it was going to end up going in—it was just something we did on a day-to-day basis."

Perhaps the lack of a rigid game plan contributed to the success of the work, as there was ample room for experimentation in the overall construction. Fortunately, from a musical standpoint the band was up to their task. Tull had toured heavily in the wake of *Aqualung*, and the quintet was now a tight ensemble that played off each other's strengths. Anderson's classical guitar and flute contrasted with Barre's meaty blues-rock guitar, while keyboardist John Evan contributed lush organ washes and piano melodies. In the wake of *Benefit*, bassist Glen Cornick and drummer Clive Bunker were replaced by Jeffrey Hammond-Hammond and Barriemore Barlow, respectively, musicians who brought a limber feel to the revitalized Jethro Tull rhythm section.

Had *Thick as a Brick* been split into individual songs, it would no doubt have been extremely successful. There was a wide audience primed by the success of *Aqualung*, and in truth the melodies and chord structures of Anderson's compositions for this album stand as some of his most striking and beautiful work. But having all of the material exist as a single work provided additional enjoyment, as the band found clever ways to twist their musical path back to themes that had been developed earlier. This reemergence of progressions effectively accentuated the cyclical nature of the album as a whole.

Despite the somewhat imposing aura created by a single-song album, *Thick as a Brick* climbed directly to the number one slot in the United States album charts. It appeared the fans had demanded a concept album that worked, and Jethro Tull had delivered.

Opening for Jethro Tull on their extravagant *Thick as a Brick* tour was Frank Zappa associate Captain Beefheart, backed by his Magic Band.

Beefheart's early albums had been outrageous avant-garde explorations, but his 1972 release, *Clear Spot*, successfully combined his experimental leanings with traditional rock and R&B styles. The album's intriguing sound was crafted by producer Ted Templeman and engineer Don Landee, a team that would record major works throughout the decade.

Songs like the exceptional "Clear Spot" and "Low Yo Yo Stuff," combined with the high-profile slot on the Tull tour, should have helped establish The Magic Band as a major band. But even the tamer music of Beefheart—who appeared on stage in a stylish Chinese coolie outfit—seemed to be a bit much for the Jethro Tull crowd.

The end of the tour left Beefheart questioning his place in the rock hierarchy, but Ian Anderson knew exactly where Jethro Tull stood in the scheme of things.

"Stylistically, I've always said that we can't be a heavy riff group because Led Zeppelin are the best in the world," Anderson admitted to Simon Frith in *Creem* magazine in 1978. "We can't be a blues-influenced R&B rock and roll group because the Stones are the best in the world. We can't be a slightly sort of airy-fairy mystical sci-fi synthesizing abstract freak-out group because Pink Floyd are the best in the world. And so what's left? And that's what we've always done. We've filled the gap."

While overall experimentation was the focus of many of rock's elite bands, the traditional voice of rock and roll—the electric guitar—was itself being expressed through an incredible variety of players who were channeling new influences and incorporating new techniques into their styles.

Roy Buchanan was an unlikely-looking laborer in the rock and roll world, but when the Arkansas guitarist's 1972 debut, *Roy Buchanan*, was released, looks obviously didn't matter. The bearded, balding musician didn't wear hip clothes, and his Fender Telecaster was a battered, no-frills plank of wood. But in Buchanan's hands, that Tele was one of the most expressive instruments to ever speak through an amplifier.

Years of playing in roadhouses and honky tonks gave Buchanan an incredible arsenal of guitar licks, and he played straight through his amps, eschewing the effects pedals that dosed so many guitarists' work of the day. The debut album's "Pete's Blue" and "The Messiah Will Come Again" were characteristic of Roy's incredible virtuosity. Though the backing band was barely there, Buchanan himself was incandescent, ably displaying most everything in his sonic palette, from piercing harmonics to quivering vibrato notes that howled in a shroud of blues.

The troubled Buchanan never ascended to levels of stardom, though he was asked to play with both The Rolling Stones and John Lennon. With the former he never showed up for the audition; with the latter he arrived too high to do more than pass out. Though it seemed Buchanan was all too skillful at sabotaging his own career, his playing inspired and intimidated any guitarist who heard that old Telecaster's cries.

Carlos Santana was another guitarist capable of inspiration, and his playing was imbued with a fiery intensity. His band was conceived in 1966 as The Santana Blues Band, but the name was shortened to Santana as the group's style developed. In their process of evolution, Santana began to successfully pioneer a potent rock sound all their own, fulfilling Carlos' vision of bringing incendiary Latin percussion to the rock world.

Much like Joe Cocker's sudden rise to stardom, an explosive performance at Woodstock was Santana's express ticket to rock nobility status. By the fall of 1969, Santana's debut album was gold and the band was on the road with Janis Joplin's Kozmic Blues Band. Two more albums followed in the driving Latin rock vein, but things took a sudden turn with 1972's *Caravanserai*.

It was obvious from the first notes that this was not the chart-friendly Santana band. Gone were tuneful hits like "Evil Ways" and "Black Magic Woman"—in their place were songs titled "Eternal Caravan of Reincarnation" and "All the Love of the Universe."

The fact that this was a band undergoing radical transformation was further evident from an aural standpoint. Opening with the soft chirping of insects, the album's entomological chorus is soon joined by the forlorn horn of Hadley Caliman, eerily blowing an echoing repeated phrase. Nearly two minutes in, an acoustic bass lazily glides into the scene, joined by dreamy keyboards and Neal Schon's gently strummed jazz chords. Greg Rolie's first vocals don't arrive until the fourth song, signaling the evolution of Santana into a primarily instrumental band. In fact, more than a dozen musicians contributed their talents to *Caravanserai*. The reason for the expanded roster was that the original Santana band had ceased to exist.

"By the third album it was like a meteor disintegrating already," Carlos Santana said. "By the time we did *Caravanserai* I had no band. Everybody was busy with buying clothes or cars or the chicks and all that stuff that goes with fame."

In the rock market of 1972, *Caravanserai* was underrated and underappreciated, with Santana's audience, frightened by change, longing for the band they used to know. Regardless of commercial reactions, though, the Santana reinvention was a successful one artistically, and this album contains some of Carlos Santana's most fulfilling playing set in a colorful, exotic soundscape. The world of *Caravanserai* was jazzy, but without the jagged edges of the Mahavishnu Orchestra's more extreme jazz and rock fusion. The new Santana maintained an earthy, organic feel but was also heady and atmospheric, mirroring the album's hazy cover photograph of a caravan crossing the desert.

Obviously no longer fulfilled by the life of rock stardom and actively seeking spiritual enlightenment, Carlos soon called an end to his band and sought guidance from John McLaughlin and his guru, Sri Chinmoy.

Meanwhile, Santana's fellow Bay Area musicians in The Grateful Dead had found their own path to spiritual enlightenment: through chemistry. Band members and their audience were no strangers to mind-expanding drug use. Out of that experimentation, The Dead had evolved their own sound, along with a rabidly loyal audience that would follow them for the band's entire career.

"We used to joke about incorporating as a religion," Grateful Dead rhythm guitarist Bob Weir once said, but joking aside, they quite likely could have pulled it off.

Their guitarist, Jerry Garcia, was a bluegrass music fan who began playing guitar at age fifteen. By the time The Grateful Dead came into existence late in 1965, Garcia was honing an unusual style of guitar that fused his bluegrass interests with folk and rock elements. Garcia seemed to play at his best on stage, where his lengthy free-form improvisations either delighted or bored listeners, depending on membership status in The Grateful Dead's congregation. On both the 1969 *Live/Dead* and 1972's *Europe '72*, Garcia was given ample vinyl acreage to document his unique explorations.

Exploration had also been the hallmark of Jimi Hendrix. And, though he'd been dead for months, this apparently wasn't stopping him from releasing new material. In actual fact, Warner Brothers was behind the marketing push that saw *Rainbow Bridge* appear late in 1971 and *In the West* and *War Heroes* materialize in 1972. Jimi's engineer, Eddie Kramer, was pretty much reaching the bottom of the near-complete-studio-material pile, especially on *War Heroes*. Thus, the real highlights of these releases were the live cuts.

From a Berkeley, California concert, *Rainbow Bridge* captured a performance of "Hear My Train a-Comin'" that rivaled "Machine Gun" from Band of Gypsys as a showcase for Hendrix's staggering talents. *In the West*—rather curiously titled, as much of the album was recorded at British performances—presented Hendrix's scorching Berkeley rendition of "Johnny B. Goode" and, from a Royal Albert Hall concert in London in 1969, a lovely, aching treatment of the ballad "Little Wing," which proved Jimi was equally proficient at songs that demanded a delicate, lyrical touch.

Lyrical was a description often applied to the solos of Free's Paul Kossoff, but his depression over the death of his idol Hendrix and his descent into addiction had only worsened in the months since Jimi died. Free had traveled a tortured path since the release of *Fire and Water*, breaking up, reforming, watching Kossoff slide further into decay and drug abuse. Finally, bassist Andy Fraser left for good in June 1972.

With Koss' condition erratic and Fraser gone, vocalist Paul Rodgers and drummer Simon Kirke had their hand forced to meet tour commitments. They brought in musicians John "Rabbit" Bundrick on keyboards and Testu Yamauchi on bass. As the fall of 1972 approached, though, Kossoff appeared to be in somewhat better health. Hoping for the best, Free booked recording time, entering the studio for what turned out to be their final sessions. The album that resulted—Free's last—was called *Heartbreaker*. The title was all too appropriate.

Recorded under the harshest of personal conditions, *Heartbreaker* could have been a disaster. Instead, it was an electrifying album that alternated between songs full of resolve and power and those seemingly resigned to an inevitable fate. Some of the most poignant songs found Kossoff discovering his full talents once again, playing with passionate emotion—ironically on songs that Rodgers may very well have written about his friend's troubled existence. In "Come Together in the Morning," as Rodgers sang, "It makes me sad to think of you, because I understand the things you do," Koss played with all of the touch and heart that characterized his greatest work.

"He was digging things up from somewhere deep inside," Rodgers said of the song in the liner notes to *Heartbreaker's* CD reissue. "His solo on 'Come Together in the Morning' is just breathtaking."

"Within the space of two years someone that you really loved and admired had gone all the way downhill, right to the very bottom," Kirke sadly recalled in David Clayton and Todd Smith's *Heavy Load*. "Very frightening. All his friends had gathered around him, they'd kicked him, cried with him, gone through every emotion. We'd put off tours, cancelled dates, done this and that and he still was . . ."

The final song on the last Free album harkened back to their darkest of material. In the lyrics of "Seven Angels," the dead stepped from their graves as Kossoff's guitar wailed in misery, interpreting the apocalyptic visions portrayed in the words. The music slowly faded, and the career of one of England's greatest bands came to an end.

"I don't think Free so much broke up as disintegrated of its own natural or unnatural causes," Rodgers said. "It was such a shambles, so chaotic at the end . . ."

Drugs, violence, poverty, gettin' over, and the big score—those were the themes of the 1972 urban drug culture film drama *Superfly*. Those topics were reflected by the film's soundtrack, crafted by Curtis Mayfield, onetime leader of The Impressions, who had gone solo in 1970.

When the film's producer and writer visited Mayfield backstage after a 1971 New York concert to ask if he would do the soundtrack for their planned film—a film for which they did not yet even have a budget—they must have been surprised when Curtis reacted with enthusiasm. But most surprising of all was the power of Mayfield's completed work.

Although *Superfly*—the story of a cocaine dealer who angles to make a million-dollar score and quit the drug game—does have its cartoon-like aspects via its depiction of black street personalities clad in huge-lapelled pimpin' finery, there was nothing funny about Mayfield's songs. He took the barest of clichéd sketches that outlined the film's characters and crafted intimate details of their lives—and, in some cases, deaths, by violence or by the needle.

Mayfield, an accomplished guitarist whose chordal approach to rhythm playing influenced Jimi Hendrix, used his regular band as the cohesive nucleus of the score. In particular, bassist Joseph Scott shines throughout, playing with a smooth, sultry feel that matches the hallucinatory urban aura at the heart of the film. His chunky, unforgettable riff supporting "Freddie's Dead (Theme from *Superfly*)" was the impetus that pushed the song into the top five in the United States pop charts. And throughout the album Mayfield's brilliant arrangements unfurled as moving settings for his intuitive lyrics.

The film's writer and visionary, Phillip Fenty, told *MOJO* magazine's Ben Edmonds of a 1990 Mayfield tribute concert based on *Superfly*.

"A group of singers took the stage and proceeded to sing the album straight through," Fenty said. "It was like a Broadway musical; the entire story was told through these songs. The completeness of the piece was extraordinary to me, a revelation years after the fact."

Superfly's glaring portrait of the decay eating away at urban America contributed to a new movement among rockers. Rather than try to change things, they simply fled to the country. It was a radical revision of 1960s all-pull-together optimism, now rewritten as self-centered introspection.

Neil Young, taking one of several extended leaves from Crosby, Stills, and Nash, released *Harvest* in 1972, an album that reflected a desire for simple themes and uncomplicated lives. Songs like "Old Man" and "Heart of Gold" were appealing in light of both Young's maturing lyrical style and the musical performance by The Stray Gators, a highly adept temporary band of studio musicians. Far less successful were two cringe-worthy piano ballads accompanied by the London Symphony Orchestra.

Harvest became the biggest selling album of the year in the United States, and "Heart of Gold" was a massive hit. The success scared Young back toward more challenging material.

"This song put me in the middle of the road," Young said of "Heart of Gold." "Traveling there soon became a bore, so I headed for the ditch. A rougher ride, but I saw more interesting people there."

Still, the musical question asked on *Harvest*—"Are you ready for the country?"—could have been rephrased to, "Is the country ready for a bunch of mellowing rock stars?" The exodus was on.

Joe Walsh had left The James Gang and packed himself off from Cleveland to Colorado. His first solo album, released later in 1972, pictured acres of rustic scenery in its gatefold packaging. Entitled *Barnstorm*, the album reunited Walsh with producer Bill Szymczyk and signaled a new direction in Walsh's music. The riff-based hard rock of The James Gang was gone; in its place were songs that took their time to develop, at their best sprawling out while maintaining a discernible force, as on the beautiful "Turn to Stone." The album was an indication that Walsh's budding songwriting skills would serve him well even though he had strayed far beyond the boundaries of the power trio environment.

The Band, having served time as Bob Dylan's backing band, was also interested in the roots of America. But rather than lounge around writing laid-back paeans to the glories of country life, The Band created vignettes of people and times in America's history, setting them to rich and timeless arrangements like those heard on *Rock of Ages*.

A live album recorded on New Year's Eve as 1972 dawned at New York's Academy of Music, *Rock of Ages* captured the group on a glorious evening. Not only were the members of The Band in fine form, but they were also augmented by an outstanding horn section that included respected jazz sax player Joe Ferrell. The horn charts by legendary New Orleans songwriter and arranger Allen Toussaint added a new dimension to The Band's sound, and this album successfully documented a very special performance just before worsening relations in the group sent them into decline.

Though The Band were inspired by the past, The Nitty Gritty Dirt Band were determined to enshrine it. Fascinated by the deep roots of American music, the band dreamed of assembling the legends of country and bluegrass music and recording them together before age and the passage of time began to inevitably claim their talents. Somehow the group made it happen, bringing together artists like "Mother" Maybelle Carter, Earl Scruggs, Doc Watson, and Merle Travis to record an elaborate, three-disc album called *Will the Circle Be Unbroken*.

Lavishly packaged, *Will the Circle Be Unbroken* collected more than three dozen of the collaborative performances. The album assured The Nitty Gritty Dirt Band of recognition of a different kind—for once, a band had selflessly acted out of its love for the work of fellow musicians. As such, the album is still highly regarded decades after its release.

What is it that gives an album its sound? Obviously, there is the tone of the singer, the choice of guitars and amplifiers, the tuning of the drums, the selection of keyboards. But all of those elements are shared with the concert experience. The unique demands of album creation hinge not just on the tools of music creation, but also on the input of the producer and the engineer's recording techniques—things like knowing how a room presents sound, how to mic a guitar amplifier, how to record drums, and myriad other intangibles. Even the studio itself may have pronounced characteristics, giving one facility a radically different voice from another.

In England in 1972, one of the decade's most significant waves of rock music was being crafted and captured at London's Trident Studios, under the guidance of producer Tony Visconti. The artists had the vision; Visconti had the sound.

The Brooklyn-born Visconti traded in his career of playing music in favor of recording it, moving to London in 1968. After working with celebrated British pop star Georgie Fame, Visconti recorded two artists with whom he would go on to craft influential work for years, Marc Bolan and David Bowie.

The first album Visconti recorded for Bolan's Tyrannosaurus Rex was *Prophets Seers and Sages*, faithfully capturing Bolan in the depths of his hippie fantasy folk-rock era. Indeed, the group was simply an acoustic duo. But by 1971, Bolan's approach had changed. Editing their name, T. Rex was now a four-member rock band, and Visconti was on hand to record an album called *Electric Warrior*, the record that would establish the group as stars.

"Marc and I had a long list of sonic tricks and musical signatures in our arsenal by now," Visconti explained in the liner notes of the CD reissue of *Electric Warrior*. "We were using tape flanging and phasing, backward guitars, cool guitar pedals, plugging the guitar directly into the console and overloading the mic preamplifiers, and even tape loops, since our second album."

The result was that *Electric Warrior* had its own distinctive sound, based on simple rock elements but presented using the entire studio vocabulary at Visconti's disposal. Songs like "Jeepster" and "Get It On" became smash hits, driven by clever touches like Visconti's usage of two cellos and a bassoon in the former song's descending chorus.

"Bolanmania" became a cultural epidemic as much of Europe went mad for T. Rex.

"I'm very erratic, but that's part of art and I consider myself to be an artist," Bolan pronounced. "I don't feel any compunction to be professional if I don't feel like it, or play if I don't want to."

A waifish guitarist with an unruly crop of long, curled hair, Bolan was the prototypical rock star, wearing detailed silk or satin jackets and colorful trousers as he sang in his breathy voice. His audience matched his attire, decking themselves out in sequins and applying glitter to their faces. The music media recognized a nascent movement when they saw one, and thus was born "glam rock."

Though the fleeting years of glam rock are often viewed as an era when style was triumphing over substance, in 1972 Visconti and Bolan left London to record T. Rex's masterpiece album, *The Slider*. From its cover photograph of Bolan in top hat—shot by Visconti, though credited to Ringo Starr—to its collection of songs about characters like "Telegram Sam" and "Buick Mackane," *The Slider* took the strengths of *Electric Warrior* and elevated them to new levels of studio artistry.

Indicative of the creative level is the album's title track, which crashes in on Bill Legend's stereo-panned drums, recorded loud and up front. Bolan and bassist Steve Currie drop in next with a grinding-yet-traditional blues/rock riff given more urgency by double-tracked guitars. Legend's bass drum thumps massively, anchoring the bottom, while Bolan's voice airily descends into the mix, recorded cleanly and clearly. Verse one ends with a half chorus, with strings and the otherworldly backing vocals of Howard Kaylan and Mark Volman—on loan from Frank Zappa—feathering over the band. After the second chorus, one of Bolan's guitars echoes an orchestrated string pattern, leading to the voice doing the same. The layout of the instrumentation is not overly complex, but it is addictively effective.

On release, the single "Metal Guru" shot to number one in the British charts, as did the album when it appeared in July. Oddly, the United States remained indifferent to T. Rex, perhaps because of the cultural clash between the States' basic-denim sensibility and Bolan's flamboyance.

Despite the lukewarm American reaction to T. Rex, Bolan's acquaintance David Bowie had arrived at a fundamental conclusion: success in the United States was critical to his plans for full-scale stardom. Though Bolan was at the height of his powers in 1972, the fey dress-up glitter of T. Rex was decidedly earthbound. It took a full-scale launch from Bowie to punch the glitter trappings of rock into orbit, shoving glam into its sci-fi future—and successfully attracting the attention of American rock fans.

Bowie had also sprung from the Visconti sphere of influence. After years of flirting with material ranging from folk to music hall, Bowie finally committed to rock in a big way with 1970's *The Man Who Sold the World*. The album, produced by Visconti and clearly boasting the Trident studio sound, marked the beginning of Bowie's alliance with guitarist Mick Ronson, a blues-influenced hard rocker in the style of the early Jeff Beck. With drummer Mick "Woody" Woodmansey and Visconti himself manning the bass, *The Man Who Sold the World's* thunderous tracks "Width of a Circle" and "Running Gun Blues" showed an entirely new David Bowie to the world. Of course, the music's heaviness did tend to conflict with the famed picture of a sexually ambiguous Bowie wearing a dress, a photo that graced certain versions of the album's cover.

Bowie returned to Trident to record 1971's *Hunky Dory*, working with Ken Scott—one of Visconti's main engineers—as producer. This album, which featured Yes' Rick Wakeman on keyboards throughout, took a giant step back from the metallic thunder of its predecessor. But when Bowie booked Trident yet again in 1972, he and Ronson had come up with a set of songs that effectively balanced the loud and the soft. And best of all, the songs worked as a theme, mixing extraterrestrials with rock and roll to tell the story of *The Rise and Fall of Ziggy Stardust and the Spiders from Mars*.

Bowie's ten original songs, plus a cover of The Kinks' "It Ain't Easy," were beautifully recorded by Scott, and the band— now consisting of Bowie, Ronson, Woodmansey, and Trevor Bolder on bass—brought the material to energetic life. The album's cover depicted Bowie, clad in a futuristic jumpsuit with guitar slung low, looking as though he had just beamed down from his mother ship to a dark London street.

There was no questioning the strength of the songs; the problem was one of generating awareness. And while Bowie had

plenty of awareness in England—declaring himself gay in the
music press and flaunting his new high-tech look at every
opportunity—on September 22 Bowie and his band, now officially christened The Spiders from Mars, took on the United
States with a brief but high-profile tour. The success of the entire American venture hung on a crucial radio concert, to be
broadcast live across the nation from Santa Monica Civic Auditorium in California.

The Americans had seen the photos of Bowie in full space
drag, hoisting Ronson aloft on stage in mock oral sex posturing
in a *Rolling Stone* photo spread. They'd heard the proclamations
of his gay lifestyle and read of his curious marriage to wife An-
gela. But all that was hype—it was time to hear if Bowie and his
band were for real.

The October 20 concert was an unqualified success. Bowie
and the Spiders were rough and raw, relaxed but focused. As a
front-man, Bowie came across as exotic and charming. And
though adorned in makeup, with streaked hair and bodies clad
in reflective glittery space wear, The Spiders From Mars proved
that their roots were more likely to be found in the British electric blues scene rather than the soil of Mars. The middle five
minutes of "Width of a Circle" was nothing less than a Cream-
like power jam capped by Ronson's brilliantly sloppy guitar
histrionics.

"I once asked John Lennon what he thought of what I do,"
Bowie said. "He said, 'It's great, but it's just rock and roll with
lipstick on.'"

Regardless, Bowie had, with one concert, established an
American beachhead that would serve him well for the remainder of his career. And he had also established allies in the
form of Mott the Hoople.

A British band on the verge of breaking up after encountering only limited success, Mott the Hoople found a fan in David
Bowie, who proceeded to bestow upon them a smash hit single,
"All the Young Dudes." The success of the song in 1972 and the
high-profile alliance with Bowie revitalized the band. After releasing the album *All the Young Dudes*—produced by Bowie—
the band went on to record the appropriately titled records
Mott and *The Hoople*, as well as a live concert album. All were
characterized by Ian Hunter's Dylan-like delivery of erudite

lyrics and the muscular hard rock guitars of first Mick Ralphs and later Luther Grosvenor, who for reasons unknown chose to go by the name Ariel Bender while in Mott's service.

Other bands began to capitalize on the burgeoning glam movement. England's Slade, managed by ex-Animal and former Jimi Hendrix manager Chas Chandler, had hit after hit in England. Slade boasted a catalog of ridiculously misspelled titles—"Mama Weer All Crazee Now," "Cum on Feel the Noize"—that were churned through a rambunctious style of pub rock. The workmanlike lads in the band were gussied up with a touch of satin for that we're-glam-too look. In the States, The New York Dolls were pushing the glam envelope even further. The Dolls were frequently seen wearing women's blouses with full makeup and big hair, and they did take a tiny-but-influential portion of Manhattan by storm as they lobbied for a record deal—and in the process created a template for latter-day rock bottom-dwellers like Motley Crue and Poison.

Some trendmongers proclaimed The Dolls to be the new Rolling Stones, which no doubt would have highly amused the real Rolling Stones. While everyone seemed to be scurrying about to align themselves with glam rock, The Stones spent the year determined to enhance their reputation as one of the best—if not *the* best—rock band in the world.

"I don't sit around saying, 'Now I'm going to write a song,'" Keith Richards said. "They come to me. I firmly believe they're all floating through the room right now. You don't create them, you find them and nurture them."

Keith had apparently been quite actively nurturing, for The Stones followed up the brilliant *Sticky Fingers* with 1972's *Exile on Main Street*, a double album comprised of eighteen songs that ran an incredible gamut of styles. In fact, it was so rich stylistically that many print reviews of the album ran before critics had a chance to fully digest the imposing collection. Hence, lukewarm opinions rather than open arms greeted the album in some quarters. In hindsight, it's almost universally regarded as one of the greatest rock albums ever recorded.

Exile featured a remarkably murky mix that somehow emerged as a shadowy-but-vibrant setting, with Mick Jagger's vocals coiled deep within a dark nest of guitars and keyboards. The sound is dense and hallucinatory, and even the more uplifting songs are presented in an atmosphere of mood-iness and unease. The pacing of the material covers a tremen-dous amount of ground, from the furious charge of "Rip This Joint" to the shambling country of "Sweet Virginia."

Interestingly, the band recorded the entire album using the very same mobile unit they had rented to Deep Purple for the recording of *Machine Head*. The Stones' use of their own truck actually was a necessity, as The Rolling Stones' popularity had pushed them into a most unfavorable tax bracket in England—proving that the perils of rock stardom were many. The band fled their homeland, taking refuge in France and summoning their mobile recording truck to follow them into exile.

Living like a drug-fueled commune, The Stones and their contributing musicians recorded *Exile on Main Street* under far-from-ideal technical conditions in the basement of Keith's man-sion in the south of France, Villa Nellcote. The dungeon-like surroundings were prone to power failures, in which case someone would be dispatched to tap into nearby train system power lines to get the recording equipment up and running. Take after take, jam upon jam was recorded as The Rolling Stones slowly assembled the sprawling album, a task that seemed endless.

"Nine months of listening to The Stones—it isn't my idea of heaven," was Mick Jagger's own less-than-enthusiastic take on the recording of *Exile on Main Street*, one of the true landmark rock albums of the 1970s.

1973

Hicks and Sophisticates

4

On January 15, 1973, Elvis Presley went global.

Already one of the most recognizable rock and roll figures in the world, Elvis had been in the news a week earlier as he turned thirty-eight—and simultaneously entered into divorce proceedings with his onetime sweetheart, Priscilla.

It may have been an unsettling personal time for the King, but duty called—within days of his birthday Elvis and entourage were winging their way to Hawaii's Honolulu International Center, where his live concert performance was beamed to a worldwide audience estimated to be as large as one and a half billion people.

If *Aloha from Hawaii* demonstrated the massive scale that rock sometimes operated on, just five days later Elvis' Sun Records cohort Jerry Lee Lewis showed how wild it could still be.

Having slowly established a country audience though a series of powerful, rootsy albums, "The Killer" had finally been invited to perform on the *Grand Ole Opry* radio show in Nashville, with one caveat: no rock and roll allowed. Never one to be told what to do, Lewis opened with his country ballad "Another Time, Another Place"—then promptly launched into a crazed rendition of "What'd I Say." Jerry Lee rocked on into the night, ignoring commercial breaks for the radio broadcast and the increasingly frantic gestures from the producers that he stop immediately.

"Let me tell ya something about Jerry Lee Lewis, ladies and gentlemen," announced Lewis. "I am a rock'n'rollin,' country and western, rhythm and blues singin' mothafucker!"

Jerry Lee was immediately banned from the Grand Ole Opry.

No matter how popular or how crazed the original rockers were, it's doubtful they could relate to much of the new rock music—and they must have watched with amazement as these seemingly incomprehensible records easily ascended to the upper reaches of the charts.

Though Jerry Lee and Elvis might not have considered rock to be an art form, less than two months after Lewis stunned the Grand Ole Opry a record considered to be one of rock's artiest statements landed in shops and quickly began rewriting the sales chart history. It was *Dark Side of the Moon* by Pink Floyd.

Pink Floyd had been assigned by the music media to a new subset of rock music, "space rock." Space rock was mystical territory found one step beyond prog rock, existing in a heady domain where the slow unfolding of musical movements was the norm.

"When we started out we found us a little niche—we found an area where there was so much to do and so many interesting ideas to be explored that other people just had not gotten into," Pink Floyd drummer Nick Mason told *Creem* magazine in 1988. "We were also very bad in some areas of this thing and we just wouldn't have made it if we had attempted to compete with other people. If we hadn't found our own thing that we were particularly good at and stuck with it and developed it, we would not have succeeded. Our musicianship just wasn't good enough in certain areas to stand up against some of these other bands."

Led by Syd Barrett since the band's formation in the mid 1960s, Pink Floyd willfully cultivated a reputation as psychedelic explorers of the first degree. Throughout 1967, though, Barrett appeared to be teetering on the edge of full-time psychedelic exploration, showing little interest in coming back to reality. With Barrett demonstrating increasing signs of mental instability in the wake of their first album, *The Piper at the Gates of Dawn*, guitarist David Gilmour was asked in 1968 to join Mason, bassist Roger Waters, keyboardist Rick Wright, and Barrett as a stabilizing influence.

Within months of Gilmour's arrival, Barrett—the band's one-time leader—was gone for good. Under their own guidance, the remaining members took a more somber and serious approach to their ventures, focusing entirely on the album market while crafting weighty, ambling records with titles like *Ummagumma* and *Atom Heart Mother*.

When the band entered Abbey Road Studios to begin recording what would become *Dark Side of the Moon*, the album material was largely already written and had been honed in live performances. Though Pink Floyd felt confident throughout the process of cutting the album, they had no reason to imagine their new release would make them superstars.

Shocking the band members, *Dark Side of the Moon* began a climb to number one on the *Billboard* album chart in the United States, then proceeded to take up near-permanent residence in that chart, hovering at various locations in the top two hundred albums for a mind-boggling fifteen and a half years.

Though *Dark Side of the Moon* was a step up in both performance and cohesiveness from its predecessors *Meddle* and *Obscured by Clouds*, sales records aside it was still a somewhat uneven album.

The record did have its share of highlights. Gilmour's introductory guitar in "Time" takes on a single-note dimension not that far removed from Ennio Morricone's spaghetti western soundtracks. The languid "Us and Them" is set off by a gorgeous chorus and Wright's keyboard solo. "Money" stumbles off at a turgid pace but is prodded awake by a tempo change and Gilmour's anxious, howling solo.

On the other hand, there was "On the Run," with its keyboardless Electronic Musical Studio VCS3 synthesizers warbling on and on and on, a repetition that was quickly mind-numbing rather than mind-expanding. An abundance of "trippy" effects did not help matters, and Claire Torry's wordless wailing in "The Great Gig in the Sky" was either effective emoting or aggravating caterwauling depending on one's point of view.

Still, millions of listeners were willing to forgive the album's faults, adding their purchases to the commercial momentum that has made *Dark Side of the Moon* the best-selling mediocre album in rock history.

Other bands working similar turf could only look on in wonder—and jealousy.

To follow up their album-long song *Thick as a Brick*, Jethro Tull utilized a similar modus operandi to create *Passion Play* in 1973. Perhaps it was the challenges inherent in issuing two such works back-to-back, but *Passion Play* lacked the seamless flow of its predecessor. Certain transitions between movements were awkward rather than elegant, and some of the movements themselves likely would have benefited from some editing.

That said, most of the melodic structures contained very interesting passages, regardless of how well they coexisted as a single piece of music. John Evan had fully incorporated the synthesizer into a starring role in his keyboard lineup, and leader Ian Anderson suddenly displayed proficiency on the saxophone—an unlikely tonal color in light of Tull's past efforts, but one that worked quite well in the new material.

"The concept of the album was Ian's thing," guitarist Martin Barre explained. "The words meant a lot to him, and he knew what he wanted. It was a very personal thing. For us, it was really just the music, and it was very hard music. It took a lot of thinking to play it."

Unfortunately the very good music in *Passion Play* was brought to a screeching halt at the album's midpoint. The jarring arrival of "The Story of the Hare Who Lost His Spectacles" can only be excused as an indulgence in Monty Python-like silliness. This grating, four-minute intermission for *Passion Play* does little for the recorded legacy of Jethro Tull other than serve as a convenient low point of reference.

Jethro Tull took *Passion Play* on the road in the summer of 1973. The concerts were elaborately staged, and they even included an appearance by the bloodied ballerina pictured on the album's cover, who danced in film footage before suddenly bursting through the screen and onto the stage to herald the band's arrival.

"We had started doing crazy things on stage at the time of *Thick as a Brick* when nobody else was doing it," Barre noted. "People didn't know what was going on. But we took it to an extreme. We used flash boxes, smoke effects, strobes, strange clothes, animal suits, films, everything. But it got to the point where we couldn't decide how to better the last tour. There wasn't anything left to do . . ."

The sold-out arenas full of witnesses to the *Passion Play* spectacle proved the work had found an audience despite the challenging aspects of the music. As for everybody else? The opinion of the masses didn't seem to concern Ian Anderson when he spoke to Cameron Crowe in *Creem* magazine in 1975.

"Before you ever get caught up in trying to figure out the deepest inner meaning of any music, much less Jethro Tull music, just remember that it's all noise. To a Martian, it's no better or worse than a buzz saw."

Although it remains unknown precisely how many Martians accounted for the sales of *Passion Play*, Anderson's oblique lyrics might have held more obvious meaning to the extraterrestrial intellect. More earthbound and direct was the years-in-the-making realization of Ray Davies' *Preservation*.

The main songwriter and singer of The Kinks, Davies was known for his literate encapsulations of British life on near-perfect pop songs like "Waterloo Sunset" and "Sunny Afternoon." But Davies had a grander vision, and it emerged over the course of *Preservation Act 1* in 1973 and *Preservation Act 2*, a double album released in 1974.

England was undergoing economic and class upheavals in the early 1970s, and the turmoil spurred Davies to set these tensions to music, as he both questioned the political future of his country and debated the fate of the cultural traditions that defined British life. In the sprawling *Preservation*, an up-from-the-streets hoodlum named Flash rises to political power, where he encounters a challenge from a strict morality movement led by one Mr. Black. Following's Black's successful coup, society sets forth with a bleak, Orwellian clean slate. Musically, *Preservation* largely sustained life thanks to the wide-ranging strengths of the band. Charged with supporting brother Ray's weighty visualizations, Dave Davies' hard rock guitar surfaced frequently enough to propel the score forward.

The Kinks proceeded to take *Preservation* on the road with their own highly theatrical presentation. Despite the opera-like construction of *Preservation*, an invitation to perform the work at the Metropolitan Opera House, as was extended to The Who during the *Tommy* era, was not proffered. By 1973, rock operas had become old hat.

When The Mahavishnu Orchestra detonated an explosive fusion of electrifying jazz and rock on their 1971 debut *Inner Mounting Flame*, it took some time for the smoke to clear. Once it did, though, a new rock landscape was emerging, one where the traditional architecture of rock song structures no longer applied. One of the first bands to set forth in pursuit of these newly expanded horizons was King Crimson. The discoveries they made in their quest for new auditory ground were documented on both 1973's *Larks' Tongues in Aspic* and *Starless and Bible Black*, recorded late in 1973.

King Crimson found success almost immediately upon formation with an early 1969 lineup featuring bassist Greg Lake on vocals, with the band gaining rave reviews from gigs on the prestigious London club circuit. A crucial defining sound of early King Crimson was crafted via an instrument that swept the prog rock world, becoming an essential weapon in the arsenal of every band doing serious work. It was known as the Mellotron.

Heard on countless recordings of the era, the Mellotron is a primary voice on King Crimson's debut, *In the Court of the Crimson King*. The small keyboard had each of its keys assigned to a loop of audiotape, creating an array from which the player could choose a choir, a violin, a flute, or another recorded instrument. If a musician chose the violin setting and held down four keys, the sound of four violins playing four different notes lasted as long as the keys were depressed. Pitch variations in the playback speeds tended to give the Mellotron its own eerie voicing, sounding less like a clearly voiced choir or orchestra and more like some indescribably ominous wall of sound.

Following the release of the second Crimson album, Greg Lake moved on to Emerson, Lake, and Palmer—offering yet more proof that the English prog rock scene was a small, incestuous circle where everyone eventually wound up playing with everyone else. Remaining behind, though, was King Crimson's founding guitarist Robert Fripp, the constant of myriad lineups since the band's inception.

Guitarist? Fripp himself might take issue with that description, as he did in the 1970s, going to great lengths to separate himself from the rock guitarist pack. Witness the comments that follow, from an infamous interview with *Guitar Player* magazine in May 1974.

"I've never really listened to guitarists, because they've never really interested me. In fact, I think the guitar is a pretty feeble instrument," Fripp insisted. "Just before I turned professional I listened to some Hendrix and Clapton, and there were one or two Hendrix things I enjoyed. Not the rocky things so much, but the slower things. I haven't been influenced by Hendrix and Clapton in the way that most people would say it. I don't think Hendrix was a guitarist. I very much doubt if he was interested in guitar playing as such. He was just a person who had something to say and got on and said it. Clapton I think is mostly quite banal, although he did some exciting things earlier in his life with Mayall. The Mayall *Blues Breakers* album is superb. Clapton does quite amazingly. I saw Cream live once and I thought they were quite awful. Clapton's work since, I think, has been excessively tedious. Jeff Beck's guitar playing I can appreciate as good fun . . . I wish him all the best of luck."

In effect, Fripp's comments boiled down a haughty sentiment: I'm above all this distasteful "rock and roll" business. To complement his elitist public persona, Fripp carefully cultivated a studious, nearly professorial image, punctuated by his round wire-rim spectacles.

No matter how infuriating Fripp's comments or how calculating his personality, though, there was little arguing that his band was functioning on a higher level. Fripp had coerced Bill Bruford away from Yes, certain that the drummer's precisely rigid style would fit well in Crimson. John Wetton, the bassist, had arrived from the well-regarded band Family, joining David Cross, who brought both keyboard and violin skills. Avantgarde percussionist Jamie Muir was with the band only for *Larks' Tongues in Aspic*, but his experimental influence on Crimson lingered long after his departure.

On *Larks' Tongues in Aspic*, Fripp and company began charting a bold new course for the band, one that contrasted delicate atmospherics with harsh attacks of near-atonal rock twisting atop Bruford's inspired drumming. If pieces like "The Talking Drum" took the lack of structure to boring extreme by dressing up jamming in avant-garde clothes, "Exiles," "Easy Money," and "Larks' Tongues in Aspic, Part Two" were thrilling adventures.

Though Muir had left Crimson when the band returned to the studio later in 1973 to record *Starless and Bible Black*, the core quartet was honing the band's sharp edge on the angular "The Great Deceiver" and the fire-and-ice tension revealed within "Lament." And in "The Night Watch," listeners discovered that Wetton's harmonious vocals and the band's restrained performance could lead challenging exploration in a new direction—toward serene beauty.

With *Bitches Brew*, Miles Davis had drawn a line indicating to what degree he would align himself with rock, and what elements of its music he would or would not use in the creation of his own work. But the young sidemen who joined Miles in those fundamental recording sessions felt no such restrictions and weren't afraid to take another giant step closer to rock. From the *Bitches Brew* sessions came the birth of three new bands, groups whose existence would help alter the future course of rock.

One of those three bands was Return to Forever, led by the exciting keyboardist Chick Corea. Corea teamed up with Philadelphia bassist Stanley Clarke, then initially brought in Mingo Lewis from Santana on percussion and legendary studio drummer Steve Gadd. Gadd and Lewis soon departed, with the powerful Lenny White inheriting the drummer throne. For the crucial position of electric guitarist, Corea accepted the recommendation of an acquaintance and luckily discovered an incredible new talent, Bill Connors.

When Connors got the call from Corea, he was already envisioning a complete convergence of jazz and rock, though the concept had yet to be realized.

"Frankly, they didn't call it fusion," Connors told *Virtual Guitar* of his musical vision. "They didn't have the word yet. I wanted to sound like Eric Clapton playing Coltrane. That remained with me forever."

Connors was outfitted equipment-wise like any rock guitar god—and due to Return to Forever's volume, he had to be.

"I got a 100-watt Marshall head and I brought that to the rehearsal," Connors recalled of an early session. "One rehearsal. You couldn't hear me. I remember that very well. So I took the 100-watt back and then I bought this 200-watt and I loved it . . . It really sang at the kind of levels that we were playing at . . . It was awesome! It was like shaking the house down. I liked that big, old, stadium sound."

When the band recorded their astonishing debut *Hymn of the Seventh Galaxy*, their massive sound was that of rock welded onto jazz. The result was dangerous and unpredictable, the true realization of fusion. Corea's aggressive Fender Rhodes piano, occasionally treated with distortion or harmonic effects, stabbed in and out of the arrangements. Clarke's bass playing amply demonstrated why he was considered a rising instrumental superstar, and White brought rock and Latin flourishes to his jazz chops, driving the band forward.

Above it all rode Connors' guitar. Though admittedly influenced by Clapton, the fiery guitarist also called to mind the brilliant Paul Kossoff. Connors would frequently cap a swift, emotional scale run with a moaning Koss-like vibrato, then rip into a series of double-stops, grabbing two notes and forcing the resulting convergence into a harmonic whole. It was passionate and fiery playing, made up of more than just notes and scales. With heart and intensity, Connors defined how potent a force the electric guitar would be in this context.

Taking a path away from the fire of Return to Forever was Weather Report, founded by *Bitches Brew* contributors Joe Zawinul on keyboards and Wayne Shorter on saxophone. An evolving cast of top-flight personnel joined the duo from the band's inception in 1971, helping Weather Report move toward more temperate sonic climates. The band was as much about atmosphere and mood as it was about demonstrating blistering musical chops.

On 1973's *Sweetnighter,* an insistent, Latin-flavored percussive groove was typically established by bassist Miroslav Vitous and drummer Eric Gravatt, with additional color splashed throughout the mix by percussionist Dom Um Romao. Upon that foundation Zawinul and Shorter would spar melodically, Zawinul's treated keyboards contrasting tonally with Shorter's fleet soprano sax.

Despite the growing critical appreciation of Weather Report and Return to Forever, the most influential of the three *Bitches Brew* "children" remained The Mahavishnu Orchestra.

A second album, *Birds of Fire,* had followed *Inner Mounting Flame* in 1972. Recorded at London's Trident Studios—the home of T. Rex and David Bowie—and engineered by Bowie associate Ken Scott, the mad Mahavishnu formula had remained much the same for their second collection. The main stylistic evolution came in the playing of keyboardist Jan Hammer, who was more heavily incorporating synthesizer into his palette, allowing him to enter more forcefully into the musical fray with guitarist John McLaughlin and violinist Jerry Goodman.

"That whole period was tremendous," McLaughlin told Bill Milkowski in the liner notes to the CD reissue of The Mahavishnu Orchestra's catalog. "Walls were coming down right, left, and center. We were making light-year jumps in terms of playing together and developing new ways of playing, new techniques and sounds."

"It wasn't a matter of just following charts," added Goodman, "it was a matter of really playing together and trying to be of one mind. The music was so intricate that that kind of rapport was necessary."

But by 1973, tensions within the band were growing. An attempt at recording a third album, again with Ken Scott at Trident, was characterized by strife, and the tapes remained unreleased for decades.

Instead, a live album, *From Nothingness to Eternity,* was released, containing concert versions of material from the aborted Trident project. Sadly, the dynamic concert recording marked the final chapter in the history of an extreme band whose lasting impact resonates over the years into the music of today.

Jan Hammer preferred to take a philosophical view of the premature dissolution of The Mahavishnu Orchestra, rather than wallow in the personality squabbles that eventually destroyed the band.

"The personal negatives that we were involved with are of much less importance than the actual music, which survives us. That's really all that matters."

In the wake of Mahavishnu Orchestra's dissolution, talented players from both the rock and jazz worlds angled to participate in the band members' next projects, further blurring the lines of demarcation between the styles of music.

One of the most intriguing of these spin-off projects was the solo album recorded by thunderous drummer Billy Cobham, *Spectrum*. Cobham's explosive chops had fueled the flights of The Mahavishnu Orchestra, providing the band with a source of energy as powerful as any rock group could possibly hope for, and his fans were anxious to hear Cobham in a new context.

Joining Cobham on *Spectrum* was his Maha-mate Jan Hammer, along with highly regarded bassist Leland Sklar. But the surprise element—proving just how deeply the fusion movement had pollinated within the rock world—was the presence of guitarist Tommy Bolin, soon to join Deep Purple. Bolin was on the verge of replacing Ritchie Blackmore in one of rock's heaviest bands, but his highly developed instrumental skills allowed him to flourish as he conquered the jazz demands of Cobham's project.

In addition to working with Billy Cobham, Jan Hammer also took his skills to the first solo album by Return to Forever bassist Stanley Clarke. Clarke was always quick to acknowledge the fact that rock had heavily influenced his own musical development.

"I grew up listening to The Beatles, early Stevie Wonder, all that soul music, Sam and Dave, Sam Cooke and, later on,

Hendrix," Clarke told Robert Duncan in *Creem* magazine in August 1979. "I really dug Jimi's stuff. Believe it or not, Jimi Hendrix's music actually inspired me to move into more progressive music, because when I heard his music I said, 'Wow, what the hell is that?' Then I started buying his records . . . I started buying them and getting more progressive and that's when I went off on my trail of playing with all the progressive artists and jazz musicians."

On *Stanley Clarke*, his solo project band honed fusion further still, while Clarke himself took great strides toward advancing the art of the electric bass, swimming easily between jazz and funk while enhancing the "popping" bass string sound cultivated by Larry Graham with Sly and the Family Stone.

Aside from Hammer, Clarke was joined by Tony Williams, the brilliant drummer whose band Lifetime—which had included Larry Young, Jack Bruce, and John McLaughlin—was an early landmark on the path to fusion's evolution. Bill Connors joined his Return to Forever band mate on guitar, recording what would prove to be the swan song of his high-volume fusion career. Connors had already quit Return to Forever by the time Clarke's album was released, leaving replacement Al DiMeola—technically gifted, but far more sterile than Connors—to reap the rewards of the commercial acclaim that began to swell around Chick Corea's band.

In the wake of The Mahavishnu Orchestra's universally praised triumvirate of albums, John McLaughlin found his own increasing commercial acclaim through a high-profile association with Carlos Santana. Santana had adopted McLaughlin's spiritual leader Sri Chinmoy as his own, so it was nearly inevitable that the two guitarists would work together. On 1973's *Love Devotion Surrender*, they did just that.

When the two guitarists entered the studio, they did so accompanied by an intriguing mix of musicians from both Santana and The Mahavishnu Orchestra. For material, they had two songs written by the legendary saxophonist John Coltrane matched with two McLaughlin originals, as well as a traditional song for which they had devised an instrumental arrangement. No one doubted that *Love Devotion Surrender* had the opportunity to become the defining statement of this bold new branch of rock music.

In the end, though, what *Love Devotion Surrender* documented was a project nowhere near as good as it looked on paper. Much of the album consisted of the two talented guitarists hurling scales at each other over interminable single-chord vamps. Due to the rushed and jamming nature of the project, the lack of preparation sadly crushed any prospect there was for these two unique musicians to create music of eternally lasting value.

Frank Zappa had been watching the evolution of fusion with interest. Though certainly not regarded as a jazz musician, he was always interested in the form, keeping an eye out for stray jazz musicians who might be willing to contribute to the ever-fluid lineup of his Mothers of Invention. On 1973's *Apostrophe*, jazz players like keyboardist George Duke and violinist Jean-Luc Ponty recorded alongside rock drummer Aynsley Dunbar and bassist Jack Bruce, who by now had an impressive résumé in both realms.

The highlight of *Apostrophe* was the title track, a furious jam between Bruce, Zappa, and ex-Derek and the Dominos drummer Jim Gordon. Zappa made the most of his opportunity to air out his underappreciated rock guitar skills, while Bruce launched volleys of the stabbing, aggressive bass playing that was the hallmark of his live work in Cream.

Unfortunately, the remainder of the album was surrendered to typically intricate Zappa compositions. In itself, that wasn't a bad thing, but the music was accompanied by juvenile lyrics that were hardly worth exploring, considering that titles like "Don't Eat the Yellow Snow" and "Stink Foot" accurately represented their content.

This was the dichotomy of Frank Zappa: moments of instrumental and compositional genius, wrapped in grade school humor that held up to repeated listening only for his fanatic followers, a group fully as dedicated as the Grateful Dead's congregation.

Frank Zappa was far from the only rock musician to enjoy an all-star jam now and again, and for better or worse many sessions were rushed to vinyl. One of the most curious such titles was *Music from Free Creek*, a double album that appeared with little fanfare in 1973 on The Famous Charisma Label, best known as the home of Genesis.

Little is known of the factual origins of this album, allegedly recorded in its entirety at the Record Plant studio in New York. If in truth it was, one would have to be curious as to why Mitch Mitchell from the Jimi Hendrix Experience, Keith Emerson from Emerson, Lake, and Palmer, Delaney Bramlett, Harvey Mandel from Canned Heat, Linda Ronstadt, Dr. John, Chris Wood from Traffic, and a few dozen more all felt inspired to get together and record songs like "Working in a Coalmine," "Girl from Ipanema," and "Lay Lady Lay." And add to the mystery the presence of one King Cool—reportedly Eric Clapton—and A. N. Other—identified as Jeff Beck. Sadly, the circumstances leading to the creation of this enigma will likely remain lost in the sands of time.

In the liner notes to *Music from Free Creek*, it is reported that participant Todd Rundgren's hair "went from blonde to green to blue to yellow to purple to magenta to crimson, and is now all seven colours at once." Actually, that was not an exaggeration. And whereas some people go gray from stress, Rundgren's rainbow tresses may have attained their condition from the whirlwind of ideas ricocheting through his mind.

Rundgren began his climb to prominence in the Philadelphia music scene as a skinny guitarist in the band Woody's Truck Stop, supporting many of rock's biggest acts at the city's prestige venue, the Electric Factory. His next project, The Nazz, brought him his first major success as the songs "Open My Eyes" and "Hello It's Me" edged into the charts in 1968.

"Destroyed Nazz, worked lights in a discotheque, lived with clothes designers, produced first record," stated Todd himself in his 1978 record label bio. "Began recording solo albums, became more commercial, became more successful, became less commercial, became less successful . . ."

Rundgren placed himself squarely in the latter two categories with 1973's *A Wizard, A True Star*. He'd garnered rave reviews in 1972 with *Something/Anything?*, a sprawling double album that was loaded with catchy rock songs and irresistible pop confections. Todd proceeded to follow up this commercial break-through with one of the most amazing—and challenging—albums of the decade.

"If you want to see these albums as reflections of my mental condition, then I'm evolving through a greater expansion of possibilities," was Rundgren's self-analysis of his state in 1973, documented in the liner notes of *The Very Best of Todd Rundgren.* "On *A Wizard, A True Star* I'm seeing possibilities in every-thing—the idea of breaking down song structure and making a continuous flow of music; starting to throw in more instru-mental stuff. *A Wizard, A True Star* represented how broad the possibilities were."

A hallucinatory, massively complicated recording, *Wizard* as a technical achievement alone is truly mind-boggling. At least partially drug-fueled, the album was the realization of creative vision in full flower, made possible in part through the support of other musicians but largely crafted by Rundgren himself decades before computerized track synching brought such dif-ficult projects within the reach of less-determined musicians. But Rundgren relied on sheer willpower to reach beyond the technical limitations of 1973; by refusing to acknowledge those limitations, they simply ceased to exist.

The album begins with "International Feel," a stirring anthem set over a stumbling rhythm, the song urged higher by waves of overdubbed vocals. Ending in a sonic cloud of stuttering voice and reverb, the noise unexpectedly falls away, leaving only the sound of a phased acoustic piano. Todd proceeds to sing "Never Never Land," joined by synthetic accompaniment as the song advances toward its spiraling conclusion. "Tic Tic Tic It Wears Off" follows, a bouncy, electronic instrumental, which suddenly yields to "You Need Your Head," where Todd's first electric gui-tar solo of the album rips across the stereo spectrum. That evolves into the roiling cauldron of instruments bubbling through "Rock and Roll Pussy," trailed by the highly processed treatment of a ca-nine confrontation on "Dogfight Giggle." The chiming, delicate "You Don't Have to Camp Around" is then abruptly replaced by a second ping-ponging electro-instrumental, "Flamingo," which itself is pierced by the sound of an electronic arrow flying across the speakers, slamming into its target and bringing the song to a sudden conclusion.

All that in the album's first thirteen minutes.

That Rundgren would risk his entire career to release such an imposing album—at fifty-six minutes in length, it pushed the limits of vinyl LP playback capabilities—symbolized the un-compromising attitude Todd had toward his art. If you wanted to listen to Rundgren, you did so on his terms.

"Most people making records today are making a living," Rundgren explained to Ben Edmonds in *Creem* magazine in 1974. "If you actually do sell records, people suddenly believe that the record which sold contains within it that magic stuff that makes them saleable, and they build on imitation from there. 'Well, there's my style, what I've been looking for, be-cause it makes me a living.' This is one of the few lines of work where that's possible. You can't be a doctor and experiment on people until you've found that magic formula."

Although many listeners were put off by Rundgren's intimi-dating genius, David Bowie was being showered with acco-lades as an accessible rock visionary. Having released the highly regarded *Ziggy Stardust* album and established The Spi-ders From Mars band as one of rock's better live outfits, it was time for Bowie to cement his reputation.

He did so by not tampering with his own magic formula. Bowie retained his sci-fi futuro look on the cover of 1973's *Al-addin Sane*, pale skin tinted pink, set off by his shock of red hair and a vibrant painted lightning bolt slashing his facial features. Not to mention the gob of . . . something, dripping off his col-larbone. The retention of Ken Scott as producer and Trident Studios as workplace contributed to a creative atmosphere of treading water.

"It was a case of not wanting to let go of something that was successful, yet another part of me really wanted to go some-where else," Bowie admitted to Kurt Loder in the liner notes to *Sound + Vision*. "Also, I had a . . . not a falling out, really, but a loss of enthusiasm with The Spiders. They really didn't want to go where I wanted to go. I was already developing a great in-terest in soul music, and experimental forms. They were pretty much into playing this straightforward rock. Which was un-derstandable—they played it very well."

Indeed, it was on the tracks where The Spiders were truly al-lowed to attack the material that *Aladdin Sane* shined with the same brilliance that had suffused its predecessor. Bowie had expanded The Spiders' core with pianist Mike Garson, a perfect musical complement to Mick Ronson's fully aggressive guitar. Ronson fueled the album's thunderous lead-off track "Watch That Man," perhaps Bowie's greatest pure hard rock song. Under the wailing, sustained metallic guitar notes, Garson contributed a lively mid-level support around the song's chords. And when the mood cooled on the following song—the album's title track—Garson relied on his jazz background, sprinkling trilly flourishes above Ronson's insistent, barely restrained rhythm chording. As always, Trevor Bolder and Woody Woodmansey provided a supple bottom, powering the Bo-Diddley-on-steroids rhythmic pulse at the heart of "Panic in Detroit," another concussive rocker.

Less successful, though, was a halfhearted stab at the Rolling Stones' "Let's Spend the Night Together." And though the overly baroque drama of "Lady Grinning Soul" pointed to Bowie's future as a quite capable balladeer, on *Aladdin Sane* he wasn't there yet.

Perhaps as a way to vent his creativity while The Spiders maintained their status quo, Bowie began to further explore his studio options. In the wake of his successful production of Mott the Hoople's *All the Young Dudes*, Bowie's management company began taking artists under its wing, among them Detroit's volatile Iggy and The Stooges. Bowie himself mixed the punishing band's landmark 1973 album *Raw Power*—although years later vocalist Iggy Pop would remix the master tapes himself, preferring a more "violent mix."

The songs and performances of *Raw Power* demanded such treatment. The band, which had been on its last legs before rock's new superstar blessed them with attention, came to the studio with a snarling batch of songs that included "Search and Destroy," "Your Pretty Face is Going to Hell," and "Death Trip." Bowie, having learned the recording craft from the carefully assembled albums of the Tony Visconti/Ken Scott alliance, was not the best choice to take on such seething, hostile material. But The Stooges had no choice but to accept the fact that their continued existence depended on Bowie's participation—and financing.

"It's always sounded fragile and rickety," Pop said of the original mix in the liner notes to his remake, "and that band was not fragile and not rickety. That band could kill any band at the time . . ."

A more sympathetic creative match for Bowie's production talents was Lou Reed, founder of the influential Velvet Underground, a band that had sprung to prominence through an artistic alliance with Andy Warhol. Bowie, with assistance from Mick Ronson and Ken Scott, took the rather sober music of Reed and cast it squarely into a rock framework on 1972's *Transformer*, yielding a hit with the slinky "Walk on the Wild Side." But less than a year later, Reed would be collaborating with yet another unusual choice of producer: Bob Ezrin, who had helped establish Alice Cooper as one of rock's biggest acts.

Ezrin and Reed assembled a stellar cast to record the album *Berlin*, bringing to the sessions young Midwestern guitarists Steve Hunter and Dick Wagner.

Ezrin first met Hunter when he produced 1971's *Detroit*, the self-titled album from a raw, forceful band assembled by famed white R&B and rock vocalist Mitch Ryder, who had found chart success with his previous band, The Detroit Wheels. Like The Stooges, Detroit the band was a rock powerhouse, rough around the edges and proud of it, driven by Hunter's aggressive guitar. Ironically, one of the strongest cuts on the album had been a cover of Reed's "Rock and Roll."

Dick Wagner had recorded three albums with Frost, a mainstay of the Detroit city scene in the late 1960s, playing alongside bands like The MC5 and The Stooges. When Frost thawed, Wagner moved to New York, where Ursa Major was formed. The power trio was paired up with Ezrin to record its self-titled debut, a rumbling slice of proto-metal that was a great artistic success even if the album languished in stores.

Though both Detroit and Ursa Major were short-lived, Ezrin knew that Hunter and Wagner were valuable discoveries, and he kept in touch with the guitarists until summoning them to the *Berlin* sessions.

When Hunter and Wagner arrived in London to begin their work with Lou Reed, the two young musicians found themselves in heady company. Joining them were bassists Jack Bruce and Tony Levin, drummers Aynsley Dunbar and Procol Harum's B. J. Wilson, organist Steve Winwood, and jazz horn brothers Michael and Randy Brecker. One might have expected such a lineup to create a thunderous rock album. But the defining element was Reed's material—this was not going be a typical rock album.

"I find my stuff is filled with compassion," Reed has said of his craft. "It's one of the things that I see thematically running through these lyrics. There's a lot of things that I'm describing that seem personal and painful but, as a literate person, I know they're universals."

Berlin was a darkly beautiful album, a tragic tale of drug abuse and infidelity, death and betrayal. And though it did not make for easy listening, it was gut-wrenching in its effectiveness. In the stark "The Kids," the song's narrator matter-of-factly relates his satisfaction at seeing his lover's children taken away by social workers. As the song's deliriously slow fade-out begins, two children wail desperately for their mother in the background. Rumors about the album spread as it neared release, including one that the two children were brought into the studio, informed that their mother was dead, and then recorded. Another account had test listeners fleeing from preview sessions in tears. Regardless, *Berlin* was unlike any other album this group of musicians had ever worked on.

Producer Ezrin, on the other hand, was likely prepared for anything after his years working with Alice Cooper.

Since the release of *Killer* in 1971, the Alice Cooper band had shocked their way to the top of the rock heap. The group's 1972 album *School's Out*—elaborately packaged in cardboard that unfolded into a grade school desk, the vinyl itself gently embraced in a pair of controversy-generating panties—featured a title track that rocketed into the charts, boosted by an adrenalized guitar introduction that was instantly approved for inclusion in the rock riff hall of fame. The album had demonstrated the studio smarts and growing musical talents of Ezrin, Cooper, and the band, even featuring a mini-*West Side Story* that set synths against the vicious guitars of Michael Bruce and Glen Buxton. Still, all parties involved felt the Alice Cooper formula might very well reach its explosive climax with the next album. They were right.

Billion Dollar Babies became one of the biggest-selling albums of 1973 and, taken as a whole, marked both the zenith of the band's creative expression and the summit of Alice Cooper's ascension to rock superstardom.

Everyone who looked at Alice Cooper in 1973 thought they knew exactly what they were seeing—but it all depended on who was doing the looking. Was Alice Cooper just a shambling rock band, decadently attractive? Were they sly, incisive analysts of pop culture? Barnum-like purveyors of showbiz chaos? Demons from hell that would be satisfied with nothing less than the destruction of American youth? Were they symbols of "anyone can make it" capitalism—or simply living advertisements for wretched excess? In reality, they were all of that—and more.

"I'm like Dali," Alice averred. "I present the image and let people react to it."

In the studio, Ezrin and the band meticulously crafted the songs of *Billion Dollar Babies*, augmenting the core band with a handful of supplemental musicians including guitarists Hunter and Wagner from the *Berlin* sessions. But the vibrant pulse of the album was still provided by the core quintet. Though they were justifiably notorious for their crazed stage show, they remained underappreciated for the intelligence and craft of their studio work.

The songs on *Billion Dollar Babies* could be as multifaceted as Alice's image. Take a song like "Raped and Freezin'"—on the surface an irresistible-if-inconsequential rock and roll trifle. But listening to how each part was assembled, how the sonic balance constantly evolves, how the band approaches one verse from one direction, the next from another—it's clear how much thought was dedicated to the creation of the album. That impression is just cemented by the clever quote from Jimi Hendrix's "Dolly Dagger" that kicks off "Elected," the spy music themes in "Unfinished Sweet," and the inspired choice of British flower power folkie Donovan as duet partner for Alice on the title track.

With *Billion Dollar Babies* flexing its muscle on the charts, the Alice Cooper band set off on one of the rock world's biggest—and greatest—tours. The show was mind-boggling, compounding itself upon all the insanity and outrage that had characterized Alice Cooper since the formative years in Hollywood. On a huge stage set, Alice stalked his audience, clad in thigh-high leopard print boots and stained, ripped white underwear, makeup running down his face in a horrifying mask. The band, Alice's own legion of doom, played with a go-for-the-throat confidence that left audiences from coast to coast exhausted. By the time Alice was ceremoniously guillotined in the show's triumphant, confetti-filled conclusion, survivors of the astounding spectacle knew they had seen a rock show unlike any other, before or since.

"We're all veteran crazies," Cooper told *Creem* magazine's Barbara Charone. "We've gone beyond crazy because we've already been crazy. We're into the second level of craziness. We're so intelligent now that you don't actually know we're crazy.

"*Billion Dollar Babies* was like *Clockwork Orange*. It looked brutal, sounded brutal, and you felt like this," Cooper described as he made a fist, "when you left the show."

Though on the surface the *Billion Dollar Babies* tour was rock at its most commanding and glorious, all was not well in Cooper's crazed kingdom. The seldom-revealed pressures of rock superstardom were having their inexorable way, beginning to plant a slow, undermining decay that private jets and luxury hotels would prove powerless to stop.

The world of touring luxury that Alice Cooper enjoyed was lustily eyed by a growing number of bands in 1973, all determined to ascend to that same level of rock and roll aristocracy. Failing that, many would settle for a good opening slot on a multiband arena tour of the States, where audiences were generally more receptive to new bands.

"European gigs were so much more formal and serious than their American boogie circus counterparts," noted King Crimson's David Cross, "and it was an uphill struggle trying to raise the excitement above that of warm approval."

Still reliably serving as a hard rock blueprint was the power trio format pioneered by Cream. Having departed for rock's Valhalla as certifiable historic legends, Cream left behind a configuration with inheritance rights that were fought for tooth and nail throughout the decade.

Cream's own producer, Felix Pappalardi, moonlighted from his deafening band Mountain to man the recording board for

Bedlam, a British guitar-bass-drums-vocals lineup that—no big surprise, considering the producer—wound up sounding just like Mountain. If known at all, Bedlam was recognized as the new home of former Jeff Beck drummer Cozy Powell and guitarist Dave Ball, who had contributed lead guitar to Procol Harum's live Edmonton symphony album. But despite the lumbering thud of "The Beast," the album's standout cut, Bedlam's self-titled debut sank without a trace.

Tempest was another virgin band on the scene in 1973, formed by drummer Jon Hiseman of Colosseum, who found himself in need of a new group when Clem Clempson departed Colosseum for the greener pastures of Humble Pie as Peter Frampton's replacement.

"We're a new band that plays the music of today and not yesterday," Hiseman said of Tempest in *Disc* magazine in 1973. "But if people want to compare us to Cream that suits me down to the ground."

Such comparisons were only logical, as Hiseman had long traveled in the same circles as Cream's members. He had replaced drummer Ginger Baker in the Graham Bond Organisation after Baker and Jack Bruce left to form Cream, and he'd also played in John Mayall's Bluesbreakers, as had both Bruce and Eric Clapton.

Sadly, though, Tempest sounded as though they were simply following in Cream's footsteps. That impression was unavoidable on songs like "Dark House," with Paul Williams' Bruce-like phrasing and the Claptonish, wah-wah effected guitar of Alan Holdsworth, for reasons unknown spelling his name "Holldsworth" on his recorded debut.

Though Holdsworth would soon gain recognition as one of fusion's leading guitarists, Tempest the band was primarily notable for two nonmusical innovations. First, they were one of the earliest bands to have a snazzy gothic logo designed for them. And second, they reinforced the concept of instructing album buyers in the proper method of listening: "This record should only be played loud," warned the cover. A similar admonishment had appeared on David Bowie's *The Rise and Fall of Ziggy Stardust and The Spiders from Mars*. Soon thereafter, variations on "made loud to be played loud" cropped up on most hard rock albums.

Stray Dog was also paddling in the power trio waters, led by Texan "Snuffy" Walden. Walden was pals with fellow Lone Star native John "Rabbit" Bundrick, who had been recruited into Free during the recording of their final album, *Heartbreaker*. When Paul Kossoff faltered in the sessions, Walden was brought in as a substitute before he moved on to form Stray Dog, signed to Emerson, Lake, and Palmer's Manticore label.

Though Walden was an outstanding guitarist, the album *Stray Dog* suffered from unexceptional material and lackluster production by Greg Lake. Tapes released decades later reveal thrilling live performances, but the lack of an attention-generating slot on a major tour contributed to Stray Dog's inability to find a home in the charts.

Straying from the "let's be Cream" formula was Sharks, the band formed by founding Free bassist Andy Fraser. Joining Fraser was guitarist Chris Spedding, who, despite recording two albums with Jack Bruce, had little Clapton influence in his playing—perhaps a selling point for Bruce's interest in working with him.

With drummer Marty Simon and vocalist Snips—a mono-named singer who sounded intimately familiar with Joe Cocker's vocal approach—Sharks' debut, *First Water*, established them as a band with an appealing batch of songs and an unusual way of recording them. Despite the potential, Fraser soon departed his own band, and the survivors recorded a single additional album—the rather unappealingly titled *Jab It in Yore Eye*—before calling it quits.

Wishbone Ash presented another variation from the power trio mold, utilizing two guitarists who harmonized their parts in gothic tales of kings, castles, and warriors. This interplay was something new, and the effective no-frills recording of 1973's *Live Dates* offered a blueprint showing how a two-lead-guitar band might function in creative harmony. The path taken by Wishbone Ash would prove to be highly influential on a later generation of heavy metal groups.

Uriah Heep had proven to be highly influenced by Yes. Not only did the group borrow Yes artist Roger Dean to craft the artwork for their albums *Demons and Wizards* and *The Magician's Birthday*, but they also took a dose of the prog rock masters' mysticism. Keyboardist Ken Hensley and guitarist Mick

Box mixed fantasy elements with their stately hard rock compositions, intricate songs that were crowned by vocalist David Byron's dramatic wails.

There was little drama or fantasy to be found in the music of Bachman Turner Overdrive, a pedestrian-if-competent hard rock band from Canada. Formed by Guess Who guitarist Randy Bachman with his drummer brother Robbie, the group also included bassist Fred Turner and an additional Guess Who refugee, Chad Allan, who was soon replaced by yet another Bachman, Tim. Songs like "Takin' Care of Business"—in which the band cheerfully gloated that, as rock stars, they had no need for real jobs—brought the group surprising chart success.

Despite all these bands clamoring for attention, they were difficult to discern over the roar of the mighty Black Sabbath. Since *Paranoid*, the band had released *Master of Reality* and *Vol 4*, in the process forcing their way to global headliner status—not necessarily the highest of honors.

"There were three toilets for half a million people," Ozzy Osbourne recalled of 1972's Indiana Soda Pop Festival, where promoters planned for 55,000 attendees and were overwhelmed by many times that number. "They were selling them aspirin to get them stoned. For ten miles along the freeway there were abandoned cars. There were cars turned over in the river. It was like someone had said, 'You've got ten seconds to get out of the city before it's destroyed.'"

So much for the rewards of stardom.

Black Sabbath had tampered with their sound very little since their inception, and as they entered the studio in 1973 they were fully seasoned road warriors. Following an exhausting period of touring activity that had lasted several years, the band, on the verge of exhaustion, had taken some time off. As a result, the material developed in the interim was fresh and powerful, still existing within the established aural realm Sabbath had constructed but boasting a compositional sophistication that elevated the songs to striking new planes.

Sabbath Bloody Sabbath was to be the band's final truly great album and, quite possibly, its best. Appropriately, the title cut may have been Sabbath's heaviest single track. Lumbering forward at full force, "Sabbath Bloody Sabbath" was a song to be listened to only as loud as one dared. Heralded by Ozzy's grueling cry, the formidable tour de force of turmoil was made all the more dangerous by a sudden midsong downshift into sonic underdrive, Black Sabbath wielding leaden momentum with a riff so massive that a generation of future heavy metal guitarists likely stirred in their infant sleep upon its creation.

In just a few short years, Ozzy Osbourne, Tony Iommi, Geezer Butler, and Bill Ward had achieved the goal that every rock band aspired to reach—they had established indelible new parameters for an entirely new genus of rock music. The darkness and power of the band would reverberate for decades, spawning countless imitators who would always fall short of the seismic brilliance of the originators. Their work done, the original Black Sabbath would soon succumb to personality conflicts, drug abuse, and general malaise after a final studio album in 1974, the prophetically named *Sabotage*.

The rock world of 1973 was drastically different from that of five years earlier, when the fabled Summer of Love was already a fading memory. For many of the bands of that earlier era, the 1970s had proved to be a harsh environment.

When *Thirty Seconds over Winterland* was released on May 23, 1973, The Jefferson Airplane had already crash-landed after encountering the disastrous turbulence of personal differences and wandering interests among the band members. The later Airplane records had seen the band's sound change, as co-lead singer Marty Balin left and violinist Papa John Creach joined. Having played with Airplane bassist Jack Casady and guitarist Jorma Kaukonen in their spin-off project Hot Tuna, Creach was a natural addition. But with Kaukonen, Casady, guitarist Paul Kantner, and vocalist Grace Slick all involved with myriad side projects, the permanent grounding of the Airplane had seemed inevitable.

To many fans, the new Airplane didn't sound like the old Airplane—which was probably true. But the new band was innovative and did have a unique timbre. The album *Thirty Seconds*, recorded during what turned out to be the Jefferson

Airplane's final two shows at San Francisco's Winterland, had its share of intriguing moments. In particular, the sound of the whole band united in "Have You Seen the Saucers," anchored by Casady's earthy bass, and Kaukonen's extended workout on "Feel So Good" indicated that disgruntled fans may have been hasty in their judgment.

Regardless, the Airplane had had a long, fascinating flight, one that had reached its final destination.

"We were incredibly lucky," Kaukonen recalled in the liner notes to *Jefferson Airplane Loves You*, a career retrospective. "We went from being nobodies to being somebodies literally overnight. Having been in the music business a long time now, you realize how rarely that happens and how really lucky it is."

With The Airplane grounded for retooling via major personnel shifts into the incarnation known as The Jefferson Starship, Hot Tuna became Kaukonen and Casady's primary focus. With drummer Sammy Piazza, the trio took a step away from the acoustic fingerstyle blues of Jack and Jorma's first album and the subtle electric blues of *First Pull Up, Then Pull Down* and *Burgers*. With Creach now Starship-bound, Hot Tuna was by default a guitar band, forced to move with the times and apply more edge and more volume to parallel the market for hard rock bands.

"The lyrics on certain songs were very interesting and intelligent and not clichéd," Casady said of the resulting *The Phosphorescent Rat* in Jeff Tamarkin's reissue liner notes. "Jorma didn't get a chance with the Airplane to have that develop and take its course."

On songs like "I See the Light" and "Easy Now," the newly power-trio'ed Tuna took their rootsy blues background and amplified it to gratifying effect. With just three musicians in the mix, each had ample aural acreage to freely create while still contributing to the ensemble's whole.

Though Jorma and Jack had moved on to their more recent full-time venture, a band of their peers from the Summer of Love, The Grateful Dead, were still hanging in together—and they were about to join two other bands for the year's biggest concert event.

On July 28, 1973, the largest crowd to ever attend a rock concert—more than 600,000 people—descended on Watkins

Glen, New York, for the Summer Jam, a concert featuring The Band, The Allman Brothers Band, and The Dead.

After losing brilliant guitarist Duane Allman, The Allman Brothers Band had made an immediate decision: to keep going. Within four weeks of Duane's funeral, the band was on the concert stage. Perhaps the biggest burden was on Dickey Betts, now the band's lone guitarist. In February 1972, *Eat a Peach* was released, and though Duane was on nearly all the tracks, the double album began with three songs recorded by the group in its missing-man formation.

As Dickey gained confidence, The Allmans began laying out plans for their next album. Then, for a second time, tragedy struck. Eerily mirroring Duane's fate, the great bassist Berry Oakley, who had tried to assume the role of band leader, was killed in a motorcycle crash on November 11, 1972.

Again, The Allman Brothers Band was faced with the decision of whether to carry on. They had just added keyboardist Chuck Leavell, who brought a new dimension to the band's sound. They'd begun recording a new album, and the material was strong. In the end, the band again decided to keep playing, bringing in Lamar Williams on bass to complete *Brothers and Sisters*—the second consecutive album to carry the legend, "Dedicated to a brother."

The album bore a distinctly different sound than fans of the band were accustomed to, as it marked Leavell's prominent debut. Yet Betts was the true star of the album, his playing becoming intensely focused and razor-sharp. His country influence came to the forefront, and where much of *Eat a Peach* had contained long jams, *Brothers and Sisters* was a tight, seven-song collection. The band was different without Berry and Duane, but Dickey, Gregg Allman, Butch Trucks, and Jaimoe were smart enough to let the changes take their own course. As a result, the new Allman Brothers Band flourished rather than floundered.

As for The Grateful Dead, they had suffered their own loss when original member "Pigpen" McKernan died on April 8, 1973, succumbing to complications from a short life of hard living.

At Watkins Glen, The Grateful Dead were the first to play that day, ambling on stage just after noon. Almost inevitably the massive crowd had been rained on, marinating in mud as The Dead played a typically long-winded five-hour set. The Band were on next, performing for three hours. The Allman Brothers Band brought up the rear with their own three-hour set, then members of all three groups added another ninety minutes to the running time with a prolonged jam.

Three days later *Brothers and Sisters* was released. The album debuted at number thirteen, but within a month The Allman Brothers Band found themselves residing at the top of the charts.

Released within hours of The Allman Brothers Band's *Brothers and Sisters*, Stevie Wonder's *Innervisions* paralleled The Allmans' run up the charts. But Wonder himself was not able to enjoy the success.

On August 6, near Winston-Salem, North Carolina, Wonder was involved in a freak car accident that nearly proved fatal. After four days in a coma, Wonder emerged into consciousness and began a slow recovery.

The blind keyboardist—who had risen to stardom in the glory days of Motown Records' pop chart domination—held a position of influence in the rock world of 1973. He had opened tours for The Rolling Stones, and Wonder's newer albums *Music of My Mind* and *Talking Book* marked fast-paced advances in soul, funk, and the use of synthesizers. He'd also provided material to rock bands like Beck, Bogert, Appice, whose rendition of "Superstition" marked one of the few highlights of the short-lived supergroup's career, and Beck himself guest-starred on *Talking Book*.

Innervisions took up where its predecessors left off, but Wonder's compositional skills had taken another leap forward. And although synths were still gimmicky noise generators in the hands of others, Wonder turned to top programmers and audio engineers to ensure that the electronic sounds on his new album were entirely musical. As a result, on tracks like "Too High" and "Higher Ground" the synths provided a sympathetic and vibrant musical foundation.

While Wonder managed to find a voicing for topical and so-cial concerns on *Innervisions* with songs like "He's Misstra Know-It-All" and "Living for the City," he filtered his observa-tions through a viewpoint that was knowing, not strident. It was a difficult balance to achieve, which explained why most pop artists preferred to evade such issues entirely.

Elton John was one of the world's top pop stars, plying piano ballads and a ridiculously flamboyant image to great success. And though Elton steered clear of weighty pronouncements, the new complexity of rock and its instrumentation did influ-ence his 1973 album *Goodbye Yellow Brick Road*. The record's ini-tial notes, grandly spilling from the speakers in a cascade of synthesizers, created an overture-like prologue to "Funeral for a Friend/Love Lies Bleeding," an eleven-minute-plus track that was certainly John's longest and most ambitious.

Length wasn't an issue for Leon Russell—when he decided to release *Leon Live* on his own Shelter label, he was free to utilize all the vinyl grooves necessary to fully represent his revival-like concert experience. The album documented Russell's exuberant ten-person band, one made up of an alluring mixture of gospel musicians and veterans of the *Mad Dogs and Englishmen* tour. When the collection arrived in stores, its songs sprawled across three albums, all contained within colorful, folk art packag-ing—and, refreshingly, in *Leon Live's* two hours of rollicking performances, there wasn't a synthesizer to be heard.

The gentleman oozes sophistication as he stands in aloof dis-interest, dressed in a white dinner jacket that contrasts his suavely styled black hair. One hand rests in his trouser pocket; the other lightly grasps a cigarette, the smoke gently wafting past his knowing half-smile.

Humphrey Bogart in *Casablanca*? No, Bryan Ferry of Roxy Music.

Six young men in full formal attire, complete with top hats, stand at ease in front of an expansive mansion, luxuriant ruf-fled curtains visible through the bay windows.

No, not a publicity still from *The Philadelphia Story*—just Procol Harum on the cover of *Grand Hotel*.

In 1973 both Roxy Music and Procol Harum released albums that were uniquely European, recordings that were spiritual cousins despite the opposing musical realms the two groups operated within. Common artistic ground was shared through the presence of Chris Thomas, who produced both albums at London's AIR Studios, and through the fact that Roxy Music's *Stranded* and Procol Harum's *Grand Hotel* stand as highlights of each band's career.

Roxy Music had splashed down in the British musical scene in 1972, releasing *Roxy Music* and *For Your Pleasure* to excited reviews in the musical press. By the summer of 1973, though, personnel changes—chiefly the departure of avant-garde experimentalist Brian Eno—had that same musical press atwitter over the creative status of the band's next album.

Stranded heralded an image makeover for the group, as they abandoned the glittery sci-fi rockabilly look that had characterized their early months in favor of the trappings of modern decadent sophisticates—a style that would serve the band well throughout the remainder of their career.

One thing that had not changed with *Stranded* was the unique strength of a most unusual band. Front and center was Bryan Ferry's curious croon of a voice, Sinatra-smooth one line, wavering Marc-Bolan-as-a-baritone the next. Guitarist Phil Manzanera was a rock guitar antihero, all texture and mood rather than blazing blues. The lonesome oboe and raw saxophone of Andy MacKay drifted through Roxy's chords, providing the band direct access to moods ranging from classical dirges to '50s dance parties. The brutal thunder of the workmanlike Paul Thompson on drums was the very foundation of Roxy Music, and Eddie Jobson—filling Eno's vacancy quite handily—supplemented his keyboard skills with electric violin, adding another atmospheric selection to the band's palette.

"We deal on so many different levels that people tend to get different things out of it," Ferry told Lisa Robinson in *Creem* magazine's May 1973 issue. "There really is something for everybody, I think. My idea is to take the audience through as many moods—to have as much variety—as possible. Some of the lyrics may be obscure to some, but the songs have a mood that people can relate to."

Stranded was an impressively diverse album, roaming from the finger-snapping electro-jive of "Street Life" to the hypnotic pulse of Ferry's beautiful composition "Mother of Pearl." And certainly one of the key tracks was "A Song for Europe," a dramatically knowing elegy in which Ferry vows that, "these cities may change, but they'll always remain my obsession." In six passionate minutes, Roxy Music surveyed Europe, crafting a melodramatic farewell to a way of life that was rapidly fading into the mists of time.

If Roxy Music delved into continental concerns in a uniquely experimental way, Procol Harum ventured across similar lyrical turf while maintaining the classical fundamentals that served to bolster their work. Chord progressions may have been shared by the two bands, but the resulting sounds were radically different.

Grand Hotel's title track opened Procol Harum's seventh album with a delicate piano phrase. Within moments, though, the song was bathed in the full fruition of Procol Harum's classical aspirations. A thunderous orchestral accompaniment swelled behind the band, pushed to even greater heights by a choir launching volleys of chilling, descending melodies. It was a fully successful deployment of disparate music, and it was an approach that was unique to Procol Harum.

The title track notwithstanding, the band was not fully addicted to reinforcement by orchestras and choirs. Chris Copping's stately organ washes provided more than ample colorings, and drummer B. J. Wilson's dramatic, halting style was brilliantly suited to set up Gary Brooker's consistently striking choruses. And on "Toujours L'Amour" and "Bringing Home the Bacon," the newest member of the band, guitarist Mick Grabham, displayed the talents of a glowing arrival on the rock scene. Many rock guitarists launch into solos by leaping for the high, piercing notes immediately; Grabham wasn't afraid to explore the realms of the middle and low notes, a region also frequently visited by ZZ Top's Billy Gibbons. Indeed, Grabham's work on this entire album stands as guitar playing of the highest caliber, fundamentally moving even if it was underacclaimed.

The *Grand Hotel* lyrics of Keith Reid were crafted with references to European elite society and continental glories. Brooker sang of "dry champagne and bursting grapes," "a villa in France," and other visions of the pedigreed and privileged. To complete the image, the cover photo session was conducted at The Grand Hotel near Lake Leman in Switzerland—ironically, the site where Deep Purple had recorded their hard rock masterpiece *Machine Head*.

If both Roxy Music and Procol Harum were using rock to celebrate the ideals and traditions of European culture, in the United States a newer band had developed their own musical style, one imbued with cultural traits that were uniquely American. They were Lynyrd Skynyrd, and they made no secret of the fact they were proud to be American by birth, Southern by the grace of God.

Hailing from the Jacksonville, Florida, area, Lynyrd Skynyrd endured a frustrating series of personnel changes and flirtations with success. Finally, they found the express path to rock stardom upon the release of their MCA Records debut, *(pronounced 'leh-nerd' skin'-nerd)* late in 1973. The source of the group's name was high school coach Leonard Skinner, who hated long hair on boys—including the future group members. Curious name aside, the band was bolstered by a thrilling guitar attack and a stout young singer named Ronnie Van Zant. Big things began to happen for Skynyrd when they took to the road in a high-profile slot opening The Who's winter 1973 tour.

Though *pronounced* contained characteristic songs that would come to symbolize the band—songs like "Simple Man" and the anthemic "Free Bird"—many more songs of equal caliber were already written, having been recorded in early sessions taped throughout the South. Indeed, recordings of a 1973 radio concert find the band confidently roaring through later album tracks like "Call Me the Breeze" and the ironic "Sweet Home Alabama."

Like that of another legendary rocker of the South, Jerry Lee Lewis, the music of Lynyrd Skynyrd was imbued with the tensions of a soul seeking peace and spiritual salvation as it tried to resist the temptations of honky tonks and hard living. Early but sophisticated Skynyrd material like "He's Alive" and "Was I Right or Wrong" played off the Bible, while "Gimme Three

Steps" and "I Ain't the One" poured from the bottle. No matter the topic, Ronnie Van Zant was well on his way to becoming one of American rock's greatest lyricists, with a direct, conversational style that communicated from the heart.

As for their performances, Lynyrd Skynyrd was doing nothing less than reestablishing the parameters of so-called Southern rock. In the wake of The Allman Brothers' success, any band whose roots stretched south of the Mason-Dixon Line found themselves unceremoniously lumped into the marketing-driven Southern rock bin, regardless of what they sounded like. But Skynyrd revealed the shallowness of such classifications, as they easily merged elements of The Allmans, Free, Jimi Hendrix, and Buck Owens in a heady brew of sounds. Lynyrd Skynyrd stalked in a rocking swagger one moment, and eased on down country roads the next.

Guitarists Gary Rossington and Allen Collins could make the sound of their instruments travel from London to Nashville in a heartbeat, but the band soon gained another dimension. Just in time for The Who's tour, Leon Wilkeson joined Skynyrd with his striking bass skills. Ed King was then free to put down the bass for his first love, giving Skynyrd a stunning three-guitar front line, fully complemented by Billy Powell's roadhouse piano. It could easily have turned into an aural disaster, with so many instruments clamoring for attention. But the band meticulously assembled their sound, using an intricate interplay of locking musical parts to ensure that every note had its place.

For all of the critical respect bestowed upon The Mahavishnu Orchestra for their bold experimentations with jazz and rock, Lynyrd Skynyrd was equally deserving of accolades. The ongoing research conducted in their rural Florida "Hell House" rehearsal space near Green Cove Springs was revolutionary in its own uniquely American way.

1974

5

Distant Early Warning

"Can anybody out there play drums?"

Pete Townshend's voice echoed off the walls of the cavernous Cow Palace arena as the British guitarist peered into the glare of the stage lights. Thousands of The Who's San Francisco fans stared back, uncertain if Townshend was serious.

The question seemed absurd—but then again, the sprawling black drum kit occupied just moments earlier by the legendary Keith Moon now sat empty.

It was November 20, 1973, a cool Tuesday night in San Francisco, and The Who were just moments into the first date of a significant United States tour. After opening with the classics "I Can't Explain," "Summertime Blues," and "My Generation"— songs the band knew easily—the foursome had turned their attention to vastly more challenging work: *Quadrophenia*.

There had always been a certain blunt simplicity to live rock and roll. Take a stack of amplifiers, add some guitars, turn on the power—and rock! The Who were now changing that perception.

To recreate their new double album on stage, The Who required an elaborate series of technical assists. There were rhythm "click tracks" to synchronize Townshend, Moon, and bassist John Entwistle, as well as instrumental backing tapes to augment their overall sound. It was a challenge for all of the musicians, but from drummer Moon it demanded total precision. Not a good idea.

Moon, renowned for his fiery percussive brilliance, was anything but a typical rock timekeeper. In the conjuring of his thunderous drum rolls and wild cymbal washes, Moon could sometimes be found surging just ahead of the beat, at other times lagging slightly behind. Where most bands relied on the drummer as the keeper of the beat, The Who were perpetually in pursuit of their mercurial band mate.

Even though Moon's offstage reputation was that of a wild man liable to do anything, his role in The Who was precious to him. He knew he was expected to don a pair of headphones so he could hear the tapes clearly over the onstage roar and perform the new album to perfection. Friends say he fretted endlessly over the new burden before leaving on tour. Simply put, Moon had stage fright. Under circumstances that are still mysterious to this day, he apparently gulped a handful of tranquilizers before clambering on stage to the cheers of the San Francisco Who fans.

Those cheers became more subdued as the concert wore on. Moon wobbled his way through the set while butchering his *Quadrophenia* parts, the effects of the drugs wreaking havoc on his ability to follow the demanding tracks.

Realizing things were taking a turn for the worse, and in an attempt to regroup, The Who turned to a familiar *Who's Next* song, "Won't Get Fooled Again." It didn't help. Though concerts by The Who had an "anything can happen" notoriety, an unfortunate new chapter for the band's legend was written this night. In the song's midst, Keith Moon passed out cold, slumping over the drum kit.

Revived and directed back to the stage, Moon collapsed again early in "Magic Bus." It was then that the guitarist for one of the world's mightiest rock bands sought a drummer from the assembled masses. Townshend didn't have to ask twice.

A chance to actually play with one of the legendary rock bands, in front of thousands of fans? Nineteen-year-old Iowan drummer Scott Halpin launched himself on stage. A brief on-the-spot job interview commenced. Townshend wanted to know if Halpin could "really play." Answering in the affirmative, Halpin was dispatched to Moon's drums with Townshend's blessings. After all, Pete reasoned, things couldn't get much worse. From behind Moon's drum kit, Halpin surveyed his environment.

"The size of the drums was ridiculous," he recalled years later in Tony Fletcher's insightful Keith Moon biography *Moon*. "The tom-toms were as big as my bass drums. Everything was locked into place; anyplace you could hit there would be something there."

Halpin lived out every amateur garage band drummer's fantasy as The Who soldiered on through several oldies before calling it a night.

The Who left San Francisco, continuing the tour with a reanimated Moon. Halpin's night of fame ensured that his name would become the answer to one of the more unusual rock trivia questions.

That The Who now found themselves on stage, chasing backing tapes and attempting to synchronize themselves not to Moon but to a series of recorded beats, symbolized the growing musical ambition of Townshend that had manifested itself with *Quadrophenia*. And despite the chaos of the 1973 tour, as 1974 dawned the double album still rode high in the American charts—even if most fans in the States didn't have a clue what the album was about.

The Who, and Townshend in particular, had always seemed nearly obsessed with the band's origins. Now with a global fan base, Pete saw an opportunity to use *Quadrophenia* to indulge his fascination with the band's history, immersing the world's listeners in the curious, trendy English subculture of the Mod movement.

Serving as the environment that cultivated the birth of The Who, the Mod culture of the early to mid-1960s was one diametrically opposed to that of the Rockers, the British kids who favored black leather and gritty rock and roll. The Mods envisioned themselves infinitely more stylish, with neat haircuts, sharp clothes, a taste for rhythm and blues, and a predilection for riding about on Vespa motor scooters. Mods also chose speed as their drug of choice, popping pills dubbed "leapers" and carousing about until they collapsed days later.

Townshend was determined to take myriad aspects of Mod culture, boil them down into a single character, and give that character all the personality facets of the four members of The

Who. Not one for imaginative names, Townshend took one small step away from the 1968 album title character *Tommy* and christened his Mod-for-all-seasons "Jimmy." Suitably blessed by Townshend with some severe personality issues, Jimmy himself allegedly wrote the album's liner notes, summing things up thusly:

"Schizophrenic? I'm bleeding Quadrophenic."

Jimmy's lengthy essay within the album's gatefold sleeve told of typical Mod trials and tribulations—stressing over obtaining fashionable clothes, obsessing over girls, riding scooters, scoring speed, and pondering one's self-worth with all of eighteen years of living under one's belt. *Quadrophenia* was illustrated with a forty-four-page book following Jimmy through the Mod realm, the grainy black-and-white photography matching Townshend's grim viewpoint. In his new songs he had focused less on the Mods' vibrancy, centering on the desperate need to belong that was often at the heart of such movements. The lyrics of the seventeen-song piece paralleled Jimmy's story, in the end leaving our hero floating about in a small boat, tossed hither and yon on life's seas, facing an uncertain future.

"The story is there. It's as simple as *Tommy*," Townshend reflected twenty-five years later in an interview with *Addicted to Noise*. "What happened with *Quadrophenia* is it's a very elegant piece of work that to an extent is confused by its grandiosity. But it's a very, very simple story. A young man has a bad day, basically, and that's really all there is. It's a series of events. He just realizes that all he has in his life is himself and some spiritual future."

Musically, The Who had followed a different path than many established rock bands, groups who came to rely on lengthy instrumental explorations. Townshend's confidence in his guitar talents was less secure than that of highly worshipped peers like Eric Clapton and Jeff Beck, and Pete preferred to turn the spotlight away from expectations of virtuoso performances and to focus instead on strong songwriting. Even when The Who did stretch out instrumentally, as in the fourteen-minute rendition of "My Generation" that had highlighted the *Live at Leeds* album, the song as a whole consisted of many small structured parts sewn together—it was not brilliant free-form improvisation. The same traits applied in the studio. The band's longest recording, "Won't Get Fooled Again," was a meticulously arranged musical work from beginning to end.

Quadrophenia displayed a growing sophistication in the band's abilities, one that raised the bar for contemporaries of The Who. Already notorious for birthing the rock opera concept with *Tommy*—and for receiving an invitation to perform the work at New York's Metropolitan Opera House—Townshend felt validated in dressing up rock with ever more grandiose trappings. To complement Jimmy's "Quadrophenic" personality, Townshend developed four musical themes that recurred throughout the album's four sides, each theme woven into the story and reflecting the band personalities. More importantly, layers of synthesizers, reflecting Pete's growing talents as an arranger, created lush electronic backings for the band to play above.

On stage, though, the burden of translating *Quadrophenia* to audiences was crushing. The severity of that was borne out by Moon's unfortunate attempt at self-medication in the face of being assimilated by Townshend's orchestral scope. And the challenge was not limited to recreating the music; Townshend spent lengthy portions of concerts in this era attempting to explain to his audience the finer points of the songs they were about to hear.

Did audiences who lived in ignorance of the Mod world really care about or understand the subject? It really didn't matter. *Quadrophenia* quickly reached gold record status, with sales figures befitting one of the elite bands of rock and roll.

In hindsight, the most fascinating aspect of *Quadrophenia* is found in the song "The Punk Meets the Godfather." Emerging from the pen of a man continually questioning his place in the world of rock and roll, the song was Townshend's insecure vision of a rock star confronted by his own audience, an audience grown repulsed by the trappings of stardom.

Townshend's use of the word "punk" in the song's title was particularly prescient—or maybe just lucky. The violent musical rift that would be associated with that particular four-letter word would begin to tear into rock and roll in just a matter of months. It was a song that would come back to haunt not only Townshend and The Who, but also the entire rock hierarchy.

If Pete Townshend was not yet regarded as a prophet in 1974, Bob Dylan certainly was. A certifiable "voice of his generation," Dylan's audience had spent more than a decade closely following the singer's journey of constant reinvention. Howling dire warnings and railing against social injustice, Dylan, in full folk singer mode, began a climb to critical respect and popularity in the early 1960s. In 1965, though, Dylan officiated at the marriage of electric guitars and folk music. To many of his fans, it wasn't a popular union.

Throughout the 1960s, large gatherings of appreciative jazz fans politely be-bopping together were a common occurrence, with shows such as the Newport Jazz Festival becoming an annual tradition. Although peaceful folk festivals were also common, Dylan's performance at the 1965 Newport Folk Festival spurred the heretofore-gentle folkies into showing an impressive mean streak.

Young Bob, as the nasally-voiced acoustic hero of the socially conscious, was an icon with a Martin acoustic guitar slung over his shoulders and a harmonica holder around his neck. Yet he took to the stage at Newport brandishing what might as well have been a semiautomatic weapon aimed at his audience— Bob Dylan held an electric guitar in his hands, and he was accompanied by a scruffy-looking band also armed with electric instruments. The Newport audience was expecting heartfelt protests carried by natural acoustic properties; what they got was a highly amplified ear blast that launched Dylan's musical persona into a new realm.

One can imagine the shrieks of indignation and outrage that swept through the crowd as Bob and his cohorts plugged in. Hundreds of folkies opened their mouths in unison to emit a chorus of boos, rivaling the amplifiers in volume as Dylan attempted to force-feed his fans a brave new direction in his mysterious career.

But Bob's flirtation with electric rock was just that. He later abandoned large amps, soon taking on the guise of a family man living a rustic lifestyle in Woodstock, New York. With conflict removed, many felt his works of the later 1960s suffered accordingly, though Dylan himself never seemed all that concerned about what anyone thought one way or another.

The one constant characterizing Bob's career since the electric days was that he did not tour. So when it was announced that Dylan would unite with his former backing group, The Band, and take to the road in 1974, it was huge news. Reportedly, six million ticket applications were made for the 660,000 seats available over the course of the tour. The outing grossed five million dollars as it rolled on through twenty-five United States and Canadian cities.

Financial aspects aside, though, Dylan's reunion with his highly regarded mates was simply the act of treading water elevated to a grand scale. The resulting studio album commemorating Dylan's return to action, *Planet Waves*, contained little in the way of revelations or groundbreaking points of view. Perhaps the most notable aspect of the lucrative tour was Bob's ego.

"It doesn't mean that much to me, really," opined Bob the Bard of the masses' excitement over his return. "I mean, who else is there to go and see?"

Well, there was certainly David Bowie.

David Bowie, in 1974, anointed himself "the spirit of the seventies," claiming that half of the people looked to him to see where the decade was heading—and offering proof that Bob Dylan did not have a lock on the ego concession.

As the year began, Bowie had presented himself with a clean creative slate. The Spiders from Mars, the backing band that had helped pilot Bowie to glam rock superstardom, crashed back to earth after Bowie's announcement of his alleged retirement from rock and roll on July 3, 1973.

"Not only is it the last show of the tour, but it's the last show that we'll ever do," the redheaded rock star announced from the stage of the Hammersmith Odeon in London. The reaction from his dedicated followers was screams of disbelief. The retirement came as news to The Spiders as well.

"I feel like I'm an actor when I'm onstage, not a rock artist," Bowie later said. "It's not much of a vocation, being a rock'n'roller."

But fans who interpreted Bowie's comments as a farewell from the singer soon found out that it was simply Bowie's farewell to the Ziggy Stardust character, the makeup-clad, space-age effeminate rock superstar guise that had served Bowie so well for two full years.

More surprising was the fact that Bowie was ending his relationship with Mick Ronson, the dealer of muscular guitar riffs who had added brawn to Bowie's fey posturing since 1971's *The Man Who Sold the World*. In the tradition of Jeff Beck and Jimmy Page, Ronson's aggressive style was pure supercharged blues; without Mick's grounding effect, it seemed quite likely that Bowie would succumb to an overdose of character-driven musical fantasies.

The music journalists who predicted such dire outcomes soon discovered that Bowie was far too clever to fall into such a trap. The Hammersmith farewell was simply Bowie's means of severing himself from his immediate past and a public image that threatened to turn stale. It was a pattern that would be repeated throughout Bowie's career.

"Now I'm doing Orwell's *1984* on television," Bowie announced early in 1974. "That's a political thesis and an impression of the way in another country. Something of that nature will have more impact on television. People having to go out to the cinema is really archaic. I'd much rather sit at home."

Far from sitting at home—and freed from Ziggy's extraterrestrial constraints—Bowie ensconced himself in the studio. Fascinated by George Orwell's vision of a depersonalized future, Bowie laid his plans to adapt *1984* into a conceptual production. There was just one problem—the Orwell estate refused to grant Bowie the rights to use *1984*. So Bowie simply adapted the grim mood of Orwell's work to a new sonic recipe of apocalyptic paranoia. The resulting creation was *Diamond Dogs*.

The album began with an ominous soliloquy, informing listeners they were about to hear a soundtrack for the end of civilization, Bowie promising that it was not rock and roll contained within the vinyl grooves—it was genocide. From those first words, it was clear that Ziggy's visions of a "Moonage

Daydream" and "Soul Love" didn't exist in the realm of *Diamond Dogs*. And even though Bowie facially still resembled Ziggy on the album's cover, his torso was attached to canine back legs. So disturbing did RCA Records find Guy Peellaert's painting that they insisted the male genitalia of the dog body be airbrushed out before they would agree to release the album. All of which conveniently made for great publicity, of course.

Bowie himself took over the guitar duties on *Diamond Dogs*, replacing Ronson's riff power with a more blunt, chordal approach that meshed well with the stripped-down rock thump of the title track and "Rebel Rebel." Mood was crucial on more atmospheric songs like "Sweet Thing" and "We Are the Dead," and Bowie relied heavily on keyboardist Mike Garson, hired for the second round of Ziggy Stardust tours and to record *Aladdin Sane*, to make the songs memorable.

Diamond Dogs climbed toward the top five of the sales charts in both the United States and England in the wake of its April release, but even as his fans wrestled with Bowie's vision of life after the collapse of civilization, David himself was already moving on.

"Ever since I got to New York I've been going down to the Apollo in Harlem," Bowie enthused to *Rock* magazine soon after arriving in Manhattan to prepare for the release of *Diamond Dogs*. "Most New Yorkers seem scared to go there if they're white, but the music's incredible. I saw The Temptations and The Spinners together on the same bill there, and next week it's Marvin Gaye—incredible!"

Indeed, Bowie's growing obsession with soul and rhythm and blues had an instantaneous effect. The tour to support *Diamond Dogs*, carefully staged to present the doomsday aspects of the album, offered the incongruous addition of Eddie Floyd's jaunty feel-good hit "Knock on Wood" in mid-set. David's clothing had come back to earth from the sci-fi Ziggy days, revealing a sharp-dressed master of ceremonies for the impending apocalypse. And Bowie's touring performances on an eighty-date trek through the United States and Canada heavily featured the reedy alto saxophone of David Sanborn, much as it once had focused on Mick Ronson's guitar pyrotechnics.

When the first leg of the tour reached its conclusion with four nights at Philadelphia's Tower Theater in mid-July, the tapes rolled for *David Live*. Released late in 1974, the album documents Bowie moving further afield from straight rock, veering towards dance-friendly rhythm and blues—even as he sings of the fall of society.

"The point is to grow into the person you grow into. I haven't a clue where I'm gonna be in a year," Bowie told *Playboy* in 1976, admitting that change was the sole constant of his career. "A raving nut, a flower child or a dictator, some kind of reverend—I don't know. That's what keeps me from getting bored."

David Bowie, in a matter of mere months, made the hugely popular Ziggy Stardust seem like ancient history. Bowie had learned a crucial lesson. He knew how to masterfully operate the tool that established his immediate metamorphosis and those he would initiate in the years to come.

"The media is either our salvation or our death," he explained. "My particular thing is discovering what can be done with media—and how it can be used."

Unlike David Bowie, using the media was something entirely alien to Yes, whose image—what little there was—came largely through the use of artist Roger Dean, whose paintings graced their album covers. Instead, Yes kept their focus on the music alone, continuing to build respectability for the realm of prog rock.

When arty rivals King Crimson lured precise percussionist Bruford away from Yes in late 1972 following the recording of *Close to the Edge*, the band recruited a drummer who brought a fundamentally different style. Alan White had first encountered rock success as a member of ex-Cream drummer Ginger Baker's Air Force, then went on to play with John Lennon, Eric Clapton, George Harrison, Joe Cocker, and many others in a host of studio sessions and live settings. He accepted the invitation to join Yes three days before a United States tour commenced in November 1972.

White insists that he's always played Yes music following a simple motto: "Let it breathe and make it swing." Of course, there were plenty of prog rock haters who would insist that the band Yes stood in complete contradiction of the term "swing." If nothing else, though, White did bring a certain percussive fluidity that flowed beneath the rigid structures created by the band.

With a solid personnel lineup finally in place, and after issuing a live recording entitled *Yessongs* in 1973—a triple-disc album that featured both Bruford and White—Yes faced the task of returning to the studio.

Much had changed since Yes had last recorded new material. In particular, The Mahavishnu Orchestra, Return to Forever, and others had changed the rock landscape with their fusion of jazz and rock. In the months since the John McLaughlin-led Orchestra had smashed the artistic barriers between the two forms of music, many other jazz musicians had begun swimming in rock waters. Prior to the commercial success of The Mahavishnu Orchestra, jazz musicians wouldn't have dreamed of sullying their reputations by playing rock—but that was definitely no longer the case. Not only could this new crop of talent apply their jazz chops to their hearts' free-form content within a rock context, but the rock market offered significantly more financial opportunity than the shopworn jazz trail of smoky clubs. Besides, the newly rocking jazzers could still play musical elitist, looking down their noses at the more primitive skills of native rockers.

Nowhere was the threat of the fusion movement taken more seriously than among the prog rock community. Yes; King Crimson; and Emerson, Lake, and Palmer had secure grips on the throne in the kingdom where complexity counts, but the odd time measures and musical explosions detonated by the fusion crowd were seen as warning shots fired over the castle walls—and invasion seemed imminent.

Yes, though, was inspired to take up the challenge. Emboldened by the commercial success they'd enjoyed with their most recent albums, and realizing that playing it safe was not a viable option, the band decided to take a tremendous risk. Some considered the end result of Yes' gamble the greatest prog rock album ever recorded. Others considered it the most pompous prog rock album ever recorded. In reality, it was quite likely both.

It was *Tales from Topographic Oceans,* and its creation began with Anderson and Howe comparing notes for song ideas. On tour in the United States, the two musicians lay the groundwork for *Tales.*

"By the time we reached Savannah, Georgia," Anderson recalled in the liner notes to the CD reissue, "things had come together very clearly. There, during one six-hour session, which carried on until 7 a.m., we worked out the vocal, lyrical, and instrumental foundation for the four movements. It was a magical experience which left both of us exhilarated for days. Chris, Rick, and Alan made very important contributions of their own as the work evolved during the five months it took to arrange, rehearse, and record."

Though *Tales* shared the "four themes" idea that The Who's *Quadrophenia* was based on, it differed in one significant way— *Tales* was one massive song, spread across four album sides.

Yes' record label, Atlantic, was less than thrilled with this development. In effect, the band was kissing off any hope of garnering radio airplay, making a risky, exploratory project all the more difficult to market, despite the band's proven popularity. To Atlantic's amazement, though, the album went top ten in the United States upon its release.

The massive work began with Anderson softly chanting over a swelling sonic background wash, his words a bizarre, freeform torrent that certainly sounded important even if their meaning was cryptic.

Then again, no one was expecting straight narrative from a band whose hit "Roundabout" contained the line, "Mountains come out of the sky and they stand there." But did it mean anything?

"I spent a year of my life just going crazy, creating a piece of music that even I didn't know what it was all about," Anderson admitted in *Yesstories: Yes in Their Own Words,* Tim Morse's collection of interviews. "I was just driven like a lunatic. Obviously the guys in the band thought that I'd lost it and hated me; it didn't matter. I knew it was this thing I had to do."

"At that time, Jon had this visionary idea that you could just walk into a studio, and if the vibes were right, that the music would be great at the end of the day," Chris Squire said in *Yesstories.* "It isn't reality."

Reality or not, Anderson's main collaborator on the project, Howe, felt the four sides were well used.

"We had so much space on that album that we were able to explore things, which I think was tremendously good for us," Howe insisted in 1992. "Side one was the most commercial or easy-listening side of *Topographic Oceans*, side two was a much lighter, folky side of Yes, side three was electronic mayhem turning into acoustic simplicity, and side four was us trying to drive the whole thing home on a biggie. So we saw them much smaller than they are in reality. Big arrangements, certainly, but we didn't see any problems with it."

As Howe noted, the third side of *Tales* did contain the band's most experimental music. The harsh, abrasive combination of electronic noise and chaotic percussion broke new ground for what could be defined as popular music—although it was definitely not popular with the critics.

"It was the most critically-knocked album we ever did," Howe acknowledged in *Yesstories*. "We were trying to paint a very big landscape, and when I hear the beginning of side three I can't believe we were going so far out."

Perhaps too far out—just weeks after the release of *Tales from Topographic Oceans*, Rick Wakeman quit Yes on June 8 to begin a solo career.

"Yes began as a five-piece unit and it got less and less a five-piece *unit*," Wakeman insisted to *Creem* magazine's Jaan Uhelszki in the February 1975 issue. "Everyone pulled further and further apart. Besides being a music-making machine, Yes became a money-making machine. . . . There's an important state that a band can get to, and Yes got to that point—where a record would go gold before it was even made. And that means people believe enough in what you've done before, and on the strength of that, are ready to accept your next thing. I didn't think that was very good. In fact, it was a very embarrassing thing. I didn't enjoy the concerts, or making records anymore."

Wakeman felt the band was now burdened by far too many pretensions. Yet in a textbook case of the pot calling the kettle black, Wakeman promptly recorded a deeply complicated musical interpretation of Jules Verne's *Journey to the Centre of the Earth* with the London Symphony Orchestra, as well as a work titled *The Myths and Legends of King Arthur and the Knights of the Round Table*, both following in the footsteps of his 1973 solo project *The Six Wives of Henry VIII*.

One of the first groundbreaking prog rock bands was The Nice, the trio that sought to meld rock directly with classical elements. When keyboard sensation Keith Emerson dumped drummer Brian Davidson and bassist Lee Jackson to form Emerson, Lake, and Palmer, the dismissed rhythm section sought another classically trained keyboardist, settling on Swiss musician Patrick Moraz. No sooner had the newly christened band Refugee entered the studio than word came of Wakeman's departure from Yes. It was an opportunity too good to pass up—Moraz became a refugee from Refugee, climbing behind the mountain of keyboards that occupied stage right at Yes shows. Davidson and Jackson, victims of keyboard betrayal for the second time, faded into rock obscurity. Moraz went on to aggressively push Yes into even more of a jazz and rock fusion.

Many of the champions of prog rock used mathematics as much as musical ability, counting sections of music that played concurrently in a battle for supremacy in the ear of the listener. The result could be pure glory or pure chaos.

"A lot of Yes music from that era and prior to that were worked out mathematically," Yes drummer Alan White explained in *Yesstories*, "where we'd say this number of bars at that tempo goes into this number of bars at this tempo and we'll meet at this point. So we'll do so many of these and you'll do so many of them and we'll end up at this point. And that's how it was worked out."

Joining Yes in the complexity sweepstakes were Emerson, Lake, and Palmer. Though by now notorious for stabbing his Hammond organs with a dagger while a member of The Nice and ELP, Keith Emerson was actually an important advocate of new keyboard technology. He worked with Dr. Bob Moog, a pioneer of the synthesizer keyboard, at a time when the ability to play multiple notes at the same time on a synth keyboard—known as polyphony in tech terminology—was considered a major advancement. Synthesizers of the era were ornery beasts, and photographs of Emerson's early rigs display a bewildering array of circuitry and patch cables that he used to conjure up the band's orchestral oeuvre.

Orchestral? Like any good prog rock band, ELP had "interpreted" their share of the classics, following up their self-titled debut of 1970 and 1971's *Tarkus* with a grand reinvention of Mussorgsky's *Pictures at an Exhibition*. Released in 1972 to great acclaim by the band's fans, it was viewed with equal horror by the classical music world. But ELP also held the distinction of being the "chick group" of prog rock. Each album by the band contained a radio-friendly ballad sung by Greg Lake, generally regarded as the trio's cutest member. The gentler songs attracted females and ensured that ELP had a string of hit singles—an unusual accomplishment for a prog rock band.

Following the release of 1972's *Trilogy*, ELP were anxious in 1974 to prove they were one of the elite bands of the entire musical spectrum, prog rock or not. *Brain Salad Surgery* was the LP that rode the charts for them, though initially the album was more notorious for its creepy, elaborate cover, designed by the disturbing Swiss surrealist artist H. R. Giger, the man who later envisioned the horrifying creature from the *Alien* movies.

Looking back on the album's musical origins, Keith Emerson alluded to the interpersonal relationships of a rock supergroup and its effect on the creative process.

"ELP were three very competitive individuals, not only in music, but in a lot of other respects as well," he said in an interview contained on the remastered disc. "When the competition was friendly, everybody would be receptive, and when it wasn't healthy, frankly it was hell. *Brain Salad Surgery* was created at a time when everyone was at their most receptive level, and it hadn't been easy getting there."

With lyrics provided by Lake and former King Crimson lyricist Pete Sinfield, the album offered a trip through a futuristic world of carnival sideshows and mechanized control, climaxing with an earth-shaking man-versus-machine battle given impetus through Emerson's wall of synths and Carl Palmer's forceful drumming. The overall performance was nearly manic as the trio rocketed from section to section at breakneck pace.

Emerson's multitude of keyboards gave him a rich palette to work with, his multitasking abilities camouflaging the fact that he was supported by just bass and drums.

Though it fell just a touch short in the length department—the album's main theme didn't kick off until the final nine minutes of side one, spilling over to take up all of side two—the band's performance of *Brain Salad Surgery* was unquestionably grand. Equally important, ELP maintained a consistent urgency that had flagged at times in the more obtuse waters of Yes' *Topographic Oceans* voyages.

"Wait another year, Utopia is here," vowed Todd Rundgren on *A Wizard, a True Star*, and the multihued one made good on his promise with *Todd Rundgren's Utopia* in 1974.

After releasing *Wizard*, Rundgren provided a futuristic, cold production to Hall and Oates' esoteric *War Babies* album, a collection of songs that was greeted with dismay by fans who expected more of the soft rhythm and blues with which the duo had established their career. His work with Hall and Oates complete, Todd hit the road with his newly formed Utopia, made up of a group of forward-thinking musicians from the axis around Bearsville Studios in upstate New York, where Todd crafted his studio wizardry.

Rundgren fans who filed into venues looking forward to the delectable pop craftsmanship of "I Saw the Light" and "Hello It's Me" from days of yore were instead confronted with a six-member band performing tracks like "Utopia Theme" and the thirty-plus-minute "The Ikon." Some audience members were willing to depart with Todd on his bold new sonic voyage; the others simply left.

On *Utopia*, the band confidently ran through a fascinating array of prog rock. The group's fourteen-minute theme song urges Todd's concept into lumbering reality, recorded live in Atlanta and powered by an insistent, dark force. Kevin Ellman, one of rock's finest percussionists, drives the piece hard with dexterous drumming throughout. Above the foundation of Ellman and bassist John Siegler, solos are traded between keyboardists Ralph Schuckett and Mark "Moogy" Klingman and the guitar of Rundgren. Todd makes the most of his opportunity to play, attacking with a fiery transcendence seldom captured on his studio recordings.

Roxy Music had relied on experimentalist Brian Eno in their early days, and in Utopia that role was played by a former monk named M. Frog Labat, who contributed an array of electronic textures to Utopia.

The green-tressed Frog had released his own experimental album, *Labat*, on Rundgren's Bearsville label in 1973. It was a strange and obscure work largely based on an esoteric concept involving the use of colors to program electronics and design sound synthesis. When Frog sang "We Are Crazy" on *Labat*, Todd's pop music fans weren't about to argue. In Utopia, Frog's domain was a huge, self-devised electronic console, the blinking bulk of which consumed much of the band's stage acreage.

The entire second side of *Utopia* was consumed by "The Ikon," a constantly evolving work that ranged from the pop sensibility so missed by Todd's traditionalist fans to full immersion in the thunderous fusion of bands like Return to Forever and Mahavishnu Orchestra. Not that Todd was all that concerned about what his fans—or ex-fans—thought of his creative actions.

"I never make records for the masses," Rundgren informed *Creem* magazine's Ben Edmonds in the November 1974 issue. "If the masses buy them, that's fine. But I actually expect that the more people buy them, the less people will understand them. Because people will begin to buy them out of habit, knee-jerk reaction. The more popular my records become, the less accessible I have to be, if only to make people question why they bought it in the first place."

A harsh assessment, but what else could be expected from a man who proved himself to be a true visionary of pop culture?

"See, the thing is that before long none of this will be so weird," Rundgren said of his own colored hair, accurately peering into the future. "Pretty soon kiddies will be pestering their parents . . . 'Aw, c'mon Mom, just a little purple on the side . . .'"

Though more conservative in appearance, the urgency of King Crimson's music matched that of Utopia and supported the British band's ascension to the status of prog rock royalty. A unique combination of power and grace characterized the three LPs released by the band in 1973 and 1974. Both *Larks' Tongues in Aspic* and *Starless and Bible Black* had established a potent aural formula: long passages of surprising beauty contrasted against abrasive fury. Those albums prepared listeners for the apex of King Crimson's output from this period. *Red*, released late in 1974, elevated King Crimson's music to such heights that it remains among the most successful of all experimentations with rock's form.

Beginning with the harsh instrumental title track, the sound of *Red* matched the cold and black technical aura of its cover artwork, art that on the rear simply showed an instrumentation gauge with its needle pegged to the right. Fripp's guitar tone was a nearly frightening force, pushed to the fore by Wetton's bass thundering up from the lower frequencies. Enmeshed within it all, the drums and percussion of Bruford pounded and skittered across the stereo spectrum, the tones of impact vividly captured. Produced by the band and engineered by Jimi Hendrix associate George Chkiantz, *Red* remains one of the best-recorded albums of rock's history, benefiting from both the clarity of the core instrumentation as well as more experimental techniques such as the reverse reverb handclaps that spill from the speakers as the band climbs to the climax of "One More Red Nightmare."

Critics of the day seemed uncertain just how to react when confronted with *Red*, although Ireland's *Belfast Telegraph* summed the album up quite efficiently: "Aggressive and loud enough to strip the wallpaper off your living room wall."

Having created a monumental album that stood victorious at the peak of the prog rock mountain—one whose influence imbues the work of modern bands such as Radiohead, Tool, Nine Inch Nails, and Fear Factory—Fripp promptly disbanded King Crimson, allegedly concerned that a civilization-wide disaster was imminent. Fripp stated that he would now be concentrating on ensuring his future survival by transforming himself into a "small, self-sufficient, mobile, intelligent unit."

If the dearly departed King Crimson had presented 1974 with progressive music at its most exhilarating, a far more earthy experimentation with traditional rhythms was coming from a vastly different source than the European classical influence—one that could not have been more different than Wakeman, Moraz, Emerson, and others of their ilk.

Whether Eric Clapton himself shared Robert Fripp's recently publicized opinion that Clapton's current work was "excessively tedious," the legendary guitarist was in fact searching for a new sound in 1974. Not surprisingly for a musician who cut his teeth on traditional blues and had recently been attracted to rural American sounds, Clapton steered clear of complex song cycles, artistic statements, and rock as a form of art. Instead, Clapton discovered the reggae of Bob Marley.

Marley, the son of a British Army captain and a Jamaican mother, began recording in Kingston, Jamaica in 1961. As the styles of Marley and his fellow Jamaican musicians developed, something entirely new emerged. Music that had been characterized by the sprightly dance hall sound of ska took on darker undertones and slowed its pace. The bass became the most prominent instrument, the rhythm loping, the other sonic elements creating a trance-inducing repetition enhanced by the musicians' fondness for smoking vast quantities of marijuana. This was reggae music.

Though Marley's 1972 album *Catch a Fire* garnered critical acclaim, both the singer and reggae music itself remained curiosities—until Eric Clapton heard Marley's "I Shot the Sheriff."

Clapton, once regularly referred to as "God" for his stunningly lyrical guitar abilities, had largely been a no-show in the 1970s. After the pressures of Cream led to that brilliant improvisational group's demise, Clapton's career floundered. He grew a beard and his appearance decayed from his glory days as a psychedelic trendsetter during Cream's peak months. And soon after the release of 1970's Derek and the Dominos *Layla* album, Eric virtually disappeared from the rock world. The reason was an addiction to heroin.

Like many people who fall under the sway of the drug, Clapton thought he could control a mere flirtation—until he realized he was dead wrong. Suddenly it became crystal clear to the guitarist why junkies act the way they do, and why they'll do anything—what ever it takes, no matter the consequences—to stay high. Clapton understood, because he himself had joined the decrepit ranks of the junkie.

After Pete Townshend helped set up a comeback concert in 1973 at London's Rainbow Theater, Clapton felt he had recovered enough from his drug problems to begin recording his first studio album in three years. His manager, Robert Stigwood, made the arrangements. Clapton insisted he wanted to work hard and make the most of his time, even though he entered the studio to begin the sessions with almost no new material. The album had to be constructed from the ground up.

Working with producer Tom Dowd at Criteria Recording Studios in Miami, Clapton recorded the Marley song he'd discovered, but had doubts that he and the American musicians had even come close to capturing the deceptively simple-sounding reggae aura. The resulting album, *461 Ocean Boulevard*, was nearly issued without the song.

"I didn't think we had it as good as Bob's version," Clapton later admitted. "I thought we'd prettied it up a lot, and just not done it justice. And that disturbed me to the point where I wasn't keen on having it on the album. I was overruled, and thank God I was because Bob, in fact, was one of the first people to say, 'Thank you.'"

Clapton presented reggae to the world on his highly publicized comeback album, and the listeners responded. "I Shot the Sheriff," authentic reggae or not, shot to number one on the American charts in July. The song reestablished Eric Clapton and opened the world's ears to Marley's music and to his revolutionary Third World message.

It was more proof that the rock world of 1974 was an amazing sonic stew of wild creativity, experimentation, and influences. There were artists creating rock operas, singers dancing their way to the apocalypse, prog rockers calculating musical measures, and ex-blues rockers swaying to island rhythms.

There was just one unanswered question: Didn't anyone want to rock for the pure enjoyment of rocking? Had the classic elements of big beats, loud guitars, and songs about girls and cars been lost to the ages?

In June, The Who settled in for a four-night stay at New York's Madison Square Garden. The shows sold out, with nearly 100,000 tickets sold in a matter of hours based on a single announcement. Despite the audience enthusiasm, the concerts were a nightmare for The Who. Even Pete Townshend, who had thrown heart and soul into *Quadrophenia*, felt as though he'd had enough. He'd overextended himself entirely, working with The Who, laboring with flamboyant director Ken Russell on a big-screen adaptation of *Tommy*, and helping Eric Clapton with his comeback concert in London.

Opening for The Who at the last of the disastrous Garden shows was a new California hard rock band, Montrose. Taking the stage with the enthusiasm that The Who were finding difficult to muster, Montrose blasted out tracks from their late 1973 debut album *Montrose* and its 1974 follow-up *Paper Money*. Many of the crowd had no idea who Montrose was, but their power was undeniable. Here at last was a basic, no-frills hard rock band.

Ronnie Montrose first came to prominence as guitarist for both Boz Scaggs and Van Morrison, playing gentler music on Morrison's classic *Tupelo Honey* album that was light-years removed from the kinetic energy he unleashed at Madison Square Garden several years later. When white-haired Texas bluesman Edgar Winter decided in 1972 to break up his rhythm and blues outfit White Trash and form a hard rock band, Montrose was recommended to Winter's manager Steve Paul. Montrose flew to New York, got the gig, and, as he puts it, got "my introduction to what we called 'coliseum rock,'" playing high-volume rock in cavernous arenas.

In early 1973, Ronnie left The Edgar Winter Group after playing on the album *They Only Come out at Night*. The record included the unlikely number-one instrumental smash "Frankenstein," a riff-heavy favorite with an instantly identifiable introduction. Ready to get back to work after his stint with Winter, Montrose set about the task of forming a new band.

"I'd been writing material for the next Edgar Winter Group album, but you either duke it out with fists and stick it out as a band or you split," Montrose recalled of his departure from the Edgar Winter Group. "I was just at a point where I needed to go out on my own and do my thing. I didn't have a clear vision, but I knew I wanted to go out and rock. Obviously, I was a huge Zeppelin fan, a Who fan, a Jeff Beck fan, a Deep Purple fan—all of those bands."

The lineup of the band that came to be known as Montrose fell into place as the guitarist found singer Sammy Hagar, drummer Denny Carmassi, and bassist Bill Church.

"Sammy Hagar had seen me with Edgar at Winterland with his band, and I put out the word that I was looking for a band and he called me up," Montrose said. "I went to see him, and Sammy knew Denny Carmassi and I had known Bill Church from Van Morrison's band. We put it together and there you have it."

Ronnie filled in for a few dates with Edgar Winter after "Frankenstein" began its chart climb, and suddenly labels were interested in the new Montrose band. A deal with Warner Brothers was signed, and Ted Templeman, producer of the Van Morrison sessions, agreed to produce the band with engineer Don Landee.

After a month of recording, the team emerged with *Montrose*. The eight songs were simple, almost blunt, but the band's sound was massive, the performances full of startling confidence. Over churning beds of power chords, Ronnie's solos spiraled with a sharp clarity, the rhythm section laying down a foundation that was formidable but nimble. And in 1974, a rock year of serious works based on assorted metaphysical musings, Hagar's lyrics about girls and cars sounded almost revolutionary.

The album was released bearing a cover photograph composed by Norman Seeff. Seeff, the "in" photographer of the moment, brought a fashion photography flair to rock subjects via his soft-focus imagery. The four Montrose men posed shirtless, the moody Seeff aura contrasted by retro-futuro lettering in harsh yellow and pink, looking as though the font had been lifted directly from the world of Flash Gordon.

Yes, the album looked modern, but more importantly it sounded modern. In an era when hard rock recordings often found instruments struggling to reach the surface of murky mixes, the *Montrose* recording lived and breathed. The bottom line was that *Montrose* was a very special high-energy rock album, one that set new standards in recording and served as a blueprint for all hard rock and heavy metal albums that would be crafted in the decades to come.

"As I look back at it," Ronnie says of the album, "an old band mate of mine, Mitchell Froom, who is a pretty successful producer, I mentioned to him, 'That first Montrose album sounds so basic and simple and raw. Sometimes I actually listen to a couple of songs and I sort of cringe, because it's just so junior as far as playing.' And Mitchell said, 'But the point is, all four of you were playing up to 100% of your ability. And when you do that, it can't be denied.' And that's the truth, and it was a very enlightening thing to hear from someone. When you're playing up to your ability, and you only know three chords, and you're giving it your all—that's it!"

Paper Money followed several months later, a record that reunited the production team of Templeman and Landee with the band. The album was notable not only for its thunderous new original songs "I Got the Fire" and "The Dreamer," but also for a moving arrangement of The Rolling Stones' "Connection." Though not as consistent as the flat-out fire and brimstone of its predecessor, the second album showed Montrose moving to expand its sound with a diversity of aural textures.

Though the band had built a foundation for further success, Montrose came to an end soon after their second album.

"Absolutely it was guitar player versus singer creative differences," Ronnie explained. "If we'd been like other guitar players and singers and duked it out we might actually have stayed together a little longer. But Sammy and I were both pretty hotheaded, and set in our ways about what we wanted."

Compared to the weighty ponderings of prog rock, the near-metal of Montrose sounded positively primitive. But there was a new band that made Montrose sound positively progressive. Their sound was stripped down, all excess chopped off and discarded. The band lived by the verse-chorus-verse-chorus-bridge-verse-chorus-end structure. They played loud and fast, and none of their songs lasted more than two minutes. They wore leather jackets and blue jeans. They all adopted the band name as their last names. They were The Ramones.

Singer Joey, guitarist Johnny, and drummer Tommy all grew up in the Forest Hills neighborhood of Queens, a borough of New York City. Bassist Dee Dee was a military brat who spent his youth in Germany but made it to Forest Hills in time for high school. All four of the future Ramones were fans of glam rock in the early 70s, and Joey even sang for a glam rock band called Sniper.

In Manhattan a scene had sprung up around The New York Dolls, the chaotic band that was as likely to wear makeup and women's clothing as they were to wear leather jackets.

"For me, it was like a new adventure," Joey Ramone said in the liner notes to the band's *Anthology* retrospective, "like something out of *A Clockwork Orange*—the crowd, the place, the way everybody looked. It was fun."

The four high school friends stayed in contact, running into each other in the revolving scene with The Dolls at its core. Realizing that the four of them had so much in common, the commitment to play was made, and The Ramones were born.

"Music was my salvation," the lanky Joey recalled. "When we started up in March of '74, it was because the bands we loved, the rock 'n' roll that we knew, had disappeared. We were playing music for ourselves."

As far as Joey was concerned, The Who of 1974 might as well not have existed. Though the band's early pop masterpieces were tremendously influential on the towering young Ramone, *Quadrophenia* was about as far removed from concise pop as you could get. So Joey and his friends took matters into their own hands.

On March 3, 1974, at a small showcase held at Performance Studio on East 20th Street in Manhattan, the Ramones played their first gig. The eight songs performed were "I Don't Wanna Go Down to the Basement," "I Don't Wanna Walk Around with You," "Now I Wanna Sniff Some Glue," "I Don't Wanna Be Learned," "I Want to be Tamed," "I Don't Wanna Get Involved with You," "I Don't Like Nobody that Don't Like Me," and

"Succubus." Clearly, the Ramones were not doing the kinds of songs favored by other rock bands.

Reaction from listeners was underwhelming, but The Ramones pressed on. Through a connection with the band Television, The Ramones managed to get booked by Hilly Kristal at his club, CBGB, in the depths of New York's decidedly unfashionable Bowery. CBGB stood for Country, Bluegrass, and Blues, but Kristal had been forced to go the rock route. Television had been playing at his club since early in 1974, and The Ramones made their first appearance on the CBGB stage on August 16, 1974.

"They were the most untogether band I'd ever heard," said Kristal. "They kept starting and stopping—equipment breaking down—and yelling at each other. They were a mess."

Despite Kristal's misgivings, The Ramones played CBGB more than twenty times the rest of the year. They were on their way.

The impact of these events would not be felt until the release of the first Ramones album in 1976, but when that impact came, it would amount to a seismic shift in the continents of the rock world. In 1974, though, the band's very existence and their residency at a seedy New York club served as a distant early warning, the first manifestation of Pete Townshend's vision in "The Punk Meets the Godfather."

If Pete Townshend truly saw storm clouds on the rock horizon in 1974, he was the only one. In fact, rock star excess and ego gratification had reached new lows.

Now Beatle-free, John Lennon frequently made the news, not for music but for idiotic drunken behavior in Los Angeles, where he had retreated while taking a break from his relationship with Yoko Ono. Lennon caroused with fellow Brits Keith Moon and Ringo Starr, and was often seen stumbling about with songwriter Harry Nilsson. At a Smothers Brothers show at the Troubadour nightclub, Lennon was ejected after repeatedly—and loudly—informing fellow patrons, "I'm John Lennon!" while modeling a sanitary napkin on his head.

In June, funk rock visionary Sly Stone decided it was time to marry his girlfriend, Kathy Silva. Milking the waning remains of superstardom, he booked the perfect romantic setting: Madison Square Garden arena in New York. By October, Silva had filed for divorce.

In August, the lead singer of The J. Geils Band, Peter Wolf, married actress superstar Faye Dunaway. When the first album by The J. Geils Band—a recording that marked a thrilling and gritty reinterpretation of urban rhythm and blues—was released in 1970, the band looked, to be kind, like a bunch of thugs. To imagine that just four years later their lead singer, known for his crazed antics on stage, would be marrying Hollywood royalty was the kind of bizarre tale that only made sense in the 1970s.

Other bands, though, were keeping their heads down and noses to the grindstone as they labored away on the endless concert trail.

Foghat was a band formed by refugees from Savoy Brown, a seminal blues-rock band known both for their music and for their myriad personal shifts. Guitarist "Lonesome" Dave Peverett, drummer Roger Earl, and bassist Tony Stevens discovered guitarist Rod Price and set about establishing themselves by hitting the road—hard. It was a process that never ended; in fact, Foghat was known to play more than 300 gigs per year at their peak—often taming restless crowds as an opening act on multiband arena tours, one of the most thankless gigs in showbiz.

Energized was the band's 1974 release, a third album that faithfully captured Foghat's high-octane blues-and-boogie sound. An accomplished slide and lead guitarist, Price crafted ever-intensifying solos over the band's unified churn, and on tracks like the furious cover of Big Joe Turner's "Honey Hush" that launched *Energized*, there was no band that rocked harder than Foghat.

Treading a similar path was Irish guitarist Rory Gallagher. Having formed the power trio Taste in London late in the 1960s, Gallagher released his self-titled solo debut in 1970. An endless succession of performances and increasingly strong albums were giving Gallagher solid career momentum in 1974.

Gallagher kept his music firmly rooted in the blues, and though songs like "Tattoo'd Lady" and "Livin' Like a

Trucker"—both anchors of his 1973 *Tattoo* album—were Gallagher's own, their roots were clearly showing.

Although *Tattoo* was in large part a potent album, in the studio the selection of less-than-stellar material can drag an album down. On stage, a go-for-the-throat attitude can transcend mediocre material. Thus, a merely listenable song like *Tattoo*'s "Who's That Comin'" became something else entirely on Rory's *Irish Tour '74*.

Gallagher's double live album captured the guitarist doing what he did best: powering through an incendiary set of hard-driving blues and rock, recorded in front of a lustily cheering mob of his countrymen. Bearing his battered-but-trusty Fender Stratocaster, Gallagher attacked the opening "Cradle Rock." From the first notes, Rory ushered volleys of harmonics and complex, fiery blues runs voiced in the Strat's characteristic bite before bearing down with killer instinct on the song's slide guitar solo. It stands as one of the most electrifying of live album openers, and Rory's faithful road band of bassist Gerry McAvoy, drummer Rod De'Ath, and keyboardist Lou Martin ensured that there was no letup throughout the entire live album.

While Gallagher and Foghat worked the road, other musicians were tempering their creative fires with a keen business sense. Led Zeppelin, under guidance from their brutal but brilliant manager, Peter Grant, demanded that Atlantic Records allow them to start their own label. With Zeppelin being one of the major superstar bands, Atlantic had little choice but to agree. Swan Song Records became the new home of Led Zeppelin as well as any acts that they or Grant felt had commercial potential.

Singer Paul Rodgers approached Grant about a new project he was assembling and, well aware of Rodgers' reputation as one of England's top vocalists, the savvy manager was interested in learning more about the musician's concept. Rodgers had just suffered through the painful decline of Free, one of England's greatest hard rock quartets, watching as his band was destroyed by personal differences and the descent into addiction of brilliant guitarist Paul Kossoff.

"Free was a creative and dynamic band and my first taste of success," Rodgers remembered in the liner notes to *The "Origi-*

nal" Bad Co. Anthology. "I was sad that it had ended in such a substance-induced haze. Coming out of that experience, I wanted a band where all the members were very together. I also wanted a band with strong management."

In other words, Rodgers wanted a band that would operate like a solid business. Joining with former Mott the Hoople guitarist Mick Ralphs, retaining drummer Simon Kirke from Free, and adding Boz Burrell on bass, Rodgers formed Bad Company. Burrell was yet another former member of King Crimson; there were nearly as many of them as there were ex-Savoy Brown members.

The band's debut on Swan Song met with instant popularity, and a rock audience conditioned to salivate over supergroups ever since Cream and Traffic merged in 1969 to form Blind Faith duly pushed *Bad Company* into the sales stratospheres. The debut and its follow-ups *Straight Shooter* and *Run with the Pack* had their moments of solid, if not mind-bending, guitar rock, but Bad Company never hit the emotional peaks of Free or matched the edge-of-chaos excitement that characterized Mott the Hoople. They were a band that almost sounded like a business. In an ironic turn, when Bad Company reformed in 2000 with all of its original members, business-oriented squabbles over the years resulted in the foursome no longer owning the rights to their own name. They were forced to tour under the lawyer-approved moniker The "Original" Bad Company.

Late in 1974, Bob Dylan was again at work in the studio. Though his reunion with The Band early in the year had yielded little more than huge concert grosses and a mediocre album, Dylan's full creative genius was about to be revealed once again.

"Everybody works in the shadow of what they're previously done," Dylan noted. "But you have to overcome that."

Blood on the Tracks, released in January 1975, was an intensely personal album, leaving the sweeping statements and social critiques of the young Bob Dylan far in the past. The insightful narratives of the album revealed a cast of real characters, people who had pasts and enduring relationships, lingering conflicts and hesitant loves that carried through the years. The album's songs—from the regret of "Tangled Up in Blue" to the bitter realizations of "Idiot Wind"—found Dylan communicating in fascinating detail stories that had beginnings, middles, and sometimes ends. Often as not, though, the songs faded out, leaving no clear resolution of the story line in their wake. It was up to the listener to imagine where the path sketched by Dylan might lead. The setting for these dramas was an intricate nest of acoustic instruments driven forward by restrained drumming, but the fact that Dylan could draw people into such intimate worlds was a testament to his incredible skill as a lyricist, and *Blood on the Tracks* stands as one of his greatest achievements.

Nearly as intriguing as Dylan's new work was the music of England's Nick Drake. The singer-songwriter had crafted a series of involved, introspective songs, heard to most arresting effect on 1972's *Pink Moon*. The accompaniment consisted largely of Drake's soft voice, recorded with unflinching clarity by influential British folk producer Joe Boyd, set to Drake's own acoustic guitar adjusted to tunings of his invention. But Drake was a deeply troubled young man, fearful of live performances, slowing sinking into the very depths given vision in his songs.

On November 26, 1974, Nick Drake died of an overdose of the medication he was taking for his depression. While artists like Foghat and Rory Gallagher thrived in the trenches of the rock wars, others like Drake and Pink Floyd's Syd Barrett were fragile souls, all too easily consumed in the name of rock music.

With the year drawing to a close, it was apparent that groups like the rather nondescript Bad Company symbolized a slow process of watering down that was taking an inexorable toll on rock music. Bands were becoming hesitant to carve new trails, deciding instead to comfortably follow the well-worn paths of those who had gone before.

Even The Rolling Stones, still without question one of the biggest acts in the rock world, began to appear as mere parodies of their most creative era. In a video for their new album late in 1974, the band appeared in natty white sailor suits, prancing about while miming to their new single, "It's Only Rock and Roll." The cavalier attitude implied in the song title carried over into their performances, so much so that in December, guitarist Mick Taylor quit the band.

"I have nothing but admiration for the group, but I feel now is the time to move on and do something new," Taylor said at the time, planning to start his own supergroup with former Cream bassist and vocalist Jack Bruce. The new band never released an album.

"He obviously has a lot of troubles—personal problems—but they're nothing to do with us," was Mick Jagger's reserved response to the exit of the band's lead guitarist, as reported in the British music newspaper *Melody Maker*. "I don't even know the true nature of them. I suppose it was a bit inconsiderate of him . . . "

That Jagger seemed unaware of any dissatisfaction within the band demonstrated the isolation and polarity that characterized the Stones in this period. Albums were cobbled together by overdubbing selections from a grab bag of partially completed songs recorded in studios around the world, and the core members of the band rarely were together in the same place at the same time. The jet set glamour life clearly did not agree with Taylor, a working musician who needed to play. Ron Wood, the talented guitarist of The Faces, a band known as much for their boozing as their music, was pleased to take Taylor's place in "The Greatest Rock and Roll Band in the World."

It's only rock and roll? Maybe. But as 1974 ended, there were a growing number of kids who saw The Rolling Stones and all the superstar bands as arrogant, out-of-touch dinosaurs. Their dissatisfaction would become the meteor that would threaten to wipe the rock dinosaurs from the musical landscape.

It would take more than a year, but the collision course was set.

1975

6

Calm before the Storm

"I can't really comment on just why we broke so big in the States," Led Zeppelin's guitarist and creative visionary Jimmy Page told *Creem* magazine's Nick Kent in 1974. "I can only think that we were aware of dynamics at a time when everyone was into that drawn-out West Coast style of playing."

American rock fans had indeed gone wild over Led Zeppelin, ecstatic about the band's high-volume, three-hour live sets that had become a staple of the stadium circuit. Proof of that came on January 7, 1975, when three Zeppelin shows booked at New York's Madison Square Garden went on sale. All three concerts sold out in a matter of minutes. Things did not go as smoothly further up the Atlantic seaboard, as thousands of anxious fans milled about in the freezing cold outside Boston Gardens waiting to buy their own tickets for Led Zeppelin's just-announced appearance. No one is sure exactly what sparked the incident, but within moments the crowd turned into an unruly mob, causing thousands of dollars worth of damage in a mindless, destructive frenzy.

Regardless of the Boston chaos, Led Zeppelin's American tour in early 1975 was one of rock's hottest tickets, the entire series of dates selling out instantly. And though there was no arguing the band was huge in the United States, their popularity was just as great overseas. It is likely that, at the dawn of 1975, Led Zeppelin was the biggest rock group in the world.

Not that one would have realized it, judging by the naysaying of most rock critics. In their oft-stated opinions, Led Zeppelin was little more than distasteful hard rock, with Robert Plant's ear-splitting caterwauling ceremoniously plopped atop the cacophony. The writers insisted the band's concerts did little more than placate legions of Quaalude-swallowing, whiskey-and-wine-swilling cretins, a vulgar audience that filled the soulless hockey rinks and municipal auditoriums of the United States—and Led Zeppelin was more to be blamed for the group's low-rent audiences than praised for their music.

The very fact that Led Zeppelin appealed to a lowest-common-denominator audience was in itself exceedingly curious. Beginning with 1973's *Houses of the Holy*, the band had become as concerned with texture and atmosphere as with blues riffs pumped through thousands of watts of amplification. By the time their newest album, *Physical Graffiti*, was released in February 1975, the change was even more pronounced. Once, the music of Led Zeppelin had been obvious—they were either heavy or acoustic. But with *Physical Graffiti* they delved into the myriad shadings that Page's guitar skills and John Paul Jones' keyboard and arranging talents made possible. It was as if they'd just become aware of a vast aural landscape stretching out before them, and with confidence they'd set out to explore it. The result of the expedition was one of the landmark albums of the decade.

The album packaging itself—building photography with cutout windows that changed views depending on how the contents were inserted—symbolized the musical diversity contained within. Though the album had its share of concussive rock in the presence of songs like "Sick Again" and "In My Time of Dying," those tracks were countered by the unusual time signatures, sweeping arrangements, and global influences of the hypnotic "Kashmir" and "In the Light."

"To be able to fuse all these styles was always my dream in the early stages," Page stated at the time, as recounted in the liner notes to the *Led Zeppelin* box set, "but now the composing side of it is just as important."

Nowhere was that more true than in "Ten Years Gone," a moving near-ballad that anchored the third side of *Physical*

Graffiti. Above rhythm guitars sketching the song's chord composition, other guitars rise to the surface for mere seconds then
depart, leaving shimmering arpeggios in their wake. Page's
solo on the song is one of his most effectual, given solid impetus through Bonham's responsive drumming.

Even on the album's basic guitar-bass-drums songs, such as
the rumbling, deeply syncopated "The Rover," rather than
chasing riffs with single-minded determination the band
demonstrated they had truly learned how to swing. Very heavily, of course, but they were swinging nevertheless.

"Usually, we'd start with the framework, we'd lay down the
tracks and Robert would do a guide vocal," Page noted of the
band's approach to their more fundamental songs. "I would
then overlay lots of different guitars, and then Robert would
come in and do a final vocal."

Though Page did have a favored Gibson Les Paul for his
stage work, in the studio his experimentations with sounds
gave each song a dramatically different timbre than the ones
that surrounded it, inspiring Plant to virtually reinvent his vocal approach for *Physical Graffiti*. Combined with Jones' more
scholarly contributions and Bonham's force-of-nature attack,
Led Zeppelin at the time of *Physical Graffiti* was one of rock's
most potent and experimental bands—regardless of what the
rock critics said.

Quite naturally, most hard rock bands of the mid-1970s
would have killed for even one-tenth of Led Zeppelin's popularity in the massive American market. But that audience could
be a fickle one. Though they quickly embraced Golden Earring's propulsive, percussive hit "Radar Love," the American
listeners soon hung the Netherlanders out to dry, leaving the
remainder of the band's material to fall on deaf ears.

Scottish quartet Nazareth also flirted with one-hit-wonder
status after the seminal power ballad "Love Hurts" laid the
groundwork for a new genus of song, one that matched lyrics
about love and heartbreak with ballad pacing and heavy gui-

tars. But that one song wasn't representative of the heady and powerful hard rock found on their 1975 album *Hair of the Dog*. That fact, combined with a burgeoning touring schedule, contributed to the band moving more than one million copies of their album.

Nazareth guitarist Manny Charlton was a fleet-fingered, inventive player, heard to best effect on *Hair of the Dog's* "Changin' Times." In its early moments, the song was in large part a spiritual cousin of the hulking opening track of Led Zeppelin's fourth album, "Black Dog." But eventually Nazareth veered off into an extended vamp finale, providing Charlton a shining opportunity to show his stuff.

Nazareth was helping lay the groundwork for all the heavy metal bands that were yet to come, but they were far from alone. Among their compatriots, Rainbow was doing their part as well.

On May 21, 1975, Deep Purple's testy guitarist Ritchie Blackmore left the band, handing over guitar duties to Tommy Bolin and recruiting leather-lunged wailer Ronnie James Dio to join him in Rainbow—or Ritchie Blackmore's Rainbow as they were initially known.

"I am a brilliant guitarist," Blackmore humbly acknowledged in 1975. "I know I can blow any other guitarist that's around today off the stage."

Fortunately, Rainbow had more going for them than just Blackmore's sizable ego. Removed from the competition for attention among Deep Purple's instrumentalists, Ritchie set himself squarely in Rainbow's spotlight—where he didn't hesitate to show off his blazing, truly inspired guitar work. Blackmore's classical leanings meshed well with the band's gothic-themed material, crafting an influential aura that would settle over much of heavy metal in the years to come.

Drummer Cozy Powell was an impressive percussionist who had departed the Jeff Beck Group to join Rainbow—in the process trading in one temperamental guitarist for another—after briefly trying to get his own Bedlam project off the ground. Powell knew he was in for a hard time amidst Blackmore's booming amplification, and he had taken appropriate action.

"I use Ludwig 3-S sticks which are extra heavy, the heaviest ones you can get," Powell revealed to *Creem* magazine's Dave

Patrick. "Basically, I've been playing pretty hard for a long time and since I've been with Ritchie, who plays particularly loud, it's become even more so. To compete with all the fuggin' amplification that the band uses I've got to play really hard. I've always used a big kit and big sticks anyway . . . I'm just a basher, really. That's all there is to it. I just hit 'em rather than tickle 'em."

Powell's former employer, Jeff Beck, had undergone a period of serious reinvention since scuttling both the final incarnation of The Jeff Beck Group and the short-lived power trio Beck, Bogert, Appice. Although Ritchie Blackmore was still quite content to strut about on stage dressed in black medieval finery, Beck felt that his music was maturing beyond the most obvious pretensions of rock stardom.

"Back in the old days, I used to just bash about on stage all the time," Beck reflected to Gordon Fletcher in the August 1975 issue of *Creem* magazine. "I had the urge to kill when I went out there and I really believed in acting it out. Now I'm much more conscious of what I'm doing and how important it is that I play really well."

Beck proved that his new attitude was more than just talk on his 1975 album *Blow by Blow*. Produced by The Beatles' longtime creative producer, George Martin, the album was one of the first successful attempts by a rock guitarist to create a cohesive instrumental album, one that consisted of strong arrangements rather than endless jamming. On tracks like "Diamond Dust" and Stevie Wonder's "Cause We've Ended as Lovers," Beck unleashed a radical new approach to his craft, still utilizing the aggressive runs that had powered The Yardbirds and The Jeff Beck Group but filtering them through a new respect for melodicism.

What had caused Beck's reevaluation of his style? It may have simply been a case of his sphere of influences broadening beyond the incestuous rock world. He had turned in a guest star role on Wonder's *Talking Book* album, and Jeff's rendition of "Cause We've Ended as Lovers" was dedicated to the wildly talented Roy Buchanan, whose style delicately pervaded the track.

If *Blow by Blow* had a flaw, it was found in its core instrumentation, accompaniment that at its worst imbued Beck with an overly smooth jazz ambience that might be described as "fusion lite." Keyboardist Max Middleton relied on a Fender Rhodes piano throughout, one of the most identifiable sounds of the 1970s. And with "disco" dance music beginning to dominate the pop charts in 1975, drummer Richard Bailey overused a litany of standard beats and accents with roots that are indelibly disco, binding an otherwise virtuoso percussion performance to a specific time frame in musical history. Still, Beck's undeniable flair and the tones of his guitars—on *Blow by Blow*, the holy guitar trinity of Gibson Les Paul, Fender Stratocaster, and Fender Telecaster—rise above the quibbles.

"*Blow by Blow* marked an important change in my life," Beck explained to Chris Gill in *Guitar World* magazine. "I was exploring an entirely different direction, but it came together almost by accident. I had always fed off of singers or guitar riffs before . . . It was like starting over again, like I had never played the guitar before."

Meanwhile, Carlos Santana was also starting over in the wake of his self-named band's dissolution and a disappointing album recorded with John McLaughlin. While Santana regrouped in 1975, his record label in Europe and Japan released *Lotus*, a three-record documentation of the New Santana Band at a 1973 concert in Osaka, Japan. Although the music did have its moments—the album captured Carlos during a phase of brittle tones and fiery note flurries—*Lotus* was most intriguing for its packaging. The word "elaborate" failed to convey the full glory of the album's artwork. The European and Japanese Santana fans—and those in the United States who purchased the album as an import—needed a fair expanse of real estate if they wished to view the album packaging in its entirety. At full extension, *Lotus* measured more than three feet in height and nearly seven and a half feet in length.

In 1973, President Richard Nixon had been driven from the presidency in disgrace as the fallout from the political debacle known as Watergate settled over Washington. Soon thereafter, the United States' leader in 1975, Gerald Ford, pardoned Nixon, thereby ensuring that the former president would endure no criminal penalties.

President Ford's pardoning skills might also have proved useful at Columbia Records, where certainly someone should have been held accountable for signing Pavlov's Dog to a multialbum recording contract. Though their debut, *Pampered Menial*, featured packaging that relied heavily on the beautiful mid-1800s engravings of Robert Vernon, contained within the album's vinyl grooves was a rather terrifying mishmash of styles ranging from heavy guitar riffing to Broadway show tune preening. This was one 1970s rock experiment that was doomed to failure. Overly dramatic to the extreme, the album was made even more alarming by the vocals of David Surkamp, whose howling pitch and affectations likely would have proven distressing to the dogs featured so prominently in Vernon's etchings.

To call Pavlov's Dog an acquired taste would be entirely accurate. And not many fans developed that taste, for after a second album, *At the Sound of the Bell*, the group returned to the kennel.

Curiously, Pavlov's Dog had been taken under the wing of Murray Krugman and Sandy Pearlman, the producers of one of the strongest and most creative bands of the mid-1970s, Blue Oyster Cult.

Originally signed as an "American Black Sabbath," after their first two albums, *Blue Oyster Cult* and *Tyranny and Mutation*, the New York band hit its stride with *Secret Treaties*. Their third album was a complex one, rooted solidly in hard rock while revealing a diverse array of moods. Based loosely on Pearlman's interest in a self-conceived "secret science," the album's lyrics were obscure. Its musical performance was not.

Blue Oyster Cult differentiated themselves from their contemporaries in a number of ways. The keyboards of Allen Lanier gave the band a unique dimension, one that emerged to support vocalist Eric Bloom when atmosphere was required more than brawn. Albert Bouchard was an impressive drummer, with a swinging touch that rode freely in tandem with his brother Joseph's bass. The Blue Oyster Cult rhythm section had a light, nimble feel that presented a totally different vibe than the plodding pounders that had become commonplace in hard rock. The brothers Bouchard could afford to approach the band's music in such manner, as the Cult's arsenal included guitarist Donald "Buck Dharma" Roeser. Roeser was nothing less than a stunning lead guitarist, skilled at unleashing spiraling descents down the fret board. More importantly, though, he never lost sight of the fact that solos have a duty to contribute to the dramatic impact of songs, and Roeser's work on *Secret Treaties* songs like "Flaming Telepaths" and "Cagey Cretins" stands among the titans in the storied history of rock guitar.

In 1975 a concert recording, *On Your Feet or On Your Knees*, presented ten tracks culled from The Blue Oyster Cult's three albums to date, supplemented by stampeding takes on the Yardbirds' "Maserati GT (I Ain't Got You)" and Steppenwolf's "Born to be Wild." The band was captured at their live peak on the double album. Though the group would continue to gain commercial acceptance with *Agents of Fortune* and *Spectres* later in the decade, The Blue Oyster Cult was at their creative zenith in 1975.

Other rock artists were seeking to recapture the glory of days gone by. Drummer Ginger Baker was back from Africa, with not a single afro-jazz note to be heard in his newest project, The Baker Gurvitz Army.

One thing was clear from the band's self-titled debut album, released early in 1975—they could use some assistance vocally. So by the time the group recorded *Elysian Encounter* later in 1975, vocalist Snips—late of the newly defunct Sharks—was enlisted as front-man. There he joined Baker, keyboardist Peter Lemer, and the brothers Gurvitz—Adrian and Paul—from the band Gun, on guitar and bass respectively.

Elysian Encounter tracks like "Time" and "People" were the most successful for the band, given a modern hard rock arrangement and powered by Baker's most flamboyant and aggressive drumming since the demise of Cream. It was a welcome return to hard-hitting form for one of rock's greatest musicians.

But the existence of Baker Gurvitz Army was to be a short one. Even the talents of Emerson, Lake, and Palmer associate Eddie Offord, who produced the group's 1976 album *Hearts on*

Fire, couldn't entice rock fans into enlisting in The Army, and Baker, characteristically, was soon following the trail of more adventurous musical pursuits.

For Alice Cooper, 1975 was a year to start over. The decay that had taken root within the Alice Cooper group during their demanding *Billion Dollar Babies* tour had begun with band disapproval over guitarist Glen Buxton's substance abuse and sloppy performances. That had spiraled into distrust and ego-driven accusations, barbs traded among all five of the band members. After recording a final album, *Muscle of Love*, the longtime friends from Phoenix went their separate ways.

The core of the band adopted the name Billion Dollar Babies, recording one poorly received album of the same name before dissolving. Meanwhile, Alice Cooper was busy planning his solo debut.

When Cooper returned to the studio, once again he did so with Bob Ezrin producing. As Ezrin had done to complement Lou Reed's *Berlin* sessions, he called on guitarists Steve Hunter and Dick Wagner to serve as the anchors of Cooper's new project. Cooper was already familiar with Hunter and Wagner, the duo having served as musical pinch-hitters on parts of *Muscle of Love*.

Alice's goal was to produce something of a concept album, one that would easily translate into his next stage extravaganza. The result was *Welcome to My Nightmare*, an album that sustained Cooper's aura of horror while dressing it up with the professional virtuosity of Hunter and Wagner.

Across the Atlantic, Paul Kossoff, the virtuoso guitarist of Free, was also reexamining his career. Emerging from the wreckage of years of self-abuse, Koss rallied to record his first solo album, *Back Street Crawler*, in 1973. Though he was joined by drummer Alan White of Yes and Free-mates Simon Kirke, Tetsu Yamauchi, and Rabbit Bundrick for the solo album, Kossoff soon decided it would be best to form another full-time band. Retaining the title of his solo debut, he christened the new group Back Street Crawler, and their recording, *The Band Plays On*, was released to a curious rock world in 1975.

From the first notes of the album, it certainly sounded as though the old Koss was back. The guitarist unleashed a brief but confident intro that assertively displayed many of his

Jo Jo Gunne was one of the true road warriors of 1970s rock, their first three albums fueled by guitarist **Matt Andes**' powerful touch. Shortly before the band's demise, Andes tired of the road and yielded his slot on stage to John Staehely.

Jefferson Airplane crash landed for good in 1973; lead singer **Marty Balin** had bailed out months earlier. But in 1974 he reunited with key members of the band—including Grace Slick and Paul Kantner—as Jefferson Starship, pursuing a less-revolutionary path to the top of the pop charts.

More than once **Ritchie Blackmore** of Deep Purple and Rainbow was quoted regarding the high esteem in which he held his own talent. The thing was, he was justified in doing so. Bringing classical scales and an intensely disciplined style to hard rock, Blackmore's influence was seismic on the next generation of heavy metal guitarists.

Marc Bolan of T. Rex demonstrates a classic rock star hip dip. Bolan was slogging it out on the road in the United States, in an attempt to generate the same "Bolanmania" that greeted T. Rex in their homeland of the United Kingdom. The campaign was only partially successful.

Nearing the end of his career as Ziggy Stardust, **David Bowie** sings "Rock 'n' Roll Suicide" in February 1973. Within five months, Bowie would retire The Spiders from Mars as his backing band—and supposedly retire from rock entirely.

Looking as though they'd just stepped off a Martian transport, **David Bowie** and Mick Ronson were the incandescent focus of Bowie's revolutionary Ziggy Stardust era. Revolution would be a constant of Bowie's career, while Ronson followed a less flamboyant musician's path until his death from cancer in 1993.

Jack Bruce and Leslie West *(see caption for West, Bruce, & Laing)*

*Drummer **Bill Bruford** has had one of modern music's most intriguing careers, bringing his technically challenging percussion to rock's most influential progressive bands. At various points in the decade, Bruford manned the drums for Yes, King Crimson, and Genesis.*

Mick Jones and the late Joe Strummer display the riveting intensity that was the hallmark of **the Clash** *in concert. Where many other bands simply went through the motions, the Clash played every show like they meant it. There was no questioning their commitment to their vision.*

Joe Cocker *lurches onward through another arena show. In the wake of a riveting performance at 1969's Woodstock festival and the hugely successful* Mad Dogs and Englishmen *grouping, the great British blues singer's stardom was assured.*

Phil Collins models rather unusual stage attire during a Genesis concert. It's 1976, singer Peter Gabriel has left the band, and Collins has been forced to abandon his refuge behind the drums to take over front man duties.

Parents who reacted in horror to the antics of Marilyn Manson in the 1990s must have forgotten all about the original master of morbid mayhem, **Alice Cooper**. Seen here on the massive Billion Dollar Babies tour in 1973, Cooper and his band set new standards for elaborate rock staging—all the better to frame electrocutions, hangings, snake handling, and general high-volume chaos.

The vitriol that seethed at the heart of **Elvis Costello**'s early material was unleashed on stage here in 1978 as the singer and his Attractions undertook their first major U.S. tour.

The Who's **Roger Daltrey** became one of rock's most enduring front men. His no-nonsense style was a diametrical contrast to the flamboyant parading of Mick Jagger and Robert Plant's occasionally feminine posturing.

Though the Kinks had become known for near-perfect pop songs that communicated a distinctly British atmosphere, **Ray Davies** saw the emerging complexity of rock in the 1970s as the opportunity to unleash character-driven works functioning as musicals. But where a musical often takes up residence in a single theater, the Kinks took their shows on the road.

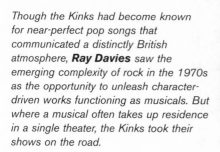

State-of-the-art concert amplification as demonstrated by **Emerson, Lake, and Palmer** in 1972. Unlike modern concert sound systems, which are usually "flown" from arena ceilings, in the 1970s the speakers were just piled up on the stage—assuring those in the front rows ringing ears the next day.

Bryan Ferry sways under the influence of his moody, cosmopolitan music. As the suave front man of Roxy Music, Ferry abandoned an early taste for pseudo-rockabilly stylings in favor of fashionable looks that matched his songs' troubled, dark elegance.

*The mind boggles at how many stages **Foghat** set foot upon throughout the 1970s. At their peak, the British group performed well over 300 gigs per year, many as an opening act on countless package tours following the rock trail across the United States.*

*Bearing a battered old Fender Stratocaster that seemingly bore witness to every stage its owner had conquered, Ireland's **Rory Gallagher** crafted music that was deeply rooted in blues. The simplicity of the genre let Gallagher's stunning talent shine.*

*1970s rock in full flight as **Hot Tuna** engages the audience at Philadelphia's 20,000-seat Spectrum in 1972. The no-frills staging of the Jefferson Airplane spin-off would soon give way to an ideal of giant sets and elaborate pyrotechnics.*

*After recording several pop-oriented songs produced by Nick Lowe, **Chrissie Hynde** aligned her Pretenders with producer Chris Thomas—who had worked with Bill Price to create the monumental sound of the Sex Pistols' debut album—for a batch of harder-edged material. Hynde's band was propelled to stardom by the momentum of that creative alliance.*

Joe Walsh and Dale Peters of **The James Gang** *in 1971, just after the release of the album* Thirds. *This would be Walsh's last tour with the band before departing to indulge in a solo career. Later, in 1976, he would join the Eagles to participate in the creation of one of the biggest selling rock albums of all time,* Hotel California.

Armed with a flute and a charismatic personality, **Jethro Tull** *leader Ian Anderson stalks the stage as guitarist Martin Barre concentrates on the increasingly complex Tull canon of 1975.*

*Paul Barrere and Lowell George bear down on one of **Little Feat**'s extended instrumental breaks. Though Little Feat took the liberty of stretching out in performance, the band's status as accomplished musicians ensured forward musical momentum was a concert constant.*

*While other guitarists concentrated on bludgeoning riffage or fleet-fingered displays of scale runs, **Phil Manzanera** pursued a path of tonal discovery and experimentation. His tasteful use of guitar effects ensured a distinctive sound for Roxy Music.*

John McLaughlin launches a volley of cerebral guitar explorations as the Mahavishnu Orchestra takes flight in 1971. Typical for the wild variety of 1970s concert bills, on this night the virtuoso Orchestra shared the stage with the jazz/blues of former John Mayall sidemen Mark-Almond and the glittery vamping of T. Rex.

Anyone who saw **Freddie Mercury** on stage with Queen knew they were seeing him in the environment he was born to inhabit. Simply put, Mercury was a star, and the fact that his huge character was graced by an astonishing voice simply made him all the more larger than life. Rock suffered a deep loss with the singer's death in 1992.

"The Animal Trainer and the Toad" was a self-penned description of the relationship between bassist Felix Pappalardi and guitarist Leslie West, a partnership that resulted in some of the heaviest hard rock in music history. Pappalardi had witnessed first-hand the tensions that destroyed Cream, and was determined to steer **Mountain** around the pitfalls.

Gary Brooker, Mick Grabham, and Keith Reid of **Procol Harum** *are joined by the author for a radio interview conducted for WVBU-FM, in a dressing room of Philadelphia's Tower Theater in 1974.*

The lead guitar position in many bands in the 1970s seemed to be equipped with a revolving door. Mick Grabham, seen here digging deep mid-solo in 1974, followed Robin Trower and Dave Ball in **Procol Harum**. His approach to the instrument was creatively the best fit of the three guitarists who held the job for the British band.

Today **Lou Reed** is revered as a voice of the New York arts community, but in 1972 he was out on the arena circuit like everyone else in the rock world. Here Reed tours in support of Transformer, the album produced by David Bowie and Mick Ronson.

*Guitarists Billy Bremner and Dave Edmunds with Nick Lowe on bass comprised the front line of **Rockpile**, but Lowe's greatest contribution to rock in the 1970s came via his production talents. He helped establish the careers of a diverse range of acts including the Damned, Graham Parker and the Rumour, and Elvis Costello and the Attractions.*

*While David Bowie turned on fey charm in his role of Ziggy Stardust, guitarist **Mick Ronson** was all blunt muscle—even if he was clothed in state-of-the-fashion glam attire. Ronson's barely-in-control lead guitar heroics supercharged Bowie tours through 1973.*

Both as a musician and as a producer, **Todd Rundgren** was a crucial element in shaping the character of 1970s rock music. Fascinated by the creative potential of technology, Rundgren became one of the first musicians to embrace video and computer graphics as the 1970s yielded to the 1980s, and he was a pioneer in music-oriented Internet utilization. Todd occasionally emerges from his home base in Hawaii for tours.

As UFO's lead guitarist, **Michael Schenker** could barely speak English. But with his imposing playing speed and wide-ranging knowledge of scales, the German guitarist forced hard rock guitar into new realms of technical expertise.

As rock grew louder and larger, **Paul Simon** and his vocalist partner Art Garfunkel entered the decade of the 1970s contrasting their chart competition with a carefully-crafted "less is more" approach. Simon's subtle guitar speaks volumes, but requires listening to discover its nuances.

*The author seems pleased to meet **Grace Slick**, while Slick seems pleased to be on tour with Jefferson Starship. The offshoot of Jefferson Airplane found greater commercial success by toning down the political rhetoric that characterized the final flights of the Airplane.*

*Shortly after the release of Easter, **The Patti Smith Group** ascended to the levels of popularity inhabited by rock's biggest stars. But Patti never lost sight of what it was like to be a true fan of rock music, and to this day her career is one characterized by dignity and passion.*

***Patti Smith**, the author, and singer Karon Bihari backstage in Philadelphia, 1977. Patti had returned to the Philadelphia area near where she was raised in southern New Jersey to perform in a free outdoor concert at the riverfront park Penn's Landing.*

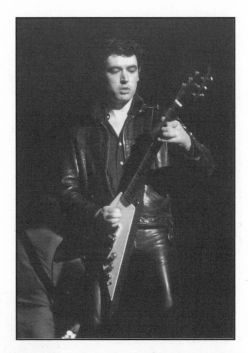

One of rock music's unsung heroes, **Chris Spedding** followed a fascinating path throughout the 1970s that saw him set off Jack Bruce's post-Cream solo career, contribute rockabilly riffs to Robert Gordon, found a unique band called Sharks, and then produce early recordings by the Sex Pistols.

Bruce Springsteen and the author prepare to celebrate New Year's Eve together in 1975, the author from his seat in the audience, Bruce from the stage of Philadelphia's Tower Theater. It would be the final show of the tour supporting Springsteen's breakthrough album Born to Run.

At a time when rock music bore an ever-growing burden of complex compositions and extravagant stage presentations, **Bruce Springsteen** came along to return the exuberance to rock and roll. With a stripped-down approach that was firmly in touch with the pulse of rock's forefathers, Springsteen and his E Street Band used traditional ideals to bold effect.

Seldom has a band had such an instantly recognizable sonic signature as Yes did, thanks to **Chris Squire**'s Rickenbacker bass guitar. Squire is seen here in 1972, on tour to support the band's new Close to the Edge album.

The rock star ideal personified, **Rod Stewart** accepts backing vocals from guitarist Jim Cregan on stage in 1977. Cregan was a frequent Stewart collaborator after the guitarist left British band Family and Stewart's own band, Faces, collapsed in disarray.

The Who's **Pete Townshend**, *seen at the Spectrum in Philadelphia during the band's* By Numbers *tour on December 15, 1975. It was the final night of a thirteen-date outing to promote the new album, one full of songs that revealed the guitarist was in a period of deep personal doubt.*

Robin Trower's rich talent first came to light in Procol Harum, but fully developed with his solo trio. One of rock's biggest acts in the 1970s, Trower had the good fortune of working in an era when musicianship was more highly valued than personality and dance routines.

Though Yes member **Rick Wakeman** was justifiably renowned for his command of an arsenal of instruments, the keyboardist here seems somewhat less coordinated. Wakeman was hamming around in a locker room at Philadelphia's 20,000 seat Spectrum arena.

West, Bruce, & Laing *was in many ways the epitome of the supergroup ideal. Featuring one half of Mountain merged with the bassist/vocalist of Cream, the potentially hi-octane trio generated tremendous excitement upon announcement of their union in 1972. But the actual material recorded by the band didn't reach the heights that seemed tantalizingly in reach, and the supergroup's career output was limited to two studio albums and an uneven live recording.*

Dan Hartman, Edgar Winter, and Ronnie Montrose thunder through a show at St. Joseph's University Fieldhouse in 1972. Though Winter was about to reach certified rock star status with his album They Only Come Out at Night, *Montrose would soon leave* ***The Edgar Winter Group*** *to form his namesake hard rock quartet with singer Sammy Hagar.*

Peter Wolf, *lead singer for the J. Geils Band, at the group's tenth anniversary show at New York's Palladium in 1977. Within months the group would be play-ing huge arenas as headliners after their* Freeze Frame *album unexpectedly claimed smash-hit status.*

trademark tricks—most crucially, his glorious vibrato. But the album was murkily recorded, and most of the material was unexceptional, largely written by keyboardist Mike Montgomery. The songs often stood as little more than frameworks for Kossoff's mid-song solos, set up as the band dropped into Free-like progressions.

Still, Koss' fire was reignited on the album's strong title track, and he brought an icy restraint to "It's a Long Way Down to the Top," a moody review of the pitfalls of the rock and roll lifestyle—many of which Kossoff himself was all too familiar with.

Aside from their guitar star, though, Back Street Crawler was nothing exceptional, and it was troubling to hear Kossoff struggle in an attempt to elevate the ordinary into the exceptional.

Back Street Crawler undertook a British tour in August to support the album, but the dates were suddenly cancelled when Kossoff suffered a heart attack. By the time he had recovered enough to return to the studio, Kossoff's old friend "Rabbit" Bundrick had been enlisted to replace Montgomery on keyboards. The recording for the second album took place largely in New York, including sessions at Electric Lady Studios—the studio built by Kossoff's idol, Jimi Hendrix.

With the new album nearly completed, Kossoff took a flight home to England on March 19, 1976. He dozed off over the Atlantic, and never woke up. Weakened from the years of abuse and personal misery, on that night Paul Kossoff's heart simply stopped beating.

When the album, *2nd Street,* emerged weeks later, it bore a simple, sad inscription: "Dedicated to Koss."

In the spring of 1975, the top of the charts was dominated by Van McCoy's instrumental "The Hustle," a rather moronic example of the burgeoning disco movement. In fact, the song was little more than a hi-hat-driven dance floor drumbeat cloaked in a grade school melody—and unfortunately, there was a bountiful crop of such songs yet to come. Disco glittered with commercial gold that was mightily tempting to funk and R&B artists.

Fortunately, there were still bands whose members were faithful disciples of the teachings of James Brown. One of those groups carrying the torch for pure, unadulterated funk was Kool and the Gang. Their insistent repetition of the word "party"—a word that had evolved from noun to verb—ushered in "Funky Stuff," just one of the big-beat funk blasts collected on their 1975 *Greatest Hits* album. Propelled along by staccato guitar and booming bass that would have made the Godfather of Soul proud, tracks like "Funky Stuff," "Jungle Boogie," and "Hollywood Swinging" were wild and raw where disco was slick and smooth. Though Kool and the Gang's sound would soften, becoming almost unrecognizable in the years to come, their early 1970s roots were as earthy as they come.

Out on the West Coast, a group called Nightshift had been supporting the fledgling singing career of former National Football League star Deacon Jones when they were selected in 1969 to back up ex-Animal Eric Burdon. Renamed War, the group stuck it out together even after the unpredictable lead singer quit in mid-tour during 1971. Soon thereafter, War unexpectedly found even greater chart success than they'd known when fronted by Burdon. War's 1975 album *Why Can't We Be Friends* was characteristic of the band, a sound of sultry grooves accented with Latin percussion and slinky bass. Working together to create an intricate ensemble sound resonating with exotic influences, War offered proof that commercial success and a creative approach could coexist.

Though funk and soul were the obvious domains of black musicians in 1975, there were a handful of players of color determined to follow the rock trail blazed by Jimi Hendrix.

With Mountain's Felix Pappalardi in the producer's chair, the all-black power trio White Lightnin' looked to have the best shot at breaking down the perceived barriers between black artists and the rock world. The odds were improved with studio time booked at the Sam Phillips Recording Studio in Memphis, the new facility operated by the man who had discovered Elvis and recorded everyone from Jerry Lee Lewis to Roy Orbison. The outlook for success was further bolstered by the fact that White Lightnin's record label, Island Records, had arranged to have the album mastered by George Marino at Sterling Sound. Marino was respected throughout the music industry, highly regarded for his skill at the unique craft of performing the final preproduction aural tweaks that made albums sound their very best.

In the end, though, the only thing heavy about White Lightnin' was their leaden pacing. Though "Joke's on You" ushered the album into existence with a heady and unrelenting blast of rock-drenched funk, the proceedings ground to a halt on "Without You," an interminable ballad that was inexplicably placed second in the running order. The album's momentum irrevocably lost—and far from regained during a dreadful cover of Garland Jeffries' "Wild in the Streets"—it became apparent that White Lightnin's material and arrangements were not of the same caliber as the support network that had been arranged for them.

Not surprisingly, enthusiasm for White Lightnin' was nonexistent. Within months of the album's release, bassist Busta Jones would join Chris Spedding and Snips in the band Sharks, just in time to participate in the collapse of that band. Brothers Woody and Donald Kinsey would wait almost a decade before forming the influential modern blues band The Kinsey Report. Island Records' belief that White Lightnin' might become the next Hendrix had turned out to be unfounded.

Of course, record labels will go to any lengths to make money, which explained why Jimi Hendrix was still in the "New Release" bin five years after his death. But on the 1975 albums *Crash Landing* and *Midnight Lightning*, Warner Brothers Records and producer Alan Douglas had descended to a distressing new low.

Dissatisfied with the performances of bassists Billy Cox and Noel Redding on the original tapes, in an astonishing act of arrogance—and with Warner Brothers' approval—Douglas hired Motown bassist Bob Babbitt to simply replace the bass parts that Jimi, Noel, and Billy had devised. The drumming of Mitch Mitchell and Buddy Miles received no greater respect, as their parts were replaced by session drummer Alan Schwartzberg. And in the crowning insult, Jimi himself was judged to be in need of support from studio guitarists Lance Quinn and Jeff Mironov. None of these musicians had ever played with Hendrix, and Douglas' actions were all the more mind-boggling in light of the fact that his efforts completely erased the original parts performed by the original musicians. There was also the matter that some versions of this product—for that was all these albums were to the company—bore Douglas' name as the co-composer of tracks with Hendrix.

"It proves only that the commercial necrophilia about Hendrix is of the most relentless and nauseating type," opined *Stereo Review*, "and that the producers of this jerk-puppet series are perhaps of the family Frankenstein."

"Is there morality in rock and roll?" questioned England's influential music newspaper *Melody Maker*. The answer was all too obvious.

The pirate smashed a large hole in the brick wall, then peered to his left. There his piercing glare encountered a clown—or perhaps it was a mime. If it was a mime, then it was surely the loudest mime known to humankind. Armed with a Gibson SG guitar, he began blasting out power chords to accompany the ensuing demolition of the wall.

A bizarre nightmare? No, simply The Sensational Alex Harvey Band, live and in concert.

Though Scottish blues singer Alex Harvey was blessed with little success by the fall of 1972, he had encountered an equally little-known band called Tear Gas. Forming an alliance to follow Harvey's grand rock vision, the band recorded their gutty debut album, *Framed*, in just six days. It was an album that mixed powerful rock, unexpected folk, and Harvey's lilting, unsteady baritone into one of the most unusual and grand combinations in rock.

Though little appreciated in the United States, by 1975 Harvey's band was beloved in England, having just released a fifth studio album, the mesmerizing *Tomorrow Belongs to Me*. What can be said of an album that features Middle Eastern motifs in its lead-off track, then proceeds to touch on Hawaiian music and boozy-and-bluesy soul, finally incorporating swelling strings and horns to relate a grade school tale of dinosaurs and earth-moving machinery in the seven-minute epic "The Tale of the Giant Stone Eater," all while rocking intensely? And if there was any doubt about the band's ability to play it straight, the eerie "Give My Compliments to the Chef" stood out as simply a brilliant rock song.

Studio strengths aside, The Sensational Alex Harvey Band—SAHB for short—became legendary for their live shows. Alex ran through a series of loosely aligned, oddball characters, pausing at stage edge to read from books and address his audience like a demented schoolteacher. Clad in black striped sailor shirt, big boots, and leather jacket, Harvey looked like a maniac—and acted like one.

"I like being on the thin edge," Alex perceptively noted, "between total madness and organization."

The soundtrack to the tantalizing mayhem was captured on *Live*, released later in 1975. Opening with "Faith Healer," The SAHB crafted a delirious swirl over Hugh McKenna's synthesizer pulse. Guitarist Zal Cleminson bore down on his notes with a evil aggression that flew in the face of his circus appearance, and drummer Ted McKenna and bassist Chris Glen were adept at following Alex's often convoluted creative paths. The full range of The SAHB was captured on *Live*, from the metallic surge of "Vambo," the tale of a mythical superhero, to the music hall sing-along of "Deliliah."

Perhaps the odd relationship between the eccentric Harvey and his rabid followers can be gleaned from this note, part of the band's 1975 tour program.

"Dear Boys and Girls," Alex printed. "As we start our British tour—be good, don't smash any windows or throw any rubbish. We look forward to seeing you because we love you and that's why we don't want you to get into any trouble. Love, Alex."

Trouble is just what Kiss found themselves mired in as they prepared to record a live album in May 1975, and the ghoulish makeup the foursome favored likely hid some frowns. The reaction to their studio efforts to date had been underwhelming, to put it mildly. But there was hope; they had been building word of mouth as a live act. Whereas The Sensational Alex Harvey Band and Alice Cooper based their theatrical shenanigans on a foundation of thrilling and unpredictable rock, Kiss music played second fiddle to a lineup of explosions, blood, and noise. In the eyes of many, Kiss' musical abilities functioned at such a deficient level that reinforcement was demanded from anything capable of distracting the audience from the dire state of the music alone.

If any rock audience was capable of being whipped into a frenzy, though, it was Detroit's. Kiss had chosen wisely in deciding to record their live album in the city. After an appropriate display of bassist Gene Simmons' blood-spitting skills, a few detonations, and enough ponderous riffage to set hard rock back several eons, Kiss had *Alive!* in the can. Former Jimi Hendrix engineer Eddie Kramer did what he could with the sound, and the album was released. To the amazement of the band—and the dismay of their critics—*Alive!* began to sell, and sell, and sell. It made its way to number nine on the charts, first reaching gold and then platinum status.

Within a matter of months, Kiss had capitalized on their success and were well on their way to evolving from rock band to marketing machine. With identically packaged solo albums—why release a single album when you can lure dedicated fans into buying four?—joining a comic book allegedly printed with "real Kiss blood," Kiss was ultimately shown to be irrelevant as musicians.

The final disintegration of any artistic respect remaining for Kiss came with *Kiss Meets the Phantom of the Park*. The television movie, starring the band members as crime fighters attempting to solve mysterious misdeeds at an amusement park, proved that Kiss members were not much better at acting than they were at playing their instruments; the group suffered from such poor diction that actors were later required to dub in much of the dialogue.

Far more stimulating from a live musical standpoint were Lou Reed's *Rock'n'Roll Animal* and *Lou Reed Live* albums. Before joining Alice Cooper for his *Welcome to My Nightmare* sessions and tour, Steve Hunter and Dick Wagner had followed up their work on Reed's *Berlin* album with an extensive tour in 1974. After assembling a full band for Reed, night after night Hunter and Wagner played high-wire guitar heroics that were captured for posterity in a concert at New York's Academy of Music.

The recording was distributed in two parts, first on 1974's *Animal* and then in 1975 on *Live*. Though the material from *Berlin* lost some of its haunting edge in translation, the sheer firepower of Hunter and Wagner's guitar-gunslingers-for-hire talent made up for it. And on songs like the basic "Sweet Jane" or "White Light/White Heat"—vintage Velvet Underground material predicated on nothing more than simple rock chords—the duo burned with brilliant intensity. Though Reed himself came across as little more than an accessory on his own albums, these two records stand, even today, as a luminous catalog of rock guitar artistry.

With the two live albums bathing Reed's material in a most commercial light, rock critics began grumbling in print that Reed was selling out for the masses. *Metal Machine Music* was his response, a double album of shrieking electronic noise and feedback. In his speed-freak-stream-of-consciousness liner notes, Reed noted, "*Rock'n'Roll Animal* makes this possible, funnily enough. The misrepresentation succeeds to the point of making possible the progenitor," before curtly noting, "My week beats your year." RCA Records was obligated to release the work and, stuck with an album that bore no songs, they proceeded to dress up the cover with photos of Reed in concert in a desperate attempt to move product. But word of the deception quickly spread, and *Metal Machine Music*—a quite interesting work of electro-texture even if it was tuneless—soon disappeared from sight.

At the opposite end of the spectrum was Jo Jo Gunne, a California hard rock band that had risen from the ashes of a split in the influential 1960s band Spirit. Led by pianist and vocalist Jay Ferguson, Jo Jo Gunne scored just enough success with the hit "Run Run Run" from their first album to ensure middle-of-the-bill booking on endless tours.

"It was just hard," Ferguson recalled of the band's work ethic in the liner notes to Rhino Handmade's catalog reissue. "It was a hard-working band. It was in the middle of that sort of, what they would call journeyman rock era where people would just go out and slog it out. You know, you'd do one hundred and twenty shows with Bad Company and you're all just trying to break your careers and we did that for a long time."

On the endless concert trail, Jo Jo Gunne shared stages with everyone from Lou Reed to Foghat, The Eagles to Yes. They were the prototypical hard rock band, but their material consistently boasted a clever edge lurking amidst the bombastic solos. Though their second and third albums, *Bite Down Hard* and *Jumpin' the Gunne*, were blessed with the production talents of Bill Szymczyk—not to mention the latter album's truly tasteless cover photo of a naked, obese woman literally jumping the Gunne— it was the group's final album that best captured their spirit.

So . . . Where's the Show? began with that most clichéd of rock songs, one with lyrics detailing just how hard it is to be a rocker on the road. But Jo Jo Gunne had earned the right to play a song like that by living the nomadic life for years, and the words rang with an authenticity often missing in similar efforts. John Staehly's guitar provided cutting-edge hard rock momentum throughout the entire album, but the life force of Jo Jo Gunne was drummer Curly Smith. Smith, the band's drummer for their entire career, was a dynamic, tough player who received little recognition for a talent that, in a perfect world, would have long since been celebrated. With Ferguson's piano bringing an additional range of tone to the band, Jo Jo Gunne seemed to be forever standing at the tantalizing border of major rock stardom, territory that in the end eluded them. Late in 1975, one of hard rock's most dependable foot soldiers simply faded away.

"There was an unspoken understanding that we were going to go out and we were going to support this and tour," Ferguson said of the last record, "but if this doesn't really break, then it's time to move on for all of us. We took stock at the end of that tour and looked at the sales and looked at the concert experiences. It really was just sort of stuck. It was time to move on, and Jo Jo Gunne was over."

Robert Plant had enjoyed all the rewards of stardom that Jo Jo Gunne never found. In the summer of 1975, as his band Led

Zeppelin took a break from shattering box office records, Plant and his family vacationed in Greece. It was there, on August 5, that Plant was nearly killed in a car crash. His severe injuries would wind up derailing the band's touring ability for more than a year as the singer slowly recovered.

Just over a week later, another major British band lost their lead singer totally when Peter Gabriel sent a letter to the music press explaining why he was leaving Genesis.

In recent months, Genesis had released the intricate *Selling England by the Pound*, following it up in late 1974 with *The Lamb Lies Down on Broadway*, a sweeping double album that was far and away the band's most ambitious effort. Collaborating in part with Brian Eno, the challenging ex-Roxy Music member known for unique electronic approaches to a new form of music he called "ambient music," Genesis had labored long and hard to record *Lamb*, setting up in Wales and recording with Island Records' Mobile Studio.

Constructed around a nearly impenetrable Gabriel story about two brothers swept into a dangerous subterranean world via a dimensional portal on Times Square, the album differed from such one-work-per-record efforts as Yes' *Tales from Topographic Oceans* or Jethro Tull's *Thick as a Brick* in that *Lamb* consisted of individual songs strung together into a whole. But the performances were no less elaborate, with Gabriel's charismatic vocals adding to the band's weighty instrumental approach. In particular, Tony Banks' spiraling synthesizer solos and washes of ponderous organ gave the sound of Genesis its character, with drummer Phil Collins perfecting a remarkable, explosive approach to prog rock drumming.

In support of the album's release on November 18, 1974, Genesis embarked on a lengthy tour, burdened with elaborate stage sets and three projection screens that enabled Gabriel to act out the entirety of *Lamb*. One of the show's more memorable moments found Gabriel crawling though a lengthy, eerily lit tube, only to emerge as one of the "Slippermen," unrecognizable in a greenish costume of hideous lumps and protuberances.

Based on Gabriel's letter of departure in August, though, not everyone had been happy playing music that many considered little more than background accompaniment for Gabriel's theatrics. His words gave a peek inside the power struggles and ego conflicts that had begun to plague Genesis.

"The vehicle we had built as a co-op to serve our songwriting became our master and cooped us up in the success we had wanted," Gabriel wrote. "To get an idea through 'Genesis the Big' meant shifting a lot more concrete than before. For any band, transferring the heart from idealistic enthusiasm to professionalism is a difficult operation. I believe the use of sound and visual images can be developed to do much more than we have done. But on a large scale it needs one clear and coherent direction, which our pseudo-democratic committee system could not provide."

Yes, a band that had certainly endured their share of personnel upheavals over the years, welcomed the year 1975 with their own new album on the charts, *Relayer*. Jazzer Patrick Moraz had been deposited behind the Yes keyboard array as a result of group personality and artistic struggles with the classically trained Rick Wakeman. Typically, though, the band continued to thrash against the confining barriers of prog rock. Moraz seemed eager to steer the band in a fusion direction, and the other members sounded willing to follow. *Relayer* was anchored by a characteristically sweeping "The Gates of Delirium," which less-patient listeners felt they'd passed through upon reaching the majestic conclusion of the twenty-two-minute opus. But the opening minutes of "Sound Chaser" had Yes fans wondering if they were listening to Mahavishnu Orchestra or Return to Forever as the group rallied behind Moraz's Fender Rhodes piano-led charge.

Far more restrained than the frantic moments of *Relayer's* frenzied peaks, Pink Floyd's own 1975 effort, *Wish You Were Here*, built on both the format and the commercial success of *Dark Side of the Moon*. It was one of the rarest of rock albums, one that was nearly flawless in both composition and performance.

Wish You Were Here ached with loneliness, depersonalization, and regrets over the loss of friends, specifically band founder Syd Barrett. To a greater degree than ever, Pink Floyd relied on the guitar textures and remarkable solos of David Gilmour, who used the darkness inherent in blues scales to bring an earthy melancholy to a decidedly non-blues context. Keyboardist Rick Wright's muted, eloquent synthesizer and organ work brought a deeper emotional context to the music, helping make the album one of the most rewarding song cycles in rock's history.

Ironically, in the midst of recording the Barrett-themed "Shine on You Crazy Diamond," an unkempt Syd himself suddenly appeared at Abbey Road Studios after seven years of disappearance. His arrival startled and shocked the band, an awkward meeting made all the more wrenching by Barrett's announcement that he stood willing to help the band—although it was obvious Syd could not even help himself rise above his mental imbalance and damage from rampant drug use. His reappearance as a ghost-like apparition only added emotional resonance to the lyrical heart of *Wish You Were Here.*

Similar introspection—and depression—weighed on Pete Townshend's heart as he crafted the lyrics to 1975's *The Who by Numbers*. "However Much I Booze" sought solace—however hollow—in the bottle, and "How Many Friends" and "In a Hand or a Face" found little comfort at all. Bassist John Entwistle's "Success Story" provided the album's only light moments, with a witty and sarcastic look at the absurd job description of professional rock star.

Interestingly, at a time when other bands were adding more and more to their sound, *By Numbers* found The Who stripping their sound down to its core. The synthesizers that had formed the foundation of both *Who's Next* and *Quadrophenia* were missing in action, with the guitar, bass, and drums supplemented only by the acoustic piano of Nicky Hopkins. Hopkins was the perfect choice to add to *By Numbers*, as he was one of the unsung heroes of session work and a vital contributor to albums by The Beatles, The Rolling Stones, The Kinks, The Jefferson Airplane, and many more.

It's quite possible The Who had stripped down their sound in an effort to avoid the inevitable fallout from two cinematic efforts helmed by the flamboyant British director Ken Russell. The first, which emerged in 1975, was a big-screen adaptation of *Tommy*, with guest stars including Elton John, Tina Turner, and Jack Nicholson. Filming was also underway that year for *Lisztomania*, a movie that sought to cast the classical music figure in the light of a rock star. Roger Daltrey played the starring roles in both films, debuting an acting style somewhat lacking in finesse. But it was difficult to notice, as *Tommy* and *Lisztomania* were so over-the-top. Both films were a disturbing pastiche of psychedelia colliding with glitter, and under the circumstances such trifles as acting ability were lost in the chaos.

The bottom line was that these embarrassing film efforts did little more than add substance to the growing impression that most rock stars were entirely out of touch with reality. While musical celebrities pranced about in campy movie appearances or fretted over whether they'd have to move to the French Riviera to avoid England's high taxes, the people expected to shell out diminishing discretionary income on those stars' new albums were facing crushing unemployment and economic inflation gone awry. Even if they had yet to voice the need, the working classes were longing for a new rock hero. They were about to get him.

"The stuff I write is what I live with," singer Bruce Springsteen said in 1974. "The stories are all around me. I just put 'em down. They're all true."

When Springsteen's second album, *The Wild, the Innocent, and the E Street Shuffle*, was released on November 5, 1973, his slowly growing fan base found a collection of songs that weren't first-person accounts of wealthy alcohol abusers. Nor were Springsteen's songs about parallel universes or topographic oceans. Instead, Bruce wrote about the things that real people saw and the events they lived through every day, happenings and characters that Springsteen reported on through keen perceptions and a deft skill at penning dramatic, moving lyrical passages. In short, Bruce Springsteen was a masterful storyteller.

Signed by Columbia Records' legendary Artist and Repertoire man John Hammond in 1972, Springsteen was expected to follow in the footsteps of Hammond's other discoveries, an imposing group of musical talent that included Bob Dylan. Things didn't go according to plan.

Upon the January 1973 release of *Greetings from Asbury Park*, Springsteen's debut Columbia album drew unfavorable comparisons to Dylan, thanks to its barrage of lyrics and semicoherent imagery. The album's lead-off track, "Blinded by the Light," comprised one hundred and twenty-four words in the first verse alone.

In a way, the lukewarm reception may have worked to Springsteen's advantage. When the second album appeared ten months later, it was clear that Bruce had reinvented his lyrical approach, self-editing dramatically and focusing on the delivery of concise narratives.

Certain key cities in the United States began to fall under Springsteen's spell, chiefly Philadelphia and Cleveland. Radio station support of songs like "Rosalita" and "Kitty's Back" began to build a buzz around Springsteen, and the rollicking strength of those songs hinted at the true power of Springsteen's biggest asset: The E Street Band.

Late in 1974, The E Street Band had grown through a series of personnel changes, arriving at a lineup of seemingly limitless ability. Not only was Springsteen's band proficient in its ability to rock, but they were also quickly becoming adept at draping texture around Springsteen's evolving lyrical talent.

The E Street Band's rhythm section was the lifeblood of the group. New drummer Max Weinberg was brutally strong but maintained precise control as he steered the direction of the music. Garry Tallent was a lyrical bassist, responsible for filling out the band's melodic presence and fundamentally moving the music rather than simply outlining chord changes.

Above Tallent and Weinberg, the dramatic combination of Danny Federici's organ and Roy Bittan's gorgeous, intricate acoustic piano provided Springsteen a tremendous palette of moods. Steven Van Zandt contributed ragged-but-right harmony vocals and confident rhythm and blues electric guitar talent, a style that meshed well with Springsteen's own rock-based guitar skills.

Anchoring The E Street Band, to the delight of Springsteen's growing army of fans, was "the Big Man," Clarence Clemons. A massive black man known for sartorial splendor, Clemons was an imposing presence. That impression was made all the more monumental via the sound of his saxophone, a raw blast from the soul that called to mind the great R&B tenor sax players, near-mythical legends like Big Jay McNeely, Paul "Hucklebuck" Williams, King Curtis, and Sam "The Man" Taylor.

The E Street Band was an unusual aggregation—and they were quickly becoming one of the most consistent and potent forces in rock.

As critics began to climb on board the accelerating Springsteen bandwagon—much to Bruce's embarrassment, Jon Landau famously wrote, "I saw rock'n'roll future and its name is Bruce Springsteen"—sessions began for what looked to be a make-or-beak third album.

Recording stretched on for months, with Springsteen restlessly approving tracks and then changing his mind. Concerts during the period found certain verses appearing in one song on one night, transplanted to a different song the next. Springsteen knew the album was crucial, and he wanted the recording to speak with its own voice.

"We approached the record the way some of the early '60s producers like Phil Spector or Brian Wilson would approach their records, which is make a record to create this sound," Bruce explained.

But that sound was proving elusive. Springsteen, who had become friends with critic Landau, finally brought him into the sessions to help provide perspective. At last, a year after the initial recording attempts had been undertaken, the new album—*Born to Run*—was released on September 1, 1975.

"After it was finished? I hated it," Springsteen fretted to Robert Duncan in the January 1976 issue of *Creem* magazine. "I couldn't stand to listen to it. I thought it was the worst piece of garbage I'd ever heard. I told Columbia I wouldn't release it. I told 'em I'd just go down to the Bottom Line gig and do all the new songs and make it a live album."

Bruce eventually came to like the sound of the album, but America required no such convincing. The Bottom Line gig—at the influential Manhattan nightclub—was a radio concert rather than a recording session, and the electricity the band communicated across the airwaves helped fuel a runaway frenzy over Springsteen.

But for once, the hype was justified. From the opening piano and harmonica of "Thunder Road" to the somber final notes of "Jungleland," *Born to Run* was an immense panorama of American rock styles, confidently spanning 1950s rockabilly and Phil Spector pop, majestic pseudoclassical progressions and streetwise rhythm and blues. It was astounding to hear the assurance with which The E Street Band followed a musical path that veered from massive walls of rock sound to the most hushed and delicate of moments. *Born to Run* was an album that covered as much stylistic ground as any work that had preceded it—and despite the assimilation of its influences, the record sounded absolutely unlike anything else.

If Springsteen himself had any doubts about how deeply his new album had impacted American rock, they were put to rest on October 27, 1975. On that date, Bruce Springsteen's face smiled out from the covers of both *Newsweek* and *Time*.

Late in what had already been an astonishing year in rock music, the benchmark for musical creativity was about to be raised yet again—this time through the release of an album that would stand as a masterpiece of composition, performance, and the art and science of recording. The album was called *A Night at the Opera*, and the group that created it was one of rock's most intriguing and unique bands, Queen.

Queen's roots stretched back to the late 1960s. Guitarist Brian May and drummer Roger Taylor were playing together in a band called Smile when they became acquainted with an aspiring singer from an exotic background. Farookh "Freddie" Bulsara had been born in Zanzibar, later moving with his family and living near Bombay, India, where he first began to learn piano and music theory. In his teen years, Freddie's family relocated to England, where Bulsara became a fan of Smile, the group having reached a limited level of prestige that saw them being given opening slots for bands like Free and Pink Floyd. Upon Smile's demise, the opportunity to start a band with May and Taylor presented itself, and Freddie leapt at the opportunity. At his insistence—and despite the dubious reactions of his band mates—the group was bestowed the name Queen. Soon thereafter, the handsome young Freddie traded Bulsara for a new stage name—Mercury—and Brian and Roger's chance introduction to young John Deacon led to his joining the band as bassist. The pieces were in place.

After struggling for survival, in March 1973 Queen signed a recording contract with EMI Records. Late in the summer, Queen was unleashed into the highly competitive hard rock marketplace. Through insistent songs like "Keep Yourself Alive" and "Liar," the band announced their arrival and began to develop a unique ensemble sound.

Key to the development and capturing of Queen's sound was Roy Thomas Baker. Baker was yet another member of the axis revolving around producer Tony Visconti and the Trident Studios culture, and he had cultivated his recording résumé by engineering albums by Ginger Baker's Air Force, Free, and Savoy Brown. After working with T. Rex on *Electric Warrior*, Baker felt ready to ascend to producer status. Having a producer with a seasoned engineering background can be an important advantage, because a good engineer knows the technical limitations of the recording process and the best way to approach any desired sound. Baker's partnership with Queen amounted to a formidable alliance, one that would change the face of rock music.

Complementing Baker's technical experience was the simple fact that there was more to Queen's members than was typically found in a rock band; they were intelligent young men with degrees in fields ranging from graphic design to physics. That intellectual capability no doubt contributed to the band's thoughtful, creative designs outlining how they wanted their records to sound.

The raw potential of Queen's talent and Baker's aptitude took a giant leap toward realization on *Queen II*, heard to greatest effect on the album's second side. There, the band created an aural roller coaster ride with a vivid, flat-out passage through seven divergent songs all working together as a breathtaking whole.

"I think we learned it from The Beatles, and Jimi Hendrix possibly also," Brian May told the BBC's Radio 1, commenting on Queen's meticulous approach to recording. "I remember going round Freddie's house when we were young and Freddie putting on the *Electric Ladyland* album and we would be running around his little stereo finding out which bits came out of which speaker at what time, and finding all these wonderful little magic things that were going on, so we were very conscious of that. And you'll never find on a Queen record that once you've heard the first verse and the first chorus, you know what's gonna happen, because we could never leave it that way. We always had to introduce new elements as the song went on . . . You'll always find something which you didn't perhaps realize was there the first few times you played it."

Also reaching full flower was Queen's ability to stun audiences in concert. Their show was dynamic and dramatic, a whirlwind of smoke, volume, light, and heat. May, playing a guitar dubbed "Red Special" that he had built with his father nearly ten years earlier, generated a soaring, sophisticated tone far removed from the typical Gibson-guitar-through-Marshall-amps blare of so many of his contemporaries, and even in the stage environment he was able to approximate the grand structures of Queen's studio work.

Yet even more crucial to Queen's growing reputation was the blossoming of Freddie Mercury into the singer who may have been rock's greatest front-man. With an innate sense of how to win over a crowd, Mercury stalked the stage, gesturing with dramatic flourishes, unleashing the full range of his remarkable voice. The fury of the band contrasted diametrically with Mercury, who flirted with fey campiness one moment and strutted like a god descended from the heavens the next.

"He was very much his own creation," Taylor reasoned in an interview with the VH1 network. "He made himself and he just got better and better. At first we thought, 'He'll never get away with this,' but he just developed and became a better singer, better and better all the time. He was a great writer from the start and absolutely inherently a musician. He was quite extraordinary."

With Deacon and Taylor anchoring the band with one of the most overwhelming rhythm sections in rock, Queen began to generate a well-deserved buzz throughout the rock world through continued touring in Europe and the United States and via the release of *Sheer Heart Attack* late in 1974.

The third Queen album proved the band's strong work ethic was paying off, as the collection climbed to number two in the British charts and nearly made the top ten in the United States. More importantly from a creative standpoint, the album helped perfect Queen's sound in the studio. May's Red Special sang with a violin-like vibrato, layered in its own orchestral overdubs. The waves of guitar played against lush banks of choir-like voices, ushering in the band's stunning choruses as Mercury's solo voice heroically arched across the stereo spectrum. Such was the sound of Queen at their most majestic and angelic—but on songs like "Brighton Rock" and "Stone Cold Crazy," a brutal personality emerged through a Hyde-like transformation. Queen could just as easily play it low-down and dirty, fueled by a blunt power that equaled the hardest of rock bands.

Yet just as rock fans felt they had come to terms with the incredible breadth of Queen's musical reach, the band unveiled a work that somehow took in all the myriad aspects of Queen's personality—and more. It was all melded into a single amazing song called "Bohemian Rhapsody," and the six-minute track contained more twists and turns than most bands' entire albums.

"Freddie was sitting in his apartment," Roy Thomas Baker recalled for the BBC, "and he said 'I've got this idea for a song' and he sort of sat down and he sort of started playing the song . . . He was playing away and he stopped and he said, 'Now dears, this is where the opera section comes in' and I went oh, my god!"

If any band could incorporate the heretofore-untouched realm of opera within a rock context, it had to be Queen.

"We left a blank piece of tape to do the opera section," Baker continued. "When we started doing the opera section properly, it just got longer and longer and we just kept adding blank tape to this thing and it got bigger and bigger and bigger. Every day we just sort of thought, 'Oh, this is it, we're done now' and Freddie would come in with another lot of lyrics and say, 'I've added a few more Galileos here, dear' and so we would put on a few more Galileos and it just got bigger and bigger and bigger and in the end it became the epic we all know."

Baker and the band were truly pushing the limits of recording technology in realizing Mercury's boundless creative vision. So often did the master tape pass through the machine heads for playback and overdub recording, legend has it that the tape was nearly worn through entirely in certain sections, barely surviving the risky recording procedure.

"Bohemian Rhapsody" became one of rock's most legendary creations, an astounding—and most unusual—hit single. From piano balladry to metallic pummeling, gentle phrasings to operatic crescendos, the song had it all. Spending nine weeks at number one in England, "Bohemian Rhapsody" generated a sales momentum that launched *A Night at the Opera* to the top of the British album charts and drove it to a peak of number four in the United States.

Other artists were quick to acknowledge the imposing genius behind Queen's quantum leap in creativity.

Brian Wilson, the compositional mastermind of The Beach Boys, told *Creem* magazine's Richard Cromelin in the October 1976 issue that "Bohemian Rhapsody" was, "to me, a fulfillment of artistic music. I studied the record, I became very familiar with it, and I'm very, very fond of it and scared of it at the same time. Oh, it's the most competitive thing that's come along in ages . . . They had enough of what was happening, and by God they went in and did their thing and stomped."

"Bohemian Rhapsody" appeared as the next-to-last song in the running order of *A Night at the Opera*. There was really only one track that could possibly follow it—Queen's sober and sweeping instrumental take on "God Save the Queen." It was an inarguable pronouncement: once again, Britannia ruled the waves of the rock ocean.

1976

7

Under Siege

As the year 1976 began, it was boom time for the recording industry. Despite a wobbly economy and the uncertainty of a presidential election that would eventually pit incumbent Gerald Ford against a self-described "Georgia peanut farmer" named Jimmy Carter, people were buying more records than ever before. The proof? The Recording Industry Association of America felt that its traditional benchmarks for exceptional sales were no longer adequate. So, in 1976, the RIAA introduced the new Platinum Award.

The first single to go platinum (to have sales of more than two million copies) was Johnny Taylor's "Disco Lady." The first album (for sales of more than one million LP copies), was *Greatest Hits 1971–1975* by California's Eagles—an album that would eventually total sales in the neighborhood of twenty-five million copies.

Aside from commercial weight, The Eagles' creative influence was pervasive in the latter half of the 1970s. Indeed, in much the way it seemed everyone who ever played British blues rock had passed through John Mayall's Bluesbreakers, so too did The Eagles and the bands that led to their formation cast a huge shadow on American contemporary rock.

The lineage of The Eagles could be traced back to The Byrds, a band that, throughout the later 1960s, brought an exciting rock sensibility to the no-frills framework of folk music. Chris Hillman, a founding member of The Byrds, became close with latter-day Byrd Gram Parsons as the band neared the end of its run. When the Byrds landed for good, Hillman and Parsons founded the equally influential Flying Burrito Brothers, one of the first bands to seriously inject country elements into the rock bloodstream. Among the group's members was guitarist Bernie Leadon, a future Eagle.

After the books closed on the career of The Flying Burrito Brothers, a quartet of musicians—Leadon, along with Glen Frey, Don Henley, and Randy Meisner—all became acquainted while recording and backing singer Linda Ronstadt. The foursome decided to create a new band—The Eagles.

Signing to a new label created by rock manager David Geffen, The Eagles recorded their debut album with famed producer Glyn Johns, whose client roster boasted names of the finest pedigree including The Who, The Rolling Stones, and Eric Clapton. With the release of their debut *Eagles* in 1972, the band was successful out of the gate, leading to the chart ascension of two top-ten singles. They immediately attracted fans with a sonic aura that evoked a laid-back, Southwestern lifestyle. Other musicians noticed both the success and the style of The Eagles, and soon a flock of like-minded Los Angeles artists were displaying their own placid recording attitudes.

Yet for a band that presented such a mellow vibe, The Eagles had more than their share of hotheads and internal strife. After clashing with Johns during the recording of their third album, the band turned to former James Gang producer Bill Szymczyk to complete the recording, in the first chapter of what would become a long creative relationship. At the same time, they added guitarist Don Felder to their lineup. Stability was fleeting, though. In the midst of a tour to support the group's fourth album, it was announced on December 20, 1975, that founder Leadon was no longer a member of the Eagles. His replacement? Former James Gang member Joe Walsh.

That Walsh and Szymczyk should be reunited at this time—as guitarist and producer of one of the world's biggest-selling bands—must have seemed ironic in light of their first association nearly a decade earlier, when Walsh had been nothing more than a college kid at Kent State, enthralled with the idea of recording a first album.

Walsh helped the band complete their world tour in the first part of 1976, then entered the studio to begin work on the Eagles' fifth album. It would turn out to be one of the best-selling albums ever recorded, somewhat justifying the eight months spent laboring over the tracks. Dedicating that much time in pursuit of a perfect album can be a dangerous proposition, as it's all too easy to perfect the life right out of a record. But Walsh's harder-edged guitar approach, honed during his years in the James Gang and as a solo artist, meshed well with Don Felder's playing. The spark from the interplay of the two guitarists brought life to *Hotel California*, displayed to shimmering effect via Szymczyk's immaculate production.

As for platinum? *Hotel California* reached that status in a single week.

A key contemporary of the Eagles was singer-songwriter Jackson Browne. Like the band, he was one of the first artists to sign with David Geffen's Asylum Records, having nurtured a track record that found his songs recorded by The Byrds and Linda Ronstadt.

Browne cowrote the Eagles' first chart single, "Take It Easy," with Glenn Frey, but it was as a solo artist that he caught the public eye. A writer of thoughtful material, his 1974 album *Late for the Sky* was a masterpiece of dark melancholy, eerie in its depth. Browne's commercial breakthrough came in 1976 with *The Pretender*, recorded soon after the suicide of his wife. Throughout his career, Browne was supported by the masterful instrumentalist David Lindley, accomplished on an array of string instruments and key to the effective moodiness of Browne's albums.

Browne was active as more than just a recording artist. Not only did he secure a record deal with Asylum for his friend Warren Zevon, but Browne also produced the self-titled album of the gruff, sarcastic songwriter. Despite lyric topics and a wry styling that contrasted sharply with many of his fellow West Coast artists, Zevon benefited from the performances of Eagles Don Henley and Glenn Frey on his album, welcoming the additional celebrity power for songs like "I'll Sleep When I'm Dead" and "Poor, Poor Pitiful Me."

Surprisingly, the roots of The Eagles were planted in ground common to two other stylistically divergent musicians, Emmylou Harris and Tom Petty.

Like most of the members of The Eagles, Harris had also been involved with projects for fellow singer Linda Ronstadt. In the process, she became friendly with Eagle Bernie Leadon, who would later help Emmylou record her own solo projects.

Harris had emerged from the Washington, D.C. area after forming a creative partnership with Gram Parsons following the final breakup of The Flying Burrito Brothers. They had met after one of the last Burrito concerts, when Parsons took the advice of band mate Chris Hillman and traveled to see Emmylou singing in a small D.C. club. He was immediately smitten by her talent and knew that she could help him realize his new vision of country music.

Parsons had already been influential in that realm. During a brief hiatus from The Burritos, Gram became friendly with Keith Richards, acting as an inspiration for The Rolling Stones' newly prominent explorations of country sounds.

Harris went on to record and tour with Parsons, but the collaboration was tragically cut short when Parsons died of an overdose in September 1973. Emmylou was forced to step out on her own. Due to the critical respect shown for her work with Parsons, Harris was able to line up a contract with Warner Brothers Records. She met producer Brian Ahern, whom she would eventually marry, and began recording her first solo album.

Equipped with a luxuriant soprano tone, Harris technically had a prettier voice than the benchmark of country music, Patsy Cline. But like the great Patsy, Emmylou was instinctively able to convey the heartache and pain existing at the core of songs like "Too Far Gone" and "Boulder to Birmingham." It was a rare gift—and even more welcome in an era when pop songs by singers like Olivia Newton-John were being passed off as "country."

But there was far more to Harris' music than the emotive nature of her mesmeric voice; backing Harris in the studio on her mid-1970s albums *Pieces of the Sky* and *Elite Hotel* was the very core of Elvis Presley's exceptional concert band, including one of America's greatest guitarists, James Burton.

Burton was first noticed as the guitarist for Ricky Nelson, the early rock idol who gained acclaim on the *Ozzy and Harriet* television series of the 1960s. By the 1970s he was Presley's main guitarist, a stunning player equally adept at ripping off fiery rockabilly runs or coaxing his Telecaster to cry out in moaning, countrified pedal-steel tones. His subtle artistry contributed much of the atmosphere that made Emmylou's albums so consistently moving.

Emmylou Harris first encountered The Eagles' sphere of influence at a fairly young age, but Tom Petty had crossed paths with members of the band far earlier in his life.

Petty grew up in Gainsville, Florida, perhaps best known as the site of the annual National Hot Rod Association Winternationals. In other words, it was not a booming metropolis. But there was a lot of music in town, and as a teenager Petty became a big fan of The Continentals. Coincidentally, the lead guitarist of the Continentals was future Eagle Don Felder. After the demise of The Continentals, Felder formed a group called, for reasons unknown, The Maundy Quintet, with yet another future Eagle, Bernie Leadon.

By the time the duo flew west to gain acclaim in California, Tom Petty had formed his own band with Leadon's younger brother, Tom. Mudcrutch was a band that, though hailing from the South, played outside the boundaries of Southern rock. They kept their songs short and were just as influenced by Emmylou Harris' partner Gram Parsons and his earlier band The Flying Burrito Brothers as they were turned on by the sounds of British rock.

Joining Petty and the younger Leadon in Mudcrutch was a quiet young guitarist named Mike Campbell. Though Mudcrutch would splinter after entering into a troublesome development association with Leon Russell's production partner Denny Cordell, the alliance of Petty and Campbell would endure. Cordell helped direct the recording project as it evolved from a Mudcrutch album into the debut of Tom Petty and The Heartbreakers, with Petty and Campbell supported by fellow Gainsville musicians Stan Lynch on drums, Benmont Tench on keyboards, and Ron Blair on bass.

Upon release in 1976, the self-titled debut album by Petty and the band looked to be a record in search of its own niche. Boasting a hard, aggressive edge in some songs, the material was just as often characterized by a Byrds-like shimmer of twelve-string guitar. Some of the harmonies were sharp rock exhortations; others long, lush wordless textures. Petty's voice contrasted those gentler moments with his bratty street-punk delivery and strained choruses. And there was a further trait that was unusual for mid-1970s rock—songs that wrapped up in two to three minutes. Petty and company came in, said what they had to say, and got out.

In particular, Campbell's guitar symbolized the less-is-more approach. Already a masterful synthesizer of rock guitar styles, Campbell's brief forays into the spotlight were models of how to play a moving-yet-economical solo, ones that left listeners wanting to hear more. His lyrical approach to playing resulted in every note being a perfect choice, serving the song construction as it emphasized a chord change or resolved a musical progression.

Tom Petty and The Heartbreakers were a rough-and-tumble entry into an American rock world that was increasingly becoming dominated by faceless-if-earnest bands from the heartland of the country. Groups like Kansas and Styx suffered from a terminal deficit of star power and charisma. Most of these musicians, despite sales reaching gold and even platinum status, could easily walk the street with no fear whatsoever of being recognized. The time was right for a savvy manager to market a pretty face, one accompanied by music that had that most desirable of elements, crossover appeal.

Just as Humble Pie was about to release their new live album in 1972, Peter Frampton suddenly abandoned his post as the band's lead guitarist. Despite the loss, within weeks Humble Pie began an ascent to new levels of popularity, thanks to enthusiasm for the concert recording.

Second thoughts? Frampton could be forgiven for having had them. But even though he'd left his former band mates with a difficult position to fill, Humble Pie's manager, the mercurial Dee Anthony, thought the handsome young man had star potential. Anthony retained Frampton as a client. A contract with A&M Records was arranged, and Frampton recorded a solo album before forming his own band. Rather curiously known as Frampton's Camel, the group included former members of Spooky Tooth and Cochise, the band that had provided Procol Harum with guitarist Mick Grabham.

Despite near-constant touring, Frampton's Camel could carry its namesake only so far over the course of three albums, and the guitarist broke up his band. Recalling the success of *Rockin' the Fillmore*—the double album live set that had rocketed Humble Pie into the forefront of the American market—Anthony, Frampton, and the record label decided to record one of Peter's first gigs with a newly assembled band.

The result, taped at San Francisco's Winterland auditorium, was *Frampton Comes Alive*. Whether it was old fans of Humble Pie, or people who had been impressed by Frampton's countless opening-for-the-headliner gigs, or simply girls smitten by the guitarist's curly hair and boyish charm—it seemed that everyone bought the record at once. Out of nowhere, *Frampton Comes Alive* became the largest-selling live album of all time, residing in the number one spot for seventeen weeks and selling more than eight million copies.

The *Frampton Comes Alive* cover was enhanced for the young girl market by a huge, flattering cover picture of the smiling Frampton, his tousled hair backlit by stage spotlights. Yes, he was certifiably dreamy. Still, at least some of the sales were explained by the rock pulse of Frampton's songs—even if, from a topical standpoint, they were studiously inoffensive.

Other bands could be excused for salivating over Frampton's remarkable success, but the odds were against them. They either didn't have Peter's glowing looks and flowing locks or they were simply unable to tone down their sonic attack. In the case of Aerosmith, they were guilty on both counts.

Like just about every other band of the day, Aerosmith had slogged through endless tours, opening for a procession of haughty headliners and slowly building an audience. Finally, with the release of the band's fourth album, *Rocks*, in 1976, there was a growing belief that the phrase "America's Rolling Stones" might be more than a catchy marketing headline.

Comparisons to Mick Jagger and company were further legitimized by the fact that Aerosmith's vocalist, Steven Tyler, was a living caricature of the Stone's front-man, all mouth and lips and sashaying scarves on stage. With the dark, dangerous

Joe Perry playing the role of Keith Richards, the Boston-based band seemed ready to get down to business.

Perry was a masterful creator of rock riffs. The kinetic power of the main phrase in "Sweet Emotion" from Aerosmith's third album was undeniable proof of that. With Perry's talents augmented by co-guitarist Brad Whitford's own six-string propulsion, Aerosmith had a truly dangerous attack. Over a reliable rhythm section anchored by drummer Joey Kramer and bassist Tom Hamilton, the two guitars sparred in high-volume combat, lashing out with solos and quick fills between Tyler's screeched lyrics.

In the studio, Aerosmith was under the wing of producer Jack Douglas. Douglas had come up through the New York studio scene, working on sessions as diverse as Lou Reed's *Berlin* and the first album by The New York Dolls. An expert at capturing a vibrant rock sound, Douglas was establishing his own reputation as he designed the foundation for Aerosmith's massive studio presence.

On *Rocks*, Aerosmith was in an exciting creative phase, pushing the boundaries that had defined their first three albums. While "Sick as a Dog" and "Rats in the Cellar" were largely standard hard rock, things took a turn toward evolution with the ominous chorus thunder of Perry's "Combination." And a collaboration between Tyler and Whitford yielded "Nobody's Fault," the next page of the modern heavy metal blueprint that was becoming more defined with each passing month. The lone obstacle preventing the band from claiming a near-prefect album arose when Tyler was left to his own compositional devices, specifically the mawkish "Home Tonight." With blue-moon exceptions, ballads are territory best avoided by hard rock bands.

Sadly, Aerosmith in 1976 was standing on the verge of a post-*Rocks* creative decline. Substance abuse and the departure of both Perry's guitar and Douglas' production skills would decimate the band.

Piper, on the other hand, was young and hungry. Orbiting around the talents of a songwriter, singer, and guitarist named Billy Squier, Piper took form when Squier began recording demos with drummer Richie Fontana and bassist Danny McGary. When Kiss manager Bill Aucoin grew interested in the project, guitarists Alan Nolan and Tommy Gunn were added to the mix, leading to a contract with A&M Records.

The band's debut album, *Piper*, arrived in 1976 with the best support available. The project was mixed by Eddie Kramer and had been mastered by audio whiz Bernie Grundman. In the grooves, the band's slightly improbable sound was akin to a more emphatic, agitated Marc Bolan singing bitter love songs in Dylan-like phrasing supported by a three-guitar harmonized attack. But despite gigs opening for Kiss and Ritchie Blackmore's Rainbow, Piper never caught on. Their follow-up *Can't Wait* proved to be their swan song.

Though Squier would go on to great solo success, his high-pitched vocals were easily topped by Geddy Lee, the bassist and lead singer of Canada's entry to the hard rock wars, Rush. Their first album was released in 1974, finding Lee, guitarist Alex Lifeson, and drummer John Rutsey playing the power trio game amidst an assortment of not-particularly-original riffage. And there was no failing to notice a serious fixation with Led Zeppelin's Robert Plant on Lee's part.

For the band's second album, Rutsey was replaced by Neil Peart. Rush began to mature as Peart perfected his awesome raw talents, the drummer driving the band in new directions until, in 1976, they hit with a commercial breakthrough, *2112*. The album relied on a science fiction lyrical approach, but more noticeable was a new sophistication in the band's compositions. To ensure everyone was aware that Rush was now to be taken seriously, quotes from *1812 Overture* were dropped into the overture portion of the album's title track. The tight ensemble playing among the trio was a framework that would serve the band well, all the while providing life support for Peart's growth into one of rock's most astounding percussionists.

Like Rush and their Canadian roots, Germany's Michael Schenker was also contributing to the international flavor of hard rock circa 1976. Lead guitarist in the hard-hitting British band UFO, Schenker communicated with his band mates in halting English—but his guitar spoke volumes in the evolving language of heavy metal.

Tapping his extensive vocabulary of scales, Schenker played with stunning dexterity as he carved a new path that diverged from the classical explorations pioneered by Ritchie Blackmore.

On the 1976 album *No Heavy Petting* and especially on 1977's *Lights Out*, Schenker foreshadows in thrilling fashion the technical skills that would be expected of a new generation of heavy metal guitarists more than a decade later.

Though Schenker was breaking new ground, Robin Trower was following the same road that had beckoned since he quit Procol Harum's lead guitar position in 1972. Key to his decision to leave the band was his composition "Song for a Dreamer," a song dedicated to Jimi Hendrix that appeared on Procol Harum's 1971 album *Broken Barricades*.

"It was a tribute to Hendrix and I wanted it to sound like Hendrix," Trower commented. "It made me see the creative possibilities of the electric guitar, and it wasn't until I came up with my own material that I got the urge to do it full-time."

With a style that was based in blues but colored by the lush tones of Hendrix at his most tranquil, Trower established his solo career in 1973 with a dazzling, sonically enticing album entitled *Twice Removed from Yesterday*. The record was produced by another Procol Harum refugee, keyboardist Matthew Fisher, whose organ work had framed the band's global calling card, "Whiter Shade of Pale."

Working with Trower was bassist and vocalist James Dewar, late of Stone the Crows. Dewar and his band had slowly established a name on the British rock scene, with the group relying on Maggie Bell's powerhouse vocals and the guitar of Les Harvey, younger brother of Alex Harvey. But Dewar saw greener pastures ahead with Trower and departed. Within months, Stones the Crows dissolved after Harvey was electrocuted in a tragic onstage incident.

Dewar's vocals called to mind Free's Paul Rodgers at his most soulful, and the Trower album's triumvirate of lead-off songs— "I Can't Wait Much Longer," "Daydream," and "Hannah"— unfolded at a stately, trance-like pace. Trower confidently walked a fine line, balancing the fire of his attack with the material's demands for dreamscape aural vistas. With solos like the two that embellished "Daydream"—among the most moving and evocative electric guitar solos to ever grace a song—the album announced that a new guitar hero had arrived.

The band's second album, *Bridge of Sighs*, was also produced by Fisher and firmly established the group in the United States.

The dark beauty of the title track, the urgent opening song "Day of the Eagle," and the heavy blues jam of "Too Rolling Stoned" commanded constant FM radio airplay throughout 1974, becoming staples for the rest of the decade.

By the 1976 release of *Live*, his fourth album, Trower was refining his guitar skills further and had also replaced drummer Reg Isidore with former Sly and the Family Stone member Bill Lordan.

Removed from the overdubbing support system of the studio, the guitarist in a power trio has a lot of foundation to support with just six strings to do the job—but *Live* captures Trower handling the daunting challenge with facility.

"We weren't planning on doing a live album," Trower admitted of the set, recorded as a broadcast for Swedish radio. "It was the only show that was recorded and it happened by accident; we didn't even know it was being recorded. Swedish Broadcasting did it and though it wasn't the best sound, it captured the mood and feeling of that particular night, so it worked out well."

Though Trower enjoyed the success of his creative labor, the endless weeks on the road took their toll. Gig after gig in city after city, always chasing the next performance—it was a numbing lifestyle that scores of his fellow musicians working the concert trail of 1976 could instantly identify with.

"You get enough time to eat," Trower confided about his own life on the road, "and sometimes enough time to sleep. But with the flying, the sound checks, and the gig you can only get maybe an hour or two to relax after a show. I was tired of it years ago. I can see a time coming when I'll choose to only work in the studio."

While Robin Trower pondered retiring to a life of studio creativity, a young man near Boston was using his own home studio in the feverish pursuit of a dream. Flying in the face of the standard path to a record contract, where bands are expected to have a pre-established fan base from abundant live concert work, Tom Scholz labored hour after hour as he meticulously assembled his vision of the perfect demo tape. The challenge was daunting, but his goal was simple: get his band signed. The fact that there really wasn't an actual band at that point in time could be dealt with later.

Scholz had attended the prestigious Massachusetts Institute of Technology, pursuing a degree in mechanical engineering, and to make ends meet he held down a day job at Polaroid. And though his perfect demo painfully yielded nothing but rejection during an agonizing period from 1972 to 1975, at long last Epic Records' Artist and Repertoire man Lennie Petze signed the band. They were to be called Boston—but first Scholz had to assemble the group. Collecting a handful of experienced hard rock musicians from the Boston scene to join him and singer Brad Delp, who had been involved in the project from the beginning, Scholz and company flew to Los Angeles in early 1976 to build an album around Tom's precious demos. The result was *Boston*, released in August 1976.

Marketed under the motto "Better Music Through Science," Boston the band watched in awe as the album met with an astonishing reaction: Boston was gold in seven weeks, platinum in eleven, double platinum in sixteen. In a plot twist that would have been dismissed as too unbelievable even for Hollywood, in mere weeks Boston roared from obscurity to superstardom, riding the biggest debut album in recording history.

Key to the band's sound was Scholz's laborious crafting of guitar overdubs. Much the way Queen's Brian May orchestrated guitar parts to create lush, near-symphonic passages, so too did Scholz build an elaborate architecture upon which the band's songs were constructed. In addition, Scholz used his education and Polaroid experience to begin building his own specialized guitar effects, providing him rich tones and infinite sustain. The only drawback to Scholz's recording science was that the heart of the band's music seemed to resonate more with craft than emotion. Regardless, Boston sounded so good—a pure sonic confection—that the massive sales were understandable.

While Boston was the new kid on the rock scene, Steely Dan had been a presence since their debut album in 1972 spun off the hits "Do It Again" and "Reelin' in the Years." As time passed and band personnel shifted, it became clear that keyboardist

and lead singer Donald Fagen and guitarist and bassist Walter
Becker were the mainstays and masterminds of the band's
sound. They guarded that sound jealously, the two men notorious for demanding standards in the studio.

By the time they began work on their fifth album, to be titled
The Royal Scam, Becker and Fagen were all that was left of the
original Steely Dan. The group now consisted largely of studio
musicians drafted to serve as temporary specialists, charged
with realizing the duo's creative visions. Among those brought
on board to record *The Royal Scam* were brilliant rhythm and
blues drummer Bernard "Pretty" Purdie, guitarists Elliot Randall
and Larry Carlton, and bassist Chuck Rainey. Of the band's original lineup, only guitarist Denny Dias, a wonderfully melodic
soloist, was still a recording participant at these 1976 sessions.

Key to the new sound of Steely Dan was Becker and Fagen's
maturing sense of harmonic sophistication, developed in large
part from studying jazz. Though their lyrics could be obscure
(One *Stereo Review* analysis noted, "The lyrics baffle me. Maybe
they know what they're talking about but I can't get a clue."),
their song structures were intricately assembled works of
beauty, with sections interacting in a harmonious momentum
that urged on songs like "Don't Take Me Alive" and "Kid
Charlemagne."

"I don't know why groups who have some good writers as
far as the lyrics go don't get bored playing the same old rock
and roll stuff," Fagen wondered in the notes to the band's *Citizen* career overview. "Even though we were really too young to
experience a lot of the golden age of jazz in the 1950s, nevertheless that's what we were into when we were young, through
recordings . . ."

Refining his own sense of studio sophistication was singer
and guitarist Boz Scaggs. The Californian played as a side man
with The Steve Miller Band in the late 1960s before moving on
to record an alluring rhythm and blues album with Duane Allman in 1969. Scaggs slowly edged toward a more dance-floor-
friendly sound, casting a sweet dash of jazz fusion over the studio tracks he concocted during 1976.

Much like Jeff Beck's *Blow by Blow*, Scaggs' tremendously successful album of that year, *Silk Degrees*, sounds firmly rooted in
the 1970s thanks to its obvious dance floor influences. Still, it's

an album every bit as stylish as the works of Roxy Music, given a fashionable, hip air through Scaggs' coolly soulful vocals and the sweeping arrangements and production of David Paich and Joe Wissert, respectively. But where Roxy Music's albums carried an undertone of gloom over Europe's fading elegance, Scaggs' music symbolized trendy west coast sophistication, a world of long nights and cocaine, palm trees and easy wealth.

Obviously, studio expression was crucial to the sound of both Steely Dan and Boz Scaggs. That was also the case with a unique band from Germany called Kraftwerk, a name that translates to "power plant." The group members were not instrumentalists in the traditional rock sense; rather, they all played electronic keyboards or operated noise-generating devices of their own design. In fact, when Kraftwerk toured, their Dusseldorf studio went with them. Klingklang Studio had been constructed modularly for portability, as all of its components were crucial to the band's sound. In Kraftwerk's case, the studio was literally their instrument.

Though the band always performed as a quartet, like Steely Dan, Kraftwerk was the creative vision of a duo. The conceptualization of Florian Schneider and Ralf Hutter ensured that Kraftwerk sounded like no other music.

"After the war, German entertainment was destroyed," Hutter noted of the pop culture vacuum in which he and Schneider grew up. Essentially, Kraftwerk began with a clean creative slate. After several recordings of experimental electronic music, Kraftwerk's first notable success was the song "Autobahn," from the 1974 album of the same name. Their efforts took a giant step forward with 1975's *Radioactivity*, an album with song titles reflecting the music's technical origins: "Airwaves," "Radioland," "The Voice of Energy," "Ohm Sweet Ohm." Although the music was largely instrumental, Kraftwerk's few vocals were supplied by Hutter in detached, near-monotone voicings. The disembodied vocals floated about in Kraftwerk's electronic sound webs—fragile, repeating structures of cool and efficient beauty.

By 1976, Kraftwerk were already performing material from their next album, *Trans-Europe Express*. The new material revealed that, as synthesizers and other electronic media evolved, so too would the sound of Kraftwerk—though they deliberately juxtaposed their new sounds against an old-fashioned suit-and-tie image.

Trans-Europe Express took the pulse of the dominant disco culture and synthesized a mutated approximation of the beats. Upon this newly updated foundation, Kraftwerk was able to craft ever more complex sound sculptures that reflected Hutter and Schneider's maturing compositional talents. And the two exquisite solos that graced "Europe Endless" proved that electronic instruments were quite capable of generating the emotional resonance of traditional instruments. Not only was Kraftwerk's music unique among their rock world contemporaries, but it would also serve as the direct blueprint for the development of modern "techno" and "electronica" music.

Roxy Music had already proven to be an influential band by 1976, though they were known primarily for their moody studio efforts. In 1976 they presented a more vibrant vision of the band with a live album, *Viva! Roxy Music.*

A significant change had occurred to Roxy Music's already distinctive sound through the incorporation of King Crimson bassist John Wetton. Crimson had dissolved after recording the stunning album *Red*, the band members possibly realizing they had recorded an album of such depth and intensity that it would be impossible to follow. Teamed with Roxy's mighty drummer Paul Thompson, Wetton brought new bottom-end power to what had become a surprisingly forceful live band.

Viva! superbly captured the myriad facets of Roxy Music, from the unsettling tension of "In Every Dream Home a Heartache" to the clever Spectorian "wall of sound" approach on "Pyjamarama." But the centerpiece of the album was a relentless rendition of "The Bogus Man," Bryan Ferry's eerie tale of a nameless, unstoppable pursuer. The majestic arrangements and evocative progressions of Roxy Music's carefully assembled studio albums hit with far greater impact as they unfolded on the grander scale of a live concert. As such, *Viva!* was a revelation, the album some consider the band's best.

Though Brian Eno had quit Roxy Music years earlier, he, too, was a participant in a 1976 live album, sharing the stage with Roxy guitarist Phil Manzanera as the latter moonlighted in a side project called 801. Splitting the original song lineup evenly between Eno and Manzanera compositions, the album also included a trance-like version of The Beatles' "Tomorrow Never Knows" as well as The Kinks' "You Really Got Me," a rather rollicking choice for musicians generally regarded as cerebral rather than sensual. True to form, though, 801's take on Ray Davies' raw classic was precise, stuttering, and carefully calculated. But 801 did have ample firepower in the form of drummer Simon Phillips, whose percussive dexterity seemed to know no bounds. Phillips' professional ranking would soon elevate to "in demand" status, and *801 Live* showed why, particularly on fusion-friendly songs like "East of Asteroid."

Eno's friend David Bowie was also returning to the stage in 1976, ending a two-year absence from the concert trail. His flirtation with Philadelphia's soul sound having drawn to a close, Bowie moved back toward rock with a new album titled *Station to Station*. Typically for Bowie, a new album demanded a new identity, and reporting for duty in 1976 was a persona that came to be known as the Thin White Duke.

For his return to live performance, Bowie had chosen a look as severe as the tour's concert staging. Fabulously emaciated, crowned by slicked-back hair, Bowie-the-Duke stood beneath harsh lighting in white shirt and black vest, his clothing matching the stark black and white setting of the stage.

"I wanted to go back to a kind of Expressionist German-film look," Bowie stated in the notes to his *Sound and Vision* career overview. "A black-and-white movies look, but with an intensity that was sort of aggressive."

Part of the aggression came from the more forceful stance of Bowie's new material. In the studio recording *Station to Station*, the core of Bowie's current live band—Dennis Davis on drums, George Murray on bass, and Carlos Alomar on guitar—was supplemented by pianist Roy Bittan, on loan from Bruce Springsteen's E Street Band, and Earl Slick, playing the role of both lead guitarist and six-string stunt man. Bowie encouraged Slick to take risks in his playing on the album.

"I got some quite extraordinary things out of Earl Slick," Bowie noted. "I think it captured his imagination to make noises on guitar, and textures, rather than playing the right notes."

Slick's experimentations are immediately apparent on the album-opening title track, as long howls of feedback and string-scraping growls lord over a simple two-note intro progression.

Though Slick proved his worth throughout the album—his solo in "Stay" is particularly noteworthy—it is Bittan whose contributions were most essential, lending percussive drive to "TVC15" and lush grandiosity to the poignant ballads "Word on a Wing" and "Wild Is the Wind."

The single constant of David Bowie's career was that he existed in an unvarying state of reinvention, perhaps afraid that remaining in one visage too long would allow the quickening pace of rock music to leave him behind. It was a pressure that was widely shared among rock's upper echelon.

"Our music may change so much in times to come that our audience does diminish," theorized Led Zeppelin singer Robert Plant, speaking to Jaan Uhelszki in *Creem* magazine's July 1977 issue. "Because I know we won't become passé, we might take things beyond what people are prepared to accept from us . . . When you think you've reached a dead end, you have to get off the horse."

Those thoughts arose during any discussion of the band's 1976 album, *Presence*. The question was one of fading popularity. After all, Led Zeppelin had been at the top of its game for most of the decade, and the critical and audience reaction to *Presence* had been disappointing.

The project had faced obstacles from the start. In the wake of Plant's car crash in Greece in August of 1975, the band's planned touring had been scuttled while the vocalist recuperated from his severe injuries. Once Plant seemed firmly on the road to recovery, manager Peter Grant suggested the band use its down time to record a new album. Shipped off to Musicland Studios in Munich, Germany, Led Zeppelin set about the task of recording their new album in a time frame of less than three weeks—an astonishingly short period by rock superstar standards.

Due to the accelerated pace of the recording sessions, *Presence* resonated with a raw live energy not present on the band's albums since the beginning of the decade.

Though the quicker pace of tracking resulted in a sound that called to mind the vibrancy of the group's first two albums, the songs themselves were different from anything Led Zeppelin had recorded. "Achilles Last Stand" and "Nobody's Fault but Mine" were complex—not quite to the twisting-and-turning extremes of the fusion bands, but unusual time signatures and sudden accents abounded. This was the province of John Bonham, whose thunderous drumming was the very heart and power of this album. And though the songs thrived on their own complexity, Jimmy Page's guitar solos were loose and inventive, the guitarist stretching out in a way he had not done for years. On *Presence's* predecessor, *Physical Graffiti*, Page's solos had been short and concise, components assembled within an elaborate structure of overdubs; on *Presence*, the improvisational feel of his solos imbued the songs with a sense of daring.

Still wheelchair-bound due to his shattered right leg, Robert Plant doubtless found the sessions a welcome distraction from the pain of rehabilitation, and his invigorating vocals contributed to the project's overall energy.

Presence was a largely successful project, even if the monotonous "Candy Store Rock" and "Hots on for Nowhere" could both have used work. But it did leave Led Zeppelin fans wondering exactly where the band was heading. So much of the group's masterpiece, *Physical Graffiti*, had depended on Page's intricate webs of guitar and John Paul Jones' atmospheric aura of keyboard textures. Yet on the new album, Page was playing with abandon and Jones' keyboards were nowhere to be heard. No one—the band included—seemed certain as to the direction of Led Zeppelin's flights in the future.

New York City's Madison Square Garden. For Led Zeppelin, the twenty-thousand-seat arena had become a home away from home, the site of some of their greatest triumphs. For every major rock band in 1976, the Garden was where you played—and hopefully sold out. It sent a message to the world, reaffirming a band's status as an equal among rock's elite.

But some forty blocks away from Madison Square Garden, in the run-down environment of a New York neighborhood known as the Bowery, radical sonic experimentation was underway. Using the rock and roll periodic table as a starting point, new kinds of rock bands were hard at work in a determined attempt to devise new elements.

Art student David Byrne had moved to New York with fellow band members Chris Frantz and Tina Weymouth, renaming his group from The Artistics to Talking Heads. At the same time, Television, built around an angular guitar approach that was quickly growing more and more sophisticated, was founded by Tom Verlaine. And a former member of Television, Richard Hell, began to follow his own raw rock visions.

In 1976, though, perhaps the brightest light of the bold New York scene was Patti Smith, a young woman from New Jersey who had already made contributions to the world of rock and roll as a writer and poet. Her words had appeared in the pages of the influential *Creem* magazine and had graced album covers by Todd Rundgren and Edgar Winter, and she, like her roommate, photographer Robert Mapplethorpe, was beginning to feel the embrace of New York's trendy art scene.

Aside from crafting words for poetry readings and print, Patti had also contributed lyrics to songs by Blue Oyster Cult. Though it seemed only natural that a poet should bring her talents to lyric writing, the concept of evolving from writer to performer had not been a driving vision.

"Before I had my own band," Smith recalled, "Blue Oyster Cult had heard me reading poetry and thought of having me involved in the band, but I had never sung and it had never occurred to me to be in a rock and roll band."

Once the idea did take hold, Smith aligned herself with writer Lenny Kaye, an aspiring guitarist and a highly regarded expert in obscure 1960s rock. With the joining of the twosome, the foundation of The Patti Smith Group was born. Augmented by keyboardist Richard Sohl, and borrowing Tom Verlaine from Television, Smith and Kaye entered Jimi Hendrix's Electric Lady Studios in June 1974 to record two songs, "Hey Joe" and "Piss Factory." Funded by Mapplethorpe, Smith took what at the time was an almost unheard-of route—she pressed her own record, circumventing the idea that an artist had to have the backing of a major label to validate his or her creations.

Still, in the wake of the single's release on her own Mer Records, a major label was drawn to Patti and the growing excitement about her work. In 1975 she signed with Arista Records based on the interest of the label's founder, legendary music industry veteran Clive Davis. Her band now bolstered by guitarist Ivan Kral and drummer Jay Dee Daugherty, Patti entered Electric Lady to record her debut album, a record produced by former Velvet Underground member John Cale.

"Three chord rock merged with the power of the word," was Patti's initial description of *Horses*. Later, in an interview with *Creem* magazine's Tony Glover in the January 1976 issue, Smith further analyzed the album.

"If there's a concept to the record, it's voyage," she surmised. "It starts with 'Gloria' and ends almost with 'Land of a Thousand Dances,' which has the same chord structure. In between, travel is the key."

Smith's torrent of words and images and a quickly maturing band made her concerts unforgettable experiences, each night presenting instant creative evolution that differed radically from the night before.

In the summer of 1976, The Patti Smith Group returned to the studio to record a second album. This time the choice of producer was something of a surprise—Jack Douglas, the hard rock producer best known for his work with Aerosmith. Industry observers expected a clash of titanic proportions if Douglas attempted to reign in Smith's rampant creativity.

Instead, when *Radio Ethiopia* was released in October 1976, the result of the collaboration was a cohesive work of sublime intensity.

Radio Ethiopia found a professional hard-hitting sound applied to a raw, experimental rock band to thrilling effect. All of Patti and the band's experimentations remained in full flower, but Douglas' production skills provided the band with an aural thump that had been missing on *Horses*. Though "Ask the Angels" and "Pumping (My Heart)" were concise blasts of pure rock power and emotion, the exotic sway of "Ain't It Strange" was erotic and hypnotic, Smith's stuttering vocal delivery chilling in its urgency. And there was no denying the white-hot emotion of romantic abandonment and betrayal that fueled "Pissing in a River."

The raw voicings of guitarists Kaye and Kral, communicated with such force by Douglas, reinforced the basic ideal at the very heart of the new Manhattan scene: to create effective rock music, the guitar dexterity of a John McLaughlin and the scales of a Ritchie Blackmore were no longer essential qualities. Patti's own triumphant battle cry at the finale of an incendiary cover of The Who's "My Generation" sounded the new rock charge: "We created it—let's take it over!"

That concept was one that had been fully embraced—and in large part invented—by The Ramones.

"I use Mosrite guitars," Johnny Ramone revealed of his guitar sound on the first album by The Ramones, released in mid-1976. "I bought the first one 'cause when I went to the store I only had fifty dollars and that was the cheapest guitar I could find."

Johnny Ramones' thrifty attitude carried over—by financial necessity—into the recording of *Ramones*. When Yes recorded *Tales from Topographic Oceans* they spent five months in the studio. The Ramones did their deed in seventeen days for $6,200. They spent all of ten hours mixing the album.

The Ramones had spent 1975 in residency at the New York club CBGB, overcoming owner Hilly Kristal's doubts upon seeing the band for the first time—"the most untogether band I ever saw"—and slowly building a burgeoning cult following. Finally, at the end of 1975, The Ramones secured a contract with Sire Records to document their unforgiving, blitzkrieg aural assault.

When the band emerged from the studio in early 1976, the primitive mix of *Ramones* called to mind the earliest of stereo recordings. The guitar and bass were piled on top of each other in pumping unison to the left, the cymbal splashes washing over the right. The pulse of the beat ran up the middle, and above it all, in complete startling clarity, was the unmistakable voice of Joey Ramone. With phrasing borrowed from The Ronnettes' Ronnie Spector—Phil Spector's idealized urban-romantic female vocalist—Joey had the most unusual and distinctive rock inflection this side of Roxy Music's Bryan Ferry. But where Ferry crooned over the Euro-gloom of Roxy's continental posturing, Joey crooned over blasting Marshall amps and simple, relentless rhythms.

"We've always been our own breed of band," Joey noted. "We concocted a unique sound and style all our own, a trademark. That's what everybody tries to achieve but so few really do."

A perfect Ramones moment? There are those who'd argue that the first album in its entirety is nothing if not perfect, but there is one brief passage in the midst of "Judy is a Punk" that sums up the world of The Ramones. Johnny and Dee Dee's guitar and bass are a unified force, thundering on in a hypnotic jackhammer roar. Tommy's drums are right in sync, as handclaps celebrate the big beat. And Joey Ramone, in his inimitable voice, plots the musical terrain ahead: "Second verse—same as the first!" With The Ramones, people either got it or they didn't.

In England, the kids really got it. On July 4, 1976, as the United States celebrated the two-hundredth anniversary of its independence from England, the Ramones brought a special gift to the British people as the band began a short tour—a tour that would leave countless repercussions resonating in its wake. The raw, blunt, and brief blasts of songs like "Beat on the Brat" and "I Don't Wanna Go Down to the Basement" validated the equally direct blueprints of a new generation of British kids already forming their own bands and spurred scores of others to join together in creating a new kind of rock music.

These kids loathed the famous superstar bands, disgusted over their extravagant lifestyles. And as for musical complexities? They saw the high standards of prog rock musicianship as a membership qualification designed to keep grass-roots bands out of the rock star club. It made them all the more determined to follow Patti Smith's declaration and reclaim rock music as their own.

The chain reaction was underway. All of the ingredients had come together in just the right manner, at just the right time. Pete Townshend had seen it coming, but no one heeded his warning. Now, it was too late to be stopped. The core elements of rock and roll in 1976—from the elaborate arrangements of the prog rockers to the spastic cadences of the fusionists, from the posturing of the hard rockers to the haughty attitudes of the rock legends—had created a fertile environment. But that environment, so celebrated for its anything-goes freedom, so profitable for its inhabitants, so established in its hierarchy, was on the knife edge, about to cascade into an era where the familiar would seemingly overnight become treacherous and unknown. Rock had given birth to something new and alien, and it was christened punk rock.

From the moment "Colonel" Tom Parker got his hands on Elvis Presley, the role of the manager has been inexorably linked with rock music. Over the years, managers like Peter Grant, who guided Led Zeppelin and Bad Company; Dee Anthony, overseer of Humble Pie, Joe Cocker, Peter Frampton, and The J. Geils Band; and Albert Grossman, manager of Bob Dylan and Janis Joplin, stood as symbols of rock glamour and, more importantly, control.

Like a moth to flame, British rock-wear store owner Malcolm McClaren was drawn to rock and roll, entertaining visions of his own management skills, convinced that his creative notions would lead to stardom—if only he could find someone to follow his guidance.

In early 1975, he convinced the on-the-verge-of-disintegration New York Dolls to allow him to try his hand at steering their floundering career. After implementing a rather bizarre makeover on the band based on Soviet Union imagery, McClaren was forced to face the fact that his Dolls project was an abject failure. Returning to England, he considered the atmosphere he'd found in New York. He'd been impressed by the look of musicians he'd encountered like Patti Smith and Richard Hell, who wore torn clothes and fashioned radically chopped hair.

McClaren's shop, once called Let It Rock and now dubbed Sex, was the hub of a tiny scene. McClaren had put the word out that he was looking for bands to work with and had thus encountered a semi-proficient outfit made up of part-time Sex employee Glen Matlock on bass, guitarist Steve Jones, and drummer Paul Cook. McClaren had even devised a name for the band: The Sex Pistols.

In August 1975, young John Lydon walked into Sex, wearing a homemade T-shirt that declared, "I hate Pink Floyd." Impressed by Lydon's obvious attitude, McClaren associate Bernie Rhodes invited Lydon to audition as lead singer of The Sex Pistols. The audition took place in a pub, where Lydon mugged outrageously as he lip-synced to a jukebox. McClaren knew The Sex Pistols had their man.

On November 6, 1975, The Sex Pistols played their first, chaotic gig. Officials at the St. Martin's Art College pulled the plug within a matter of minutes—a reaction to Lydon's antics and the band's music that would become all too familiar.

McClaren had decided the path to better days for The Sex Pistols was to be one modeled on the formative years of the Alice Cooper group. He counseled the band on maximizing their opportunities for confrontations and displays of aggression. Taking a cue from the rock styles he'd seen in New York, McClaren encouraged a de-evolution in clothing and hairstyles in the band. The crowning touch was Lydon, now renamed Johnny Rotten and poised to become the lightning rod for the outrage the band was certain to create.

Throughout 1976, The Sex Pistols played anywhere they could, and they slowly began to attract a following drawn to the band's crazed look and general disregard for established superstar rock bands.

"They insulted the audience well enough and pulled back just in time," said Ron Wells, who booked the band at the influential 100 Club, "to let me know they were in control of what they were doing. They did have a definite idea of presentation."

An underground buzz was building around punk rock, and gradually the media became aware that something was going on. As photos began to appear of spiky hair and safety-pinned clothing, the record companies started warily poking their noses into brackish waters that were unlike any they had encountered before. A scene was obviously evolving, centered around The Pistols. But the movement was growing, beginning to absorb other loud, amateurish, outrageous bands like The Damned and The Clash, now playing their own formative gigs.

On October 8, 1976, EMI Records took McClaren's bait and signed The Sex Pistols. Just over six weeks later, on November 26, the first Sex Pistols single was released. "Anarchy in the

UK" found Johnny Rotten making the most of his studio debut, howling as he informed the world that he was both an antichrist and an anarchist, while Jones, Cook, and Matlock pounded away behind him at the basic—but very effective—chords.

On December 1, Thames TV called The Sex Pistols' office, inquiring if the band could appear that day on a talk show with interviewer Bill Grundy. It was impossible to know it, but rock and roll was about to change.

The band and their attitude were in full flower on *Today*, a show that aired live in family teatime. Grundy appeared to loathe the band from the instant the broadcast began, goading them into outrageous replies to his antagonistic questions. Within moments, the interview had degraded into an obscenity-laden fiasco.

"Go on. You've got another five seconds," Grundy said as time expired. "Say something outrageous."

"You dirty bastard," offered Steve Jones.

"Go on, again," urged Grundy.

"You dirty fucker," obliged Jones.

"What a clever boy," noted Grundy as he closed the show, noting to the band, "I hope I'm not seeing you again."

The reaction to the live broadcast was swift and vitriolic. The Sex Pistols could only hope there was truth in the old saying that there was no such thing as bad publicity.

"The Punk Rock Horror Show—TV Fury at Rock Cult Filth," screamed the headline of the *Daily Mirror*. The *Daily Mail* exclaimed, "Four-Letter Punk Rock Group in TV Storm."

The British public at large was outraged over the Grundy incident—but they hadn't seen anything yet.

The late 1970s was to be the most disconcerting yet exciting era in the history of rock music. Listeners were accustomed to encountering musical sounds unlike anything they'd heard before, and new branches of rock bore unexpected fruit throughout the decade. But as the ten-year period neared its close, the creative pace began to quicken.

Among the aural visionaries playing a crucial role was Brian Eno. Eno's own bold music was intriguing in itself, but a collaboration with David Bowie yielded two albums that bookended 1977. Strange, disturbing records of intense and twisted beauty, *Low* and *"Heroes"* stood like sentries keeping a wary eye on the musical chaos spanning the months between them.

In the years since quitting his job as Roxy Music's resident synthesist and avant-garde visionary, Eno had grown to become one of England's most influential musicians. He had pioneered what he called "ambient" music—music that could serve as either background or foreground music, composed of atmospheres of tones and sonic colors. He had also developed "oblique strategies" for the creation of more traditional music, at times even utilizing a random card system to guide compositions. Eno's results were anything but conventional.

"We are no longer concerned with making horizontal music," Eno had informed *Creem* magazine's Frank Rose in July 1975, "by which I mean music that starts at Point A, develops through

Point B and ends at Point C in a kind of logical or semi-logical progression. What's more interesting is constructing music that is a solid block of interactions. This then leaves your brain free to make some of those interactions more important than others and to find which particular ones it wants to speak to."

Eno's record sales may not have paralleled the high esteem he was held in, but he had little trouble assembling interesting casts of musicians to accompany him in the studio. Among those serving Eno's creative visions were Roxy Music's Phil Manzanera, Andy MacKay, and Paul Thompson; Busta Jones and Chris Spedding of Sharks; John Wetton and Robert Fripp of King Crimson; and Phil Collins of Genesis.

Before and After Science, Eno's 1977 release, was the most fascinating and stylistically wide-ranging record of his 1970s rock period. Eno overcame his vocal range limitations by multitracking his lead lines. In the process, he revealed a keen sense of vocal harmonies, used to great effect on the drifting dreaminess of "Here He Comes" and "Julie With . . ." More heated music emerged from Eno's guests on the phased funk fusion of "No-One Receiving" and "Kurt's Rejoinder," while the foot stomping and atonal piano accompanying the shouted vocals and Fripp guitar solo of "King's Lead Hat" cast the song in a positively rollicking light. Further depth was shown in the childlike rhythmic rhyming and alliteration of the insistent, infectious "Backwater," and through the suite of three songs that closed the album on a delicate, hauntingly exquisite note, "By This River," "Through Hollow Lands," and "Spider & I."

"What really interests me is a combination of horizontal and vertical where it would be possible for both of them to exist at once," Eno said of his music. "That's an experiment in progress."

Such experimentation yielded glorious, if unsettling, results through Eno's first creative collaboration with David Bowie, *Low,* released on January 14, 1977.

In preparation for recording, the album's material was partially devised by the two musicians. At that juncture, longtime Bowie associate Tony Visconti was brought in as coproducer to get the sessions underway at the Chateau d'Herouville studio near Paris.

Not only was the album's material different, but its very sound was revolutionary. This came through the use of new technologies, such as the Harmonizer effect that Visconti used on Dennis Davis' drum kit. Davis heard the Harmonizer live as he played, but then Visconti later retreated the parts during the mixing sessions.

"The drummer always had the Harmonizer in his headphones," Visconti explained to Larry Crane in *Tape Op* magazine, "and it has some kind of envelope trigger in there. If you hit it harder the pitch will drop off more severely. If you hit it softer it will give you a few little flutters. . . . So if you put a Harmonizer on a snare drum in the mix it's a totally different animal, because it's arbitrary."

This effect is heard immediately on the first of seven short songs making up side one of *Low*. "Speed of Life" had a drum sound unlike any yet heard, but the other instrumentation throughout was equally revelatory. Eno personally contributed through the use of exotic-sounding musical machinery including Splinter Mini-Moog and Report ARP synthesizers. But even traditional instruments—the guitars of Ricky Gardener and Carlos Alomar, the bass of George Murray, Bowie's own woody-voiced sax—sounded as though they'd arrived from another planet. Equally unusual was the fact that two of the seven songs were instrumentals—unprecedented for a major release by a singer. And then things got truly strange on the album's second side.

With the recording of side one complete, Eno, Bowie, and Visconti dismissed the other musicians and set about creating an entirely instrumental suite of ambient music, following the methods devised by Eno.

"It was just Brian, myself and David doing the ambient side, side two, which was really a three-way thing," Visconti told Crane of the process, recorded long before modern computer synchronization via the technology known as SMPTE of tracking was a reality. "I played a lot of those instruments and I was also the click track. It was before the days of SMPTE and any time code and all that, so we just set a metronome clicking and I had to go on microphone and say, 'One, two, three . . .' all the way up to like 176. That's how they were writing those compositions. . . . So they'd say, 'OK, the synth choir will come in on 86." And that wasn't bar 86, it was click 86 . . . Brian, by his own admission, is a primitive musician, so he doesn't know from bars and keys and stuff. He just does what he does and he paints these lovely aural pictures."

The four ambient tracks—"Warszawa," "Art Decade," "Weeping Wall," and "Subterraneans"—were indeed lovely, polished to their final sheen by Bowie and Visconti after a move to Berlin to mix the album.

But the public failed to see the beauty of *Low*. Indeed, the album was greeted with horror by an audience expecting the next step in an accessible progression from *Young Americans* to *Station to Station*. Even the album cover was intimidating; the front depicted a gaunt Bowie in profile set against a sky of flame-colored clouds, while the back was simply an expanse of orange, broken only by record label logo and catalog number.

The team that had created *Low* was just getting started, however. Working throughout the year on the groundbreaking album's follow-up, Bowie, Eno, and Visconti saw to it that *"Heroes"* took matters even further. The base of operations for the entire project was Hansa by the Wall studio in Berlin, a German city that at the time was literally divided down the middle between communist East and democratic West Germany.

"I have to pick a city with friction in it," Bowie said. "It has to be a city that I don't know how it works. I've got to be at odds with it. As soon as I feel comfortable, I can't write in it anymore."

As Berlin was the front line of the Cold War between the United States and the Soviet Union, Bowie had little reason to worry about getting too comfortable during his stay in the city.

Joining the core band of Alomar, Davis, Murray, and Eno for the recording of *"Heroes"* was Robert Fripp. His individualistic approach to electric guitar was ideal for songs of confused aggression like "Blackout" and "Joe the Lion."

The entire album was characterized by a prickly angularity. Even the album's title track, distinctive in the context of *"Heroes"* in that it utilized a somewhat traditional structure, was recorded using a series of noise gates on microphones placed at varying distances from Bowie. Which of the microphones was recording at any given moment came down to how hard

Bowie was singing a particular phrase. And as for the phrases themselves?

"I had no melody, so I only sang the lines I'd written for four or five bars at a time," Bowie recalled of the song. "Having sung one line, I'd take a breath and do the same thing again, and so on to the end. I never knew the complete melody until I'd finished the song and played the whole thing back."

Soaring on a mass of treated instrumentation and sustained beds of "Frippertronics"—Fripp's own description of his technical artistry—"Heroes" was an intense, stirring song. It was given emotional weight both lyrically and musically by the paranoia and uncertainty ever-present in the troubled city that hosted the recording.

Once again, mass audiences were less than enthralled by the cold charm of a new David Bowie album. They were equally unenthusiastic over the sterile, stark beauty found in *"Heroes'"* own suite of side-two instrumentals. The eerily moving aural landscapes, replete with the sounds of wind, faint electronic dogs barking in the distance, and planes flying high overhead, sadly held little appeal to most rock listeners.

Though many of his fans seemed unable to comprehend Bowie's current career trajectory, to the artist himself it all made perfect sense.

"I was really trying to push my musicians in experimental music," Bowie recalled in the notes to his *Sound and Vision* career overview. *"Station to Station* was really the rock-format version of what was to come with *Low* and *"Heroes."* I was at the time well into German electronic music. . . . And Kraftwerk had made a big impression on me. I thought they were quite wonderful."

Bowie's enthusiasm for the steely new sounds he had invented in Berlin carried over into his production of two albums for Iggy Pop. With Iggy's original group, The Stooges, having finally been relegated to disbanded status, Pop had once again turned to Bowie for creative direction at a time when the Detroit singer's career seemed to be floundering.

The Idiot—with Visconti engineering and mixing the final product—and *Lust for Life* were both produced by Bowie, and the two albums shared the musicians who contributed to the *Low* and *"Heroes"* sessions. The players were augmented by the brotherly rhythm section of bassist Tony and drummer Hunt

Sales, the sons of American television entertainer Soupy Sales and two of Todd Rundgren's earliest musical collaborators.

Due to the recording environment, Iggy's albums were stylistic first cousins to Bowie's own efforts, with Pop's snarl replacing David's croon. The Iggy albums had an abundance of their own icy highlights—"Sister Midnight," "Funtime," "Baby," "Lust for Life," "Some Weird Sin," "The Passenger," "Neighborhood Threat"—all cowritten by Pop and Bowie. Still, if a major star like Bowie found his experiments greeted by cold shoulders, Iggy couldn't have been expecting mass popularity for his own efforts.

But the association with Bowie—including Bowie's decision to play keyboards on Iggy's tour supporting the albums—gave Iggy Pop a new credibility. It showed him to be more than a screaming, bloodied lead singer famed for rolling in broken glass—as Iggy had once done while in the throes of demented inspiration generated by The Stooges' aggressive madness.

While David Bowie and Iggy Pop were reveling in their brave new world, Bryan Ferry was continuing to establish a solo career that coexisted with his duties as lead singer and visionary of Roxy Music. Indeed, Roxy members Paul Thompson and Phil Manzanera, also guests on Brian Eno's projects, were on hand to join Ferry on his 1977 album *In Your Mind*.

Ferry's solo albums afforded him the opportunity to indulge in material that was a touch more pop-oriented than Roxy Music's experimental leanings, and the crisp performances on *In Your Mind* make this album an upbeat highlight of Ferry's career.

When the singer mounted a tour in support of the record, Ferry assembled an imposing band anchored by Thompson's drumming and featuring guitarists Manzanera and Chris Spedding. A lengthy soloing trade-off between Manzanera and Spedding during the Ferry composition "Love Me Madly Again" was a nightly tour highlight, offering proof that harmonious two-guitar approaches could thrive in environments other than Southern rock.

In the wake of his solo excursions Bryan Ferry always returned to the Roxy fold; Genesis, however, had come to terms with the fact that Peter Gabriel was gone for good.

After auditions failed to yield a satisfactory replacement for Gabriel, in an unusual development the band decided to elevate drummer Phil Collins to front-man status. After all, he'd been Gabriel's lead harmonizer, and both men's voices were in similar ranges.

Thus redeployed, Genesis released *Trick of the Tail* late in 1975 and *Wind and Wuthering* in 1976. Though sonically intact, the band was lyrically diminished without Gabriel's abstract vision. Newer songs like "Robbery, Assault, and Battery" and "All in a Mouse's Night" were too-cute literal tales of Cockney safecrackers and mischievous rodents, and they proved to be a let-down for the band's Gabriel-era fans who pined for apocalyptic material along the lines of "Watcher of the Skies."

Aside from topical matters, Genesis faced a logistical problem for live concert duty. How could Collins bash away behind the drum kit while entertaining the crowd as front-man? The answer was clear: he couldn't. So Genesis drafted into service former Yes and King Crimson drummer Bill Bruford on their first post-Gabriel tour. For their next stage venture, they called on former Frank Zappa and Weather Report percussionist Chester Thompson. The results of both lineup variations were documented on 1977's live double album *Seconds Out*.

"From the best live band in the world, the best live album," crowed the Atlantic Records' ad copy. Perhaps not.

The problem was not that the replacement drummers weren't up to the task of carrying Genesis. Despite their stylistic differences—Bruford specialized in angular precision while Thompson was more free-swinging—both men did a fine job.

Still, it was well known how crucial drumming was to the grand scale of Genesis music. Compositionally, a song like "Firth of Fifth" from 1973's *Selling England by the Pound* sounded as though it had been constructed in the studio specifically to allow Collins to show off his skills. But *Seconds Out*—and the necessity for Bruford and Thompson as substitutes—signaled the continuing de-emphasis of Collins' percussion role. He had brought his own unique percussive creativity to Genesis, a vital contribution to the band's overall sound rather than mere rhythmic support. That contribution was now largely missing.

Though Collins did go so far as to found the fusion band Brand X as a drumming outlet in 1976 and 1977, his role as Genesis lead singer, and later as solo vocalist, sadly overshadowed his value as instrumentalist.

Though Genesis had continued issuing albums almost immediately after Gabriel's departure, Peter himself had virtually dropped off rock's radar screen. Finally, though, late in 1976 Gabriel returned to the studio. A number of surprises resulted.

Perhaps the most shocking aspect of his highly anticipated solo debut was his choice of creative partner. Gabriel's producer was none other than Bob Ezrin, who had guided the aural careers of Alice Cooper and Lou Reed. Ezrin's clients were certainly established artists, but they existed in realms far removed from Gabriel's rather eccentric artistry. It seemed a real possibility that Ezrin's showy production style might collide rather than mesh with Gabriel's creative vision.

Instead, 1977's *Peter Gabriel* documented an incredibly creative artist trying to decide what direction to follow by trying them all out. In the process, Gabriel thankfully got some genres out of his system for good. Few would miss the barbershop harmonies of "Excuse Me" or the standard slow blues of "Waiting for the Big One," even if the latter provided guitarist Steve Hunter a platform for a torrid solo toward song's end.

Somewhat more successful was the orchestral rock of "Down the Dolce Vita," which redefined "bombastic," and the modern rock of "Modern Love," which was closer in spirit to Alice Cooper than Genesis. And the jaunty, folksier feel of "Solsbury Hill" translated well into radio airplay for Gabriel.

But the real indicators of Gabriel's future path came on the songs "Humdrum" and "Here Comes the Flood." The former eases in on stark Fender Rhodes piano before taking wing on an eerie and unlikely cha-cha rhythm. A sudden drop into a stately, momentous passage leads to song's end. The hymn-like "Here Comes the Flood" mixes atmosphere and majesty in equal parts, a song of bitter hope. Written in a time when nuclear annihilation was very much an immediate threat, the song's theme of innocence destroyed in an act of mass destruction was one Gabriel would revisit throughout this career.

Shortly after the release of his album, Peter Gabriel embarked on a tour with one of the more unusual backing bands of the 1970s. Including most of the musicians who had contributed to *Peter Gabriel*, the lineup included both hard rocker Steve Hunter and avant rocker Robert Fripp on guitars. Joining them were experimentalist bassist Tony Levin and synthesizer expert Larry Fast, whose own project, Synergy, aligned with the efforts of Kraftwerk in pushing electronic instrumental music in exciting new directions.

To symbolize his wish to break down the barriers between artist and audience, Gabriel began his shows seated incognito among the crowd, rising with microphone in hand and slowly making his way to the stage.

The opening act on this groundbreaking tour was Television, leading lights of New York's experimental rock scene.

Television—the first of the new movement of New York bands to play at the now-notorious club CBGB—had recorded demos produced by Brian Eno for Island Records in 1975, at a time when Richard Hell was the band's bassist. But the momentum of the New York scene was still gaining impetus, and nothing came of the early sessions. Hell soon quit the band to form his own project, Richard Hell and The Voidoids. Television replaced Hell with Fred Smith, though not the MC5 guitarist of the same name.

In 1977, with the success of Patti Smith and The Ramones, and with a growing interest in the other inhabitants of the ever-intensifying scene swirling around CBGB, Elektra Records signed Television. The band entered the studio with producer Andy Johns. Johns established his career as an engineer with a client list that included Free, Led Zeppelin, and The Rolling Stones, for whom he had recorded *Exile on Main Street* under virtual combat conditions.

Johns and Television leader Tom Verlaine chose to record the album with a straightforward approach, allowing the pure sound of the guitars to go straight to tape. Indeed, the first sound heard on the album—a surging rhythm guitar that drives "See No Evil"—is recorded with a startling clarity. The effect is as if the amplifier is mere inches away from the listener, broadcasting the pure, unadorned tones of the guitar's voice.

The essence of Television was not that far removed spiritually from the first incarnation of The Allman Brothers Band, except their sensibility was updated urban rather than rural Southern, and they operated within the confines of set structures rather than free-form jams. But there was no denying the excitement of the interplay between Verlaine and coguitarist Richard Lloyd, both musicians playing off each other with the same incandescence that had characterized Duane Allman and Dickey Betts' explorations. Lloyd's style was more lyrical and spiraling, whereas Verlaine tended toward more abstract attacks, as heard in the staccato Dick-Dale-on-octaves runs that ascend through the solo of "Friction." Smith's syncopated bass lines probed beneath the guitars, while Billy Ficca created a solid drum foundation. Verlaine's vocals, delivered in phrasing nearly identical to that of his good friend Patti Smith, evoked a mood of awkward passion.

Though Television emerged from a scene increasingly accused of being antimusical, the band was justifiably proud of their work. When *Marquee Moon* was released in May 1977, the individual solos were credited by guitarist in the album's liner notes.

Former Television member Richard Hell also saw the release of his debut album early in 1977. "Blank Generation," the album's title track, acted as a lyrical focus for the burgeoning punk movement but also served as the introduction for a thrilling new guitarist, Robert Quine. On that song and throughout *Blank Generation*, The Voidoids' lead guitarist displayed an aggressive, stuttering attack that was unpredictable and strangely moving.

If the work of both Television and Richard Hell and The Voidoids was elevating the reputation of the musicians of lower Manhattan, it appeared The Dead Boys wanted little more than to toss that notoriety into a dumpster. Signed to Sire Records like The Voidoids, The Dead Boys couldn't have been more of a contrast.

Originally hailing from Cleveland in the form of an unappreciated, raw band known as Frankenstein, the newly rechristened Dead Boys made a move to New York after witnessing The Ramones in performance. There they made their way to the stage at CBGB. Club owner Hilly Kristal thought they had potential and decided to manage the band, whose attitude is best summed up by the title of their first album, *Young, Loud, and Snotty.*

Over Stiv Bators' snarl of a voice—belligerent, complaining, and threatening to "kill the next hippie I see"—The Dead Boys thunder through their debut playing blunt, stripped-down rock, heard to greatest effect on the roaring lead-off cut, "Sonic Reducer." Ironically, the album sounds a lot like Alice Cooper's *Love it to Death* played double-time.

The early punk bands of the United States tended to behave with the same attitude characterized in a crucial scene in the 1954 motorcycle rebel movie *The Wild One.* In the film, bad boy biker Marlon Brando is asked what he's rebelling against. "What have you got?" Brando replies.

In England, though, the punk kids knew exactly what they were rebelling against—the blinders-on nationalism of the Royal Jubilee, staggering unemployment, and a social support system that was grinding to a halt. Punk rock in the U.K. had reached a roiling boil, gaining strength in a nation where the semiaffluent suburban boredom that fueled the obnoxiousness of The Dead Boys was an alien concept. In England, punk wasn't just music; it was becoming a vision and a lifestyle.

The first major musical explosion of the year 1977 hit Great Britain on April 8, in the form of *The Clash.*

Clash lead singer and rhythm guitarist Joe Strummer had been a member of The 101ers, a "pub rock" band playing high energy R&B and rock, when he met Malcolm McLaren associate Bernie Rhodes. The pub rock bands specialized in basic American-styled music, presented with a working-class, no-nonsense attitude, and Rhodes likely figured that pub rock wasn't that far removed from punk rock. So Rhodes told Strummer he was helping assemble a new band based around guitarists Mick Jones and Keith Levene with bassist Paul Simonon, the remnants of the provocatively named but short-lived London S.S. He asked Strummer if he'd consider joining the new group. Strummer felt The 101ers were going nowhere, and—intrigued by the look of Rhodes' charges—agreed to come on board. Thus was born one the most significant of the hundreds of bands formed in the latter half of the 1970s, The Clash.

Having already recorded and gigged regularly with The 101ers, Strummer had actually done the very things his new band mates dreamed of accomplishing. That made him something of an intimidating presence.

"I'd seen Joe play quite a few times," Mick Jones told Clash associate Kosmo Vinyl in the liner notes to the *Clash on Broadway* box set. "We didn't think we could get him, to us he was really up there. The day Keith brought Joe round to David Road we were all terrified."

But almost immediately, the elusive chemistry that distills into a great rock band began to flow through The Clash. Things happened quickly: Levene left the band, Terry Chimes joined as drummer, material was written, cover songs were carefully selected. Two months in, the band played their first gig, opening for The Sex Pistols in Sheffield. As the group developed, Bernie Rhodes helped them focus their direction.

"He steered us away from lovey-dovey stuff like 'She's Sitting at the Party'," Strummer told Vinyl, "I think because he realized it was overdone, and he steered us toward writing something that was more real. He kept saying write about what affects you."

The Clash were also developing a bold look, their clothing splattered with paint and stenciled boldly with provocative expressions like "Hate and War" and "White Riot."

Entering the studio, the band cut *The Clash* in three four-day sessions, setting up as though they were on stage and blasting through their basic material.

Both the recording and the performances were blunt and breathless, with the guitar solo in "Protex Blue" lasting all of six seconds. Produced by The 101ers' soundman Mickey Foote, the extent of recording gimmicks was a flange effect in "Cheat." Other than that, it was flat-out Clash—and that was enough. The sound of Strummer and Jones sawing away at their guitars over Simonon's rudimentary bass lines would have been nothing but amateurish had it not detonated in such a cataclysmic blast of enthusiasm, excitement, and commitment.

Over the din of the songs' brief bursts of propulsive noise, Joe Strummer's hoarse bark of a voice cajoled and commanded, sometimes overwhelmed with outrage, other moments resigned with bitter acceptance. The rough edges of Strummer's vocals lent his phrases a charismatic warmth; listeners heard the voice of a common man, and it gave his words an air of credibility. Strummer's utterances contrasted with Mick Jones' own solo verses and higher harmonies. Though neither band member was technically a good singer, they were imminently believable.

While The Clash were establishing their presence with their album, The Sex Pistols spent much of 1977 earning a living by signing with record companies and then frightening them until they were paid to go away. In early January, in the wake of the Bill Grundy television interview that had so scandalized the nation, EMI sent the Pistols packing—after agreeing with manager Malcolm McLaren to pay 30,000 pounds in addition to the 20,000-pound advance already paid. And in March, a six-day association with A&M Records resulted in the band keeping a 75,000-pound advance.

"When the Pistols first started we found it impossible to get gigs," singer Johnny Rotten told *Record Mirror*. "The business bends over backwards to help the big bands. If you're not established you've got no chance. But by hook or crook we forced gigs onto people. And now we're in. All the big bosses think they've got us sussed—no way. They only took us on because they could see something was going on. But now we're fighting them from the inside."

With just two singles available through May of 1977—and the latter hastily pulled by A&M Records—The Pistols played what gigs they could.

"The only point I could make about The Pistols, being an eyewitness, is that they could absolutely play," Joe Strummer recalled. "The four of them could get on a shite stage on a shite Tuesday night and the sound you'd hear was total."

Meanwhile, Rotten—perpetually sneering, his short, orange spiky hair pointing in myriad directions—continued to lay out the band's agenda.

"We have got to fight the entire super band system," Rotten insisted. "Groups like The Who and The Stones are revolting. They have nothing to offer the kids any more. All they're good for is making money. . . . Life has really become safe for them. They are just so pathetic."

In February 1977, the endless circus around The Pistols became too much for bassist Glen Matlock, whose songwriting skills had contributed greatly to the band's sound. He'd grown tired of dealing with Rotten and felt that guitarist Steve Jones and drummer Paul Cook were merely along for a high-profile ride. In turn, The Pistols announced that the band's new bassist would be Sid Vicious, a failed drummer in the early days of Siouxsie and The Banshees with no apparent background as a bass player whatsoever.

It was in this turbulent atmosphere that the band finally signed with Virgin Records in May, and began putting the finishing touches on the album they had begun several months earlier. One of the producers chosen to work with the band by manager Malcolm McLaren seemed an unlikely choice, Chris Thomas.

Thomas, earlier in the decade, had overseen the production of two records that mourned the decline of European sophistication and tradition, Roxy Music's *Stranded* and Procol Harum's *Grand Hotel*. Now he was to oversee what many expected would become a soundtrack to the fall of the British rock empire.

Bill Price was also doing production work with The Sex Pistols. Price was an engineer who had worked with rock's top bands, names like Paul McCartney's Wings, Mott the Hoople, Roxy Music, and many more. In 1977, he'd engineered the debut album by The Clash, and he had a good feel for capturing punk's vital energy.

"The simple facts of the matter were that Chris was hired by Malcolm to do a series of singles for The Sex Pistols," Price recalled in an interview with *Mix* magazine. "I was hired by Malcolm to do a series of album tracks with The Sex Pistols. Life got slightly complicated, because I did a few album tracks that Chris remade as singles. Also, Chris started a couple of tracks, which got abandoned as singles, which I remade to be used as album tracks. On quite a large number of songs, when we'd finished the album, we had two versions of the song."

The two producers eventually realized that crafty manager McLaren was attempting to avoid paying either man for his work by completely confusing the issue of who had done what. Thomas and Price put up a united front and demanded payment, splitting the compensation privately. In the end, the production credit printed on the album's original pressings read "Producers: Chris Thomas & Bill Price."

When *Never Mind the Bollocks—Here's the Sex Pistols* was finally released by Virgin in October, its lurid yellow and pink cover contained a record that wielded an explosive impact.

On early Sex Pistols studio sessions produced by guitarist Chris Spedding, the sound had been simple, more or less documenting the Matlock-era band's live approach. Thomas and Price took a different tack, using the studio to full effect and essentially creating the proverbial "wall of sound." The term *wall of sound* had become an oft-used description for "big" music since the days of Phil Spector's busy productions. But in the case of *Bollocks*, it was the only conceivable description able to hint at the titanic sounds barely contained within the album's grooves.

Essentially recording as a trio, with Jones handling much of the bass work due to Vicious' rather prominent lack of bass facility, The Sex Pistols used simple but brutally effective touches to craft the album. The producers had to walk a fine line, aware that The Pistols were not virtuoso instrumentalists and that energy was crucial to their sound. So they coached Jones in the creation of huge overdubbed slabs of guitar and bass that rode over Cook's drumming. The solos that Jones played were mixed so deeply that it's sometimes hard to hear exactly what notes he's playing—the runs are felt and intuited more than they are actually heard, lurking deep within the sonic maelstrom. But one listen to the call-and-response guitar break of "No Feelings" offered testament to the soundness of both the vision of Thomas and Price as well as Jones' underestimated skill as a guitarist.

As for Johnny Rotten? *Bollocks* contained one the greatest vocal performances in rock history. Seldom before had a singer's limited range been so thoroughly overcome, Rotten ignoring the boundaries and unleashing his voice with astonishing force. Rotten snarled and growled, howling in anger and frustration. But he was just as likely to drop into a mocking singsong, or crack his voice, or even unexpectedly roll his R's. His performance was slyly witty and totally committed, an unpredictable, thrilling vocal feat.

With choruses threatening there was "no future for you," bolstered by Rotten's vocals and the huge instrumental sound, it seemed that all of the loud warnings trumpeted by the skittish media over The Sex Pistols and the rise of punk rock were fully justified. From the sound of this album, The Sex Pistols truly were dangerous—and thrillingly magnificent.

Despite the raging excitement of the Sex Pistols' debut, Rotten's public persona characteristically professed indifference toward the idea of having made an album.

"I hate art," he lamented. "I can't stand it! It's treating something that's supposed to be good as precious. And it ain't precious. Anyone can make a record."

That idea—that fans could easily metamorphose into musicians—was a crucial component of The Pistols' party line.

"I want more bands like us," Johnny Rotten told the newspaper *Sounds*. "I want people to go out and start something, to see us and start something, or else I'm just wasting my time."

Rotten needn't have worried. With The Sex Pistols and The Clash having kicked open the doors of the music industry, a motley array of bash-and-crash rabble rushed the rock castle. Some lacked the furious commitment of The Clash or The Pistols' pounding brutality, but that didn't stop bands like X Ray Spex, Eater, The Subway Sect, The Adverts, and Alternative TV from launching their own records and performances into the ever-growing fray. And bands like The Vibrators quickly chopped off their hair and threw on the leather and pins in a transparent attempt to achieve punk credibility.

Even within punk's stripped-down confines, there was a diversity of styles and approaches. When The Clash mounted a tour of England in 1977, they brought along the all-female Slits as opening band, a group just beginning to perfect their tribal stomp onslaught. On the same tour were The Buzzcocks, a far more musically advanced young band with a highly evolved sense of brisk punk-pop composition. The appropriately named Billy Idol—whose good looks and bottle-blond hair contrasted diametrically with glamour-challenged front-men like Strummer and Rotten—led Generation X's own pop-flavored punk charge. And The Jam, perhaps the least threatening of the "New Wave" of bands, seemed intent on reliving

The Who's past, dressing in "My Generation"-era suits and openly airing their admiration for R&B stylings.

While The Sex Pistols and most of their fellow punk bands were disrupting rock's status quo through their actions and images as much as through their noise, England's Wire needed nothing more than their sound.

"We weren't really a punk group," Wire vocalist and guitarist Colin Newman said. "We were doing stuff that was weird for punk people."

Determined to be different, Wire's experimentalism placed them in a role similar to that of Television in New York's punk scene. But Wire could be far more abrasive than Verlaine's band.

"One of the first things I remember is playing to an audience in Liverpool where they were literally standing in a semi-circle against the wall. They were crowded as far away from us as they could, like they were petrified of us."

Wire was not inclined to indulge in the lyrical guitar solos that characterized Television. In fact, the very brevity of their songs was one of Wire's primary calling cards.

"When the text ran out, it stopped," said guitarist Bruce Gilbert. "We hadn't thought of the songs as being any length."

That approach found songs on Wire's 1977 debut *Pink Flag* ranging from three minutes, fifty seconds for the title track down to twenty-eight seconds for "Field Day for the Sundays," with most of the album's twenty-one tracks running just over a minute.

Pink Flag opened on an unsettling note with "Reuters," a correspondent's chilling account of society collapsing in warfare, predating actual events that would occur years later in Sarajevo and Bosnia. With mood established, Wire proceeded to run the gamut from tuneful, infectious blasts like "Ex Lion Tamer" to the deliberately shambolic "1.2.X.U." Passing through hypnotic syncopations and shouted choruses, using trebly, slashing guitars and the most elemental of beats and construction, Wire's unique, minimalist approach saw them successful in their determined attempts to devolve punk even further.

It was clear that rock music was in the throes of upheaval, but the questions raised were many. Was this just a tiny cult movement, doomed to wither away, or was it something more fundamental? Was punk mere entertainment, or was it really a

new lifestyle? And most importantly, was there actually an audience receptive to this snarling, unwashed, and apparently
dangerous new offspring of rock and roll?

The answer to the latter was a resounding "yes." *Never Mind
the Bollocks* had advance orders of more than 125,000 copies in
England alone, and immediately upon release, the album was
awarded gold status. And across the ocean? Not released in the
United States until months after its European debut, *The Clash*
had become the biggest-selling import album in history, moving more than 100,000 hard-to-find copies.

The superstar rock bands could have been excused for feeling a cold shiver of fear run along their spines. Punk rock had
risen from out of nowhere, suddenly becoming a razor-sharp
wedge that divided bands and audiences into two distinct
camps: those who embraced punk, and those who mocked it.

"What the fuck do we want to sound like The Sex Pistols
for?" wondered The Rolling Stones' Keith Richards. "What's
the point of listening to that shit? It's for mass media consumption anyway."

But Patti Smith publicly and prominently extolled the virtues
of The Clash. And Neil Young noted, "I never met Johnny Rotten, but I like what he did to people."

Quite naturally, the division carried over into the media.
There were critics filled with genuine excitement about the new
bands, who joyously leapt from the Genesis and Pink Floyd
bandwagons into uncertain fates, led in large part by influential American writer Lester Bangs. But for some critics these tu-
multuous days presented a major dilemma. The endorsement
of Patti Smith's work had been nearly universal, but for some
critics the praise had been a self-conscious attempt to look hip.
Now those writers were in the uncomfortable position of further endorsing a group of noisy riff-raff who they ordinarily
would have dismissed out of hand.

Regardless, punk rock had been turned loose upon the rock
landscape—and now there was nothing to do but see what
happened.

Patti Smith was aware of the role that her own group as well
as The Ramones had played as pollinators of the new culture.

"We were trying to set the stage, create space for the future,
for new people, and stir up people so they could do things on

their own," Patti Smith said years later, speaking in *Entertainment Weekly* magazine of punk's birth. "When we started we always told people, 'Now that you've seen us, don't even come back. Do something on your own if it moves you. Don't buy our records, make your own records.' If we contributed anything in that period, it was that we helped to create space. The actual movement was created by other bands and by the people themselves."

Chris Thomas and Bill Price had their hands full producing The Sex Pistols, but for those who earned a living laboring in recording studios, adapting to the new sounds was crucial from a professional perspective. After producing Television, though, Andy Johns took a step back toward more traditional rock through his work with Detective.

Signed to Led Zeppelin's own Swan Song label, Detective wasn't quite a supergroup, though its core trio had been members of fairly well known bands: vocalist Michael Des Barres was a member of Silverhead, guitarist Michael Monarch came from Steppenwolf, and Tony Kaye had been the original keyboard player of Yes.

When Johns completed production on the band's self-titled 1977 debut, one might have believed Swan Song held the patent on Led Zeppelin drummer John Bonham's cavernous sound, for the pounding of Detective's Jon Hyde rang with the same booming authority. Yet even though "Grim Reaper" stalked with a Zeppelin-like syncopation, Detective were in pursuit of their own sound. Their influences were wide-ranging, and the group even flirted with a touch of Jeff-Beck-era *Blow by Blow* fusion lite on "Recognition."

Image-wise, Detective wanted to be seen as a sophisticated rock band, hence their tailored suits and an album cover boasting fashionable photography. But it was to no avail; the band members' Swan Song livelihood was to last for just one more album. *It Takes One to Know One* followed its predecessor later in the year, and though the band continued to refine its sound—the rambling Faces-like opener "Help Me Up" and the halting, monolithic "Dynamite" made a very strong case for the group's continuing existence—new hard rock bands found 1977 to be a hostile environment in which to attempt career building.

With unknowns having trouble breaking into the market, record labels found it easier to circle the promotional wagons around established artists. In turn—and especially in the United States—many record buyers preferred to stick with known quantities rather than try to sort out the confusing punk rock chaos that had infected Europe. These conditions were about to play quite profitably into the hands of Fleetwood Mac.

Originally known as something of a schizoid act in the late 1960s—one moment playing Buddy Holly–like pop when fronted by Jeremy Spencer, the next digging into gritty blues at the behest of the brilliant, fiery guitarist Peter Green—Fleetwood Mac's personnel lineup had seldom solidified for more than a single album. By the mid-1970's, Green was long since retired from the band after mental illness effectively de-railed his career, Spencer was a memory, and many more play-ers had come and gone. Most recently guitarist Bob Welch had elected to depart, in favor of a new band called Paris, formed with Jethro Tull bassist Glen Cornick. Miraculously, though, in 1975 Fleetwood Mac had actually settled on a stable lineup. Stable? That was debatable, as the group's internal workings were in a state of constant emotional crisis due to the presence of two romantically involved couples in the roster.

Towering, lanky drummer Mick Fleetwood was the source of the first half of the band's name, and former John Mayall Blues-breaker bassist John McVie contributed the back half. McVie's wife, keyboardist Christine, had also joined the band several years earlier. But the greatest sparks—both commercially and emotionally—came with the incorporation of singing duo Buckingham–Nicks into the ranks of Fleetwood Mac.

The newly remodeled Fleetwood Mac recorded a self-titled album in 1975, but shortly thereafter singer and guitarist Lind-sey Buckingham and his longtime girlfriend, vocalist Stevie Nicks, found themselves in the process of painfully splitting apart. At the same time, the McVies were divorcing. Mick Fleetwood was also getting a divorce, but at least his wife wasn't in the band.

"We were all trying to break up and when you break up with someone you don't want to see him," Nicks told Sally Rayl in the July 1977 *Creem* magazine. "You especially don't want to eat breakfast with him the next morning, see him all day and all night, and all day the day after . . ."

It was in that nervous atmosphere that Fleetwood Mac spent the majority of 1976 recording their new album *Rumours*.

The album began a spirited assault on the record charts upon its release in February 1977. Acrid lyrics like those that comprised "Go Your Own Way" and "The Chain" were set to infectious compositions as Fleetwood Mac tunefully recounted the betrayals, jealousies, and bitterness raging unchecked within the quintet. With Christine McVie's smoky voice and romantic adult pop mixed with Nicks' delirious, fairy-tale temptress imagery, Fleetwood Mac became a music-selling juggernaut of epic proportions, racking up *Rumours* sales of more than seventeen million copies in the United States alone.

"As far as all this recent success," John McVie told *Creem*, "it was timing and a combination of all things connected with this band. All of a sudden we had the properties that the public wanted at the right time."

Like Fleetwood Mac, it seemed that an unlikely character named Meat Loaf—one of the few new artists to barge into the charts—had his own public properties at the right time, to paraphrase McVie.

The stocky singer—famously referred to as "Mr. Loaf" by *The New York Times*—had a blowtorch voice that had first come to public attention via the horror spoof movie *Rocky Horror Picture Show*. Partnering with songwriter Jim Steinman, who specialized in a dramatic show tune sensibility melded with rock and roll attitude, Meat Loaf entered the studio. He seemed to be an improbable presence with little hope of capturing the whims of the public. But an over-the-top production by Todd Rundgren—then taking a break from Utopia—ensured that pure bombast was the hallmark of Meat's debut. Though the album was slow to gain marketplace momentum, once it got going it was virtually unstoppable.

Rundgren himself provided lead guitar on the record, joined by two of his band mates from the newly revised Utopia, Roger Powell on synthesizer and Kasim Sulton on bass. Roy Bittan from The E Street Band contributed suitably grand piano crescendos, and the addition of orchestration completed the operatic extravagance.

"It's an unlikely success," Rundgren admitted, "but not really more unlikely that anything else I've done. Meat Loaf's voice has a real commercial edge, histrionic as it is."

That kind of commercial edge was to play a critical role in the career of a new band that was in its infancy in England, a group that would help establish a safe offshoot of the punk chaos.

Drummer Stewart Copeland had been a member of the prog rock band Curved Air, but when that outfit collapsed Copeland started playing with a local bassist named Gordon Sumner and a guitarist named Henri Padovani. Soon thereafter Sumner took the name Sting, the band took the name The Police, and a second guitarist, Andy Summers, was added to the fold. Summers had a deep English rock pedigree, having been one of the British musicians to meet Jimi Hendrix on the day Hendrix first arrived in the country. By August, 1977, Padovani had left and The Police were reduced to a trio, the group slowly establishing itself on the pub and club circuit.

Within months The Police would not only begin recording their first album, but they would also appear—with identically dyed blond hair—in a Wrigley's chewing gum television commercial. People noticed that, even though the Police had spiky hair like the punks, they didn't come across as ferocious little beasties. And though their music may have borrowed from punk's stripped-down-to-the-basics idealism, the songs played by The Police were tuneful and catchy. Those were the early traits of what came to be known as New Wave music, a more commercial dilution of punk rock.

Though there was no strict definition of exactly what was or was not New Wave, it became a term liberally applied. Generally, any band emerging after 1977 that grew spiky hair and wore skinny ties or day-glo animal pattern prints was New Wave. If it looked or sounded punkish but was somewhat cuddly as opposed to nearly rabid, it was filed under New Wave.

Though new bands that played traditional hard rock were having a rough go of it in 1977, other British bands noticed which way the punk winds were blowing and took appropriate action. Although they didn't go so far as to adapt the complete punk rock makeover, they did strip down their sound and rough up their images. One such band was The Motors, made up of two veterans of the British pub rock scene.

Guitarist Nick Garvey and bassist Andy McMaster were both former members of pub rockers Ducks Deluxe. Like Joe Strummer's The 101ers, Ducks Deluxe played their stripped-down rock with an attitude that had no room for pretensions. But Garvey and McMaster were ready to head in a weightier direction, and upon the demise of Ducks Deluxe they assembled The Motors.

Recruited into the band were the rather punkishly named Ricky Slaughter and Bram Tchaikovsky on drums and guitar, respectively. Yet even though Garvey and McMaster had developed a taste for the harder stuff, the lead-off cut of their 1977 self-titled album packed a tuneful wallop. "Dancing the Night Away" was six and a half minutes loaded with multiple guitar-driven passages, stylistically roaming from airy arpeggios to curt octave runs over a pounding surge of rhythm. "Freeze" built on the momentum with a solid, leaden thumping and gang-like vocals, but the album's real first-side highlight was next, "Cold Love." An early example of punk and New Wave's fascination with Jamaican reggae, on "Cold Love" The Motors took a nearly heavy metal tack as they navigated the staggered Caribbean rhythms.

Throughout the remainder of the album, The Motors infused a raw, punk energy on Garvey and McMaster's pub rock heritage, with a strong dash of mid-period The Who tossed into the pot. The more melodic aspects of the project were likely endorsed by the producer of *The Motors*, Robert John Lange, better known as "Mutt." As one of his first productions, *The Motors* turned out to be an early step in what would prove to be a most significant music industry career.

The hard and basic ethos of the new sounds had an obvious influence on pub rockers, yet surprisingly it also acted as a siren call to lure some older rockers out of the shadows they'd been lurking in for more than a decade.

Among them were The Pirates, who in 1977 released *Out of Their Skulls*, their first album in more than fifteen years. Predating The Beatles and The Rolling Stones, from 1959 to 1966 Johnny Kidd and The Pirates played gritty, hard rockabilly and R&B at a time when proponents of those forms of music were virtually invisible in England. But when lead singer Kidd was killed in an October 1966 car crash, the book seemed to close on The Pirates.

A decade later, though, the spotlight was shining on a new British band called Dr. Feelgood. They were called pub rockers by some, but their no-frills attack predated punk while working the same stylistic turf pillaged by The Pirates in the 1960s. Wilko Johnson, the group's guitarist, openly admitted being heavily influenced by The Pirates' Mick Green. Johnson began lobbying The Pirates for a reunion, and in early 1977 it happened. What might be called the very first power trio returned to action.

Half of *Out of Their Skulls* was recorded in studio sessions, but the sparks begin to fly on the as-it-happened live side. Brusquely blasting through rock standards like "Please Don't Touch," "Milk Cow Blues," and the classic "Peter Gunn" theme, The Pirates showed they were definitely back at full power, led by Green's fierce rhythm and lead style.

Across the ocean in the United States, another early rock guitar great was about to return to the muscular, pile-driving style that had won him admirers like The Who's Pete Townshend.

Link Wray hailed from North Carolina, but he moved to the Washington, D.C. area as he began to perfect a unique style of revved-up guitar instrumental music. His first hit came in 1958, with a snarling blast of raw guitar called "Rumble." Follow-ups "Rawhide" and "Jack the Ripper" boasted more rude rock sounds. But commercial fortunes turned against Wray, and he spent much of the 1960s and 1970s recording little-appreciated material that roamed across the musical map.

Meanwhile, young Robert Gordon had been a member of The Tuff Darts, a band on the fringes of the New York CBGB landscape. But Gordon wasn't enthralled with the nascent punk scene—he loved hard 1950s-style rock and roll. And it didn't come any harder than in the form of Wray, still regarded by his cult following as one of guitar's true wild men.

In 1977, *Robert Gordon with Link Wray* was released on the Private Stock Records label, and Wray was back in the public limelight. His solos—taut blasts of sound and fury—lit a fire under Gordon's vocals on rampaging, rockabilly-inspired songs like "Flying Saucers Rock & Roll" and "Red Hot."

The unlikely partnership lasted for one more album, *Fresh Fish Special*, a record containing the song "Fire," written by Bruce Springsteen as a token of his esteem for Wray and Gordon's efforts. After splitting with Gordon—taking Gordon's band with him as the singer started fresh in partnership with Chris Spedding—Wray proved he still had an appetite for high-octane rock on both his solo studio album *Bullshot* and on a flat-out concert recording from Amsterdam, *Live at the Paradiso*. The live album in particular offered a no-frills snapshot of Wray's devastating technique.

Not that Wray had cornered the market on sonic brutality. There was one British rock band that doubtless was the toughest new contender of them all. They were called Motorhead.

"If Motorhead moved in next to you, your lawn would probably die," speculated band leader Lemmy Kilmister. It probably wasn't far from the truth. Motorhead looked and sounded like they would happily dismember any punk band that dared cross their path. Their image was pure outlaw biker, and if they owned any clothing that wasn't black, it never saw the light of day.

Lemmy—as he was generally known—had impeccable rock pedigree. He'd first been a roadie for The Jimi Hendrix Experience, then took to stages himself as bassist in Hawkwind. One of England's second wave of prog rock bands, Hawkwind had differed from more pensive groups like Pink Floyd thanks to Lemmy's driving bass. He gave the group a drastically more insistent rhythm section, one that stalked rather than meandered. On tour in the United States in 1975, Lemmy was arrested for possession of amphetamines, "speed" being his drug of choice. He was booted from Hawkwind, the band virtually signing a death certificate for their own creative energy.

Back in England, an angry Lemmy vowed to form his own band, and he knew exactly how he wanted it to sound.

"We will concentrate on very basic music," he insisted at the time. "Loud, fast, city, raucous, arrogant, paranoid, speed-freak rock 'n' roll."

Lemmy first attempted to get Motorhead on the road with ex-Pink Fairy guitarist Larry Wallis and drummer Lucas Fox. That lineup floundered, but Lemmy finally found his men when the trio evolved into the classic roster of Lemmy, Phil "the Animal" Taylor on drums, and guitarist "Fast Eddie" Clark. Planning to release nothing more than a single on the smaller Chiswick Records label, the project blossomed into the band's self-titled 1977 album.

Produced in part by Speedy Keen, mastermind behind the late 1960s band Thunderclap Newman and their hit "Something in the Air," *Motorhead* was greeted by reviews such as one that noted, "subtlety was not invited to the recording session." Nor was it needed. What listeners heard was a thunderous new offshoot of rock, the first blast in what became known as "the New Wave of British Heavy Metal."

Lemmy favored a Rickenbacker bass, the same distinctive-sounding instrument that Chris Squire utilized to create the distinguishing bass lines of Yes. But in Lemmy's hands the Rick became something else entirely, a fearsome squalling noise that was both treble and bass at once. Taylor defined the role of the high-powered, relentless heavy metal drummer, and "Fast Eddie" was indeed fast, using the enormous foundation of Lemmy's bass as a launching point for furious rhythm and lead guitar. A case in point was the monolithic cover of "Train Kept A-Rollin'" that rendered earlier versions by both The Yardbirds and Aerosmith laughably feeble in comparison. The term "power trio" was sadly inadequate when it came to conveying the brutal, noisy fury of Motorhead.

The breakneck tempos and roughneck lyrics of songs like "Iron Horse/Born to Lose" and the self-descriptive "Motorhead" drove the album up the British charts, and it reached number thirty-seven in its second week of release—impressive for an album on a small, independent label.

To prove that the band's prowess was as imposing in concert as in the studio, Motorhead embarked on their appropriately titled Beyond the Threshold of Pain tour. Their intent, as Taylor explained at the time, was simple: "We like to send our fans home with their ears ringing."

Though Motorhead's high-volume conflagrations were inarguably ground-shaking, they came in the wake of an era when every band was expected to take to the stage with amps set to stun. But the challenge to musicians was to consistently maintain the sense of aggression needed to fuel such noise while making its substance more than mere racket.

After years of pummeling audiences, Jeff Beck's music had taken a turn in 1975 with *Blow by Blow*. Having ended his power trio Beck, Bogert, Appice, he sailed smooth jazz fusion currents on his solo album, exploring melodies that could even be called delicate.

It was all very nice, but Beck began to miss the fire and fury that more aggressive material can inspire. So when he returned to the studio in 1976—again with The Beatles' producer George Martin—Beck had a new lineup of players. Gone was the rhythm section of bassist Phil Chenn and drummer Richard Bailey. In their place was jazz and R&B bassist Wilbur Bascomb and Narada Michael Walden, the drummer in John McLaughlin's second iteration of The Mahavishnu Orchestra. Rounding out the core band was original Mahavishnu Orchestra keyboardist Jan Hammer, paired with longtime Beck associate Max Middleton.

Middleton had composed several of the jazzy tunes on *Blow by Blow*, but his edgy "Led Boots" launched *Wired* upon its 1976 release. The allusion to Led Zeppelin was appropriate—the three slashing chords of the opening seconds descend into brutal syncopation, making it obvious that Beck was on hand to flex his muscles. Unlike Bailey's smooth drumming on *Wired*'s predecessor, Walden's drums thundered with complex detonations throughout, bringing a state-of-the-art fusion edge to the album.

Though Beck did back off the volume for the ballads "Goodbye Pork Pie Hat" and "Love Is Green," the harsher setting of

Wired allowed him to show off his stunning abilities in bold
new scenery. His vibrato bar attacks soared and dove in unpredictable currents, and the sheer boldness of Beck's totally un-
conventional approach to soloing was beautifully captured by
producer Martin.

"To me, the best formula is one where what you're playing is
in no way beneath you," Beck commented, "but at the same
time keeps you and your audience on its toes. Most performers
just turn things out to be consumed and digested."

With interest in Jeff Beck being high, the guitarist's scarcity of
live work in recent years required remedy. But Beck was tired
of being an unsuccessful band leader—at least, unsuccessful as
far as dealing with personnel issues. The solution? A tour with
Jan Hammer's own Jan Hammer Group, which required Beck
to merely step into the spotlight.

The results were documented on 1977's *Jeff Beck with the Jan
Hammer Group Live*. Though migrating into a preformed band
situation was attractive to Beck at the time, in hindsight the results were disappointing.

Had Beck assembled his own outfit, even to simply back him
for a single tour, the musicians might have displayed more def-
erence to their employer than the guitarist was afforded here.
Hammer was at a point in his career at which he labored in a
determined quest to make his synthesizer sound like a guitar,
complete with simulated string bends. That contrasted with his
groundbreaking work in The Mahavishnu Orchestra, where
Hammer had relied on a Fender Rhodes electric piano and on
early synthesizers—instruments with their own distinctive
sounds. On *Live*, though, tonally he was treading within Beck's
own sonic range. The result? Rather than supporting Beck, the
keyboardist's overplayed challenges collide with the guitar and
mar the album. The proceedings weren't helped by the inferior
vocal tracks sung by Hammer and drummer Tony Smith,
"Earth (Our Only Home)" and "Full Moon Boogie."

Jeff Beck's short association with The Jan Hammer Group
seemed to point out a rock and roll truism: with few democratic
exceptions, for a band to work, somebody had to be in charge.
In fact, that was the Golden Rule in the career of an American
guitarist who had clawed his way to the very top of the hard

rock charts. His name was Ted Nugent, and he had single-handedly rewritten the definition of the guitar wild man in extreme new terms.

"The way I see it is the big time has come and now is the time to drop the hammer even further," Nugent told Kat Gisi in a *Creem* magazine cover story.

"I realize I'm very obstinate and one-directional," he continued, referring to his my-way-or-the-highway band leadership. "But I just can't think any other way. Certain aspects of music and the rock 'n' roll life must be that way . . . Everyone around me is well aware of my desires and I ain't gonna fuckin' budge. You gotta have discipline."

Discipline characterized Nugent's antidrug and antidrinking lifestyle, even when those around him in the seminal late 1960s Detroit group The Amboy Dukes were tripping and toking. As band members came and went the group became known as Ted Nugent and The Amboy Dukes. Finally, Nugent dropped the group name entirely in the mid-1970s. After all, the show was unquestionably all about Ted.

Through dedicated road work and wild concert antics that found the frenetic Nugent swinging Tarzan-style onto the stage—while clad in loincloth and thigh-high boots, of course—his name became synonymous with hard rock.

With success came inevitable personnel issues. When singer and rhythm guitarist Derek St. Holmes began complaining about a lack of democracy in the band, Nugent the Boss practiced what he preached. St. Holmes was promptly invited to hit the road, successful band or not. Which explained the presence of a pre-fame Meat Loaf on 1976's *Free for All*.

Knowing he'd left a sure thing, St. Holmes swallowed his pride, mending fences with his "Motor City Madman" employer. Back in the fold, St. Holmes helped Nugent record what may be Ted's greatest studio album, 1977's *Cat Scratch Fever*. But perhaps as a final who-needs-who reminder to St. Holmes, Nugent chose to sing the album's title track himself. With Nugent emoting in his characteristic Midwestern twang, "Cat Scratch Fever" became a smash hit, mauling its way into existence on one of the most ferocious—and recognizable—guitar riffs in rock history.

Nugent followed up *Cat Scratch Fever* with a frantic live album, *Double Live Gonzo*, cementing his reputation as hard
rock's toughest and most crazed road warrior.

Whether the subject was his music or his personality, there
was little middle ground opinion about Nugent. But those who
were terrified by his maniacal behavior totally missed the fact
that Nugent was a brilliant, agile guitarist with a canny sense
of hard rock dynamics. His six-string weapon of choice—the
jazz-inspired Gibson Byrdland hollow-body—would generate
little more than out-of-control feedback in the hands of anyone
other than Nugent under his extreme-volume stage conditions.
Yet for Ted, the guitar sang sweetly—if lustily—in a unique
voice that his audience came to crave.

"Am I the world's greatest guitarist?" Nugent pondered in
the liner notes to his *Out of Control* career overview. "Depends.
As far as pure, unadulterated, spontaneous, uninhibited guitar
sound reaction goes, nobody comes close. My playing comes
from a perfect combination of heart, soul, guts, balls, attitude,
sass, spirit, angst, sex, instinct, and sense of humor. Big on the
humor. If it ain't fun, I'm outta here . . ."

On August 16, 1977 the rock world reeled from the loss of its
greatest icon, Elvis Presley. One month later, on September 16,
the career of T. Rex came to an end when Marc Bolan was killed
in a car crash.

It had been a year of strange sounds, sometimes violent and
sometimes beautiful, seemingly brought about by the spontaneous generation of a new galaxy of rock musicians. Now, two
of the best-known artists from opposing yet fundamental rock
eras had been taken.

Strangely enough, one of the constants through the turbulent
years leading to 1977 had been Lynyrd Skynyrd. The band had
ascended to superstar status on both shores of the Atlantic since
making the most their opening slot on The Who's 1974 tour.

Skynyrd had released a series of five earthy, no-nonsense albums that seemed to strike a universal chord in audiences re-

gardless of the band's rural Florida roots. Late in the summer of 1977, Lynyrd Skynyrd put the finishing touches on their new album, *Street Survivors*.

The band had become a more potent force with the addition of a young guitarist named Steve Gaines. Gaines had been worked into the band's sound via an aggressive live schedule throughout 1976, but it was in the studio that he began to really stand out. A clever songwriter who brought a touch of swing to Skynyrd's honky tonk sensibility, Gaines added a new dimension to a band that had already demonstrated mastery of a variety of styles.

The familiar Skynyrd sound was rolled out on the rollicking opening track of *Street Survivors*, "What's Your Name," and the band then made full use of their three-guitar palette on "That Smell." But the latter song's somber examination of lifestyles on the edge revealed a darker perspective in singer Ronnie Van Zant's lyrics.

Van Zant was blessed with a perceptive eye, and his lyrical gifts shined when it came time to put those perceptions to music. That had been the case from the band's earliest days, as evidenced by the inclusion of an old recording of an early song, "One More Time." But the three years of fame gave Van Zant pause, with a growing reflective air infusing his thoughts.

Newcomer Gaines wrote or cowrote four of the album's eight tracks, one of them being "I Never Dreamed." The rapid evolution of moods in the first moments of the song hinted at the expanded and quickly maturing musical capabilities of the revamped Lynyrd Skynyrd lineup.

Inside the *Street Survivors* album, an insert listed the schedule for "Lynyrd Skynyrd TOTS 1977–1978," the dates for the band's forty-show Tour of the Survivors. The tour successfully got underway on Skynyrd home turf with three dates in Florida. The band then played Greenville, South Carolina, and climbed on board their chartered plane to travel to the tour's fifth stop in Baton Rouge, Louisiana. They never made it.

In the darkness of the skies of the deep South, Lynyrd Skynyrd's plane encountered devastating mechanical failure. The aircraft streaked downward, crashing into a swamp near Gillsburg, Mississippi. Those uninjured enough to be mobile set off on a desperate quest for help through the remote area, but it was too late for Ronnie Van Zant, Steve Gaines, and his vocalist sister, Cassie. Tour manager Dean Kilpatrick also died in the October 20 crash.

In the days after the tragedy, MCA Records hastily recalled *Street Survivors* to reissue the album with a different cover. David Alexander's original cover photograph depicted the band standing in the middle of a darkened street, a raging fire consuming buildings around them. In the center of the photograph, Steve Gaines stood peacefully, hands at his side, eyes closed, flames wrapped around his body.

1978

9

Forward in All Directions

As 1977 staggered to a close, rock and roll had been taught a lesson in its own mortality, with Elvis Presley, Marc Bolan, and the core of Lynyrd Skynyrd never to set foot on stage again.

The losses were a blow, but to many rock musicians the danger at hand was the unpredictable punk rock movement. Its roots had been cultivated through the momentous 1976 tour of an all-American band, The Ramones. Now, though, what had been largely a British movement until 1978 threatened to leap back across the Atlantic to disrupt rock and roll American style.

The United States came very close to getting a firsthand look at the scourge of the U.K. when The Sex Pistols were booked on NBC's *Saturday Night Live* late in 1977. But the band encountered visa difficulties, sending show producers scrambling for a replacement punk. They found one in Elvis Costello and his band, The Attractions.

When *Saturday Night Live* hit the airwaves on December 17, 1977, Costello was largely viewed as though he was something out of a zoo. But the national audience knew enough about punks to expect some kind of disruption, so no one was too surprised when that's just what they got. Costello threw a wrench into live television by starting his second allotted song and then abruptly bringing the performance to a stop. The bespectacled one announced there was no reason to perform the song just begun, then proceeded to launch into an unreleased song called "Radio, Radio." Elvis spat out his scathing indictment of formulaic commercial radio formats as the show producers frantically gestured for him to halt.

Who was this Elvis Costello character, peering out of America's televisions through thick black-framed glasses, wearing what seemed to be an eternal scowl? His real name was Declan McManus, the son of British band leader Ross McManus. And though he was lumped into the punk rock movement, in reality all Elvis Costello and Johnny Rotten had in common was a jolting dose of vitriol flowing through their songs.

"I could never imagine a lot of people wanting this ugly geek in glasses ramming his songs down their throats," Costello once said, but that didn't stop him from tirelessly lobbying for a recording contract. His efforts paid off when he hand-delivered a demo tape on the day independent label Stiff Records opened for business in 1977.

Costello's first single, "Less Than Zero," was released in April of that year and promptly went nowhere. Despite a follow-up single sharing the same fate, label boss Jake Riviera gave Elvis the go-ahead to complete an album. Produced by fellow Stiff musician Nick Lowe, Costello's musical backing was provided by a California band of Lowe's acquaintance, Clover—a group containing musicians that would later form the core of pop group Huey Lewis and The News.

My Aim Is True hit the British stores in the summer and climbed to number fourteen in the charts. Columbia Records, warily sniffing around the chaotic English music scene, would eventually distribute the album throughout the United States late in the year. By following the same delayed-release strategy they'd used with The Clash, they once again lost considerable profits due to thousands of import sales made to American music fans eager to hear cutting-edge sounds from the U.K.

Meanwhile, Costello had formed his own backing band, The Attractions. Pete Thomas on drums and Bruce Thomas on bass were no relation, but they quickly bonded as a rhythm section, integrating musically beneath Steve Nieve's keyboards and Costello's own stuttering guitar.

Hitting the road on the Live Stiffs tour of the United Kingdom beginning October 3, 1977, Costello joined fellow Stiff-mates Lowe and Ian Dury and The Blockheads on an influential package tour. The jackets and narrow ties favored by Costello and

The Attractions gave them a throwback look, but the energy surge behind the rapidly evolving band was purely modern.

Through late 1977 and the first weeks of 1978, Costello and The Attractions labored in the studio, again paired with Lowe as producer, recording Costello's second album, *This Year's Model*. Jake Riviera had split from Stiff to start another label, Radar Records, in the process taking Costello and Lowe with him. Costello's new album would be Radar's debut.

From the first seconds of the album's opening cut, "No Action," it was clear this was a radically different album from *My Aim Is True*. Although Clover had provided adequate musical support, they were merely hired hands. The Attractions had played a flurry of gigs with Costello, new material taking shape in sweaty clubs and on stages throughout England. The sense of intuition that blossoms in a good band was quickly emerging in The Attractions, and the confidence and sophistication they displayed on *This Year's Model* found them light years ahead of the by-definition amateurish punk bands so prevalent in 1978.

Those bands could be forgiven for reaping the rewards offered by lemming-like record companies waving contracts— after all, the record labels themselves were determined to mine whatever they could out of "this punk thing." But Elvis Costello and The Attractions were the real thing.

This Year's Model was characterized by a raw, but beautifully recorded overall sound, with Bruce Thomas' bass front and center. In fact, his inventive prominence marked a reappearance of the "lead bass" approach that had been the hallmark of bands like Cream and Free. On songs like "This Year's Girl" and "(I Don't Want to Go to) Chelsea" Thomas' runs frame the entire structure of the song, urging the momentum along via rich tone and ingenious chord-change setups.

The Attractions as a whole were an integral unit, the four pieces meshing together seamlessly. Most bands at the time were typified by a heavily distorted guitar dominating the entire mix, but Costello used a halting style on his brief accents, like a "punch and get out" strategy in boxing. Rarely soloing, Costello instead focused on the most effective way to present each song's structure. Nieve's organ and piano work was atmospheric and urgent at the same time, and he had a unique ability to sonically illustrate Costello's lyrics with sympathetic lines that became central to each song's mood. And Pete Thomas was simply one of the most explosive drummers to emerge on the British scene in years, the master of a remarkable balance between power and precision.

Aside from the talents of the band as musicians, the songs of *This Year's Model* were far more refined than on Costello's debut, often taking unexpected diversions as they played out his lyrical visions. Those visions were given voice by Costello's seething delivery on songs like "Hand in Hand" and the contemptuous "Lipstick Vogue," blunt communiqués of emotional anguish, jealousy, and romantic betrayals.

Costello and his Attractions offered proof that there were artistic means available for the conveyance of bitterness other than screaming into a microphone over a two-chord backing track. In both performance and presentation, *This Year's Model* stood as an album unlike any other in 1978.

While Elvis Costello was breaking in his Attractions on the Live Stiffs tour of 1977, Ian Dury was using the same outing to get to know The Blockheads, his own recently assembled band.

The sound of Ian Dury and The Blockheads was one of the most unusual of the late 1970s, being an unlikely amalgamation of pub rock, disco, and British music hall styles, with the lyrics delivered by Dury in a heavy Cockney accent.

Though his body had been damaged by a childhood bout of polio, Dury stalked the stage with assurance. The force of his personality, and the swinging skill of The Blockheads, helped drive several singles and the album *New Boots and Panties!* to the top of the British charts. Arista Records hoped to cash in on Dury's charisma in the United States, but American buyers appeared to be immune to Dury's charm. The album racked up dismal sales outside Europe.

Dury's British smash hit "Sex & Drugs & Rock'n'Roll" outlined the singer's interests quite clearly, yet there were other new bands viewing life with a politically charged outlook.

"TRB is a rock band formed Jan.77: through series of lucky breaks + much support from diehard fans we landed recording contract that Aug. and British hit Oct./Nov. with '2-4-6-8 Motorway.' This is our first album."

Those were the simple, to-the-point liner notes of The Tom Robinson Band's debut, *Power in the Darkness*. Robinson saw the freewheeling atmosphere around punk as the ideal opportunity to launch serious political discussions within a rock context, and his cause was helped by the fact that TRB was easily among the most musically talented bands of the burgeoning British punk and New Wave movement.

Openly gay, bassist Robinson—supported by his band mates Dolphin Taylor on drums, Danny Kustow on guitar, and Mark Ambler on keyboards—wrote songs with an incisive, biting edge.

"I'm a middle-class kiddie but I know where I stand," Robinson announced in the highly charged "Ain't Gonna Take It." Commenting on the growing political conservatism mounting in England and his fears over the ascension of groups like the semi-Fascist National Front, Robinson was something of a politicized Ray Davies, focusing on day-to-day British concerns and worries much as Davies' Kinks had done five years earlier with their *Preservation* suite.

Produced by Chris Thomas and engineered by Bill Price, both fresh from their efforts on The Sex Pistols' *Never Mind the Bollocks*, *Power in the Darkness* avoided the danger of becoming nothing more than a litany of Robinson's political agendas. For all of its social consciousness, TRB could rock hard, as they proved in the thunderous opener "Up Against the Wall."

Throughout the album, Robinson's every-man voice played off Kustow's guitar, the latter sounding remarkably like The Spiders from Mars' Mick Ronson supercharged by a punk idealism. The extended breaks of "The Winter of '79," "Better Decide Which Side You're On," and "Man You Never Saw" contained thrilling slices of pure guitar solo power, an endangered species in the punk/New Wave hierarchy. Keyboardist Ambler was also in top-notch form, unleashing an incendiary organ solo on the album's title track above the smash-and-bash rhythm section of Robinson and Taylor.

From the rampant paranoia about government agencies that characterized "Man You Never Saw" to the postapocalypse visions of "You Gotta Survive," TRB delivered their message in hard-hitting bursts of well-constructed rock. And unlike many of the punks who wanted nothing more than to destroy rock's heritage, TRB held an appreciation for musical elders, as witnessed by the Van Morrison-like "Moondance" setting that coolly imbued "Too Good to Be True."

"I got no illusions about the political left any more than the right; just a shrewd idea of which side's gonna stomp on us first," Robinson told British music newspaper *New Musical Express*. "All of us—you, me, rock 'n' rollers, punks, longhairs, dope smokers, squatters, students, unmarried mothers, prisoners, gays, the jobless, immigrants, gypsies . . . to stand aside is to take sides. If music can ease even a tiny fraction of the prejudice and intolerance in this world, then it's worth trying. I don't call that 'unnecessary overtones of violence.' I call it standing up for your rights.

"And if we fail, if we all get swallowed up by big business before we achieve a thing, then we'll have to face the scorn of tomorrow's generation. But we're gonna have a good try."

In line with Robinson's views, the kids who most wholly bought into the punk movement as a lifestyle considered themselves to be a disaffected segment of the English population. On a spiritual level, that gave them something in common with Rastafarians, the sociological subset from Jamaica that viewed marijuana as a religious tool and believed African leader Haile Sellasie to be a spiritual deity. The "hymns" of the Rastas were reggae songs—deep, hypnotic works by recording artists like Burning Spear.

In England, the growing Jamaican population maintained a direct pipeline between the music business headquartered in Kingston and the urban subculture in cities like London. That gave the punks an opportunity to not only support the spiky-hair-and-safety-pin bands, but to also get turned on to the music of Junior Murvin, Lee Perry, Peter Tosh, Bunny Wailer, Jimmy Cliff, Toots and The Maytals, and many more of reggae's brightest lights. The Clash had even featured a cover version of Murvin's "Police and Thieves" prominently on their debut album.

Yet there was one Rasta who was creating reggae on a level of white-hot creativity. For most music listeners, Bob Marley became the very definition of reggae music.

Marley had been propelled into popular culture stardom in part by Eric Clapton's cover of "I Shot the Sheriff," but his popularity was far more profound than that of a typical rock idol. Throughout large parts of the Third World, he was viewed as a virtual prophet, one bearing tidings of equality and a better life through determination and faith.

So influential was the opinion of Bob Marley in the chaotic world of Jamaican politics that, days before he was to appear at the "Smile Jamaica" concert in Kingston on December 5, 1976, gunmen burst into his house and practice studio complex, firing wildly in an assassination attempt. Marley, wife Rita, and manager Don Taylor were all hit, but miraculously survived. Marley's agreement to appear at the concert had been seen as an endorsement of the People's National Party and their socialist leader Michael "Joshua" Manley. In turn, the assassination attempt was viewed to be the work of supporters of rival leader Edward Seaga's Jamaican Labor Party.

Incredibly, Bob Marley and The Wailers performed at "Smile Jamaica," the singer raising his shirt to expose his wounds and laughing defiantly at the mortal danger he faced.

With each successive studio album, Marley and The Wailers found greater global acclaim, and the legend of the band's charismatic, dreadlocked leader seemed to grow exponentially. But it was on stage that the incredible power of the band was fully revealed, proving Marley's Wailers to be a group every bit as formidable as Bruce Springsteen's E Street Band. A July 18, 1975 concert recording from London's Lyceum, *LIVE!*, had acted as a breakthrough to the rock audience conditioned to accept live recordings as an excellent barometer of a band's true capabilities. But by 1978's *Babylon by Bus*, The Wailers were an even more potent presence on the world's stages.

A crucial change in the band's lineup was the addition of guitarist Junior Marvin, who joined in time for the recording of 1977's *Exodus*. Marvin brought an appreciation of rock guitar and effects usage to the dark, loping sound of The Wailers. The return of former Wailers guitarist Al Anderson and the addition of keyboardist Earl "Wire" Lindo completed the revised Wailers package.

On *Babylon by Bus*, Marley and his band presented a thrilling set of material recorded at various European gigs early in 1978. The album documents the fact that The Wailers were a true

musical juggernaut, a supple, crafty, and powerful unit consisting of two keyboardists, a bassist, a drummer, a percussionist, three backup vocalists, and three guitarists, including
Marley's own rhythm playing.

Opening the set with "Positive Vibration," the deceptively
simple song reveals undercurrents of rhythm and bass that are
ever-changing and intriguingly complex. Listening to drummer Carlton Barrett's hi-hat cymbal work alone revealed a cun-
ning, seemingly erratic pattern that tugged against the band's
instrumentation. Carlton's brother, bassist Aston "Familyman"
Barrett, showed he was one of reggae's greatest musicians, a
virtuoso in a format of music entirely dependent on bass. His
rich, propulsive tones wrapped around his brother's rhythms,
painting rumbling, bottom-end vistas of melody.

Longtime Wailer Tyrone Downie and newcomer Lindo
meshed in the creation of interlocking patterns of keyboards,
Downie's thrusting organ and piano contrasting the staccato
notes of Lindo's clavinet. Solos by lead guitarists Marvin and
Anderson rose up from the deep tropical rhythms, solid rock
and R&B lines sounding revolutionary as a result of their trans-
plantation into such an exotic setting.

Over the lush rhythmic tundra of the Wailers, Marley's gritty
spiritual exhortations were unleashed, some expressed in right-
eous bitterness, others in jubilation. Joining his lead vocals
were The I-Threes, the vocal trio of Judy Mowatt, Marcia Grif-
fiths, and Rita Marley, essential voices in the overall sound of
the band. Their clever arrangements at times echoed Marley's
lines in traditional fashion, but were just as likely to preview
his next line, or even offer contrasting lyrics.

Bob Marley was an astute observer of culture and music,
and he realized that punk rock afforded an opportunity to expose a new audience to reggae and Rastafarianism. So where
others reacted to punk rock with revulsion, Marley embraced
it wholly, even releasing a single titled "Punky Reggae Party,"
which The Wailers recorded live for *Babylon by Bus*. In its
lyrics, Marley gleefully called out for a joining together of reggae artists like The Wailers and The Maytals with The Jam,
The Damned, and The Clash, assuring "no boring old farts
will be there!" And the I-Threes' chant behind Marley's vocals? "Do re mi fa, so la ti do," they crooned, in a clever ac-

knowledgment of punk's determination to break rock music down to its most basic elements.

Bob Marley may have been able to envision punk and reggae living in harmony, but, significantly, he did not name The Sex Pistols in the lyrics of "Punky Reggae Party." And life in The Pistols was proving to be anything but harmonious.

Having missed out on their chance to infect the United States in one fell swoop via an appearance on *Saturday Night Live*, The Sex Pistols faced the daunting challenge of handling the task one city at a time. And the first half of their 1977–1978 tour of the United States had already been cancelled due to the delays in the band's arrival. Finally resolving the visa issues that held them up, early in January 1978 the Pistols flew across the ocean to take on the United States. In the end, the United States would win.

Steve Jones, Paul Cook, Sid Vicious, and Johnny Rotten stepped onto an American stage for the first time on January 5, 1978, at the Great Southeast Music Hall in Atlanta. They found an audience of five hundred that was a bizarre array of followers, curiosity-seekers, and rock fans determined to heckle the band back to England. They'd already faced a barrage of barbed questions from television and media reporters determined to file sensationalized accounts of The Pistols' antics.

"It's different here in the States," Rotten told *Creem* magazine's Patrick Goldstein in the midst of the tour. "They treat us like we're some kind of circus act. It's really a load of bollocks—everybody wants my fucking autograph."

Rotten was far from impressed by the audiences he encountered in the United States.

"American kids are really pathetic," he noted. "They put bands like Kiss on a pedestal. Then they sit on their hands and demand a freak show. Well, fuck 'em. If they're gonna be like that, I'm going out of my way to disappoint them."

"You can all stop staring at us now," Rotten informed the Atlanta audience. "We're ugly and we know it."

The Sex Pistols straggled their way across the country, on a tour that manager Malcolm McLaren seemed to have carefully booked to hit only secondary markets, including Baton Rouge, Louisiana; Tulsa, Oklahoma; and San Antonio, Texas. The latter show was particularly abusive, Sid being hit in the face and finishing the set with blood smeared across his mouth and chest. After ten days of relentless media coverage, being spit upon and screamed at, The Sex Pistols arrived in San Francisco for the final gig of the brief seven-date tour.

On Saturday, January 14, The Sex Pistols took the stage of the Winterland Ballroom before a restless crowd of 5,000—bigger than all the other tour dates combined. Sick of each other and sick of the tour, The Sex Pistols imploded on stage.

Sid, who'd taken to heroin with relish, was totally wasted, slamming his bass in tuneless rhythms that had little to do with the drumming of Cook or with Jones' guitar notes. Vicious eventually keeled over.

"Tell us, what's it like to have bad taste?" Rotten taunted, but by show's end the spark had ebbed. During the encore of "No Fun," he gave up singing, instead mumbling, "This no fun, no fun, it is no fun at all . . ."

"Ever get the feeling you've been cheated?" Rotten asked. Then he walked off the stage, leaving The Sex Pistols behind him.

With that, the band that caused such an uproar and ignited so many controversies succumbed to a messy dissolution.

In the wake of the debacle, Sid promptly overdosed on a flight from San Francisco to New York, interrupting his planned return to London. Meanwhile Johnny Rotten took refuge in New York.

"I didn't quit them, they all just decided to quit me at once," he told *Creem* magazine's Susan Whitall days after the San Francisco disaster. "It was really quite pathetic; I met them all at the lift in the hotel, leaving. . . . There's no point in being miserable about it—I'm a free man! I'm quite pleased."

Years later, John Lydon—long since having shed the "Rotten" moniker—knew where to place the blame.

"It was all very easy for Malcolm to sit behind a desk or behind a phone and pontificate, saying, 'We're troublemakers,' and, 'We're into violence,'" Lydon noted. "I was the sod who had to live the violence on the street, get beaten up. Thank you, Malcolm."

The punk movement was already showing its first signs of disintegration, even as record companies continued to throw wads of money and contracts at anything they thought was punk or New Wave, particularly in England. Unable to discern the talented from the incompetent within the confines of punk's context, the businessmen of music regularly made fools of themselves signing the garbage with the gold, chasing a trend they had little capacity for understanding.

Yet leading the punk rock lifestyle could be hazardous, particularly in one of the high-profile groups where band members were targets as much as they were musicians—a lesson The Sex Pistols had learned the hard way. But the toughest punk band of them all, The Ramones, continued to thrive.

"Since we were the first group doing this, we had to be like the fall guys for everybody else," Joey Ramone noted. "We had to be the example."

The Ramones' 1976 tour of England had proven to be the brightest spark of all in detonating a nascent punk rock movement—and the band was proud to take the credit.

"That was the beginning of the world explosion in England— and then the world changed," Joey said. "Everything changed drastically for the better. '76–'77 was like '64–'65 and the English invasion. We put the spirit and guts back into rock and roll."

The Ramones were still doing just that in 1978, with their third album, *Rocket to Russia*, edging into the charts. By this time the band had honed their sound into a high-velocity blunt object, one that was wielded with a greater degree of vibrancy than heard on their earlier efforts. As the band learned to use the studio, songs like "Cretin Hop," "Sheena is a Punk Rocker," and "Teenage Lobotomy" cruised along with the thunderous energy of the band's earth-shaking live performances while still allowing Joey to apply his beloved Phil Spector pop touches to choruses and harmonies.

On stage, though, The Ramones in concert were all about momentum. On New Year's Eve 1977, the foursome stood before a near-feral audience of British punkdom at London's Rainbow Theatre, surveying all that they had in large part created.

"Hey! We're The Ramones, and this one's called 'Rockaway Beach,'" Joey announced, bassist Dee Dee nearly simultaneously screaming out a frenetic "OneTwoThreeFour!" count—and The Ramones were off on an a blitzkrieg assault of twenty-eight songs from their three albums.

When the Rainbow concert recording was released in England in 1979 as *It's Alive*, it stood as the perfect documentation of The Ramones at the very peak of their powers. It also offered an aural explanation of something that was more difficult to explain—why a short tour by a little known American band a year and a half earlier had left England's kids reeling, consumed by a determination to shake the world of rock music.

Nearly as influential in igniting the punk rock detonation, The Patti Smith Group released their own third album, *Easter*, in 1978.

In the months since the release of *Radio Ethiopia*, Smith had been forced to endure a period of inactivity. In January 1977, while performing "Ain't It Strange" in Tampa, Florida, Patti had tumbled from the stage. Her injuries were severe, with two vertebrae in her neck cracked, and she had been fortunate not to suffer paralysis. But Smith refused to let her injuries stop her.

"Out of traction, back in action!" Patti announced from the stage of CBGB six months after her fall. Still wearing a neck brace, Smith and her band chose familiar territory to make a low-profile return to the rock wars. But one thing was immediately obvious—The Patti Smith Group was a more potent force than ever.

"Musically, we are getting more sophisticated," Patti told Lisa Robinson in the March 1978 issue of *Hit Parader*. "I'm getting more sophisticated even though I don't want to. It just happens—it's like when you play long enough, you learn stuff. I can sing better, and it's happened in spite of myself."

Perhaps the biggest surprise of all was that Smith's new album was accompanied by a hit single. *Easter* producer Jimmy Iovine, who had an extensive background as an engineer, had worked in the past with Bruce Springsteen. Springsteen was also acquainted with Patti, having even joined The Patti Smith Group on stage at New York's Bottom Line. But still, the idea of The Patti Smith Group covering a Springsteen song was a novel one. Regardless, the dramatic "Because the Night" cast Smith in the light of passionate chanteuse and struck a chord with listeners. The single climbed to number thirteen in the United States and reached the top five in England.

"Because the Night" also exposed thousands of new listeners to the band's undeniable strengths. Simply because there was a growing maturity in the ranks of The Patti Smith Group—and a single climbing the charts—did not mean there had been an abandonment of the ideals that had fueled the group since its inception. Rather, whereas once the band wandered in chaotic improvisation, as on *Radio Ethiopia*'s title track, The Patti Smith Group now focused and delivered a coherent package on adventurous material like "25th Floor." And on songs like the urgent "Till Victory" and the breathtaking "Privilege (Set Me Free)" Patti and her group simply rocked with the ease and the power and the all-consuming confidence that were the defining characteristics of the world's greatest rock and roll bands.

The success of "Because the Night" was fundamental in forcing American rock audiences to become more receptive to the idea of punk and New Wave, but there was another New York band from the CBGB orbit that would prove to be the most commercially successful of them all.

With origins stretching back to 1974, the lineup of Blondie began to solidify in 1977 as the band recorded its second album. Formed by the charismatically exotic blonde vocalist Deborah Harry and guitarist Chris Stein, the band had recorded their debut album *Blondie* for the small Private Stock label in 1976. Chrysalis Records, the home of established bands like Jethro Tull and Robin Trower, then settled on Blondie as their New Wave signing, releasing the band's second album, *Plastic Letters*. The decision of Chrysalis boss Terry Ellis to sign the band would soon pay tremendous dividends.

Blondie dipped their toes in any number of stylistic waters, touching on 1960s girl group pop, campy kitsch, 1950s glamour ideals, as well as punk energy, all in pursuit of a unique image that was modern and retro at the same time.

"I did identify with Marilyn," Harry noted of her stylistic influences. "But it was more the blonde thing in general. Blonde hair we equate with glamour, success, desire. It was just a great look."

With the striking Harry in the center of the spotlight, and a strong band that aligned Stein with co-guitarist Frank Infante, Nigel Harrison on bass, Jimmy Destri on keyboards, and the explosively driving Clem Burke on drums, Blondie had all of the elements required for success—they simply needed to assemble them. Mike Chapman was the man who could help them.

Best known as a songwriter who had composed smash hits like "Ballroom Blitz" for British power-pop rockers Sweet, Chapman and his partner Nicky Chinn had begun taking on production duties as well, beginning with albums for singer Suzi Quatro. With Chapman's pop sensibility well established, the Australian's proposed alliance with Blondie looked to be full of potential.

When *Parallel Lines* was released in 1978, it was the right album at the right time, full of deliriously delectable power pop. Alternating between the angst of heartbreak and a lust that had only been implied in the hits of the girl groups from years gone by, Harry seductively cooed and growled her way through the infectious collection of songs.

The fiery backing of the band on *Parallel Lines* was diverted by a pair of stylistic forays. One, the atmospheric "Fade Away and Radiate," featured a typically eerie solo by guest guitarist Robert Fripp, whose presence served as a link to serious rock credibility. The other proved to be the band's establishing hit, a disco-tinged pop confection called "Heart of Glass."

With Harry in a white dress on the album's cover, joined by her smiling band mates dressed in black suits and white shirts with skinny ties, the album presented a consumer-friendly New Wave image that made it safe for anyone to climb on the new music bandwagon. And thousands upon thousands promptly did just that, as *Parallel Lines* reached number one in England and number six in the United States. Released as a single, "Heart of Glass" topped both nations' charts.

Also seeking such commercial success was singer David Johansen. Having shed the trappings of chaotic collapse that were the hallmark of the final months of his New York Dolls, Johansen appeared cleaned up but urban-hip on the cover of his self-titled 1978 solo debut, produced by Richard Robinson with Steve Paul listed as "director."

Paul had been an influential character in New York since the late 1960s, when he managed The McCoys—whose members included Rick Derringer, later to play with both Johnny and Edgar Winter. Paul also ran the Scene, a nightclub/hangout that was one of Jimi Hendrix's favorite spots for a late-night jam session. With vast music industry contacts, Paul was acquainted with everyone from Tiny Tim to Jim Morrison.

Robinson had also long been involved in New York's music scene. With his rock writer wife, Lisa, he had worked with Lenny Kaye long before Kaye became a founding member of The Patti Smith Group. They had established the breezy and breathless magazine *Rock Scene*, a publication that frequently championed The New York Dolls. The persistent efforts of the Robinsons to convince Lou Reed to return to the studio in the wake of The Velvet Underground's collapse finally paid dividends in 1972 when Reed recorded his first solo album with Richard as producer.

Despite all of the musicians that Johansen likely could have attracted to his project, the only "rock star" brought aboard was Aerosmith's Joe Perry, and that was only for two tracks. Johansen's selection of the earthy, rough guest guitarist signified the direction of the entire project, for which he and Robinson relied on local New York musicians. With guitarists Johnny Rao and Thomas Trask carving out swaggering rhythm and biting leads, Johansen's oversized, near-caricature voice rambled through city-smart songs like "Cool Metro" and "Funky but Chic" with a polish and a presence that had never been fully developed in The New York Dolls.

With *David Johansen*, the singer showed that it was possible to emerge artistically intact from the ruins of a poorly managed, drug-infested band that was often decadently celebrated for those very reasons. It would be a blueprint that others would need to study for their very survival when cracks inevitably led to collapse in some of punk rock's most notorious bands.

As rock's New Wave spread, it became commonplace for bands to adopt the skinny-tie look. But for Kraftwerk, such affectations bordered on trademark infringement. The foursome from Dusseldorf had always looked like conservative businessmen who had been magically transported from the 1930s into the 1970s, but in order to visually distance themselves from New Wave minions like Blondie and Elvis Costello, the Germans were forced to enhance their own image.

When the band released their 1978 album, *The Man-Machine*, the bookish atmosphere that had characterized the art of their earlier releases was replaced by a severe, Soviet-influenced look dominated by black, red, and white. Using a stern font to proclaim the band's name and the album's title in several languages, the cover depicted Kraftwerk's foursome of Ralf, Florian, Karl, and Wolfgang lined up on a stairwell, identically dressed in gray trousers, black ties, and lustrous red shirts. In a particularly unsettling touch, all four man-machines were adorned with blood red lipstick.

What did it mean? No one but Kraftwerk knew for sure, but one thing was clear—the band had continued their revolutionary advancements in creating distinctive electronic music. Tracks like the soaring "Spacelab" and the somber "Metropolis" boasted new textures and sounds as the band pursued emerging technologies in sound generation.

That David Bowie was influenced tremendously by Kraftwerk was no surprise; he had admitted as much in interviews, and even composed "V-2 Schneider" from *"Heroes"* as a token of esteem for Kraftwerk member Florian Schneider. But Bowie now faced a challenge: how to translate the Kraftwerk-influenced music of *Low* and *"Heroes"* into concert-friendly material. Record buyers had somewhat warmed to the title track of *"Heroes,"* but it was doubtful that a stadium full of fans would be clamoring to hear the instrumentals "Warsawza" or "Sense of Doubt."

Bowie pondered his return to the concert trail. Obviously, the prudent course would be to roll out the hits and give the people what they wanted. But Bowie was rarely prudent when it came to career matters.

When the singer stepped on the stage of Philadelphia's Spectrum for two shows on April 28 and 29, 1978, the RCA Records mobile recording truck was on hand. Its task was to document the event for the double live album released later in the year, *Stage*. Clearly Bowie considered Philadelphia an excellent place to get work done, having recorded his first live album in the city some four years earlier, and having used the city's Sigma Sound Studios to create the *Young Americans* album. If any audience would give his new material a chance, it was the 18,000 fans who packed the Spectrum each night.

Cannily, Bowie won over the crowd with a string of five straight songs from *The Rise and Fall of Ziggy Stardust and The Spiders from Mars*, opening with the full-throttle "Hang on to Yourself." Though the songs were familiar, they were endowed with a modern sheen by Bowie's new band. Still based on the core of Carlos Alomar on rhythm guitar, Dennis Davis on drums, and George Murray on bass, Bowie augmented the trio with bold personnel selections. There was guitarist Adrian Belew, one of Frank Zappa's key collaborators and an instrumentalist known for pushing the boundaries of the electric guitar through the employment of new effects and techniques. And Roger Powell came to the Bowie band on loan from his duties as the primary synthesist in the second iteration of Todd Rundgren's Utopia. By also including Simon House on violin and Sean Mayes on additional keyboards, Bowie had assembled a thoroughly modern-sounding seven-piece band capable of crafting an array of intriguing sounds.

And they did just that to begin the concert's second half. After intermission, the band focused entirely on the material from *Low* and *"Heroes,"* first passing through four of the long, moody instrumentals composed by Bowie and Brian Eno. With Bowie joining in on a Chamberlain electronic keyboard, the eight musicians recreated the moving atmosphere that characterized the two albums' second sides. The vocal tracks that followed received slight reinventions, the sheer energy of the live performances giving "What in the World" and "Beauty and the Beast" an animated, kinetic feel.

All in all, *Stage* documented the migration of material from a Berlin studio to an American arena, with everyone going home happy—despite odds to the contrary.

Though David Bowie was notorious for radical revisions to his sound, the impact of the new electronic bands like Kraftwerk on the music of England's Be Bop Deluxe was less expected.

Be Bop Deluxe had, since their inception, been a difficult band to categorize. Bill Nelson was a brilliant guitarist, but he didn't really fit the mold of the traditional guitar hero. And though the band was no stranger to harder-edged material, as heard on their *Sunburst Finish* album of 1976, they were more than just a hard rock band; there was always an element just a bit "outside" infusing their music.

On the band's fifth album, *Drastic Plastic*, the idealized visions of the future that had populated past Be Bop Deluxe studio albums were shoehorned into a more austere, technical environment. It was immediately obvious that, like David Bowie, Nelson was under the influence of the new German techno pop scene. Treatments on Nelson's voice, burbling synths, and the stilted machine rhythms of "Electrical Language" pointed to new directions to be explored, and, even though the band's career closed with this album, Nelson's own restless experimentations would continue over the years.

The willingness to experiment with sound was the defining characteristic of Brian Eno's work, and while David Bowie toured the world with the music that he and Eno had crafted in Berlin, Eno himself was taking on production tasks. Although a planned association with Television had not panned out, events went more smoothly when Eno took on one of the most curious bands surfing rock's New Wave, Devo.

Hailing from Akron, Ohio, Devo was—not surprisingly—the brainchild of art students. The band members bore no resemblance to rock gods such as Ted Nugent and used that fact to their advantage. Devo presented the image of demented young scientists, espousing their theory of "devolution," which decried society's descent into a lemming-like mentality. These doctrines were presented by the band while attired in a number of absurd outfits, such as the yellow plastic jumpsuits trimmed in black harnesses modeled on the album sleeve of their debut, *Q: Are We Not Men? A: We are DEVO!*

Devo's big break from nerdish obscurity to New Wave prominence came in 1976, when David Bowie and Iggy Pop happened to see the Devo-based *The Truth about De-Evolution* at the Ann Arbor Film Festival. Their recommendation to Warner Brothers secured a contract for Devo's debut.

So Warner had signed a band from mid-America that bore a geek-like countenance, wore ridiculous costumes while decrying the regression of society, and set it all to jerky, robotic rhythms and electronic noises. This was right up Brian Eno's alley.

Eno and the band—whose members were officially listed as Mark, Alan, Jerry, Bob1, and Bob2—whisked off to Koln, Germany, where sessions for *Are We Not Men* began at Conny's Studio, owned by longtime Kraftwerk associate Conrad Planck, who served as engineer.

The eleven songs presented on their debut were by definition quirky. "Uncontrollable Urge" began the collection, with Mark Mothersbaugh's high, reedy voice awkwardly bouncing within the basic punkish environment. The simple construction was twisted by elementary electronics highly reminiscent of Eno's own contributions to early Roxy Music songs like "Re-Make/Re-Model" and "Virginia Plain." But devolution got underway in earnest with a deconstruction of the Rolling Stones' "Satisfaction." When Devo had completed their redesign, Jagger's heated, self-pitying burst of frustration was reduced to a chilled stagger.

Much of Devo's material relied on a hypnotic repetition of phrases, the trance-like patterns unexpectedly broken by shouted choruses or random electronic chaos—all built on a foundation of elementary guitar/bass/drums not far removed from the most basic of punk constructions.

The shining apex of *Are We Not Men* was found on "Jocko Homo," a wildly propulsive, call-and-response recounting of the devolvic philosophy, one that served as a lament over a world full of "monkey men all in business suit."

With Devo finding a major label home for their extreme art, somehow the idea of middle ground began to seem foreign to the record industry—until it was proposed by The Cars. Guitarist Ric Ocasek and bassist Benjamin Orr had met in Ohio but soon afterward had moved to the more fertile music scene of

Boston. There the final band lineup of The Cars was assembled, and a strong demo tape led to the group signing with Elektra Records.

Elektra had the good sense to approve an alliance of their newly signed band with Queen producer Roy Thomas Baker. Always a master of studio creativity, Baker helped the band craft a modern, sleek sound that merged the techno and mechanical elements of Devo and Kraftwerk with strong songwriting and a can't-go-wrong incorporation of traditional rock elements. Coupled with a strong sense of fashion and the contrast between the dark, gawky Ocasek and Orr's blond good looks, The Cars were positioned to boldly go where no other band had gone before.

The clever melding of disparate elements that characterized 1978's *The Cars* led to astonishing success for the band, chiefly because the stodgy album-oriented radio stations—which had in large part attempted to ignore punk and New Wave—finally were confronted with new music that they couldn't help but play. *The Cars* became an incredible hit-spawning album, and its songs are still staples of rock radio today.

The fact that new music was getting airplay at all—New Wave or not—was somewhat remarkable. As of April 1978, four of the top five United States singles were produced or composed by The Bee Gees, who had been omnipotent chart-wise since the release of the disco movie *Saturday Night Fever*. In fact, the soundtrack album from the movie had taken possession of the number one album slot, remaining in that rarified air for twenty-four straight weeks and selling more than thirty million copies.

Eventually, though, the music industry signaled that it was willing to recognize the less-threatening cousin of punk rock, New Wave. When the nominees for the 1978 Grammy Awards were announced, both The Cars and Elvis Costello and The Attractions were nominated for Best New Artist. Choosing between a new singer-songwriter from England whose albums were gaining critical respect, versus a band merging the old and the new into a format that already was having a major impact on rock radio, the Grammy voters had their work cut out for them in making such a difficult decision.

The overseers of the Grammys, the National Academy of Recording Arts and Sciences, had long been considered out-of-touch by inhabitants of the rock realm, but many thought the 1978 nomination tally was an attempt to show that voters were still able to recognize bright new talent. So the rockers watched with interest when the envelope was opened. And the award went to: A Taste of Honey, for their gimmicky disco song "Boogie Oogie Oogie." The selection simply proved that some things never seemed to change.

In 1978, the future of The Rolling Stones was very much in doubt. And the threat posed by punk rock had nothing to do with their predicament.

Arriving in Toronto, Canada on February 27, 1977 to record shows for the album *Love You Live*, Keith Richards had been arrested for heroin possession. The quantity of the drug was so great that Richards had been charged with intent to distribute, and the possibility that the guitarist might go to jail for years was a very real peril.

Under those trying circumstances, with Keith's trial scheduled to begin late in 1978, The Rolling Stones recorded their next studio album, *Some Girls*, which was released in June 1978.

Amazingly, the band used the uncertainty clouding their future to fuel a raging, rocking album that had every bit of the intensity missing from their work since *Sticky Fingers* and *Exile on Main Street*.

Perhaps The Stones had borrowed a bit of the much-vaunted punk energy floating through the 1978 air. It was a known fact that Mick Jagger was impressed by punk, even if he was the most frequent target of the punks' rebellion. Despite Mick's interest, Keith couldn't be bothered.

"I don't think that Mick needs to be so conscious of what the rest of the rock hierarchy are doing," Richards groused in 1976. "Jagger always wants to know what everyone else is doing. Sometimes I get the feeling that he measures himself against others."

Regardless of the source of inspiration, though, there was no question that The Rolling Stones were again playing like a band possessed. On songs like "When the Whip Comes Down" and "Respectable," the guitars of Richards and Ron Wood intertwined into a tangled bed of pure rock propulsion. The surge was driven by the crack of Charlie Watts' snare drum and Bill Wyman's resonating bass, as Mick Jagger howled above the sonic maelstrom. Revitalized and energized, the title of "world's greatest rock and roll band" was back within The Stones' reach.

In the United States, though, many would have argued that Bruce Springsteen and The E Street Band deserved that particular honor. The only problem: Bruce hadn't been doing much to state his case. Not that he'd been able to. A seemingly endless lawsuit filed by his former manager, Mike Appel, led to month after month of recording inactivity. Springsteen found himself facing the worst torment a recording artist in his prime could imagine: he was legally barred from the studio by the court until the case was finally settled on May 28, 1977.

On June 6, 1978, *Darkness on the Edge of Town* was finally released. Some observers were amazed that it took Springsteen a full year to prepare his next album. After all, he'd crafted plenty of new material during the months the lawsuit dragged on, and much of it had already been played live by The E Street Band. But when it came to recording, Bruce Springsteen was an admitted perfectionist.

"There's so many records coming out, there's so much stuff on the shelves, why put out something that you don't feel is what it should be?" Springsteen reflected to *Creem* magazine's Dave DiMartino. "It's like from the very beginning, I just never believed in doing things that way. You make your record like it's the last record you'll ever make."

Produced by Jon Landau and Springsteen with an assist from E Street Band guitarist Steve Van Zandt, and recorded by Patti Smith producer Jimmy Iovine, *Darkness on the Edge of Town* bore little resemblance to its predecessor, *Born to Run*. That record was largely full of characters expressing determination and hope; *Darkness* played out as though some of those characters had come to grim terms with the fact that things don't always work out for the best. Despite the guarded optimism of new tracks like "Badlands" and "The Promised Land," songs like the title track and "Streets of Fire" contained bitter doses of reality. And in "Racing in the Street," Springsteen sang of a girl who stares into the night "with the eyes of one who hates for just being born."

The new material challenged The E Street Band to adapt to Springsteen's more somber moods, and they did so in moving fashion, rooted by Garry Tallent's beautifully melodic bass and Roy Bittan's shimmering piano. And when the tempos went up, the familiar E Street power was still in evidence, as was a new focus on Bruce's own underrated lead guitar abilities.

While Springsteen was determinedly reestablishing his temporarily derailed recording career, over in rock's high-rent district, Pete Townshend was putting the final touches on the next effort from The Who.

Where 1975's *The Who by Numbers* had revealed the band in lean and mean form, on *Who Are You*—released in August, 1978—The Who were back in orchestrated territory, wallowing in a sea of synthesizers.

An album with too many songs following a similar leaden pacing, *Who Are You* presented Daltrey at his most melodramatic. From the opening notes of the album's first track, "New Song," the singer seemed to thrive on the new material's bombast. Such was not the case with drummer Keith Moon.

Townshend's weighty new material worked against Moon's still-formidable strengths, seemingly validating the rumors of substance abuse that had many suspecting that Moon's talents were on the wane. But with Townshend's customary introspection restored into highly arranged compositions like the overblown "Music Must Change" and "Guitar and Pen," Moon was cornered once again in the role of beat keeper. It had always been the side of his drumming that was least attractive. Sadly, on *Who Are You*, the dynamic drummer's true talents were fully unleashed only on "Sister Disco," "Trick of the Light," and "Who Are You." One of the world's greatest rock bands stood trapped within the confines of their leader's overwrought compositions.

In the end, *Who Are You* sounded as if Townshend was writing more for Broadway than for a rock band. It was an album loaded with precisely the kind of pompous self-indulgence that made the punk rockers loathe the "dinosaur groups."

Despite the turgid aspects of The Who's new album, Moon was held in high esteem by a large segment of the punks.

Though he'd turned thirty-two on August 23, 1978, Keith's wit and wildness won over many kids who thought Townshend's music was the prattling of a self-important bore. But in spite of his public charm, Moon struggled mightily with drugs and alcohol, and his life was filled with personal wreckage.

After the release of *Who Are You*, Moon and the band turned their attention to finishing off a film depicting the history of The Who. The movie was to be called *The Kids Are Alright*, named after one of the group's earliest hits. But completing the project proved problematic for Moon. While working on the current-era segment of the film, Keith was in such rough shape that, when called upon to drum, he could barely play parts that at one time would have required little exertion.

On September 6, Moon and his girlfriend Annette Walter-Lax attended the premier of *The Buddy Holly Story* in London. It was his final public appearance. Within hours, Keith Moon, rock's greatest drummer, was dead from an overdose of the very medication prescribed to help him withdraw from a dependency on alcohol.

Soon after releasing *Some Girls*, The Rolling Stones prepared to find out if they had a future. It was October 1978, and Keith Richards' heroin possession trial was beginning in Toronto.

But Keith wasn't the only rocker in the news—ex-Sex Pistol Sid Vicious was arrested in New York on October 13 for murder in connection with the death of his girlfriend, Nancy Spungen.

"He's trying to steal my headlines," growled Richards, no fan of Vicious or The Sex Pistols.

On October 24, the verdict in Keith's trial was announced: Richards would be required to do nothing more than play a concert benefiting the blind to atone for his poor judgment. As for Vicious? Within five months, he was dead of an overdose.

Such bizarre doings were far outside the job description of most rock musicians, who understandably preferred to avoid such high-profile entanglements. Among that relatively sedate crowd was West Coast rocker Steve Miller.

People could be forgiven for thinking that Free's "All Right Now" had returned to the airwaves in 1976. In reality, it was simply Miller borrowing the British band's hook for his own "Rock'N Me."

The practice of freely using the riffs of one's rock and roll predecessors was common, but Miller was something of rock's thieving magpie. His albums sometimes left listeners wondering, "Where have I heard that before?" Whether it was the slightly altered Joe Walsh "Rocky Mountain Way" progression at the heart of "The Stake" or the Eric Clapton "Crossroads" phrase transposed to set up "Jet Airliner," Miller's modus operandi at times appeared to hinge on finding the catchiest hook of another song and adapting it to his own purposes.

Miller's somewhat recycled material made up one of 1978's biggest-selling albums, *The Steve Miller Band Greatest Hits 1974–78*. It was soothing rock for those hiding from the seismic shifts occurring elsewhere in music: basic, predictable, and well crafted despite some painful rhymes and awkward phrasings. With his unexceptional voice bolstered via multitrack overdubs and any soloing kept to a minimum, Miller served up lowest-common-denominator rock that went down easy, and the album eventually went multiplatinum.

California's Little Feat had never come close to going platinum in their near-decade of existence. In 1978 they were closing on the conclusion of a journey that had seen them evolve from laid-back West Coast roots into a challenging live alliance of exceptional musicians, including band founder Lowell George.

George had been a member of Frank Zappa's Mothers of Invention, but late in 1969 Zappa—never one to hold his band members back from other opportunities—suggested that George start his own band. The result was Little Feat, in which George was joined by Roy Estrada, The Mothers' bassist; keyboardist Bill Payne, who had once failed an audition with Zappa, and Richie Hayward, a drummer George had played with prior to his Zappa affiliation.

This lineup recorded Little Feat's self-titled debut in 1971 and *Sailin' Shoes* in 1972. But then a crucial change occurred to the band. Estrada left to join Captain Beefheart's Magic Band, and he was replaced by Delaney Bramlett Band bassist Kenny Gradney. With Gradney came percussionist Sam Clayton, and soon guitarist Paul Barrere was recruited to complement George's slide guitar skills.

Over the course of their next four intriguing albums, Little Feat quickly matured. They successfully incorporated a wide range of American styles ranging from New Orleans rhythms to jazz and blues into their sound, then served it all up on a rock and roll platter. Through their freewheeling creativity Little Feat carried over ideals that had characterized the no-boundaries aspects of the 1960s rock scene.

"The abundance of great music, the culture of drugs, and the politics of Richard Nixon, which had everybody polarized and created more of a sense of community, all contributed to this incredible feeling that somehow we were on a collective journey," Payne noted in the liner notes to the reissue of the band's 1978 live album, *Waiting for Columbus.* "*Waiting for Columbus* is one of the last parts of that journey, and among the last vestiges of that scene."

As the years passed, the inevitable personal tensions that plague nearly all bands descended on Little Feat. Lowell George was a halfhearted participant in his own group by the dawn of 1977. By then, most of the songwriting duties had fallen to Payne and Barrere. But early that year, George proposed that the band record a live album. The other members of Little Feat embraced the idea, hopeful that the project might rehabilitate their decaying internal relationships.

Recorded at a series of shows in London and Washington, D.C., *Waiting for Columbus* found Little Feat standing tall in the face of years of road and studio work. Augmented by the Tower of Power horn section, Little Feat's live album paralleled The Band's *Rock of Ages*, a recording that found Bob Dylan's former backing band bolstered by Alan Toussaint's horn arrangements.

Though Little Feat was far earthier than The Band, *Waiting for Columbus* documents the group's highly evolved improvisational skills, skills that in some aspects surpassed those of The Band. Bassist Gradney is a wonder throughout, his low-end melodicism pushing the band in tandem with Hayward's relentlessly adroit drumming. The guitars of Barrere and George dance in a restless interplay with Payne's keyboards, solos being crafted and handed off from one player to the next with a facility calling to mind The Allman Brothers Band at the height of their powers. The sound of George's slide guitar locking notes with the saxophone of Lenny Pickett, as the band cooked in sultry support, captured the essence of Little Feat.

If *Waiting for Columbus* had a flaw, it was that Little Feat's engaging raw edge was missing in action from the grooves of their live album. Its pristine sound lent a near-sterile air to the immaculate performances, ones that somehow missed the touch of rough, low-down playing that infused notorious Little Feat bootlegs like *Electrif Lycanthrope*. Still, the smart arrangements and brilliant skills captured on the album stand as a fine testament to one of the United States' greatest rock bands.

Sadly, *Waiting for Columbus* marked the end for Little Feat in the 1970s. After touring to support the album, Lowell George left the band for good in search of a solo career. Months later, on June 29, 1979, he was found dead of a heart attack in an Arlington, Virginia motel. The night before, he had played a sold-out concert at the Lisner Auditorium, ironically the same venue where much of *Waiting for Columbus* had been recorded.

Old-fashioned American rock and roll had always held particular appeal in England, and in 1978 Dave Edmunds was reaping the benefits of that fact through an association with Nick Lowe. Lowe was in on the ground floor of the punk and New Wave movement at Stiff Records, acting as an in-house producer of acts like The Damned and Elvis Costello. So when former Love Sculpture guitarist Edmunds joined Lowe in the band Rockpile, they received a much warmer welcome than might have been expected for older rockers playing music rooted solidly in the 1950s.

Edmunds, who signed an offered contract with Led Zeppelin's Swan Song Records after singer Robert Plant happened to hear some of the guitarist's in-progress work, used Rockpile as his backup band on 1978's rollicking *Tracks on Wax 4*. The album showed Edmunds' ample skills as both a vocalist and a scorching guitarist, particularly on "Trouble Boys" and a hyperkinetic blast through Lowe's "Heart of the City."

Much like Edmunds, Joe Ely must have been thanking his lucky stars for the emergence of punk rock. Not that the Texan singer and songwriter's country music had anything to do with spiky hair and safety pins, but when The Clash set out on tour in 1978 they asked Ely to open for them. It exposed the warm-voiced Ely to an entirely new audience.

Featuring a superb band that could shift gears from Tex-Mex to Cajun in a heartbeat, and boasting the talents of splendid guitarist Jesse Taylor, Ely's self-titled first album of 1977 and 1978's *Honky Tonk Masquerade* pointed to new directions for country music miles removed from the false glitter of the Nashville establishment.

The New Wave atmosphere also made it easier for Cheap Trick to establish their career—although it took a trip to Japan to wake up rock fans back home to the full brilliance of the band's supercharged pop rock. Guitarist Rick Nielsen wrote songs that mixed the sweetness of The Beatles with the roar of The Who in their prime, yielding a heady hybrid sound that reached full boil with *At Budokan*, a 1978 recording from Japan. In the Far East, the cartoonish quartet were held in rabid esteem by their young Japanese fans, and the shrieking and screaming of the manic audience lent a Beatlemania aura to Cheap Trick's surging performance.

There was no denying that Cheap Trick looked funny. Diametrically contrasting the "pretty boy" images of vocalist Robin Zander and bassist Tom Petersson, the cardigan sweater-clad Nielsen was a dead ringer for The Bowery Boys' Huntz Hall, and drummer Bun E. Carlos looked like a down-on-his-luck computer programmer. But there was nothing comedic about the pure power the quartet could generate. That was amply proven on the 1978 studio release *Heaven Tonight*, on which Zander's stunning vocals and Nielsen's to-the-point soloing drove home a memorable collection of songs. Led off by "Surrender," one of the most infectious rock songs ever recorded, the album showed dedication to craft in a hard rock setting where mere pummeling was often acceptable.

Like Cheap Trick, British hard rock band Thin Lizzy had decided to release a live album, and they wanted Tony Visconti to oversee the project. But when Visconti agreed to helm *Live and Dangerous*, he had no idea what he was getting into.

Thin Lizzy had risen to prominence in 1976 with their album *Jailbreak*, which yielded a hit single called "The Boys are Back in Town." But the band was well regarded as a strong live concert act, and Lizzy bassist and lead singer Phil Lynott wanted to show off that side of his band.

Lynott unceremoniously presented Visconti with a pile of tapes—some sixteen-track, others twenty-four-track, all recorded at slightly varying speeds. And once the album's song candidates were selected from the myriad performances, Lynott felt that there were minor bass parts that needed touching up. But since the exact in-concert bass sound couldn't be replicated in the studio, Lynott had to rerecord his entire bass track. Then he wanted to redo certain vocals. And once the guitar players learned what was going on . . .

In the end, Thin Lizzy's live album ended up being, by Visconti's estimate, twenty percent live and eighty percent over-dubbed in the studio.

Despite the recovery work, *Live and Dangerous* is regarded as a seminal album. The potential power of two-guitar hard rock harmonizing was fully realized through the interplay on-slaught of superb stringsmen Brian Robertson and Scott Gorham.

Gorham and Robertson were just two of hundreds of hard rock guitarists earning a living on the stages of the world. None of them could have known that the parameters of their craft were about to be fundamentally reset by a young guitarist from California named Eddie Van Halen.

When *Van Halen* was released by Warner Brothers Records in 1978, hard rock in general and its nascent offshoot, heavy metal, were fundamentally altered. Simply one of the most powerful and propulsive debut albums ever released, *Van Halen* was electrifying from beginning to end.

Showboating extrovert front-man David Lee Roth, bassist Michael Anthony, and thunderous drummer Alex Van Halen all played their roles with relish, but it was Alex's younger brother, Eddie, who detonated the real musical fireworks—and no doubt struck fear into the heart of every other rock guitarist.

Using a mongrel, self-built guitar, Eddie had the biggest impact on his instrument of choice since the emergence of Jimi Hendrix, developing his own mind-bending combination of light-speed finger tapping on strings, unique scale selection, and an approach to rhythm playing that overwhelmed via its sheer exhilaration. Thanks largely to Van Halen, the pitch-bending tremolo arm was soon referred to universally as the whammy bar, and Eddie's bottom-dropping-out dives and howling pitch bends upward were an integral part of his innovative technique.

Even Van Halen's guitar tone was revolutionary, achieved through altered Marshall amps. Referred to as the "brown sound," it was heavily overdriven but crunchy and crisp, with a biting treble given weight by a solid thump of bass frequencies. Eddie's attack was recorded with state-of-the-art vibrancy by producer Ted Templeman and engineer Don Landee, perfecting the hard rock experimentation they'd begun with Ronnie Montrose's *Montrose* debut four years earlier.

Setting the stage for Van Halen's blistering cover of The Kinks' "You Really Got Me" was a breathtaking instrumental appropriately titled "Eruption." The avalanche of cascading guitar notes was like nothing that had ever been heard before. Until Eddie showed off his unique style in concert, many believed it was impossible for a guitarist to play so fast. Some insisted it was studio trickery of the sort employed by Les Paul decades earlier to seemingly double his playing speed.

Van Halen's volatile debut was inarguable proof that there were still new realms to be explored within rock music's confines. Just when it seemed that every possible rock nuance had been wrung out of the handful of notes that make up all music, someone like Eddie Van Halen managed to discover a new way of doing things. Change—often fundamental—was still the sole constant of rock in the 1970s.

On Christmas Day 1978, Johnny Rotten rose from the ashes of The Sex Pistols when his new band, Public Image Ltd., played their public debut. Having reverted back to his real name, John Lydon, the singer was joined by guitarist Keith Levene, a founding member of The Clash who'd moved on before the band established their reputation. Bassist Jah Wobble and drummer Jim Walker completed Lydon's new quartet. Despite releasing an energetic single, "Public Image," the band's real specialty seemed to be the creation of long, droning sound-scapes that served as a foundation for Lydon's rants.

While Lydon had obviously survived life as a Sex Pistol, Sid Vicious was not so lucky. On February 2, 1979, months after being charged as the lead suspect in the bloody stabbing death of girlfriend Nancy Spungen, Vicious' sad, often-pathetic existence came to an end via a heroin overdose. A typical epitaph from the rock establishment was delivered by David Bowie.

"Sid Vicious was just a mindless twerp," judged Bowie. "I didn't find anything at all romantic about him, or even interesting."

The wretched passing of one of punk's icons pointed to a predicament for bands that had been part of the first great wave of punk rock, one that made 1979 quite an uncertain time. Most of those groups had blasted out debuts full of scathing energy, raging and railing at society in general and rock superstars in particular. That ground having been covered, for the bands still in existence the question became: "Now what?"

The Damned had issued what is generally regarded as the first British punk rock single, the Nick Lowe-produced "New Rose," back in 1976. But they gained little respect, critics judging them to be little more than court jesters in the world of punk. After a brief existence sharing much of the same chaos that surrounded The Sex Pistols, The Damned split up in 1978. The end had come in the wake of contentious studio sessions for *Music for Pleasure*, the band's second album—produced by Pink Floyd's Nick Mason, of all people.

When the core of the band—vampiric singer Dave Vanian, drummer Rat Scabies, and bassist and guitarist Captain Sensible—announced The Damned's reunion in 1979, the news was met with skepticism, especially as founding guitarist Brian James was not involved. But the real surprise came when a new album, *Machine Gun Etiquette*, was released. People began to realize that one of the bands held in lower punk esteem had unexpectedly created a very strong record.

Machine Gun Etiquette offered an intriguing mix of basic punk rock heritage, British music hall influences, and a solid and surprising dose of trippy, psychedelic pop that called to mind the early singles of Pink Floyd. Perhaps Mason had not been such a strange choice of producer, after all, though on *Etiquette* the recording was overseen by the band itself and their associate Roger Armstrong. The unlikely combination of influences that populated this album showed just how far the doors to the music library had been kicked open.

Among the highlights was the rumbling, sing-along "Love Song," released as a single before the album's release. There was an old-fashioned guitar rave-up leading to the climax of "Looking at You," while "Smash It Up" was the embodiment of punk's spirit. The percussion bed and insistent instrumental heart of "Anti-Pope" called to mind the musical explorations of 1967's fabled Summer of Love, but unlike some of the mindless explorations of that era, the insistent rhythm beneath the song kept it on track. *Machine Gun Etiquette* was a melding of the best of several worlds, and it had come from an unlikely source— a band that many considered little more than a joke, and a bad one at that.

Siouxsie and The Banshees had faced joke taunts of their own since forming in 1976. Founded by a tight-knit group of Sex Pistols fans, the band originally started out with Sid Vicious on drums. But after signing up a more able drummer in the person of Kenny Morris, the band began to build a serious reputation. Guitarist John McKay joined Morris and the band's core duo, bassist Steve Severin and dynamic vocalist Siouxsie Sioux, to record a debut single in 1978. "Hong Kong Garden" climbed all the way into the British top ten.

With McKay writing new material in partnership with Siouxsie and Severin, The Banshees proceeded to work with up-and-coming producer Steve Lillywhite to record their ruthless debut album *The Scream*. The 1978 record was crowned by a scorching attack on The Beatles' "Helter Skelter." A second album, *Join Hands*, found the group losing creative momentum in the studio, before a devastating blow was struck later in 1979 when McKay and Morris both quit in the midst of a British tour. But the group was to survive, thanks to the determination of Siouxsie and Severin. They recruited drummer Budgie from The Slits and survived using guest guitarists—including ex-Sex Pistol Steve Jones—until settling on the atmospheric talents of John McGeoch from Magazine.

When The Banshees' founders had still been teenage Sex Pistol fans learning to dance the pogo—the curious up-and-down, bouncing-in-place dance that characterized the early punk world—The Stranglers had already logged more than two years of gigs.

Older than most all of the punk bands, The Stranglers faced derision as debate swirled over the topic of whether the band actually qualified as "punk." Regardless, they'd been on the scene since the beginning of the movement, having actually opened for The Ramones at their first London show back in 1976.

A guitar, bass, drums, and keyboards quartet that blasted away in pile-driving style, The Stranglers seemed to specialize in the art of crafting offensive lyrics, taking equal delight in aggravating punks and non-punks alike. And then there was the infamous matter of the band augmenting their lineup with topless girls during a Battersea Park outdoor concert . . .

Which made it something of a surprise that *The Raven*, the band's fourth studio album, revealed The Stranglers of 1979 heading in an intriguingly experimental direction. From touches of The Doors to angular melodic progressions, *The Raven* covered territory far more wide-ranging than that traversed on the group's earlier, more primitive albums. Jean Jacques Burnel's bass still pulsed along in ominous, weighty tandem with Jet Black's insistent drumming, but the instrumental interplay between guitarist Hugh Cornwell and keyboardist Dave Greenfield had evolved from confrontational to investigational. From the brief opening instrumental "Longships" on through the album's surging title track and the glorious "Duchess," The Stranglers proved that there were heady discoveries to be encountered within their newly developed sound.

While The Stranglers experimented, other bands took a pass on the concept of blazing new trails. The best of those simply blazed away with all of the fire and fury that had made punk so bracing in the first place. Chief among this group was Ireland's Stiff Little Fingers.

Hailing from the troubled city of Belfast, the band had pressed just over three hundred copies of their first single in late 1977. The record, on their own Rigid Digits label, paired the songs "Suspect Device" and "Wasted Life." One copy fortuitously made its way to the British Broadcasting Corporation. Disc jockey John Peel, long one of British rock's most important tastemakers and a true friend to struggling young bands with real talent, began to air "Suspect Device." The enthusiastic reaction of listeners led to Stiff Little Fingers getting a distribution deal for their record, signing with fundamental British independent record label Rough Trade.

After a second single by the band appeared in 1978, the songs issued to date and new material were collected on the appropriately titled *Inflammable Material*, released in 1979.

Writing about what they saw every day—an existence played out in an impoverished city that was virtually under military occupation by England—Stiff Little Fingers infused their material with an undeniable air of urgency, their songs acting as vital, high-volume dispatches from a troubled region. Jake Burns' rough, gargled vocals on songs like "Alternative Ulster" and "Law and Order" were far from the emoting of a polished singer; rather, they were burning shouts of desperate, pure communication acting on an emotional level as much as a musical one.

Despite their understandably bleak setting, Stiff Little Fingers' songs on both *Inflammable Material* and the album the band recorded in 1979, *Nobody's Heroes*, reflected a determination to survive, thrive, and press for change. With their thundering guitar-bass-drums propulsion cast within a framework of basic chord construction, Stiff Little Fingers provided a last honest blast of punk rock fundamentalism.

Though an association with punk had helped establish Elvis Costello's career, the persistent critical allusions to his music as "punk rock" were laughable given the rapidly maturing pace of his material in 1979.

"What I wanted to do," Costello noted, "was approach the music with the same attitude, the same attack as punk, without sacrificing all of the things I liked about music. As a result, I had a goody-goody image to a lot of people."

If punk energy had abounded on Costello's 1978 album *This Year's Model*, fueling songs like "No Action" and "Pump It Up," by the time of 1979's *Armed Forces* his emphasis had shifted to performance dynamics and impressive songwriting.

Recorded over six weeks at London's Eden Studios, *Armed Forces* found Costello and his Attractions produced once again by Nick Lowe in the creation of one of the strongest albums of the era. From the stately structure and rich harmonies of "Accidents Will Happen" to the pressing throb of "Goon Squad," the record revealed Costello's talent growing at an astonishing rate. Once, the most basic of chord sequences had served as completed songs; now they were simply a foundation for intriguing progressions like those encountered within "Big Boys" and "Chemistry Class."

The Attractions were fully up to the task of realizing Costello's burgeoning visions. The abundance of musical talent shared among Pete Thomas, Steve Nieve, and Bruce Thomas made the group one of the most inventive and responsive new bands to emerge from this chaotic period of rock music.

The temptation to link Costello with punk had faded in England; in the United States, though, the less musically astute still assumed that Elvis Costello and Sid Vicious were just about one and the same. Fear of musical change and an inability to process new sounds were at least partially to blame for a barroom brawl that occurred during Elvis Costello and The Attractions' 1979 tour of the United States, as the Brits faced off with Bonnie Bramlett and Steve Stills' road crew in a drunken donnybrook.

Bramlett immediately called in the media, insisting that Costello had referred to James Brown and Ray Charles as "niggers." She claimed that she personally had assaulted Elvis in defense of American music's honor.

"That woman has made one reputation off one E.C.," Costello stated in *New Musical Express*, referring to Eric Clapton's brief alliance with Delaney and Bonnie and Friends early in the decade. "She's fuckin' well not going to get more publicity off of another one."

Unfortunately, Elvis underestimated the devastatingly efficient workings of the American media when it comes to reporting scandal. Bramlett got plenty of publicity, all of it casting Costello in a negative light. And though Elvis denied the racial accusations, little interest was shown in reporting his side of the story. Almost inevitably, Costello began to get death threats, necessitating the presence of two bodyguards for the remainder of the tour.

Though that March 1979 incident set tongues wagging, people soon had bigger fish to fry when the city of Philadelphia was nearly fried later that month.

On March 28, the Three Mile Island nuclear power plant came uncomfortably close to melting down, an event that would have had catastrophic implications for the Pennsylvania cities of Harrisburg, located closest to the plant, and Philadelphia, located due east.

The Clash's Joe Strummer pondered the event and incorporated it into the lyrics of "Clampdown," one of the brilliant new songs the band recorded for their double album, *London Calling*.

The Clash were at a career crossroads in 1979. Their second album, *Give 'em Enough Rope*, had been released in 1978 to conflicting reviews, largely engendered by the presence of producer Sandy Pearlman. The first album by The Clash had been recorded by Strummer's old cohort from the 101ers, soundman Micky Foote. In contrast, The Sex Pistols' *Bollocks* album had been crafted by two highly regarded studio veterans, Chris Thomas and Bill Price. The difference in sound quality between the two records had been substantial, so the plan for Clash album number two was to pair the band up with a real audio pro.

Pearlman was renowned in the United States as producer for Blue Oyster Cult, but the concept of teaming his arena-rock ideals with abrasive punk rock was far from a sure thing.

In the end, *Give 'em Enough Rope* was a qualified success. The lead-off trio of songs—"Safe European Home," "English Civil War," and "Tommy Gun"—comprised what quite likely was the most thrilling ten minutes of punk rock ever recorded, pure thunder carried on breathtaking momentum. But that momentum lagged somewhat on the album's second side, as The Clash struggled with the challenge of developing new material under hectic conditions.

Having learned what they could with Pearlman, for their third album the band chose to be paired with producer Guy Stevens. Stevens had worked with everyone from Free to Mott the Hoople, but he was equally well known for an eccentric approach to getting the most out of his clients.

"Guy was a very unusual record producer," Bill Price told Chris Michie in *Mix* magazine. Price was studio manager and chief engineer at Wessex Studios, where The Clash labored over *London Calling*. "He believed that the record producer's job was to maximize the emotion and feeling that an artist revealed on mic in the studio when doing the song. And Guy did this by what I call 'direct injection'—he would challenge the artist verbally and physically, tackle him and bring him to the ground and punch him and stuff, in order to get more emotion out of him when he performed."

Amazingly, Stevens' guerilla production tactics meshed well with The Clash's work ethic, and Price began to capture the sounds that would result in the creation of one of rock's greatest albums.

London Calling revealed a range and a songwriting sophistication that many considered unimaginable coming from a so-called punk band. The Clash journeyed through supercharged rockabilly on "Brand New Cadillac," reggae on "Guns of Brixton," jazzy blues on "Jimmy Jazz," and sprightly Jamaican dancehall on "Wrong 'em Boyo."

But The Clash had not fully abandoned the committed rage that characterized early songs like "London's Burning" and "White Riot." Instead, they honed its edge further. Rather than ranting and railing, Strummer refined his approach, crafting keen lyrics that slyly made their point. The words were then melded to the pressing pulse of songs like "Death or Glory," "Clampdown," and the album's title track.

The range of The Clash's aural research continued to grow as time went on, and a further partnership with Bill Price would yield the sprawling triple album *Sandinista!* in 1980. But the fact that virtually none of *London Calling*'s experiments failed elevates it to the truly rarified atmosphere of such double album masterworks as The Who's *Quadrophenia* and The Rolling Stones' *Exile on Main Street*.

One of the most visible supporters of The Clash as they established their career had been Patti Smith, and in 1979 she issued her fourth album, produced by Todd Rundgren. What no one realized at the time was that *Wave* would turn out to be a wave goodbye.

Smith's influence on rock music since her debut four years earlier had been seismic. Like Janis Joplin, she had been a woman functioning as a band leader in a male-dominated culture. But her femininity differed from that displayed by other late-1970s female rockers. Heart's Wilson sisters rocked as hard as the boys on "Barracuda," the powerful single from their tremendously successful *Little Queen* album, as did Pat Benatar on "Heartbreaker" from her 1979 debut *In the Heat of the Night*. But their images were traditional ones of female showbiz sensuality. Patti's sexuality came in her rock swagger, the same cocky, in-control vibe that imbued the stage work of The Who's Roger Daltrey and The Stones' Mick Jagger.

Within that context, she presented influences from and references to forms of art not previously associated with rock. In Patti's realm, Arthur Rimbaud was as important as Jimi Hendrix, William Burroughs as fundamental as Brian Jones. Smith's outlook was one of "anything goes" creativity—and spiritually, hadn't that been the whole point behind punk rock in the first place?

Thus, Patti Smith was one of the most fascinating—and improbable—rock stars to ever step on stage. Unlike other performers, who self-consciously referred only to their own work, Smith was open and enthusiastic in her admiration for other artists, and the sense that she was truly a fan of rock and roll was always at the very heart of her own art.

Patti's appreciation of the power of rock and her own status as a recording artist fueled some of the most stirring moments on *Wave*, in songs like "Citizen Ship," "Frederick," and the exotic pulse of "Dancing Barefoot." But that sense virtually defined The Patti Smith Group's furious take on The Byrds' classic "So You Want To Be (A Rock'n'Roll Star)." The song, a siren call to Smith in her own youth, was now used by Patti to reach out to the next generation. "Hey you! Come here, get up—this is the era where everybody creates!" she improvised in mid-verse, heralding the song's rush toward a pulverizing climax on the concussive, Keith Moon-like drumming of Jay Dee Daugherty.

And then suddenly, The Patti Smith Group was gone.

In the fall of 1979, the band played what turned out to be their final concert, before a crowd of 70,000 in Florence, Italy. Upon returning to the United States, Smith moved from New York to Detroit to be with the man she had fallen in love with, former MC5 guitarist Fred "Sonic" Smith. On March 1, 1980, the two were married.

Patti Smith left the rock world at the peak of her powers, but the bold sounds she had created, the encouragement she had shown, and the ideals she had espoused would continue to reverberate through the years.

If you asked Brian Eno his opinion about "art rock" bands, as Lee Moore did in *Creem* magazine's November 1978 issue, you got a mouthful.

"It's got tainted by so many connections with really dumb bands who've tried to make a kind of academic form out of rock music, and who've tried to subtract from it its sensual aspect," Eno judged. "Their attitude is 'Well, all that is just base and vulgar, we should be more intellectual in our approach.' Of course, you can be more intellectual, but it doesn't mean at the same time you have to be less sensual. So the appellation 'art band' normally has this connotation of trusting intellect to the exclusion of senses or intuition, whereas for me, a real art band would be able to make use of all these sensibilities without making them fight with one another."

Combining those sensibilities was the goal of Eno's ongoing production work with Talking Heads. On 1978's *More Songs about Buildings and Food* and on 1979's *Fear of Music*, the New York experimentalists' rather precocious artiness was reinvented through a gentle nudge toward the dance floor on songs like the slinky "Take Me to the River" and the postapocalyptic disco of "Life During War Time."

But the music of Talking Heads was just one flavor to be found in an exotic buffet of musical tastes on offer in the postpunk world. The raging storm may have passed, but as the clouds lifted, an environment was revealed in which all manner of strange sounds might be encountered.

Eno's own work with David Bowie, as well as the technical tunes of Kraftwerk, had proved influential to young Gary Numan. His band, Tubeway Army, was heavily reliant on synthesizers in the creation of their early 1979 album *Replicas* and its smash British single, "Are 'Friends' Electric?" Later in the year, Numan's solo effort *The Pleasure Principle* would find his sound spreading around the world thanks to the icy charm of "Cars," which surprisingly made its way into the American singles top ten chart. Numan was heralded as the mentor of a new movement dubbed "synth pop."

Though Numan's work was machine-based, there were other new bands whose earthier material took the occasionally morose aspects of punk and elevated such outlooks into an art form.

"The whole idea of punk, which I came out of, was that you didn't have to be able to play," said Robert Smith, guitarist and founder of The Cure. "And I couldn't. That was the charm and the joy of it."

Charm and joy aside, Smith actually could play, though perhaps not in the soloing vein of Eric Clapton or Jeff Beck. Instead, after the release of The Cure's *Three Imaginary Boys* debut in 1979, Smith set about refining a quite inventive approach to rhythmic guitar lines involving subtle effects usage. In fact, while on tour opening for Siouxsie and The Banshees, it was Smith who was asked to step in on lead guitar when John McKay abandoned The Banshees.

Smith's guitar abilities and his songwriting matured rapidly, coming into their own on The Cure's second album, *Seventeen Seconds*, recorded late in 1979. His lyrics of loneliness and isolation were set to austere songs, structures so stark that they bordered on claustrophobic.

Isolation was also a predominant theme in the music of Joy Division. In fact, their debut, *Unknown Pleasures*, was relentlessly chilling, a journey into the darkest depths of the human psyche. With rising producer Martin Hannett overseeing the project, the band worked well within the limits of their technical performance abilities, maturing beyond the more punk-like thrashing of their early singles. Over the barren accompaniment, lead singer Ian Curtis' singing becomes the very embodiment of despair on songs like "New Dawn Fades," "Disorder," and "She's Lost Control."

Unlike Joy Division, Gang of Four's despair was fueled by political dissatisfaction rather than personal introspection, as expressed on their wryly titled *Entertainment!* Their harsh, abrasive minimalism occupied the same musical neighborhood as Wire, though the lyrics of songs like "At Home He's a Tourist" and "To Hell with Poverty" served a clear-cut rhetorical agenda that differed from Wire's oblique missives.

Fortunately, not all of the post-punk sounds were relentlessly bleak. From the rubble of punk arose a British youth revival of ska music, the bouncy Jamaican style that had acted as a precursor to the slower, loping sounds of reggae.

The revival was led by The Specials, who had put the "do it yourself" work ethic into action through the formation of their own record label, 2-Tone. As the ska movement caught on, other bands came aboard, and soon the insistent rhythms and trombone-driven horn bursts of ska had taken England by storm. Among the prominent bands later aligned with The Specials were Madness, The Selector, and The English Beat.

Although the sounds of ska had little to do with the punk wave that had washed over rock music, a new band from Ireland had been fundamentally affected by the music of the past two years.

"We came from punk and that wasn't very funny," stated Bono, known as Paul Hewson before he became the singer for U2. "Johnny Rotten was very funny in interviews, but The

Clash weren't funny. And the immediate aftermath of punk, Joy Division and that funereal, fugue-like music, that was the music we came out of."

That a band like Joy Division—whose debut album arrived in May 1979—could impact the creative direction of a band like U2, whose own debut arrived just months later, demonstrated how quickly influences were traveling through rock and roll in the dynamic days following punk.

Boy was produced by Steve Lillywhite, soon to gain professional notoriety for his work with Peter Gabriel. The album's style differed radically from the music of U2's Irish cohorts Stiff Little Fingers. Where the Belfast-based Stiff Little Fingers used a blazing assault fully imbued with the punk anger that had been the hallmark of The Sex Pistols and early Clash, the Dublin-based U2 was much more atmospheric. On *Boy*, Bono's dramatic vocals soared over the guitar of The Edge, born David Evans. The Edge favored a minimalist playing style, the resulting notes fed through an echo-generating effect that built lush settings for the band's soundscapes.

Meanwhile, in the United States where punk's influence had been less fundamental, it was the loosely defined New Wave that was cresting in 1979. The charts were owned—for the short term, anyway—by a white-bread approximation of New Wave ideals called The Knack.

The Knack was considered something of a New Wave Monkees by rock media that were loathe to accept the results of Capital Records' devastatingly successful marketing campaign. The band's "My Sharona" was an unavoidable slice of power-pop that dominated 1979's airwaves. Along with Blondie's earlier "Heart of Glass," The Knack's smash hit made it acceptable for the average listener to like New Wave.

Considerably more original were Athens, Georgia's B-52s. The band was named after Southern slang for bouffant hairdos, a look that was retro-stylishly modeled within the B-52s by vocalist and keyboardist Kate Pierson and vocalist Cindy Wilson. Wilson's brother, Ricky, was the B-52s' guitarist, and the band was rounded out by drummer Keith Strickland and manic front-man Fred Schneider. The group pressed an independent single of their song "Rock Lobster" and headed for New York.

After a first gig at the Max's Kansas City nightclub, followed by a move downtown to CBGB for subsequent performances, The B-52s flew onto the world's rock scene via a deal with Warner Brothers in the United States and Island Records in the U.K. The band could not have asked for a better producer, as Island Records' founder Chris Blackwell agreed to helm the project at Compass Point Studios in the Bahamas.

Admittedly amateurish in the musicianship department, The B-52s used their limitations to their advantage. They created simple, wacky rock that existed in a world of equal parts retro, sci-fi, and B-movie camp. Schneider's talk-sing approach was sweetly surrounded by the vocals of Pierson and Wilson, and the fun factor of the band's hyperactive live performances went a long way toward breaking the band.

"We always appealed to people outside the mainstream," Kate Pierson said of The B-52s' near-instant success, "and I think there are more people outside the mainstream these days."

In California, though, there was a growing movement that was much further outside the mainstream than the B-52s' cartoonish rock parties. The blunt assault of punk's first wave had washed over the nation, but in Los Angeles and San Francisco the thunder still reverberated, morphing into what became known as hardcore punk.

One of the founding charters of West Coast hardcore came with the 1979 release of a four-song EP by The Avengers, on the small Los Angeles label White Noise. The Avengers had opened for The Sex Pistols at their final show, which helped explain Steve Jones' production credit on the EP. And one listen to the record showed the band's roots: "The American in Me" blasted into existence like an outtake from *Never Mind the Bollocks—Here's the Sex Pistols*, with Penelope Houston's high-octane harangue in place of Johnny Rotten's snarl.

San Francisco's The Nuns had also opened at The Pistols' demise. Throughout 1978 and 1979 the band cultivated a growing fan base for their aggressive-yet-melodic punk, music that featured the talents of vocalists Jeff Olener and the alluring Jennifer Miro.

The Nuns were one of the bands participating in an album that in large part acted as a directional indicator for hardcore, *Rodney on the ROQ*. Los Angeles DJ Rodney Bingenheimer had long been a supporter of new sounds in California, beginning years earlier in the glam era. But he opened his ears to punk rock and provided an outlet for local bands on his Los Angeles radio show, carried by station KROQ.

R.O.T.R. became a grass roots joint project of Bingenheimer, Posh Boy Records, and the new music magazine *Flipside*. Robbie Fields' Posh Boy label had issued its first recordings in 1978, but *R.O.T.R.* would prove to be among the most influential. Though released in 1980, the fourteen bands collected on the album were all active in 1979, many releasing their own singles as part of the burgeoning California movement. *R.O.T.R.* presented seminal works by young, hard-hitting bands including U.X.A., Agent Orange, The Circle Jerks, The Adolescents, and Black Flag.

Of those bands, Black Flag would prove most influential. Guitarist Greg Ginn had already formed his own independent label, SST Records, in 1978, a label that would thrive throughout the hardcore era and provide a platform for some of the most inventive and aggressive music of the 1980s. But SST's first release was Black Flag's own four-song *Nervous Breakdown* EP. On it, the band charts its future course with an electrifying assault characterized by Ginn's individualistic, near-out-of-control guitar and a rhythm section that sounded cohesive yet on the edge of collapse at the same time. Over the noise, singer Keith Morris howled his way through the four direct blasts of "Nervous Breakdown," "I've Had It," "Fix Me," and "Wasted."

Though Black Flag's lineup changed several times over the next decade, Greg Ginn's dedication to and belief in his no-compromises music was already obvious. The foundation for one of hardcore's greatest and most stylistically diverse bands was firmly in place.

Out on the fringes of rock music, punk rock had more or less passed by David Bowie and Peter Gabriel without a second glance. Neither artist was guilty of conduct that might have assigned them target status by the likes of Johnny Rotten. Likewise, neither singer was predisposed to succumb to the temptation of casting their new music in a punk or New Wave light. Bowie and Gabriel were individualists existing on their own aural planes, and any influences on their music were more likely to come from far more exotic sources than a snotty teenager braying into a microphone.

In 1978, David Bowie had ventured back onto the tour circuit accompanied by a strong seven-piece band, along the way recording the live album *Stage* in Philadelphia. The avant-garde edge of *Low* and *"Heroes"* had translated surprisingly well to the concert environment, so Bowie saw no reason for full-scale revisions; for his next studio album, the *Stage* band would join him in his third consecutive partnership with Brian Eno and producer Tony Visconti.

"Bowie and I both have the feeling that this next album is going to be the synthesis and more of the best ideas of the last two," Brian Eno told *Creem* magazine's Lee Moore in the November 1978 issue. "I think it's possible, because he's working with the same band that he's been on tour with. They're extraordinary people who are bound to generate material that won't be commonplace."

As predicted by Eno, *Lodger*—Bowie's 1979 release—did not have commonplace material. Unfortunately, it also did not have the aura that had made *Low* and *"Heroes"* such unforgettable albums.

With recording for *Lodger* taking place in Montreux, Switzerland instead of its predecessors' Germanic environment, a sonic change was inevitable. The fact that *Lodger* was a collection of ten songs—with no instrumentals—was interpreted by some as an indication that Bowie was moving away from the more difficult sounds of his last two albums. Yet even though Bowie and Eno came up with a batch of songs that were tunefully oblique, the actual recording of the album might best be described as "normal." The record's sound was warmer and cleaner, lacking the metallic sheen that wrapped around the first sides of *Low* and *"Heroes."*

In the end, though *Low* and *"Heroes"* were uninviting they were enthralling; *Lodger* was uninvolving, despite its more welcoming air.

Peter Gabriel was on an opposing course. His first album had been a sonic smorgasbord; his second title had also been

stylistically diverse, yet it seemed to have even less focus, despite the presence of shining moments like the opening "On
the Air." The fact that the album had been produced by
Robert Fripp generated expectations of a prog rock masterpiece. Instead, it seemed that Bob Ezrin had done a better job
capturing the singer's aural psyche on Gabriel's all-over-the-
musical-map debut.

But Gabriel was poised to enter into an adventurous, even
revolutionary phase. For his third album—the third in a row to
be titled simply *Peter Gabriel*—Gabriel teamed up with producer Steve Lillywhite and engineer Hugh Padgham.

Lillywhite had begun his recording career as an engineer,
and after working with bands like Golden Earring he revealed
his potential as a producer via a strong demo for the band Ultravox. Not only did Ultravox win a contract with Island
Records, but the label also brought Lillywhite aboard as a staff
producer. He then worked with Brian Eno in the creation of *Ultravox*, the rich synth-based pop of the band laying the groundwork for Lillywhite's reputation as a producer open to working
with new bands and sounds. By the time Gabriel came calling,
Lillywhite had already produced Siouxsie and The Banshee's
The Scream, U2's *Boy*, and XTC's *Drums & Wires*.

Gabriel and his team were taking an exciting approach to his
third album: deconstructing the idea of "songs" and starting
from ground zero.

"Sometimes you have to impose your own limits," Gabriel
noted in *Musician* magazine. "Like with the third album, I said,
'Okay, what happens to the drums if you say no cymbals?
Cymbals seem to occupy a lot of high frequencies here. Take
them away and see what happens.'"

Gabriel also imposed restrictions on his own songwriting to
break himself out of normal patterns. For example, he might
write a chorus for a song—but only sing it one time.

Gabriel, Lillywhite, and Padgham labored over the album
throughout the summer and fall of 1979. When it was released
in early 1980, it was, like Bowie's *Low*, an album unlike anything heard before.

The sonic bearing of the work was given a blunt push by the
drums on the opening "Intruder," an alarming tale of a preda-
tor creeping through a home with ill intent. The drums of Phil

Collins, on hand to help his former vocalist from Genesis, were processed through noise and reverb gates that gave them a pounding, massive-but-eerie sound.

In fact, throughout the entire album, it's the treatment of the drums that lent the album such an odd character. Gabriel enforced his "no cymbals" policy on Collins and fellow drummer Jerry Marotta, a very highly regarded studio drummer. There's no question that restricting a drummer from the use of fundamental aspects of his tool kit will indeed change the way he plays. Gabriel used that to his creative advantage.

Yet there were myriad other aspects to *Peter Gabriel* that contributed to its inventive sound. From oddly mutated vocal effects to the incorporation of instruments like synthetic bagpipes and Tony Levin's performance on "I Don't Remember" using a Stick—the unique string instrument invented by Emmett Chapman—*Peter Gabriel* was truly an album walking the outer boundaries of rock music.

In fact, it walked so far outside rock music's confines that the big bosses at Gabriel's record label, Atlantic Records, were mortified when the finished work was presented for their inspection. Atlantic president Ahmet Ertegun reportedly wondered if Gabriel was mentally ill. Atlantic Records immediately dropped Peter Gabriel after hearing the album, allowing Mercury Records the honor of releasing one of rock music's most influential albums.

Creating an album like *Peter Gabriel*—one that contains wholly new sounds and proves to be highly influential to rock music—is the dream of every recording artist. But for new bands, simply establishing a career can be challenging enough. The Pretenders overcame that obstacle with a commanding debut album that topped the British charts and reached the top ten in the United States.

"I don't want to be recognized, I don't want to be hassled," Chrissie Hynde said of the motives behind her formation of The Pretenders. "I just want to play guitar in a rock and roll band."

Hynde was an American who left her Akron, Ohio roots far
behind via a move to London in the 1970s. Befriending rock
journalist Nick Kent, she began writing for the British music
newspaper *New Musical Express*. To make ends meet, Hynde
also worked at Malcolm McLaren's shop Sex, witnessing firsthand the punk cauldron preparing to boil.

But writing about music was one thing; what Hynde really
wanted to do was perform it. One of her earliest attempts came
as a backup vocalist on a session for guitarist Chris Spedding.
While at the studio date, she met producer Chris Thomas.
Thomas thought she had a great voice but suggested she take
some time to write material and then form a band. Hynde followed the advice, eventually forming The Pretenders in 1978
with guitarist James Honeyman-Scott, bassist Pete Farndon,
and drummer Martin Chambers.

With Nick Lowe producing, The Pretenders recorded their
first single, a shimmering pop song called "Stop Your Sobbing,"
written by The Kinks' Ray Davies. No sooner had Chris
Thomas heard the song on the radio than Hynde contacted him,
requesting his production talents for the band's debut album.
In the end, Thomas reunited with his *Never Mind the Bollocks—
Here's the Sex Pistols* partner Bill Price at Wessex Studios to
record *Pretenders*.

Pretenders is a schizoid album, half bluster and thunder and
half atmosphere and pop, split almost evenly down the middle
between the album's two sides. But despite the stylistic differences, nearly all of the material is first rate.

The album's first side—the hard side—begins with the
scorching "Precious." Over Hynde's own sawing rhythm guitar,
Honeyman-Scott brings a rugged riff-based approach to the
band, calling to mind Mick Ronson's muscular guitar work with
David Bowie's Spiders from Mars. Chambers' swinging rhythm
urges the song along at breakneck speed, and Hynde's vocals—
both coy and dangerous at once—sway and swoop through the
verses. The song is a heady mix of both punk and metal influences, setting up the rest of the side. The highlights are constant,
from the bold new structure of "The Phone Call" to the hazy,
dream-like "Up the Neck," Hynde's detached recounting of a
sexual encounter that "was all very run of the mill."

On the record's flip side the emphasis shifts radically, the danger and raw emotion replaced by the lush pop of Lowe's "Stop Your Sobbing." "Kid" mines a similar vein before The Pretenders ease into the updated reggae flavors of "Private Life." "Brass in Pocket" and "Lovers of Today" return to soothing territory before a last burst of aggressive rock crowns the album with "Mystery Achievement."

Though *Pretenders* justifiably logged serious chart action, attempts to make Joe Jackson and Graham Parker into superstars were less successful. Parker was first signed to Mercury Records; Jackson to A&M, both labels likely hoping they'd found their own vitriolic singer and songwriter in the mold of Elvis Costello.

Joe Jackson had a background that may have been too sophisticated for the base world of pop and rock—he had attended the Royal Academy of Music for three years, studying composition and music theory. But a strong demo suite won him a deal with A&M, leading to the 1979 release of *Look Sharp*.

On songs like "One More Time" and "Happy Loving Couples," the redheaded Jackson spat out the lyrics with venomous disdain, backed by a tight trio enlivened in particular by Graham Maby's crisp bass. Though the single "Is She Really Going out with Him?" did fairly well, from a career standpoint Jackson's writing and arranging skills would prove more valuable to him than bitter New Wave salvos.

While Jackson was hoping to break in a new career, in 1979 Graham Parker had just changed labels—and must have realized he was running out of opportunities to hit the big time. His band, The Rumour, was one of rock's most critically respected, a tight-knit batch of pub rock veterans who hailed from bands like Brinsley Schwarz and Ducks Deluxe, capable of handling everything from soul to reggae to flat-out rock.

But critical respect didn't necessarily translate to record sales. Despite the musical firepower, a three-year association with Mercury Records had gone nowhere, the partnership ending on such acrimonious terms that Parker recorded and often performed in concert a song called "Mercury Poisoning." Parker signed to Arista Records in an attempt to establish his stardom once and for all. He came close.

Production of Parker's four albums for Mercury had been split between Mutt Lange or the ubiquitous Nick Lowe. For *Squeezing out Sparks*, though, Arista paired Parker with Jack Nitzsche, the mercurial American producer who had worked with artists ranging from The Rolling Stones to Neil Young after first gaining acclaim as an arranger with Phil Spector.

As a result, the album bore a modern, extravagant sheen that sounded drastically different from the earthy subtlety characteristic of records produced by Lange and Lowe. The songs themselves were more forceful, with tracks like "Discovering Japan," "Passion Is No Ordinary Word," and "Protection" demanding a more determined attack by The Rumour. The band rose to the challenge, particularly guitarist Brinsley Schwarz, and Parker responded with fervent readings of the lyrics.

Squeezing Out Sparks made it into the American top forty, and Parker seemed poised to follow it up with the album that would finally cement the stardom that had proved so elusive. But it didn't work out that way. Though the commercially hot Jimmy Iovine oversaw *The Up Escalator*, the 1980 project went down in sales and proved to be the end of Parker's association with his Rumour.

But Graham Parker was far from the only one to miss the stardom his material surely deserved. Singer and guitarist Jimmie O'Neill formed Fingerprintz in 1978, and the quartet promptly recorded a high-energy debut. The grainy, high-contrast black-and-white back cover photograph of O'Neill's Fender Telecaster leaning against a Vox AC30 amp was indicative of the sounds within.

But in 1979, Fingerprintz put on the brakes a touch, slowing the material and allowing O'Neill's deft sense of pop song construction to work into the momentum. The result was *Distinguishing Marks*, a sadly unheralded album produced by The Motors' Nick Garvey that offered delirious power pop over the course of ten taut songs. Riding Bogdan Wiczling's surging drums and Kenny Alton's rock-solid bass, the shimmering guitars of O'Neill and Cha Burnz rang out in glorious open chords that framed O'Neill's infectious compositions.

Fingerprintz would try one more time with 1981's *Beat Noir*—with just as little commercial success being the result—but *Distinguishing Marks* would stand as their finest hour.

Though the career of Fingerprintz was unjustly short-lived, Australia's AC/DC had built a solid fan foundation, weathered the punk storm, and were just hitting their musical stride. Their seventh album, *Highway to Hell*, was produced by Mutt Lange, who had in turn produced The Motors' album for Fingerprintz producer Nick Garvey. But the success of the AC/DC album far surpassed the limited appeal of The Motors or Fingerprintz.

AC/DC released their first album at home in Australia in 1974. They soon became known as purveyors of fine hard rock, simply recorded yet brutally effective. The band slowly expanded their popularity from an initial cult audience as dogged road work and a "never quit" attitude served the band well—not to mention lead guitarist Angus Young's propensity for wearing schoolboy-in-shorts stage outfits. Five years after their formation, *Highway to Hell* was to be the group's commercial breakthrough to rock elite status.

Protectors of public morals and the religious right in the United States insisted the band's name stood for Anti-Christ/ Devil Child. The group devilishly played off those rumors with both *Highway to Hell*'s title and the cover art, depicting a sneering Angus with devil horns sprouting through his hair and with barbed tail in hand. Though that was a peek into the band's lighter side, when AC/DC began to play it was all business.

The album's title track serves as a textbook example of the AC/DC approach. A short, choppy rhythm guitar pattern is first to arrive on the scene, soon bolstered by an elementary drum pattern. Singer Bon Scott blusters in next, finally joined by bass, more guitar, and shouted backup vocals as the band lumbers into the hook-laden chorus. And though lead guitarist Young's solos were to-the-point and biting, throughout the record it was brother Malcolm Young's vital rhythm guitar that acted as the pumping heart of AC/DC.

Highway to Hell offered all of the best qualities of earlier AC/DC albums—the spacious recording that left room between the instruments to allow the mix to breathe, the classic rock and roll open-chord progressions, the naughty double entendre lyrics, the relentless drive of the band as a unit—in a package that was consistently excellent from beginning to end. The album thundered to number eight in England, soared into the top twenty in the United States, and sold more than a million copies.

Just months later, AC/DC faced an end to their ride when
Bon Scott literally drank himself to death on February 20, 1980.
But the group immediately rallied, filling Bon's post with Brian
Johnson, singer of the hard-rocking British band Geordie.
AC/DC then showed their intensely loyal roots by recording a
high-volume tribute to their fallen comrade Scott. *Back in Black*,
released in 1980, has since sold nearly twenty million copies in
the United States alone.

"Rock and roll is like a drug," Neil Young once admitted. "I
don't take very much, but when I do rock and roll, I fuckin' *do*
it. But I don't want to do it all the time 'cause it will kill me."

It was interesting—and somehow wholly appropriate—that
Neil Young, a man who had welcomed the 1970s with one of
the gentlest of albums, *Harvest*, should see out the decade with
one of its most abrasive albums, *Rust Never Sleeps*.

Utilizing the firepower of his occasional cohorts Crazy
Horse and an electric guitar sound so distorted and full that
vinyl grooves struggled to communicate it, Young offered a
burly collection of tracks like "Powderfinger" and the wobbly
"Sedan Delivery." But his vision was most acute when he surveyed the debris-filled landscape of rock on the bookending
songs "My My, Hey Hey (Out of the Blue)" and "Hey Hey,
My My (Into the Black)."

"The king is gone but he's not forgotten—is this the story of
Johnny Rotten?" Young howled as the album thundered to a
close, Crazy Horse's instruments ringing out in a barely restrained cacophony.

In those songs Neil Young sang of the fundamental rock and
roll ideal: it's better to burn out than to fade away. But inciner-
ation by rock and roll—a fate that greeted The Sex Pistols and
countless more—was a destiny that Young managed to avoid.
Indeed, there were several major artists who had survived the
breadth of the 1970s as functional entities.

Among these survivors was "that little ol' band from Texas,"
ZZ Top. *Deguello* marked the 1979 return of the band to the rock
trenches after a three-year layoff.

In 1976 the band had mounted their "World-wide Texas Tour," the bearded trio playing on a stage that was a little slice of the Lone Star State—complete with indigenous livestock. But then ZZ Top disappeared, laying low while the punk storm blew in.

When they returned, they did so cleverly poised for a second decade of existence. Although the songs of *Deguello* revisited typical Top themes—fast cars and faster women viewed through a haze of barbecue smoke—the group's reemergence revealed a brand new look. Though still relatively young men, guitarist Billy Gibbons and bassist Dusty Hill had grown their beards long, now looking like elderly eccentrics who'd wandered down from the hills. This image played into the band's hands with amazing success: as the years passed by, ZZ Top never seemed to age.

The only downside to ZZ Top's cartoonish visage was that they were seldom taken seriously. Truthfully, Top lyrics don't require much careful analysis; as in the lyrics of AC/DC, the sexual double entendre rules the roost. But critics and fans alike were often too distracted by Gibbons' corny antics to appreciate the fact that he was one of the United States' greatest guitarists, a brilliant interpreter of blues influences and a tireless innovator in the quest for new guitar tones.

Fleetwood Mac apparently were also tireless, based on the amount of studio time they consumed while recording their 1979 double album, *Tusk*. The wacky world of ZZ Top would likely have been ignored—or even secretly admired—by most punks, but the conspicuous consumption of Fleetwood Mac was precisely the attitude punk rock had railed against.

Not that the members of Fleetwood Mac cared. The multi-platinum status that *Rumours* had enjoyed certainly allowed for studio indulgence, particularly on the part of guitarist Lindsey Buckingham, the main *Tusk* sculptor.

"It lasted thirteen months and it took every bit of inner strength we had," singer Stevie Nicks said of the sessions in *US* magazine in 1980. "It was very hard on us, like being a hostage in Iran, and to an extent, Lindsey was the Ayatollah."

Referring to the fifty American embassy hostages held in Iran after the collapse of the Shah's régime in 1979, perhaps Nicks was a bit overzealous in depicting the rigors of recording a rock album—although it's certainly possible for projects to go off track when studio time is limitless.

The months and months of recording lent *Tusk* an air of mystique. Some have heralded the album as a surreal pop masterpiece, bordering on avant-garde; in reality, though, it's a fairly ordinary album. Aside from a couple of aural experiments here and a few sonic gimmicks there, *Tusk* is what it is: a Fleetwood Mac album.

Not that that's all bad. Buckingham offers a scorching outro guitar solo on "Sisters of the Moon," Christine McVie's stark "Never Make Me Cry" is poignant, and Nicks' typically haunting vocals on the lush "Sara" certainly more than justified the song's hit status.

But if the presence of a marching band on the song "Tusk" and the usage of pitch-shifting squonkiness on "The Ledge" qualify an album for avant-garde status, perhaps that status should be reevaluated. Compared to Fleetwood Mac's 1979 chart competition—which included disco chanteuse Donna Summer, piano man Billy Joel, Springsteen-from-the-heartland John Cougar, and soft rock crooning couple Carly Simon and James Taylor—*Tusk* may have sounded revolutionary; next to *Peter Gabriel*, it was safe as milk.

Less safe was Pink Floyd's magnum opus of 1979, *The Wall*. With Bob Ezrin producing—certainly no stranger to projects demanding vast soundscapes—Pink Floyd's double album found the band succumbing to the control of bassist and vocalist Roger Waters.

"Messages become a drag, like preaching," stated Floyd drummer Nick Mason, who had actually used his down time from the band pre-*The Wall* to produce The Damned. "I think one of the worst possible beliefs is that pop stars know any more about life than anyone else."

He should have tried expressing that attitude to his rhythm section partner Waters. Or perhaps he did. Regardless, the haranguing of the most noxious punk—like Johnny Rotten, who'd once worn a t-shirt proclaiming "I Hate Pink Floyd"—certainly had a rival in Waters and his heavy-handed lyrics, a torrent of words that berated rather than related. The best moments of 1975's *Wish You Were Here* had resonated on a profound level of deep communication, echoing with longing and regret, but *The Wall* was more like a therapy session in which Waters laboriously analyzed his own troubled upbringing in postwar England.

The Wall was a grim album, far too weighty to be elevated by its one moment of undeniable brilliance, the song "Comfortably Numb." One of the most beautiful tracks from this era of rock, it was given an uplifting performance by the band, sparked by lustrous guitar work from David Gilmour.

Pink Floyd had joined Fleetwood Mac in the double album sweepstakes, splurging on vinyl as superstars were wont to do. But for one of the last major releases of 1979, the mighty Led Zeppelin followed a single-disc theory. And based on the quality of *In through the Out Door*, that was just as well.

In Through the Out Door came packaged in a brown paper bag, an idea that would have been a unique one had Jefferson Airplane not released 1971's *Bark* in just such a configuration. That was the first hint that perhaps Led Zeppelin's creativity was not firing on all cylinders.

A second indication was the presence of two songs on *In through the Out Door* that did not bear founder Jimmy Page's name as writer or cowriter, an unprecedented occurrence in the band's history. That Led Zeppelin served Page's creative vision had been a given in the past; that he did not even cowrite nearly one-third of this album was unusual. The gap was filled by John Paul Jones, who received the writer's credit on six of the album's seven songs. The bassist and keyboardist was a brilliant musician and arranger, but on *Presence* he'd received only a single cowriting credit.

In through the Out Door got off to a serviceable start with "In the Evening," a mid-tempo, no-surprises song that tended toward monotony. Page passed on the opportunity to unleash guitar fire on the album-opening cut, though drummer John Bonham is reliable as always. "South Bound Saurez" presented a keyboard-driven sashay, but it was not until "Fool in the Rain" that the album was finally livened up by Bonham's counterrhythms in the second verse, though the turgid pacing of the overall song was far from inspirational. "Hot Dog" offered a countrified, two-step trifle, and "All My Love" featured Robert Plant emoting his way through a sagging, over-long ballad. "I'm Gonna Crawl" cast itself in an after-hours R&B feel, lit at last by a stirring Page solo.

In the entirety of Led Zeppelin's eighth studio album, it was only in "Carouselambra" that the band's characteristic, brutal swagger returned. Inhabiting a titanic structure built on Jones' impelling bass and Bonham's precise pummeling, the ten-minute song passed through a barren stretch of atmospheric spaciness before rallying to a surging, synth-fueled resolution.

Though *In through the Out Door* may not have contained the electrifying, Valhallan thunder of past Led Zeppelin releases, at least "Carouselambra" gave their fans hope for a return to brilliant form in the future.

It would not come to pass.

On September 25, 1980, a year after *In through the Out Door* hit the shelves and following a summer of touring, John Paul Jones went to roust John Bonham from his slumber at Jimmy Page's mansion. The burly drummer had made his way to Page's estate after a night of intense drinking. Jones was horrified at what he found—Bonham was dead, having choked on his own vomit during the night. The awesome thunder at the heart of Led Zeppelin had been stilled for good.

To the credit of Jimmy Page, Robert Plant, and John Paul Jones, an announcement was made on December 4, 1980: Led Zeppelin, one of rock's greatest and most influential bands, had officially come to its end.

Led Zeppelin's decision to cease operation cast the band's members in a far different light than The Who. Soon after the great Keith Moon's death, former Faces drummer Kenny Jones was installed behind the kit by Pete Townshend, Roger Daltrey, and John Entwistle. An able-if-basic rock drummer, Jones had no chance of matching Moon's· unpredictable arsenal of fire-power and didn't really try, instead applying his own no-frills style to the group's back catalog.

Thus reconstituted, and augmented with former Free member Rabbit Bundrick on keyboards, The Who returned to the road on May 5, 1979 at London's Rainbow Theatre. The band toured throughout the rest of the year, making their way to the United States for several shows at New York's Madison Square Garden in September, then returning to England for dates in November.

On December 3, The Who found themselves in Cincinnati for a gig at Riverfront Coliseum, in the midst of a thirteen-date winter tour of the United States. On that day things had been running behind schedule, and it was already evening and close to the announced show time when The Who blasted through their sound check.

Outside the venue, in the cold night air, thousands of fans milled about the building, impatiently awaiting the opening of the doors. Suddenly, the muffled sounds of The Who, obviously playing live, came drifting out of the arena. The waiting fans, estimated to number between eight and ten thousand by this time, began a manic rush toward the source of the music. But the doors of the building had not yet been opened. By the time they were, eleven fans of The Who had been crushed to death in the mindless stampede.

"A wave swept me to the left and when I regained my stance I felt that I was standing on someone," recalled Ron Duristch, one of those trapped close to the Coliseum's doors. "The helplessness and frustration of this moment sent a wave of panic through me. I screamed with all my strength that I was standing on someone. I couldn't move. I could only scream."

In spite of the deadly chaos, the concert went on. The Who were not informed of the tragedy until their set was over. The following night, at New York's Buffalo Memorial Auditorium, singer Roger Daltrey acknowledged the terrible events of the previous evening.

"You all heard what happened yesterday," Daltrey said from the stage. "We feel totally shattered. We lost a lot of family yesterday. This show's for them."

A concert dedication was precious little consolation, but there was nothing else for the band to do but go on—as rock and roll always seems to do.

The lethal horror of The Who's Cincinnati concert was the last major incident of the fraught-with-peril path that rock music had followed through the 1970s.

The decade was over.

The Who never fully recovered from the loss of Keith Moon, and the deaths of their Cincinnati fans seemed to send the group into a downward spiral. Pete Townshend entered into a worsening phase of severe drug and alcohol abuse. The melodrama of the band's final album with Moon, *Who Are You*, carried over into 1981's portentous *Face Dances*, and The Who's career as a recording band came to an end with 1982's wretched *It's Hard*.

The band proceeded to mount a farewell tour—though time would prove that billing to be inaccurate—and Pete Townshend selected The Clash to open the tour of huge stadiums. Many saw Townshend's gesture as a transfer of power to Joe Strummer and company, a coronation of the next "world's greatest rock band." After their tour with The Who, though, The Clash promptly broke up.

The deaths of both Keith Moon and John Bonham sadly heralded the end of an era, that of the great rock drummers. Through the incorporation of jazz and other influences—or just sheer brute power—Bonham, Moon, Ginger Baker of Cream and Blind Faith, and Mitch Mitchell of The Jimi Hendrix Experience had been the skin-pounding aristocracy of rock, setting the standards while a legion of drummers followed in their wake. But the loss of both Moon and Bonham was a fatal blow to the concept of inventive rock drumming, an art form already largely swept away by the basic beats of punk rock.

But drumming was far from the only aspect of rock music to have undergone fundamental disruption.

At one time, a guitarist was expected to have the musical facility to walk on a stage and captivate an audience for five, ten, or even fifteen minutes while soloing. With a few exceptions, the passing of the 1970s was largely the passing of the Rock Guitar Hero.

Indeed, the very concept of instrumental prowess now carries less weight when band qualifications are judged, a factor found far down on a list where "marketing potential" reigns supreme.

Of course, marketing was crucial to killing off the very format by which rock artists expressed themselves in the 1970s, the vinyl record. Ry Cooder recorded the first all-digital album, *Bop 'til You Drop*, and released it on July 11, 1979—the first shot of the digital revolution. The compact disc was lurking right behind, its debut coming in 1983.

The release of Vanilla Ice's *To the Extreme* in 1990—the first chart-topping recording to enter stores solely on CD, with no vinyl pressing—completed the compact disc coup d'etat. But that was just the beginning of an ingenious and never-ending marketing campaign: once consumers had an album on CD, they were expected to buy it again when it was remastered, then replace that copy when the title appeared in HDCD high-definition format, then swap that for the DTC surround version, and on and on in an eternal dance of latest-and-greatest tail chasing.

In the glory days of vinyl at the beginning of the 1970s, rock in large part was still a sizzling mass of kinetic energy, plugged into the untamed experimentation of its founding fathers. The irrepressible wild streak that was the essence of Jerry Lee Lewis was the same demonic energy fueling The Who's *Live at Leeds*; the sheer joy of cutting loose that sent young Elvis' hips shaking was the same force that propelled Mick Jagger across The Rolling Stones' stage.

But those magnificent seconds of mind-melding emotional transmission from the past to the present to the hearts of the listeners would sadly grow rare, becoming an ecstasy seldom encountered. And as far as the record industry was concerned, good riddance; as everyone had seen, unpredictable results can occur from such difficult-to-manage powers.

Rock's most fundamental channel for the conduction of this extraordinary creative life-force was Jimi Hendrix. Men who themselves had felt this very force pass through their own creations—Pete Townshend, Paul McCartney, Eric Clapton, Jeff Beck, Mick Jagger, and hundreds more—found themselves inexorably drawn to the aura surrounding Hendrix. And even now, as they try to describe him more than three decades later, the words fail them—because what it was can't possibly be described. To watch Hendrix in full flight was to see currents flowing through a man possessed by untainted creativity, a visceral communication of pure expression. In moments such as those, rock and roll is revealed in its full splendor.

It's easy to hand down books from generation to generation, but how can rock and roll be passed on? You could write down

the lyrics, print the notes—but there was always that inde-
scribable something else, a thing mysterious and all-powerful,
with elemental parameters that couldn't really be defined. If
you didn't *get* it, something crucial was lost in the translation. Musical offspring that were missing that all-too-crucial
genetic factor looked like rock and sounded like rock—but
had no chance of provoking like rock, thrilling like rock, or inspiring like rock.

For some, that was just fine. Having first endured uncontrolled creation through the first part of the 1970s, then having
been battered by a movement determined to destroy it in the
latter half, the record industry faced the 1980s bloodied but
more omnipotent than ever. No matter what musical developments and evolution might be occurring in studios, rehearsal
halls, and garages around the world, one irrevocable fact had
become all too clear: the industry would now maintain a wary,
unblinking eye on all aspects of popular music. Yes, it would allow trends to develop—then, when the time was right, it would
swoop in to market them and reap the profits. It mattered not
how extreme or unorthodox the product—the issue was one of
control. Properly packaged and consumed according to marketing directions, rock really wasn't so dangerous after all.

"The strict formatting isn't good for the future of music," Joe
Strummer of The Clash noted shortly before his untimely death
caused by a heart attack late in 2002. "Everything's been airbrushed down into the same thing. It's stagnating."

"When the rulebook is applied to something that's artistic by
nature, whatever it is can't grow," Tom Petty stated in the
Philadelphia Inquirer. "You see it very plainly in music: these ex-
ecutives only want young acts that are willing to be molded
and play the game without questioning anything. . . . The performers in what they call 'rock' these days, they're exactly the
people you got in a rock band to get away from."

"The music business right now, across the board, is characterized by a lethal sameness that comes as a result of a lack of
understanding and vision at the top of the industry," Bob Ezrin,
producer of Alice Cooper, Lou Reed, Pink Floyd, and scores
more told Roman Sokal in *Tape Op* magazine late in 2002.
"Right now we are worried about the results first and shoe-
horning the talent into that. Every record made now has to

have that certain producer, certain mixer, has to be a certain length, has to be in a certain guitar tuning, has to have a certain vocal sound."

Marketing control had become the key principle of musical life as the 1980s began. That was a hard fact to accept for many who had witnessed the wild era of unchecked creativity that occurred in the ten years from 1970 to 1979. They knew that their time had passed—and that nothing like it would ever be seen again.

Indeed, rock music of the 1970s was soon being nostalgically marketed as little more than a sonic relic from a quaint era of punk rockers, disco dancers, and outlandish guitar players wearing silly clothes.

"I got a letter inviting me to a ceremony in L.A.," Gerry Stickells, road manager for Jimi Hendrix, recalled. "They put a star for him in Hollywood Boulevard. That would have been about the biggest insult imaginable . . . to suggest to him that one day, Jimi, you will be such a part of the establishment, they will put a star for you on Hollywood Boulevard.

"It was as if everything he had stood against and played against was being forced upon him after he'd died."

Appendix

Milestones:
Fifty Landmark Rock Recordings of the 1970s

Listening to these recordings provides direct access to the rampant creativity that abounded throughout 1970s rock music. But as a side note, many of the artists who appear in the pages of this book still work the concert trail. Though many writers are all too quick to joke about rockers in wheelchairs, in the case of musicians like Jeff Beck and ZZ Top's Billy Gibbons, the passing years have found these artists restlessly honing their skills, and often the musician you see today is far more accomplished than the one you would have heard thirty years ago. Don't pass up the opportunity to share the concert experience with rock's greatest musicians. As Jimi Hendrix once said, "Get experienced!"

AC/DC—*Highway to Hell* was the album that launched these Australians into rock superstardom, although singer Bon Scott did not live long enough to enjoy the accolades. Pile-driving rhythms, sex-obsessed lyrics, and heavy-but-clever hard rock chord progressions abound.

Aerosmith—*Toys in the Attic* pushed the band toward superstar status, but on *Rocks* the combination of Jack Douglas' production and a raging lead-and-rhythm guitar attack resulted in a hard rock masterpiece, created just before substance abuse wreaked havoc on the group.

Allman Brothers Band—*At Fillmore East* stands today as one of the greatest of all live albums. The confidence and assurance displayed by the entire band only comes after playing hundreds of live gigs, but in particular the stunning guitar work of young Duane Allman clearly demonstrates what a huge loss his death was to rock music.

Jeff Beck—Though *Blow by Blow* is Beck's most celebrated album of the decade, *Wired* more effectively conducts the guitarist's creative current. The hard edge of this album's fusion-influenced atmosphere spurs Beck to meld the melodicism of *Blow by Blow* with the aggressive attacks of his late-1960s hard rock efforts. The result is a display of breathtaking creativity.

Black Sabbath—The most influential hard rock album ever recorded, *Paranoid* remains a frightening collection of relentless heaviness, broken only by the spacey "Planet Caravan." Those who consider Ozzy Osbourne to be nothing more than a cartoon-like figure of the new millennium are advised to investigate the howling, doom-shouting Ozzy of 1970. In *Paranoid*, Black Sabbath created a soundtrack for the apocalypse.

Blondie—On *Parallel Lines*, Blondie took the brisk beats of rock's New Wave and muscled them into a batch of thoroughly infectious songs. Though there's no denying the sensual appeal of Debbie Harry's vocals, additional thrills are provided by drummer Clem Burke, who powers the album with a Keith Moon-like authority.

Blue Oyster Cult—The group hit chart success thanks to "Don't Fear the Reaper," but the album that preceded *Agents of Fortune* was the band's finest hour. *Secret Treaties* presents smart songwriting, focused performances, and Buck Dharma's soaring, melodic guitar solos.

David Bowie—One of the most active artists of the decade, Bowie's material covered an astonishing amount of creative territory. Of all this work, *"Heroes"* remains the most unusual Bowie album, one that sounds like absolutely nothing else from its era—or any other era, for that matter. The cold, frightening intensity of the album's first side is balanced by the austere, slowly evolving instrumentals of the second side.

The Clash—There is no denying the thrilling power and aggression of the band's first two albums, but on *London Calling*, The Clash became a truly great rock band, bringing new influences and styles to the studio in the creation of one of rock's most significant double albums.

Alice Cooper—*Billion Dollar Babies* captures the Alice Cooper band at their creative apex, building on their reputation as one of rock's biggest—and most controversial—groups. The Detroit-inspired hard rock of this album would succumb to stardom-induced inertia after this final concentrated blast.

Elvis Costello—At a time when many Americans still held the ill-informed opinion that Costello was nothing more than an obnoxious punk rocker, Elvis was recording *Armed Forces*, a bitterly passionate yet tuneful collection of songs that featured an inspired performance by The Attractions.

Deep Purple—Though the album *Made in Japan* admirably presented Deep Purple's high-octane stage show, over-long solos dragged down the proceedings. *Machine Head*, the band's breakthrough studio album, is concise and authoritative from beginning to end. The classically inspired interplay of guitarist Ritchie Blackmore and organist Jon Lord proved vastly influential when cast within *Machine Head*'s hard rock setting.

Derek and The Dominos—Eric Clapton seemed to be adrift after the demise of Cream, and he even tried out side man status in Delaney and Bonnie and Friends. But borrowing musicians from that group, Clapton formed The Dominos and jetted off to Miami, unsuccessfully fleeing his feelings for George Harrison's wife, Patti. The passion he felt for his then-unattainable object of affection—along with gallons of booze and pounds of drugs—spurred the creation of this, Clapton's most emotional, committed album.

The Doors—Jim Morrison was considered by many to be virtually washed up, a victim of excessive alcohol consumption, when *L.A. Woman* was released. Which made Morrison's confident, assured performance all the more remarkable. The relaxed circumstances of the recording and the control wielded by the band makes this one of the highlights of The Doors' too-brief career, spanning the late 1960s and early 1970s.

Bob Dylan—Followers of Bob Dylan came to expect constant reinvention from the singer, though his work in the 1970s had fallen short of the peaks of his 1960s material—until *Blood on the Tracks* was released. Nearly hypnotic, particularly in its fascinating first-person tales of diverse characters and their relationships, the album proved that Dylan's talents were maturing and laid the groundwork for his justifiably esteemed status today.

Emerson, Lake, and Palmer—Though Keith Emerson was a leading advocate of Dr. Robert Moog and his synthesizer, it wasn't until *Brain Salad Surgery* that the functionality of the new keyboard instrument was finally capable of realizing Emerson's vision. Once that happened, though, the keyboardist and his rhythm section cultivated a sci-fi-influenced masterpiece of future paranoia.

Brian Eno—Though justifiably recognized as one of the key shapers of 1970s music through his productions and other associations, Eno's own music is too often ignored. *Before and After Science* is a remarkably wide-ranging album, delving into experimental fusion funk at one end of the spectrum; hushed, near-ambient dreamscapes at the other.

Free—Guitarist Paul Kossoff ultimately became one of rock's most tragic figures, but his playing was a vital outlet during his too-brief career. *Fire and Water* presents Koss at his most focused, with impassioned vocals by Paul Rodgers adding to the mix. Before personality differences split them apart, Rodgers and bassist Andy Fraser were a remarkable songwriting team, and this album presents a powerful collection of songs including the gritty rock of the title track and moving ballads like the haunting "Heavy Load."

Peter Gabriel—After departing Genesis, Gabriel set about establishing one of the most individualistic careers in rock.

Though all of his albums contain moments of bold creativity, his third effort—with its "no cymbals" rule forcing Phil Collins and Jerry Marotta to rethink their drumming approach—was his most inventive statement of the 1970s.

Genesis—*The Lamb Lies Down on Broadway* was the result of combining one of the most accomplished assemblages of prog rock musicians with one of the most unique prog rock personalities, Peter Gabriel. The final Genesis album with Gabriel as vocalist was a dense, fascinating record loaded with hallucinatory lyrical visions and stunning displays of musical ability, in part flavored via the participation of Brian Eno.

Jimi Hendrix—After burning his guitar at the Monterey festival in 1967 and issuing seminal singles like "Purple Haze" and "Fire," Jimi Hendrix found that his audience was determined to shackle him to the Summer of Love. But on *Band of Gypsys*, Hendrix broke free with some of the most remarkable playing ever recorded by a guitarist, and the spectacular "Machine Gun" still stands as the summit of rock guitar evolution and invention.

Humble Pie—While many rock bands were on a quest to elevate prog rock to new artistic standards, Humble Pie put the emphasis on "rock" throughout their live album, *Performance—Rockin' the Fillmore*. Peter Frampton's fleet solos show his hard rock pedigree, one that would be deemphasized upon his later reinvention as a cuddly solo artist. But on this album, Frampton and his band mates Steve Marriott, Jerry Shirley, and Greg Ridley rock with kinetic authority.

James Gang—Ohio's James Gang brought an American style to the classic power trio lineup, and though the band is justifiably celebrated for the guitar work of Joe Walsh, the drumming of Jim Fox is an equally potent weapon in The Gang's arsenal. Fox drives the *Live in Concert* album with forceful percussion that rages beneath the suitably heavy guitar heroics of Walsh.

Jethro Tull—Despite the commercial momentum of *Aqualung*, an album the band was not thrilled with, Jethro Tull opted for a risky path in creating the single-song *Thick as a Brick*. But a wealth of memorable melodies and a driving performance by the whole band elevate *Brick* to the top of the Tull canon.

Janis Joplin—Though her reputation was based on the blow-torch vocal performances of her brief career with Big Brother and The Holding Company, *Pearl* reveals Janis making the most of vocal dynamics on an album that was nearly complete at the time of her death. Her comfort with her new Full Tilt Boogie Band is obvious throughout the record.

King Crimson—Though King Crimson's career arc saw the band's lineup augmented by members specializing in instruments ranging from Mellotron to saxophone, it's interesting that the group's most explosive album finds a stripped-down power trio format. Founding guitarist Robert Fripp, bassist John Wetton, and drummer Bill Bruford ensured that *Red* was simply one of the most powerful albums ever recorded, a thunderous final chapter of King Crimson's initial era of activity.

Kraftwerk—On *The Man-Machine*, Kraftwerk deftly realized all of the potential they had revealed on this album's predecessors. Perhaps it was due to the sophistication of technology finally maturing to the standards required by the German quartet, but songs like "Neon Lights" and "Spacelab" boast a richness of tone and beautiful melodies that explain why this electronic band was so influential to musicians like David Bowie.

Led Zeppelin—With impeccable pedigree thanks to Jimmy Page's high-profile stint with The Yardbirds, Led Zeppelin hit the rock scene hard with their 1969 debut album. Five albums later they released *Physical Graffiti*, a record that showed just how much the band had grown. Everything from the thunder of the band's early era to the exotic strains of Middle Eastern music was contained within the four sides of this double album, one that still sounds as fresh as it did nearly thirty years ago.

Lynyrd Skynyrd—That *Street Survivors* would be Lynyrd Skynyrd's final album was unimaginable before their plane went down on that terrible night in 1977, but it stands as a fine memorial to one of the United States' greatest bands. From British hard rock to honky tonk country, the Florida band assimilated myriad influences in the cultivation of their own unique style.

Mahavishnu Orchestra—No one had ever heard anything like The Mahavishnu Orchestra before they astonished the rock world—and there's been nothing like them since. Their second album, *Birds of Fire*, presents the band at their absolute peak, riding frenetic volleys of percussion while trading truly mind-bending solos.

Bob Marley and The Wailers—Though Marley's studio albums have a confident grace in the delivery of his lyrical messages, The Wailers were first and foremost a live band. The expanded lineup of musicians heard on *Babylon by Bus* provide their leader with a supple and exotic foundation, rooted by the incredible rhythm section of brothers Aston "Familyman" Barrett on bass and the late Carlton Barrett on drums.

Montrose—Hard rock albums of the 1970s were often muddy-sounding affairs, until guitarist Ronnie Montrose presented his new band to producer Ted Templeman and engineer Don Landee. *Montrose* was the result, a high-energy blast of rock that set new standards in performance and sound.

Mountain—Though *Nantucket Sleighride* is Mountain's most consistent studio effort, the half-live *Flowers of Evil* provides nearly thirty minutes of the heaviest hard rock improvisation of the 1970s. Sadly, a Mountain reunion is an impossibility—Felix Pappalardi was murdered by his wife, Gail Collins, in 1983.

Ted Nugent—The "Motor City Madman" lives up to his nickname on *Double Live Gonzo*, but the over-the-top hysteria can make it hard to focus on Nugent's imposing guitar talents. They're heard to best advantage on Ted's greatest studio album, *Cat Scratch Fever*, beginning with the title track's monstrous, unforgettable opening riff.

Pink Floyd—Fans immediately think of *Dark Side of the Moon* or *The Wall* when Pink Floyd is mentioned. Curious, considering that the seamless *Wish You Were Here* is a far superior album. Resonating with emotion and featuring David Gilmour's guitar work at its most sublime, *Wish You Were Here* neatly sidesteps the prog rock tedium that haunted parts of *Moon* and the haranguing attitude of *The Wall*.

The Pretenders—Like Patti Smith, Chrissie Hynde was an American girl who wanted to rock on her own terms. To make her dream a reality, she assembled a forceful band sparked by the raw, early-Jeff Beck guitar of James Honeyman-Scott. *Pretenders* balances the band's pop-singles efforts, produced by Nick Lowe, with Chris Thomas' arresting production of Hynde's aggressive material.

Procol Harum—The incorporation of classical elements was a hallmark of Procol Harum's sound by the time *Grand Hotel* was released. Though the album does have its symphonic moments, in the end it's the strengths of the group that shine through, particularly the solos of guitarist Mick Grabham and Gary Brooker's ardent vocals.

Queen—Though *A Night at the Opera* contained Queen's greatest single work in "Bohemian Rhapsody," that album's predecessor gets the nod for overall consistency. *Sheer Heart Attack* contains blustery hard rock anthems like "Brighton Rock" and the frantic "Stone Cold Crazy," but it also allows Freddie Mercury's wide-ranging interests to crop up on the old-timey "Bring Back that Leroy Brown." A roller coaster ride of an album.

The Ramones—Although *The Ramones* was this influential group's initial blast of primal punk energy, their third album, *Rocket to Russia*, finds the band's material refined but still retaining all of its power. Songs like "Teenage Lobotomy," "Rockaway Beach," and "Cretin Hop" cruise along effortlessly with breakneck pacing.

The Rolling Stones—*Exile on Main Street* was not warmly received by critics upon its release. But with so much stylistic diversity in evidence, it's no surprise that it took time to warm to the double album now generally regarded as the Stones' masterwork. The fact that it was recorded in the murky basement of an old French estate only adds to the vibe.

Roxy Music—Though the group had suffered the departure creative visionary Brian Eno, Roxy Music bounced back with the strongest album of their career, *Stranded*. Bryan Ferry's persona had fully evolved into that of a European sophisticate, and he delivered melodramatic tomes like "Song for Europe" and the beautiful "Mother of Pearl" with characteristic panache.

Todd Rundgren—It's frightening to think how much work must have gone into *A Wizard, a True Star*, Rundgren's solo masterpiece. On an album recorded long before digital recording technology would have facilitated such an imposing project, Rundgren acts as tour guide, leading the listener through an astonishing array of styles, all knitted into a single sonic entity.

The Sex Pistols—Producers Chris Thomas and Bill Price worked separately on their pieces of *Never Mind the Bollocks— Here's the Sex Pistols*, but when the components were assembled the result was one monstrous album. Johnny Rotten unleashes one of rock's greatest vocal performances, over runaway rhythms framed by massive guitar tones. A vital, intense album.

The Patti Smith Group—With *Horses* and *Radio Ethiopia*, Smith had established her transcendent visions and influenced the punk revolution in both the U.S. and the U.K. On *Easter*, care and craft joined experimentation and aggression in the creation of a superb album from beginning to end.

Bruce Springsteen—*Born to Run* was a largely uplifting commercial smash, but when Springsteen was finally able to return to the studio after a protracted legal battle with his former manager, the resulting album was far more sober. *Darkness on the Edge of Town* is as moody as its title indicates, with The E Street Band providing exceptionally sympathetic backing. This record of grim acceptance and haunted dreams established themes Springsteen continues to revisit to this day.

T. Rex—Though *Electric Warrior* was Marc Bolan's commercial breakthrough, the true glories of rock stardom ring through every note of its follow-up, *The Slider*. Paired once again with influential producer Tony Visconti, Bolan and band rock regally through heady glam tracks like "Metal Guru" and the infectiously propulsive "Telegram Sam."

Robin Trower—On Trower's first solo album after departing Procol Harum, *Twice Removed from Yesterday*, the British guitarist luxuriated in slow-paced, stately songs that he filled with lush, atmospheric solos. Trower's rich tonal palette is heard to moving effect throughout the entire album.

Van Halen—Rock fans who thought they'd heard everything got a rude awakening from the opening notes of *Van Halen*, the group's incendiary debut. Eddie Van Halen's astonishing fret board work pointed hard rock and heavy metal in new directions, even as singer David Lee Roth perfected the role of rock and roll wild man.

The Who—Though *Live at Leeds* presented the band at its most emphatic and chaotic, The Who's *Quadrophenia* remains Pete Townshend's masterpiece. From the blunt rock simplicity of "The Real Me" to the sonic structures of "Doctor Jimmy," this massive undertaking presents all aspects of one of rock's greatest bands.

Yes—If any single album sums up the adventurous spirit of the 1970s, it is *Tales from Topographic Oceans*. The sixth studio album of Yes' career, *Tales* is a single piece of music sprawling across four album sides. It runs the gamut from harsh electronic percussive experimentation to achingly gorgeous passages of sheer majesty. Overblown? Absolutely, and glorious because of that very fact.

Index

About the Author

An interest in things that go fast and make a lot of noise has characterized the writing efforts of Frank Moriarty. The author, who lives in southern New Jersey with his wife, Leigh Anne, and a Rhodesian Ridgeback named Astro, has written more than a dozen award-winning books covering the realms of popular music and motor sports.

Born in White Plains, New York, Frank began his elementary school years near Chicago, where he first heard the music of The Beatles and The Dave Clark Five. In fourth grade, Frank found himself in Memphis, Tennessee, following another family move. During an after-school bike ride there, he was blessed with a wave from the King, Elvis Presley. The family later moved to the Philadelphia area—where Frank has since remained—just in time for him to see The Jimi Hendrix Experience perform. For the thirteen-year-old adolescent, it was a night that ignited a lifelong fascination with the creative power of rock music.

While writing about music for his high school newspaper, Frank became a freelance contributor to publications around the country, interviewing artists such as Robin Trower and the members of Jethro Tull. That eventually led to a decade-long stint as music columnist at Philadelphia's *City Paper*, followed by several years of being associated with *Philadelphia Weekly*. He has written biographies of Jimi Hendrix, Johnny Cash, and Bruce Springsteen and has contributed to a number of magazines.

The opportunity to write an article about legendary driver Dale Earnhardt's crew chief (a Philadelphia native) introduced him on a professional level to the world of NASCAR. Several popular books have been the result of Moriarty's enthrallment with speed and racing technology.

Aside from writing books and articles about rock music, Moriarty was lead guitarist with the seminal Philadelphia recording and touring bands Informed Sources and Bunnydrums in the 1980s. More recently, he led and produced the hard-rock, alien-themed band Third Stone Invasion in the recording of their concept CD, which was released by J-Bird Records.

Visit Frank's Web page at mywebpages.comcast.net/loudfast/